Culture, Catastrophe, and Ri

## Studies in Rhetoric and Culture

Edited by **Ivo Strecker,** Johannes Gutenberg University Mainz and Addis Ababa University, **Stephen Tyler,** Rice University, and **Robert Hariman,** Northwestern University

Our minds are filled with images and ideas, but these remain unstable and incomplete as long as we do not manage to persuade both ourselves and others of their meanings. It is this inward and outward rhetoric which allows us to give some kind of shape and structure to our understanding of the world and which becomes central to the formation of individual and collective consciousness. This series is dedicated to the study of the interaction of rhetoric and culture and focuses on the concrete practices of discourse in which and through which the diverse and often also fantastic patterns of culture—including our own—are created, maintained, and contested.

**Volume 1**
*Culture and Rhetoric*
Edited by Ivo Strecker and Stephen Tyler

**Volume 2**
*Culture, Rhetoric, and the Vicissitudes of Life*
Edited by Michael Carrithers

**Volume 3**
*Economic Persuasions*
Edited by Stephen Gudeman

**Volume 4**
*The Rhetorical Emergence of Culture*
Edited by Christian Meyer and Felix Girke

**Volume 5**
*Astonishment and Evocation: The Spell of Culture in Art and Anthropology*
Edited by Ivo Strecker and Markus Verne

**Volume 6**
*Chiasmus and Culture*
Edited by Boris Wiseman and Anthony Paul

**Volume 7**
*Culture, Catastrophe, and Rhetoric: The Texture of Political Action*
Edited by Robert Hariman and Ralph Cintron

# CULTURE, CATASTROPHE, AND RHETORIC

THE TEXTURE OF POLITICAL ACTION

■ ■ ■

Edited by
ROBERT HARIMAN AND RALPH CINTRON

berghahn
NEW YORK • OXFORD
www.berghahnbooks.com

First published in 2015 by

Berghahn Books

www.berghahnbooks.com

©2015, 2020 Robert Hariman and Ralph Cintron
First paperback edition published in 2020

All rights reserved. Except for the quotation of short passages for the purposes of criticism and review, no part of this book may be reproduced in any form or by any means, electronic or mechanical, including photocopying, recording, or any information storage and retrieval system now known or to be invented, without written permission of the publisher.

**Library of Congress Cataloging-in-Publication Data**

A C.I.P. cataloging record is available from the Library of Congress

**British Library Cataloguing in Publication Data**

A catalogue record for this book is available from the British Library

Printed on acid-free paper

ISBN 978-1-78238-746-6 hardback
ISBN 978-1-78920-823-8 paperback
ISBN 978-1-78238-747-3 ebook

# Contents

■ ■ ■ ■ ■ ■

List of Illustrations   vii

Preface   viii

Introduction   1
    *Robert Hariman*

1. The Communal Dilemma as a Cultural Resource in Hungarian Political Expression   25
    *David Boromisza-Habashi*

2. Chronotopes of the Political: Public Discourse, News Media, and Mass Action in Postconflict Macedonia   47
    *Andrew Graan*

3. The In-Between States: Enduring Catastrophes as Sources of Democracy's Deadlocks in Kosovo   68
    *Naser Miftari*

4. Occupy Wall Street as Rhetorical Citizenship: The Ongoing Relevance of Pragmatism for Deliberative Democracy   87
    *Robert Danisch*

5. Contemporary Social Movements and the Emergent Nomadic Political Logic   106
    *Peter N. Funke and Todd Wolfson*

6. "Project Heat" and Sensory Politics in Redeveloping Chicago
   Public Housing 122
   *Catherine Fennell*

7. Reading between the Digital Lines: The Political Rhetoric of
   Ethical Consumption 149
   *Eleftheria J. Lekakis*

8. The Uncertainty of Power and the Certainty of Irony:
   Encountering the State in Kara, Southern Ethiopia 168
   *Felix Girke*

9. Grassroots Rhetorics in Times of Scarcity: Debating the 2004
   Locust Plague in Northwestern Senegal and the World 194
   *Christian Meyer*

10. *Too Too Much Much*: Presence and Catastrophe in
    Contemporary Art 220
    *Monica Westin*

Conclusion: What Next? Modernity, Revolution, and the "Turn"
to Catastrophe 231
   *Ralph Cintron*

Index 256

# Illustrations

## Figures

2.1. One of the postcard designs used to protest the Council of Europe's stringent guidelines on how to refer to Macedonia within the organization's documents.     61

6.1. Laundry, recreation, and heat facilities promote "comfort" and "happiness," circa 1950 (CHA n.d.b). Image courtesy of the Chicago History Museum.     128

6.2. Residential building and heat plant at Chicago's Stateway Gardens, January 2006. This plant was similar to the one that stood at The Henry Horner Homes.     129

8.1. Ethnic groups in South Omo.     169

10.1. Thomas Hirschhorn, *Too Too Much Much*, Museum Dhondt-Dhaenens, 2010     221

## Table

7.1. A continuum of stories in fair trade activism.     156

# Preface

∎ ∎ ∎ ∎ ∎ ∎

This volume is an example of the strange relationship between planning and contingency. When Ivo Strecker and Stephen Tyler announced the series of symposia that were to articulate the Rhetoric Culture project, they envisioned a core configuration of ideas regarding the discursive constitution of culture within specific domains of collective activity such as the economy, religion, and politics. As it turned out, the core ideas have now been set out in several volumes and become more varied for that, while some important domains may never receive the attention they deserve. In addition, a significant number of scholars who were not part of the original meetings have joined the project, bringing both additional energy and additional diversity in theory and method. This history is evident in the current volume, which is dedicated to understanding political action through the binocular vision of rhetoric and culture.

By focusing on politics, the authors in this volume are addressing the primal scene in the tradition of rhetoric, while taking an approach that would be unfamiliar to many scholars in both anthropology and political science. Anthropologists might point out that most cultures do not share the assumptions of Western political thought, and that many do not even have a comparable concept of the political as a separate dimension of collective life. Why, then, assume that the classical art of political speech is shaping decisions about leadership, distribution of common resources, and conflict resolution, much less other important features of collective identity? Political scientists would be likely to look for explicitly political functions, but probably expect them to be embedded in institutions and shaped by specific material constraints and advantages within universal conditions of competition. Why, then, assume that political behavior is determined by nebulous and epiphenomenal factors such as culture, which can be shared by both winners and losers, or that entrenched power is likely to give way to variations in rhetorical performance?

These stock objections have their own histories, not least because they are representative of characteristic developments in modern thought. In this latter regard they share a common distribution of labor, with "culture" and "politics" marking separate domains of human experience and separate disciplines of academic study. "Rhetoric" is also part of that history, albeit in a marginal position with respect to these and other major disciplines. Thus, the conjunction of "rhetoric," "culture," and "politics" brings with it multiple frictions and aporias; in the chapters that follow, we hope to show how such initial dissonance can be reworked to good effect. The intention is not to overturn more established paradigms, but to better understand phenomena that otherwise are overlooked, undervalued, or misrecognized. Indeed, labels such as "politics," "culture," and "rhetoric" can themselves only capture part of the complexity of collective action, and so we employ them here in order to explore their intersections.

This volume was first envisioned as part of the Rhetoric Culture symposium at Johannes Gutenberg University of Mainz in 2005; that meeting was possible due to the generous support of the Volkswagen Foundation. As the volumes from the other Rhetoric Culture symposia began to appear, this one began to develop a life of its own. That winding path then led to a symposium on Power, Rhetoric, and Political Culture, which was held at Northwestern University in 2012; that gathering was possible due to the generous support of the School of Communication, the Center for Global Culture and Communication, the Department of Communication Studies, and the Alice Kaplan Institute for the Humanities, all at Northwestern University. As it happens, the volume's editors attended different symposia in Mainz, but we had met long before at the Project on the Rhetoric of Inquiry at the University of Iowa, and we shared a deep appreciation for the interdisciplinary collaboration experienced there. As coincidence would have it again, we now both work at universities in the Chicago metro area, and this volume reflects the renewed relationship that has developed through that conjunction.

So it is that the volume has acquired its own texture. Indeed, the editors find that our ideas have become braided together to an extent that they no longer belong to either of us alone. Hariman brought in the themes of texture and catastrophe, while Cintron provided the emphasis on culture along with an interest in economics, but each theme was developed in part by the other. The same holds for the rest of the project, from locating the authors to doing the revisions. In short, it has become clear to us that scholarship rightly goes well beyond economic models of self-interested ownership and market exchange.

However it did work, the plan for this volume has been undone and redone several times, but we believe it is better for that. We think that Ivo and

Stephen would agree, not least because, in their story, first there was the contingency of their chance meeting, with the plan only emerging through an extended conversation that grew to include a still widening circle of scholars in multiple disciplines. We are very pleased to be part of that story as well, and welcome the reader to join the narrative—and the conversation.

# Introduction

*Robert Hariman*

■ ■ ■ ■ ■ ■

This volume addresses a critical problem in understanding the contemporary historical moment: identifying how large-scale and potentially catastrophic economic, social, and political processes are articulated and negotiated in the practice of everyday life. On the one hand, there is comprehensive evidence that capitalism, technological development, and neoliberal state practices have produced massive rates of change across the globe. On the other hand, advances in the qualitative sciences have produced remarkably fine-grained accounts of social experience that cannot be easily coordinated with the structural determination of collective association. The picture that emerges is paradoxical: one sees both highly nuanced examples of human agency and powerful constraints on any attempt to interfere with system dominance.

Thus, there is need for work that can advance understanding of how systemic change is experienced, negotiated, and perhaps resisted in specific settings that define a society's capacity for political action. To that end, this volume provides a series of chapters grounded in three principles of analysis: they rethink the concept of *political culture,* by emphasizing the *texture* of political action, with respect to *understanding the catastrophic dimension* of the global social order that is emerging in the twenty-first century.

The focus on political culture involves emphasizing the importance of shared habits of communication, interaction, and display in the constitution of political communities and collective action. "Culture" is itself a contested term, of course, and not taken here as a fixed source of meaning or motivation. Rather, the intention is to consider how political intelligibility, legitimacy, and capacity are constructed and complicated by being articulated through distinctively coherent repertoires of social practice. By seeing how political subjectivity grows out of situated conversations in specific localities, flows across the surface of society, becomes embedded in public arts, or is relayed through digital technologies, one can identify how politics depends on aesthetically inflected concentrations of social energy that in turn suggest varied theory-practice relationships.

The specific focus within this context is on the "texture" of political practices. Politics is understood to be more richly articulated than abstract relations of power, more extensive than governmental practices, and determined not only by necessity and self-interest but also by modes of performance. Although still structured by the constraints and advantages of economic resources, social organization, and other systemic factors, political judgment and action are also the outcomes of finely woven habits of speech, interaction, and artistic display. Although capable of representing structural conditions and coordinating large populations, these patterns are known only through their particularity. Thus, cultural analysis becomes focused on the surface of things—the observable features of social performance as they are embedded in texts and other artifacts—and can consider "horizontal" logics of articulation along with surface-structure relationships (Alexander 2008; Bartmanski and Alexander 2012; Hariman and Lucaites 2014). From this perspective, the relative autonomy of political thought is not necessarily given: instead, the focus is on how political consciousness is being modulated across a spectrum of social and cultural activities, while the ability to control the definition of political action can be crucial.

The commitment to theoretical argument regarding the continuing development of modernity is obviously ambitious and perhaps quixotic, but we believe it is also an intellectual obligation. The contemporary focus and small scale of our work cannot sustain comprehensive claims, but we believe scholars need to address the question of how situated knowledge can contribute to understanding large-scale historical phenomena that are putting considerable pressure on all societies today. These widespread changes include the "creative destruction" of traditional economic and social practices; population displacement and hyperurbanization; cultural hybridization and global system integration; and ecological, economic, and political disasters. Within this context, the chapters in this volume will suggest how the interaction of social structure and individual agency can be identified in the nuanced articulations of situated speech bounded by global predicaments. At the same time, we are attempting to stay abreast of corresponding changes in both academic and public discourses that attempt to track comprehensive change. These shifts in the discursive horizon include globalization, which has expanded from economic reality to civic ideology; hegemony, which may be entering a paradoxical phase that depends on disruption for system maintenance; and catastrophe, which has displaced revolution as a master trope for dramatic change.

This last point is particularly salient. While completing this book, we watched demonstrations in the Ukraine flip in days from a restoration of democratic values to the pretext for Russian conquest of the Crimea. Similar reversals are being cemented into place in Egypt and other sites of the Arab Spring, just as anticolonial revolutions have often led to another order of domination or spasms of predation between warlords battling for resource monopolies. Self-determination has been overrun by international markets in guns, drugs, and human trafficking, as well as other examples of violence going global. Revolutions still exist, but only, it seems, to become examples of how systems of exploitation can reassert themselves. Modernization, liberalization, and other markers of "Western" civilization continue to expand globally, and thus make the geographic label increasingly dated, yet twenty-first-century modernity seems to be defined less and less by a narrative of revolutionary progress, and more by terror attacks, financial crashes, natural disasters, and other catastrophes. In place of revolutionary change, we have restoration of the status quo ante amid the wreckage, and in place of progress, risk management. One might well wonder, who can really change anything?

Although "agency" and "structure" are well-worn concepts within modern scholarship, the problem of their relationship continues to challenge those attempting to comprehend the everyday experience of historical change. By bringing together scholars in anthropology, rhetoric, and other disciplines, this volume provides close readings of specific events, practices, and cultures to identify some of the characteristic constraints and possibilities defining communicative action in the twenty-first century. The volume will not provide a unified system of explanation, but we hope to get closer to the current "pulse" of the lifeworld: a sense that order and disorder have become barely separable, while political agency is to be found less in democratic institutions or social movements, and more in how ordinary people negotiate complex cultural fields that not only are structured by global forces, but also provide small spaces for making a difference.

## Rhetoric, Culture, and Texture

Rhetoric, considered as the art of amoral manipulation, has long been a defining feature of politics. Whether courtiers or democratic representatives, success seems to come to those who possess more verbal craft than conscience. Politicians of any stripe are considered "moral menials" because of their habits of dissimulation and pandering on behalf of those who hire them (Miller 1997). The study of rhetoric, then, becomes a handbook on beguilement, and any scholar would rightly avoid becoming contaminated by a mentality that aims for persuasion, even if based on false belief, rather than knowledge.

Fortunately, scholars in many disciplines now understand (more or less explicitly) that this is not the whole story, that "rhetoric" has from the beginning been an essentially contested term, and that the intellectual history of the art covers a much wider range of political and literary phenomena, many of which are essential constituents of any important collective enterprise or cultural practice. Even so, the conventional wisdom remains widely distributed—not least because it is accurate some of the time—and it can seem intuitively valid when dealing with political controversies or dysfunctional polities. Even those familiar with the Rhetoric Culture project might understandably harbor suspicions about the study of political discourse.

Both those who would fault rhetorical skill and those who would praise it agree that it is consequential. If the objection is ethical, it is there only on the assumption that political action can be shaped by verbal performance. If the ethical objection is set aside or countered, that is done on the assumption that the performance has not been adequately described or explained through the conventional account. Of course, political behavior is the result of many other factors as well, including power relations, social hierarchies and networks, geography, wealth, religion, and so forth, and all of these can appear as either fixed conditions or matters of extreme contingency. Because persuasion typically involves the representation and negotiation of such factors, the study of rhetoric should avoid single-bullet explanations. That said, important determinants of the success and failure of entire communities are not likely to be correctly identified or understood without attention to the rhetorical dimension of political action.

The chapters in this volume reflect no commitment to a single definition, theory, or doctrine of rhetoric. Indeed, because of the work of the Rhetoric Culture project, they benefit from being able to jump right into the study of specific cases of discursive action without being encumbered by academic controversies or definitional arguments. The context that enables this work is one that the editors have been a part of for several decades, and I can briefly summarize a few key commitments in that regard. The first is to begin with a capacious and affirmative understanding of rhetoric as the study of how language, images, and other symbolic materials operate as a form of action to secure agreement and other goods necessary for collective association. The interests are analytical, theoretical, and normative: that is, to identify how people communicate for social, political, or cultural effect; to explain why they do so and how their actions affect subsequent actions, policies, or practices; and to assess how choices embedded in communicative artifacts and practices constrain or enable the normative infrastructure for a decent society, not least its commitments to human rights, justice, compassion, peace, and similar ideals regarding the general welfare. One need not sign on to a given ideology or an exclusively Western worldview, but one does ask how persuasive success or failure serves some conception of human interest.

The second general feature of our approach is to bring together what have often been two separate tracks in the history of rhetoric: the study of rhetoric as a civic art, and the study of rhetoric as an art of literary composition. Both tracks have focused on the close reading of discursive technique, but against very different horizons of meaning, defined by either the political community or the literary tradition, by an emphasis on argument or on style, and by anxieties about ethical malfeasance or anxieties about authorial innovation, among many other such considerations. These have been blended powerfully in the past—Cicero and his Renaissance readers remain leading examples—but in the modern period they have been channeled into different literatures, practices, pedagogies, and disciplines. With the postmodern turn, however, productive integrations have happened on each side. The study of literary composition has acquired a decidedly political orientation, while study of the civic art has included studies of political performance, political aesthetics, and other figural analyses of the composition of political experience. The focus in the Rhetoric Culture project on the role of rhetoric in the emergence of culture is obviously another example of attempting to understand phenomena that are simultaneously aesthetic and political, decorative and consequential. That project draws on a rich tradition in anthropology of studying the use of figuration in the negotiation of difference and conflict within the discourses of ordinary life and in anthropological writing itself (Strecker and Tyler 2009: 1–3, 15–18). Thus, the reflexive conjunction of aesthetic and political mentalities makes the study of rhetoric into a study of culture.

By focusing on such aesthetic variables as genre, form, figuration, narration, gesture, mood, tone, and the like, and on corresponding variables of response and interaction in the coproduction of meaning, one acquires a critical lexicon for getting inside the discursive construction of political experience. Were these merely formalist categories, the work might remain too distant from the pragmatic consequences that define political action, but working within an explicitly rhetorical context links compositional technique and political orientation. Equally important, this focus on the "political aesthetic"—that is, rhetorical—dimension of experience provides a way to work across modernist categorizations that would define politics, society, and culture as largely autonomous fields of behavior covered by separate disciplines of study (Hariman 1995; Ankersmit 1996; Rancière 2004; Brummett 2008; Bleiker 2009; Panagia 2009; Sartwell 2010).

In our project, culture is neither a pervasive ground encompassing all political activity—and therefore often irrelevant to political discriminations—

nor a relatively sophisticated overlay of meaning and reflexivity—and therefore epiphenomenal to relations of power and impositions of force. Instead, "culture" refers to the assemblage of habits, conventions, and meanings that shape communication in any particular realm of interaction (Carey 2009). Culture functions as both context and content for communication: its media, arts, genres, styles, and other patterns provide constraints on and affordances for specific modes of communication, and the conversations, texts, and other interactions that ensue draw on those symbolic materials as sources of invention and identification when forming and relaying message content. Likewise, any given interaction can be under the horizon of a dominant culture, and it can be a point where multiple cultures intersect and vie for influence. Some cultures can be denominated as political cultures—the culture of the Tea Party, the statehouse, and so forth—while others are less explicitly organized around a political nodal point but are politically consequential nonetheless. The analysis of political cultures in this larger sense could include attention to how action coalesces within, for example, neighborhoods, ethnic groups, or states, along with many other practices such as the military, humanitarian, occupational, and entertainment networks that can become arrayed around a controversy. The point is not to define everything as a culture, but rather to use culture as a means for identifying the complexity shaping political action that might be overlooked or undervalued by analysis focused only on explicitly political variables or material conditions.

This attention to political culture also includes an attempt to account for the contingency of political action. Rather than give too much significance to either structural factors or individual agency, the analysis of political culture considers how political decisions are made "in solution," that is, in gray areas of indeterminacy and maneuver defined by rhetorical conventions that are shared, contested, provisional, and at times inadequate. This is not to deny the value of subsequent explication, but it attempts to understand how important considerations may be experienced only intuitively, indirectly, partially, or under another name and yet be in play nonetheless. Stated otherwise, to the extent that individual or collective agency is available in some objective sense, it will not be used unless it is available within the experience of the political actors, and that experience is always shaped by the context and content of their communicative technologies, habits, interactions, messages, and the like: in short, by the complex interplay of media and meanings that can be labeled the "rhetorical" or "aesthetic" resources of a culture. Thus, the study of political culture is an attempt to discern how actors become equipped for action, how they can use available resources, how effectiveness can depend on timing and other situational or performative skills, how intended actions can have unintended consequences, and similar considerations of how political scenarios are not wholly legible because they are necessarily collective and radically contingent.

This lack of legibility is no small factor when the stakes are high, as they often are when making political decisions. The importance and difficulty of drawing on experience that is collective, contingent, and tacit has been recognized since Aristotle's discussion of the enthymeme. That term refers to one of the primary forms of inference in public argument, and specifically to deductive inference where one of the premises is supplied by the audience (Sloane 2001: 247–50; Rapp 2010; Poster 2000). This coproduction of meaning and agreement is largely tacit (today polls and focus groups try to tap it). The speaker has to rely on the audience providing what goes without saying, and one of the problems is that a lot goes without saying. Thus, speakers and audiences need to be able to share cues, conventions, and the like: the materials of a culture (Miller and McHoul 1998: 179). Nor are these skills limited to elites, for they are the conditions of communicative competency for everyone in a society, and they can be distributed across all media, speakers, and audiences.

They are not distributed equally, however. The focus on shared cultural resources for political argument is easily taken to be a program for consensus politics, with a corresponding denial of systemic inequity. That may be a characteristic risk of our approach, but it is not an inevitable outcome. Symbolic resources are not distributed equally, as societies are stratified by class and other power relations. Likewise, cultures are not seamless veils of unanimity but instead are riven with differences, many of which are used to maintain regimes of domination and exploitation. Social inscriptions—for example, blue for boys and pink for girls in the maternity ward—are not politically innocent and are harder to resist the more widely distributed they become. Cultural capital, which could be widely empowering, is hoarded by those already possessing wealth, status, and other advantages. Modes of communication across social and cultural divisions then become complexly and deceptively coded, as when the "official transcript" masks what is expressed in the "hidden transcript" of any group's discourse (Scott 1990). The study of political culture has to include attention to both ideology and resistance, and to both competency and equity.

That said, relations of power are complicated by at least two factors specific to the role that language and culture play in maintaining social order: social ascriptions have to be partially evident on the surface of things; and there have to be some common conventions for communicating (and ruling, and resisting) across social divisions. The differences between in-groups and outsiders, elites and masses, or any other stratification will have to be coded into speech and other cultural materials if they are to be maintained or mobilized. Once coded, they can be manipulated, made an object of scrutiny, ridiculed, and otherwise put at variance with experience. To naturalize convention, discourse has to remain conventional; its operations are always subject to critique, whether through scholarly study or the slightest change in expression. And because all groups have to communicate with others, there have to be terms and discourses that can work across (or without) the most parochial social knowledge held by each group. These broader vocabularies become especially important as groups become interdependent and as relationships become unequal: as dominant groups come to depend on fictions of equality, reciprocity, and the like to maintain the social order to their benefit, the negotiation of what is said and its relationship to what goes unsaid becomes particularly important to all sides. Outside of total domination, the terms of political speech need to be ambivalent or ambiguous, which makes both control and resistance depend on variations in use (Edelman 1964, 1971; Scott 1985, 1990; Bailey 1983, 2009). So it is that texture matters.

By texture we mean the manner in which social context is evident on the surface of an event, and how that modulation is one dimension of the overdetermined, performative, and dynamic quality of social experience. Just as material surfaces are rough or smooth, so are social surfaces rich or poor, relaxed or tense, bureaucratic or sentimental, and so forth, and each of these textures carries a history of how it got that way. A frayed hem may be due to poverty or personal inattention to fashion or the "disingenuous mistake" of a high-end designer brand, but it means something. More than usual use of the collective personal pronoun may be due to professional habit, celebrity affectation, or megalomania, but rarely is it accidental. It may be unwitting, of course, in the sense that the social actor is not aware of the variation from the norm or is not calculating its effects, but that is simply evidence that the practice is intensively cultural rather than merely intentional.

In the same way, surfaces in any scene are more or less coordinated or uncoordinated, resonant or dissonant, homologous or dissimilar, and often unconsciously so. By paying attention to the texturing of the communicative environment, one can discern what past conditions and practices have been shaping the scene, and what resources for the composition of experience are available to the actors within the scene. When military officers are in the groove at their habitual early morning meetings while the civilians present are sleep deprived and otherwise disoriented by the time shift from their schedules, that asymmetry is likely to be evident in the small variations in dress, deportment, facial expressions, and other minutia that signal what can be consequential disparities in attention and solidarity. When conservative politicians stage events with music by artists they otherwise would include among the "liberal elite" destroying the values of the "real America," that seeming incongruity invites analysis in conjunction with other elements of the spectacle that may be evidence of either deeper continuity or a more comprehensive hypocrisy, but in either case it might provide a key for unlocking some of the puzzlement about contemporary populism. Thus, by attending to the texture of political action, one can perhaps discern how that action is shaped by contextual factors that may not be explicitly stated or explicitly political. These include how various social networks or cultural materials are braided together in a particular moment or movement; how elements necessary for the interpretation of political discourse are evident in the stylistic features of that discourse and the media and other environments affecting reception; how political experience is being shaped by the contingent conjunction of these factors; and how they provide constraints and affordances for other actors and subsequent actions.

These features of political experience can be isolated by application of a variety of methods. Discourse analytics, ethnography, semiotics, rhetoric, iconography—these and other conceptual protocols have made substantial contributions to the analysis of individual agency in materially situated contexts. We do not see the need to provide a brief for any of them. The attention to texture does, however, bend any method away from abstraction and toward a more engaged encounter with particularity. Texture provides an initial suspension of larger conceptions of structural determination; such forces are still present, but not necessarily the prime determinates of action that also can be highly contingent and turn on the smallest things. In Kathleen Stewart's eloquent statement:

> [T]he terms neoliberalism, advanced capitalism, and globalization that index this emergent present and the five or seven or ten characteristics used to summarize and define it in shorthand, do not in themselves begin to describe the situation we find ourselves in. The notion of a totalized system, of which everything is always already somehow a part, is not helpful (to say the least) in the effort to approach a weighted and reeling present. (2007: 1)

What is needed instead is an adaptation of one's method to become attuned to the nascent potentialities in any situation, and to how any event is the specific activation of some set of connections that could have been (and sometimes still can be) otherwise. Classical rhetoric emphasized the control of probabilities in crafting discourse and judgment, but this modern optic is grounded more in individual subjectivity and a phenomenology of experience: "Modes of attending to scenes and events spawn socialities, identities, dream worlds, bodily states and public feelings of all kinds" (Stewart 2007: 10). Stewart emphasizes how this attentiveness is lodged in ordinary life and yet also capable of becoming a modality for social thought. In each case, one is observing, experiencing, and thinking about resonances and other affective surges and connections. Our conception of texture can aspire to this search for "the potential stored in ordinary things.... Fleeting and amorphous, it lives as a residue or resonance in an emergent assemblage of disparate forms and realms of life. Yet it can be as palpable as a physical trace" (Stewart 2007: 21). What often is fleeting, of course, is not the artifact or the routinized practice, but the energy that both can and need not flow through that circuit. Structural pressure and surface variation, but also circuit and flow; intention and constraint, but also timing and chance: these and similar configurations are possible developments of any method that is devoted to discerning how action is a precipitate of potentialities, which in turn can involve large forces being channeled or deflected by small things.

Of course, a method devoted to identifying traces and reading signs that can carry multiple meanings, and often in highly constrained media such as official documents, institutional decor, or popular iconography, is fraught with opportunities for error. Were these merely literary exercises, some might not care, but with politics the stakes are high. We note, however, that the problems of the analyst are precisely those encountered by ordinary actors all the time. Scholars or other professionals supply additional requirements for interpretive validity, but there is no higher knowledge that eliminates the basic dilemma of having to act on the basis of incomplete information, conflicting values, and contingent circumstances. Political actors have to be attuned to the texture of their world if they are to draw on the resources for persuasion that their culture provides. And they have to do this when it matters most; ultimately, when they are trying to stave off or contend with disaster.

## Catastrophe

One might expect the study of political action to focus at some point on revolution, that is, on the paradigmatic example of radical action and deep change. Given the alignment of revolution with progress and both democratic and socialist ideologies in the modern era, both scholarship and public commentary continue to speak of revolutions in the making, revolutionary causes, or the need to reform lest more revolutionary alternatives become necessary. Even for those not happy about progressive tendencies, revolution has been the epitome of political change and something to be avoided for that reason. Although this framework for organizing or interpreting political action will persist, we believe that it has become unrepresentative of both the conditions and character of political action in the twenty-first century. Revolution no longer captures key elements of political imagination or agency, while it reinscribes a conception of autonomous political action that is increasingly unrealistic in the contemporary economic environment. Moreover, another form of violent upheaval is displacing it as the representative figure of need and mobilization. As revolutions have become precursors to disappointment (Greenberg 2014)—and, ironically, stories of literal revolution, that is, of change that returns to the same place—catastrophe has become a master trope for historical discontinuity.

Curiously, catastrophes can contain many of the features of the revolutionary ideal: a great rupturing of the established order, a sweeping process of change that affects all classes, enhanced solidarity as people create new modes of living together, and emerging awareness of a new horizon of meaning, with all of it exceeding prior practices of prediction and control. This depiction is idealized, of course, but so was the revolutionary model. There are also important differences. Catastrophe—from the Greek *katastrephein*, which is related through the root to the rhetorical term *trope*—features overturning or destructive transformation, but with no fixed intention or end. Catastrophe can also refer in classical drama to the transition from the climax to the conclusion, and so perhaps a moment—an endlessly recurring moment—within the ongoing drama of modernity. That would be the moment when control collapses, fatality is exposed, and humanity can "experience its own annihilation as a supreme aesthetic pleasure" (Benjamin 2008: 42). But that particular staging is not obligatory, and catastrophe has been developing its own iconography, rituals, and distinctive capacity for representation and reflection. Whatever the inflection, catastrophe pitches everyone into a condition of rupture where society's basic capacity to function is called into question; in that condition, no new social order is provided to replace the ancien régime, inaction does not restore the status quo ante, action is both unusually difficult and absolutely required, and the outcome is not known.

Even this construction can be too dramatic, however. Ultimately, the divergence from revolutionary action comes from moving beyond the cataclysm itself to more extended conditions that can be both more pessimistic and more open to alternative forms of political agency. Walter Benjamin hinted at this predicament when he said, "Catastrophe—to have missed the opportunity. Critical moment—the status quo threatens to be preserved" (1999: 474). He was seeing catastrophe through the lens of revolution, which could come only by seizing the opportunity provided by the crisis, but his insight goes well beyond the revolutionary attitude or his historical moment. Catastrophes are often experienced as sudden occurrences, but they can develop slowly, can be maintained indefinitely, and can operate in conjunction with the social order even as they destabilize it. So it is that concepts such as "slow violence" or the "regime-made disaster" have emerged to describe the production of catastrophic economic and political regimes, while celebrations of successful environmental reclamation efforts and more efficient energy production can become part of the texture of a civilization refusing to rein in its characteristic hubris (Nixon 2011; Azoulay 2012, 2013).

Thus, catastrophe is emerging as a representative rhetorical figure for twenty-first-century social thought. One sign of the shift in attitude is the enormous popularity of postapocalyptic narratives in television, film, and video games and in science fiction, fantasy, and gothic genres in any medium (Clarke 2005; Paik 2010). Whether in popular culture or public discourse, the trope describes crucial features of the risks, costs, and defining events of global modernization, and it provides a nodal point for thinking about processes of change and collective organization in that world. That engagement with modernity includes refiguration of the era's central myth of progress. That myth imagined inevitable improvement driven by Enlightenment mentalities in every sphere of human endeavor, albeit with some need for occasional revolutions in politics, society, the arts, and even science. Indeed, modernity was a revolutionary project, wresting itself out of the feudal order and advancing through perpetual revolutions (the Protestant revolution, the Darwinian revolution, the Russian Revolution, etc.). The catastrophic model comes without that teleology: progress can occur, but the processes of modernization can also lead to disaster and decline. Thus, catastrophe is not limited to the occurrence of unexpected and unintended negative outcomes, but rather extends to those breakdowns that expose the fragility and teleological vacuity of modern economic, technological, and political systems. As Peter Sloterdijk has observed, "[M]odernity is losing, in addition to its feeling of vitality, the distinction between crisis and stability" (1987: 124). (The claim about vitality would seem to be patently mistaken, but consider that it might include the sense that modernity cannot deliver on its promises, that it can no longer ward off its negative consequences, that it is losing control of development on its own terms, or that it cannot be renewed and extended via revolutions. More to the point, it might suggest that the apparent signs of vitality—heightened market activity and the busyness and acceleration of everyday life—are but frenetic distractions from an underlying cynicism.) As modern technologies and economic practices achieve system dominance, catastrophe shifts from being a frontier phenomenon (the loss of an army or an astronaut) to becoming embedded in the constitution of modern civilization as it can be found anywhere, such as in the "normal accidents" of a "risk society" (Beck 1992; Perrow 1999; Davis 1999; Larabee 2000; Posner 2004; Sarat and Lezaun 2009; Wright 2004). For example, one might consider how modern societies have bought into "modernity's gamble," the wager that the disastrous consequences of modern technology use can be avoided through additional innovation (Hariman and Lucaites 2007: 244). It is not an obviously bad bet, and that is where the smart money is in the near term, but the important point is that it is a bet. Modernity is no longer a narrative of the continuing mastery of nature, but rather a social order organized around a dangerous form of deep play.

This volume brings these and other variations on the trope of catastrophe to bear in several ways. The primary focus is on examining how the experience of catastrophe informs the lives of ordinary people, and more specifically how it textures the actions that they take to try to cope with conditions of economic and political instability. Thus, ongoing economic disruptions and deprivations can make ordinary life closer to the aftermath of a natural disaster than either traditional rural or affluent urban social experience, and political action can be thwarted by all manner of system breakdowns while also being affected in various directions by external interventions that are closer to disaster relief than they are to serious investments in community sustainability. As bubbles burst, states fail, humanitarian interventions assist regimes of domination, modernization projects doom traditional communities, global markets escalate income inequity both within and between societies, and the environmental costs of affluence rise ominously, more and more people are coping with the paradoxical condition of normal system operation becoming indistinguishable from system breakdown. And typically they are coping with remarkable creativity and resilience (Birkland 2009: 125–28; Solnit 2009), though not often to overcome much larger structural deficits and betrayals—the larger catastrophes revealed by seemingly local disasters.

At the last, however, we return to a more general level of theoretical argument, tracing the history and implications of the shift from revolution to catastrophe as a master trope in social thought. The result is not another grand theory, but rather a cautionary note. Perhaps the requirement for a progressive response to a catastrophic modernity is to imagine a politics that is less dramatic than the revolutionary ethos, but more radical for that. If so, the key may be to see how the gaps in system control are to be found in the little things, that is, by being more attentive to the complex and perhaps unexpected relationships between large but unstable structures and the texture of those small places that can be changed for the better.

## The Case Studies

The case studies in this volume are not defined by a common disciplinary orientation, theoretical argument, topic, or method. For example, some of the authors do ethnographic research and focus on face-to-face interaction, while others examine political or commercial advertising to provide critical interpretations of those public texts. Some follow the protocols of conversational discourse analysis, some examine metaphor, irony, or other techniques from the lexicon of rhetorical study, some draw on Bakhtin or other literary theorists, some emphasize historical and philosophical contextualizations, and many draw on several of these approaches. Each of the chapters provides a distinctive configuration of context, theory, and method to address a shared preoccupation with the themes of political culture, texture, and catastrophe. As we hope to show through the diversity and range of these case studies, these concepts provide important challenges and resources for the continued development and relevance of the human sciences.

The first chapter foregrounds a number of factors that are evident across the volume. Hungarian public discourse exemplifies many of the liminal characteristics of a political culture at the borders between national identity and imperial hegemony, between a violent past and unstable present, and between democratization and the crosscurrents of populism and liberalization. Within this context, David Boromisza-Habashi features a more fundamental liminality within public speech itself: the process by which a public expression becomes a political expression. The liberal democratic public sphere is one where it seems just about anything can move from being "nonpolitical" (a simple commercial advertisement, for example) to "political" (say, an ad that offends a minority) and back again. By focusing on the topic of hate speech, Boromisza-Habashi looks at one area of public discourse where the stakes are very high—indeed, where the question in Hungary is whether the polity can prevent an "impending social catastrophe." Through an "ethnorhetorical" analysis of several speech genres, the study identifies a specific technique for texturing public discourse: by constructing an explicit dilemma, the interlocutors can both shift from public to political speech and articulate a common resource for conflict resolution.

Macedonia provides another example of a political community defined by difficult questions of transformation. Following independence in 1991, the country has been contending with the challenges of national state formation, economic transformation from socialism to capitalism, war on its northern border, political conflict with Greece, and violent ethnic insurgencies. This complexity is reflected in the many different discourses of private life, business, government, media coverage, and so forth. Andrew Graan attempts to identify how public discourse addresses these problems in a manner that constructs political experience and enables or disables a sense of individual agency. Graan draws on Mikhail Bakhtin's theory of the chronotope, which marks how discursive genres can direct narrative composition according to specific ideological paths; thus, any coherent configuration of time and place can carry with it conceptions of character, relationships, and action that make specific responses more or less available, intelligible, and legitimate. Graan focuses on two chronotopes in Macedonian discourse, signified by the terms "transition" and "Europe." By charting these terms across several controversies and through different media, Graan shows how the two chronotopes provide contrasting visions of the nation and contrasting attitudes toward political action. Equally important, he demonstrates how they involve reciprocal interaction between media performances and everyday experience. Through analysis of these "orienting devices" in public discourse, one can understand how political culture acquires a specific texture that can shape subjective experience and political praxis.

Macedonia's problems might seem small to those elsewhere in the Balkans, and Naser Miftari's synopsis of political culture in Kosovo reflects a more pessimistic assessment of the possibilities for democratic sustainability. By looking beyond the impression management of public scandals for the basic "scripts" for elite political transactions, Miftari identifies a habit of discursive vagueness that allows near-term trade-offs between contending parties that set the polity on the path to becoming a failed state. Rhetorics of change thus become part of the ritual repetition of established power relationships, and rhetorics of democratization become the lingua franca for external management by international organizations. Nor are these developments unique to Kosovo, as Miftari argues that they stem from endemic problems of the "in-between states." Because modern democratic concepts of rights and transparency are fundamentally abstract, enactment and uptake requires drawing on the deep social networks that preceded democratization and often resist it; indeed, democratic sustainability requires relying on the social and cultural habits that it intends to change, and not surprisingly often without success. The same texturing of democratic practices that is necessary for their uptake in everyday life plays into the hands of political elites, who then thwart political transition while hijacking economic development. To avoid the pending catastrophe for the nation, it appears that one has to look past institution building to see how the social fabric is already being reappropriated to empower some and sideline many others.

One might expect that public discourse in larger and more established states would be less provisional or more uniform than in a small state fraught with transition, but every nation is caught within processes of change today, and public discourse in the United States has hardly been a model of rational deliberation. The Occupy Wall Street movement brought these tensions to a head, as it confronted a profound economic transformation that is reshaping American society, and did so in a manner that was intentionally not legible according to the conventions of political advocacy. A movement without apparent leaders, doctrines, goals, or policy proposals, and one that seemed much more interested in talking to itself than to the press or the political establishment, Occupy was easily dismissed as odd and ineffectual. Yet, it changed the agenda of political debate and remains a leading example of radical praxis. Robert Danisch explains how the movement becomes legible once it is seen in the context of American pragmatism. This legibility comes not from a gloss of political philosophy, however, but from seeing how the fine-grained communication practices of the group enacted a specific form of "rhetorical citizenship." This mode of public discourse attempts to embody egalitarian social democracy through specific communication practices that extend the social contract beyond rights to ground citizenship in collective participation and solidarity. Thus, the key to understanding Occupy is to see how the participants textured public communication according to protocols such as speaking order, audience hand signals, and other techniques designed to create a social democratic political culture.

Occupy has since moved on, and that is not surprising. As with many other social movements today, it is difficult to measure the character and influence of the movement according to conventional metrics of either progressive politics or social movement theory. Peter N. Funke and Todd Wolfson set out an argument that can explain this shift in movement strategies while providing tools for close analysis of specific organizational efforts or demonstrations. The chapter goes beyond the Occupy movement's focus on the income gap to address the more comprehensive framework of neoliberal capitalism. This economic transformation provides not only the object for democratic protests but also the structural conditions that motivate changes in progressive organization and advocacy. As logics of capital accumulation combine with information and communication technologies, progressives have become increasingly nomadic. This nomadic culture is articulated along three dimensions: a flattening of forms in organizational structure; a flattening of fronts by incorporating diverse struggles and groups; and a flattening of governance that emphasizes grassroots and consensual decision making. Thus, even if movement ideals may be relatively unchanged over time, the contemporary movements have a texture that differs from previous generations of Left activism—and raises objections across generational lines. Funke and Wolfson see the wisdom on each side, and argue that just as the new political culture is an important adaptation for confronting neoliberal capitalism, it is also hampered by that relationship and could benefit from reflection on its limitations in respect to earlier movement strategies.

This emphasis on adaptation to neoliberal political and economic policies is continued in Catherine Fennell's study of negotiations over heat within low-income communities in Chicago. Public housing projects, which had been a fixture in modern urban social welfare policy, have been destroyed and replaced with subsidized dispersion into the apartments and other dwellings available in the housing market. Whatever the problems with the "projects," former residents fondly recall the high levels of heat that were a constant comfort during Chicago winters. By contrast, now the low-income renter has to provide enough heat to sustain the familial and social housing patterns that were also part of life in the projects, but with subsidies that fail to anticipate actual costs. Subsequent negotiations over heat with family, friends, landlords, and officials become part of a new fabric of life, one that both distributes risk downward while interfering with individuals' capacity to care for others who are also struggling with poverty. Just as the projects were the subject of complicated and polarized reactions, Fennell identifies a number of ideological, administrative, and political considerations that converge in the politics of market-oriented reform. Her account is distinguished by emphasis on the political texturing of the sensorium, and her suggestions for a sensory politics allow one to more keenly identify both "intensifying fields of physical and social risk" and alternate conceptions of citizenship.

This attention to sensory experience and everyday obligations as they can infuse political action is continued in Eleftheria J. Lekakis's study of the rhetoric of fair trade coffee consumption. By examination of the narratives, allegories, and metaphors of online publicity for fair trade practices, Lekakis tracks how a political culture is created and deployed. Once within that culture, consumption becomes a specifically textured form of political action. Contrary to some arguments for both economic justice and unfettered free markets, this culture is not one where fair trade and free trade are opposing practices; instead, they are woven together, and the results can include both a strong call for justice and a strong market dependency. As with other chapters, this analysis of fair trade rhetoric demonstrates how one's sense of political participation and agency can be shaped by fine-grained interactions between media production and everyday life. Similarly, it provides another example of how the discursive tactics for progressive advocacy are shaped by the historical transformations it would resist, and how the choice for contemporary activists is often one of learning how to ride the tiger that would devour them.

The attempt to create equitable, sustainable relationships between local practices and larger processes of economic and political transformation becomes especially fraught when the encounter is between indigenous societies and top-down state modernization. As James C. Scott (2009) has demonstrated, when the state has been relatively weak and the geography conducive to escape strategies, traditional societies have been able to preserve an acceptable level of autonomy. Felix Girke thickens that idea with his study of the Kara people of southern Ethiopia. The Kara's relationship with the Ethiopian government includes ritualized negotiations constituting a political culture that is dysfunctional by some measures yet also characterized by highly sophisticated performances that allow the Kara to maintain their dignity. By attending to the texture of those ritualized encounters between state officials and Kara speakers, and particularly to the adroit use of irony and other performative tactics, Girke is able to identify important values, practices, and strategies for sustaining the political relationships that protect the Kara. Even so, Girke is equally attentive to the fact that this "peripheral wisdom" may finally be conquered by the forces of economic development: construction of a dam that would end the annual flooding necessary for Kara agriculture, which would then leave them with the prospect of either resettlement or becoming low-wage laborers for the plantations already plotted across their territory. This catastrophe is not one that their rhetorical skills can confront head-on, even as it presents the ultimate test, though not a fair one, for their political culture.

This predicament is not unique, nor does it exhaust the discursive resources for coping. Christian Meyer examines another community's response to disaster, in this case a locust plague that devastated the fields of the Wolof people in northwestern Senegal. As Meyer notes, disasters are now a regular feature of the global discourse of modernization. Although an embarrassment because of how they reveal the incompleteness or fragility of modernity, disasters also prompt mobilization across multiple networks, state intervention to manage the situation and provide aid, and, not incidentally, a lot of talk about what is to be done. Meyer provides a fine-grained analysis of conversation among the villagers directly affected by the plague, and finds strong correspondences between a global discourse of disaster management and the local conversations about the locust's encroachment, the responses of local actors and the state, and related concerns. The Wolof employ sequenced functions of disaster communication, topoi of risk assessment, figural representations, and more contentious claims of social inequality that can lead to political action. Thus, Meyer finds that the local and global discourses of disaster management both intersect and diverge. The political culture that is evident in the villagers' response to catastrophe is one that can be legible to global organizations and institutional actors, while remaining focused on finding opportunities for local control and sustainability.

It might seem odd to some that the Wolof do not have a term for disaster; as this volume suggests, that category (of disaster or catastrophe) is becoming increasingly salient in the global discourse of modernity. Even with that category, however, problems of representation remain. Indeed, one predicament in capital- and technology-intensive societies is not being able to mark the "everyday catastrophes" that result from excessive consumption. Resource depletions, toxin accumulations, species die-offs, antibiotic-resistant pathogens, public health problems such as obesity and type 2 diabetes, more and more social energy diverted to buying, storing, discarding, and recycling consumer goods—these and other conditions are signs of overconsumption, yet the lived experience of the relevant economic and social practices is often one of convenience, short-term gratification, novelty, or other simple pleasures. To address this problem, Monica Westin examines Thomas Hirschhorn's artwork *Too Too Much Much*. Hirschhorn's installation consists of many thousands of aluminum beverage cans piled up through the museum space and flowing out the door like a glacier of trash. By confronting the spectator with an experience of scale that usually is invisible, the work also evokes an aesthetic uniquely suited to the representation of rupture and excess: the sublime. This aesthetic experience is also suited to understanding catastrophe, and so Hirschhorn is able to transform the everyday world of consumer consumption into an ongoing disaster in the making. Westin takes this provocation further still by focusing on material embodiment of what are otherwise abstractions. The encounter with the texture of excess gives excess a rhetorical presence that shifts from logics of symbolic representation to political interpellation. In short, we are called to be subjects who already have been making a mess of the world.

The artist's attempt to confront large-scale economic processes is complemented by the Conclusion's return to social theory, as Ralph Cintron examines the intertwined histories of revolutionary and catastrophic mentalities. Modern economics in particular has been unusually receptive to concepts of rupture, and a political aesthetic of revolution energized both Left and Right ideologies of political economy. With the rise of neoliberalism as both revanchist ideology and global policy, another rupture has occurred, this time in the notion of disruption itself. By incorporating catastrophic change into the successful operation of capital, the logic of civilizational development has been redefined in a way that undercuts prior practices of critique and mobilization. The exhaustion of the Left as the engine of progressive social change is one symptom of that shift; another is the paradoxical capability of the Right to redefine system breakdown as a basis for reinvestment in destructive economic practices. Cintron concludes where we began, by suggesting that local political actors are not helpless in this condition, if they can become more attentive to the discursive possibilities for re-creating culture and community in a world that is defined as much by paradox as by progress. If modernity is to be both just and sustainable, those who have the capability to act must be willing to accept not only that ruins can be transformed into gleaming monuments to progress, but also that progress is already in ruins.

## Coda: Political Action among the Ruins

Catastrophe can be a resource for rethinking the relationship between structural determination and individual agency. On the one hand, system breakdown should create new possibilities for action. The shattered cityscape is also a place of social fissures and emptied spaces now open to new possibilities—in more than one blockbuster movie and perhaps elsewhere as well. On the other hand, a much more comprehensive disaster might be underway: as modern societies are torqued by large-scale forces, the intermediate spaces and shared contexts that sustain democratic politics are slowly being obliterated. As Sloterdijk suggests, when that happens individual subjectivity and social effectivity become dangerously disjointed.

> The present-day servant of the system can very well do with the right hand what the left hand never allowed. By day, colonizer, at night colonized; by occupation, valorizer and administrator, during leisure time, valorized and administered; officially a cynical functionary, privately a sensitive soul; at the office a giver of orders, ideologically a discussant; outwardly a follower of the reality principle, inwardly a subject oriented toward pleasure; functionally an agent of capital, intentionally a democrat; with respect to the system a functionary of reification, with respect to the *Lebenswelt* (lifeword), someone who achieves self-realization; objectively a strategist of destruction, subjectively a pacifist; basically someone who triggers catastrophes, in one's own view, innocence personified. (1987: 113)

Sloterdijk is identifying a deep fissure between functional roles and private consciousness, with nothing like an emergent, intermediate mentality—call it political, public, civic, or something else—to mediate between self and system, much less society and the state. When the public realm disintegrates, one gets this neoliberal conjunction of two forms of the private sphere—corporations and corporatist states on the one side and personal life on the other—and the power imbalance and split subjectivity that comes with that. This "schizoid" condition reflects fundamental contradictions between modernity's development as a global system of wealth production and its promises of freedom, self-determination, and happiness. In Sloterdijk's account, the challenge is to overcome the inevitable result of this ongoing catastrophe, which is the pervasive cynicism that is, after all, a rational response to a system that is both dominant and producing the disasters it is supposed to prevent.

In other words, both politics and social theory now lie athwart an ongoing catastrophe. This volume suggests one response to that predicament: if anyone is to bridge the widening chasm between individual agency and large-scale destructiveness, they must become attuned to more varied, provisional, and vernacular forms of communication and culture. As we have suggested, this is where forms of adaptation, resistance, and renewal are being worked out, however fitfully, and where attention to the texture of political action might become particularly helpful. Texture is important in part precisely because of the changes that Jürgen Habermas has identified in the public sphere, including such factors as the rise of consumer consumption, democratic institutionalization, and the "wildness" of noninstitutional speech (Habermas 1989, 1996). Given the pluralism, hybridity, and unchecked circulation characterizing public discourse today, as well as the varied contexts for reception, the room to move toward solidarity and effective critique is often found in the small spaces opened up by seemingly trivial variations in social performance. These spaces can be found within glittering office towers and traditional social practices, and they can include doors to more equitable relationships within existing structures, but also to alternative modernities (Gaonkar 2001).

These are also the conditions Soterdijk identifies as a "life philosophy of crisis": "moderation of expectations, adaptability, presence of mind, attention to what the moment offers," and a "current of warmth" that includes "principled hope" and "creative friendliness toward life" (1987: 123, 126). His attitude is melancholic (with an allegorical method to match), but there is no need to settle there. In our account, ruin is not the end point of the Enlightenment narrative, but rather a paradoxical concomitant to progress that is always present, whether as an actual disaster or potential collapse. Like a doppelgänger that can limn distant or future events, catastrophe shadows modernity, and by discerning how this paradoxical condition is woven into everyday life, one can perhaps discern which way the balance is shifting. Of course, this paradoxical condition applies across the board, and no one is exempt from creating unintended consequences. One result might be that action itself has to be cut down a notch, say, by being linked with modes of patience and reflexivity that can be found within the disaster (Blanchot 1986), or by becoming attuned to solidarities that can be found in both small acts of acknowledgment (Stewart 2007) and modes of spectatorship (Azoulay 2008). If dramatic action and endless innovation on behalf of progress are now tarnished dreams, one need not succumb to merely surviving among the ruins. Political imagination, shared responsibility, public accountability, the common good—these and other elements of a just and sustainable political culture are renewable resources.

**Robert Hariman** is a professor in the Department of Communication Studies at Northwestern University. He is the author of *Political Style: The Artistry of Power* (University of Chicago Press, 1995) and *No Caption Needed: Iconic Photographs, Public Culture, and Liberal Democracy* (University of Chicago Press, 2007), which was coauthored with John Louis Lucaites. He has also published three edited volumes and numerous book chapters and journal articles in several disciplines, and his work has been translated into French and Chinese. He and coauthor John Louis Lucaites post regularly at nocaptionneeded.com, their blog on photojournalism, politics, and culture.

## Bibliography

Alexander, Jeffrey C. 2008. "Iconic Consciousness: The Material Feeling of Meaning." *Environment and Planning D: Society and Space* 26: 782–94.
Ankersmit, F. R. 1996. *Aesthetic Politics: Political Philosophy Beyond Fact and Value*. Stanford, CA: Stanford University Press.
Azoulay, Ariella. 2008. *The Civil Contract of Photography*. New York: Zone Books.
———. 2012. "Regime-Made Disaster: On the Possibility of Nongovernmental Viewing." In *Sensible Politics: The Visual Culture of Nongovernmental Politics*, ed. Meg McLagan and Yates McKee, 29–41. New York: Zone Books.
———. 2013. "A Tour of the Museum of Regime-Made Disasters." *Humanity: An International Journal of Human Rights, Humanitarianism, and Development* 4: 345–63.
Bailey, F. G. 1983. *The Tactical Uses of Passion: An Essay on Power, Reason, and Reality*. Ithaca, NY: Cornell University Press.
———. 2009. "The Palestrael Aspect of Rhetoric." In *Culture, Rhetoric and the Vicissitudes of Life*, ed. Michael Carrithers, 107–20. New York: Berghahn Books.
Bartmanski, Dominik, and Jeffrey C. Alexander. 2012. "Materiality and Meaning in Social Life: Toward an Iconic Turn in Cultural Sociology." In *Iconic Power: Materiality and Meaning in Social Life*, ed. Jeffrey C. Alexander, Dominik Bartmanski, and Bernhard Giesen, 1–12. New York: Palgrave Macmillan.
Beck, Ulrich. 1992. *Risk Society: Towards a New Modernity*. Trans. Mark Ritter. London: Sage.
Benjamin, Walter. 1999. *The Arcades Project*. Trans. Howard Eiland and Kevin McLaughlin. Cambridge, MA: Belknap Press.
———. 2008. "The Work of Art in the Age of Its Technological Reproducibility." In *The Work of Art in the Age of Its Technological Reproducibility and Other Writings on Media*, ed. Michael W. Jennings, Brigid Doherty, and Thomas Y. Levin, 19–55. Cambridge, MA: Belknap Press.
Birkland, Thomas A. 2009. "Emergency Management and the Courts in the Wake of Hurricane Katrina." In *Catastrophe: Law, Politics, and the Humanitarian Impulse*, ed. Austin Sarat and Javier Lezaun, 116–45. Amherst: University of Massachusetts Press.
Blanchot, Maurice. 1986. *The Writing of the Disaster*. Trans. Ann Smock. Lincoln: University of Nebraska Press.
Bleiker, Roland. 2009. *Aesthetics and World Politics*. Houndmills, UK: Palgrave Macmillan.
Brummett, Barry. 2008. *A Rhetoric of Style*. Carbondale: University of Southern Illinois Press.
Carey, James W. 2009. *Communication as Culture: Essays on Media and Society*. Rev. ed. New York: Routledge.
Clarke, Lee. 2005. *Worst Cases: Terror and Catastrophe in the Popular Imagination*. Chicago: University of Chicago Press.
Davis, Mike. 1999. *Ecology of Fear: Los Angeles and the Imagination of Disaster*. New York: Vintage Books.

Edelman, Murray J. 1964. *The Symbolic Uses Politics*. Urbana: University of Illinois Press.
———. 1971. *Politics as Symbolic Action: Mass Arousal and Quiescence*. Chicago: Markham.
Gaonkar, Dilip Parameshwar, ed. 2001. *Alternative Modernities*. Durham, NC: Duke University Press.
Greenberg, Jessica. 2014. *After the Revolution: Youth, Democracy, and the Politics of Disappointment in Serbia*. Stanford, CA: Stanford University Press.
Habermas, Jürgen. 1989. *The Structural Transformation of the Public Sphere: An Inquiry into a Category of Bourgeois Society*. Trans. Thomas Burger and Frederick Lawrence. Cambridge, MA: MIT Press.
———. 1996. *Between Facts and Norms: Contributions to a Discourse Theory of Law and Democracy*. Trans. William Rehg. Cambridge, MA: MIT Press.
Hariman, Robert. 1995. *Political Style: The Artistry of Power*. Chicago: University of Chicago Press.
Hariman, Robert, and John Louis Lucaites. 2007. *No Caption Needed: Iconic Photographs, Public Culture, and Liberal Democracy*. Chicago: University of Chicago Press, 2007.
———. 2015. "Image, Icon, and Cultural Critique." *Sociologica* 1: 1-32. http://www.sociologica.mulino.it/journal/article/index/Article/Journal:ARTICLE:827/Item/Journal:ARTICLE:827 (accessed 21 August 2015).
Larabee, Ann. 2000. *Decade of Disaster*. Urbana: University of Illinois Press.
Miller, Toby, and Alec McHoul. 1998. *Popular Culture and Everyday Life*. London: Sage.
Miller, William Ian. 1997. *The Anatomy of Disgust*. Cambridge, MA: Harvard University Press.
Nixon, Rob. 2011. *Slow Violence and the Environmentalism of the Poor*. Cambridge, MA: Harvard University Press.
Paik, Peter Y. 2010. *From Utopia to Apocalypse: Science Fiction and the Politics of Catastrophe*. Minneapolis: University of Minnesota Press.
Panagia, Davide. 2009. *The Political Life of Sensation*. Durham, NC: Duke University Press.
Perrow, Charles. 1999. *Normal Accidents: Living with High-Risk Technologies*. Princeton, NJ: Princeton University Press.
Posner, Richard A. 2004. *Catastrophe: Risk and Response*. New York: Oxford University Press.
Poster, Carol. 2000. "The Enthymeme: An Interdisciplinary Bibliography of Critical Studies." *The Journal for the Study of Rhetorical Criticism of the New Testament*. http://rhetjournal.net/RhetJournal/Enthymemes.html (accessed 23 June 2015).
Rancière, Jacques. 2004. *The Politics of Aesthetics: The Distribution of the Sensible*. Trans. Gabriel Rockhill. New York: Continuum.
Rapp, Christof. 2010. "Aristotle's Rhetoric." *Stanford Encyclopedia of Philosophy* (Spring 2010 edition), ed. Edward N. Salta. http://plato.stanford.edu/archives/spr2010/entries/aristotle-rhetoric/ (accessed 23 June 2015).
Sarat, Austin, and Javier Lezaun, eds. 2009. *Catastrophe: Law, Politics, and the Humanitarian Impulse*. Amherst: University of Massachusetts Press.
Sartwell, Crispin. 2010. *Political Aesthetics*. Ithaca, NY: Cornell University Press.
Scott, James C. 1985. *Weapons of the Weak: Everyday Forms of Peasant Resistance*. New Haven, CT: Yale University Press.
———. 1990. *Domination and the Arts of Resistance: Hidden Transcripts*. New Haven, CT: Yale University Press.
———. 2009. *The Art of Not Being Governed: An Anarchist History of Upland Southeast Asia*. New Haven, CT: Yale University Press.
Sloane, Thomas O., ed. 2001. *Encyclopedia of Rhetoric*. New York: Oxford University Press.

Sloterdijk, Peter. 1987. *Critique of Cynical Reason.* Trans. Michael Eldred. Minneapolis: University of Minnesota Press.
Solnit, Rebecca. 2009. *A Paradise Built in Hell: The Extraordinary Communities that Arise in Disaster.* New York: Viking.
Stewart, Kathleen. 2007. *Ordinary Affects.* Durham, NC: Duke University Press.
Strecker, Ivo, and Stephen Tyler, eds. 2009. *Culture and Rhetoric.* New York: Berghahn Books.
Wright, Ronald. 2004. *A Short History of Progress.* Cambridge, MA: Da Capo Press.

CHAPTER 1

# The Communal Dilemma as a Cultural Resource in Hungarian Political Expression

*David Boromisza-Habashi*

■ ■ ■ ■ ■ ■

Let us begin with a seemingly simple question: how does public expression become political expression? There are simple, commonsense answers to this question. For example, when professional politicians speak in public, what they say constitutes political expression. When someone speaks publicly in an institutional setting commonly recognized as political—at a political rally, in a congressional committee meeting, or in the general assembly of a nation's parliament—we regard their speech as political expression. Public expression addressing political matters is also generally regarded as political talk. Often, the identity of the speaker, the institutional setting, and the topic of expression are indeed reliable indicators that political expression is taking place. However, there are cases in which the political nature of expression is less obvious. Consider the widely publicized "private" conversation between the presidents of France and the United States at the G20 meeting in November 2011. Oblivious to an open microphone in their vicinity, President Sarkozy referred to Israeli Prime Minister Netanyahu as a "liar," and President Obama complained about "having to deal with" Netanyahu "every day." Once made public, did the utterances of these prominent political figures constitute political expression? Or when the president of the United States acknowledges an invited "ordinary citizen" during a State of the Union address and the citizen smiles, is that smile political speech? What about high school debaters addressing political issues like national defense and foreign policy at a debating tournament? Are they producing political expression?

For the cultural analyst of language use, the immediate response to the question of how public expression becomes political expression is a question of point of view: political from whose perspective? Who, indeed, is in the best position to determine whether a strip of public talk counts as political expression? It is possible to advance a cultural view of discourse according to which "all talk is social and political" (Bailey 2007: 271), as all observable talk indexes established sociopolitical and historical relations. This view, however, can lose sight of moments in public talk where participants, using subtle, locally available interactional cues, signal that they have switched to a political mode of expression.

The ethnorhetorical approach (Boromisza-Habashi 2011; Carbaugh and Boromisza-Habashi 2011) was designed to show that local, cultural systems of expression and meaning bring coherence to, and find their own articulation in, rhetorical discourse. Rhetorical discourse is understood as the meaningful use of communicative (especially discursive, symbolic) resources to "shape practical action [and] mold cultural beliefs about communication itself" (Carbaugh and Boromisza-Habashi 2011: 104–5). The term "ethnorhetoric" points to the observation that humans often rely on locally available communicative resources in their attempts to shape human conduct and social relations, and do so within locally observed limits of intelligibility and propriety. Fascination with the order-making capacity of communication is an intellectual orientation the ethnorhetorical approach shares with the Rhetoric Culture project (Tyler and Strecker 2009) and, more broadly speaking, with those who study culture as human praxis (Bauman 1999).

The ethnorhetorical approach maintains that any analytical claim about the meaning of observable rhetorical discourse must represent, as closely as possible, the perspective of the speaker and their speech community. The task of the analyst is to capture locally available communicative resources cultural members use to make sense of, and participate in, social life in particular historical contexts. Cultural symbols (such as key terms and concepts), symbolic forms (such as rituals or social dramas), and the meanings of symbols and symbolic forms (such as basic cultural assumptions, beliefs, and norms) function as resources for sense making and participation (Carbaugh 2007, 2011; Philipsen 1992).

The ethnorhetoric concept suggests a third way to ask the question that serves as the intellectual engine of this chapter: how do public speakers use locally available communicative resources to impose a political order on ongoing communicative action and relevant social relations? Answering this question about a rhetorical strategy requires the study of actual political discourse, particularly the ethnographically informed study of political expression as the ordering of conduct and social relations (e.g., see Agar 1994; Albert 1972; Bauman and Briggs 2003; Bloch and Lemish 2005; Carbaugh 1988, 1996, 2002; Gal 1991; Huspek and Kendall 1991; Lippi-Green 1997; Urla 1995; Witteborn 2004).

The task of this chapter is to capture one particular, Hungarian resource, the strategic invocation of a communal dilemma (*dilemma* in Hungarian) about hate speech legislation. A second, related task is to reconstruct the local function of this rhetorical strategy. The ethnography of communication (Cameron 2001; Carbaugh 2008; Hymes 1972; Saville-Troike 2003) suggests a theoretically informed approach to social interaction. Ethnographers use theories of communicative activity to notice local activities, strive to interpret the local significance (or insignificance) of those activities, and return to the theory or theories of choice in order to assess their explanatory power in the light of cultural interpretation (Carbaugh and Hastings 1992). The communication activity theory I bring to the analysis of dilemma invocations is the theory of frames. Frames are communicative cues that help participants of the same communicative situation develop a shared definition of the situation and, in interaction, coordinate their communicative activities according to that shared definition (Goffman 1974). What I set out to show is that Hungarian speakers sometimes invoke communal dilemmas in order to frame the ongoing interaction—or an ongoing communicative process beyond the boundaries of a single interaction—as a political one.

What is a "political" frame? How do we know that someone has just invoked one, and that communicative action and social relations in that frame should be regarded as "political"? There are at least two ways to muster evidence for the claim that in a specific communicative process a political frame is active. On the one hand, social groups develop political forums (village or town hall meetings), political identities (elders, senators, or registered party members), and political genres of talk (stump speeches, presidential addresses, the concession speeches of candidates for political office) that are widely recognized as such. Overt reference to these forums, identities, and genres by means of words, spatial arrangements, or visual aids (national flags, Doric columns, balloons, etc.) can be used to frame communicative situations and actions as political. There are, however, more subtle cues at speakers' disposal to switch to a political footing (Goffman 1981) to introduce a markedly political definition of the situation and related communicative action. My goal in this chapter is to show that the invocation of a communal dilemma is a resource to accomplish such a definition.

After a very brief overview of the hate speech debate in Hungary, I investigate the meaning of communal dilemma invocations by highlighting two relevant contexts in which those invocations take on significance for Hungarian speakers. Borrowing a distinction from Goodwin and Duranti (1992), I first focus on language use as the context of dilemma invocations. This type of analysis seeks to establish the local meanings of linguistic resources (such as the dilemma) by identifying their communicative functions within the context of ongoing social interaction or broader, sequential communicative processes (such as media controversies extended over days or weeks). Second, I discuss how the dilemma acquires meaning, and the dilemma invocation rhetorical force, in what Goodwin and Duranti (1992) call the extrasituational context of language use, the context of interaction constituted by sociocultural background knowledge and broader frames of reference. I discuss one particular sociocultural meaning of the dilemma that informs particular interactions or communicative processes. Finally, I spell out the relationship between political texturing and political participation.

## The Hate Speech Debate in Hungary

The wave of concern about hate speech that marked the 1990s in the United States reached Hungary in the early 2000s. That wave was, indeed, a tidal wave: Hungarian political discourse was awash with allegations and counterallegations of "hate speech" (*gyűlöletbeszéd*) by 2003 (see Boromisza-Habashi 2013). Consensus about the meaning of the term was very limited—in fact, many public speakers thrived on the contestation of meanings. It was easy to counter an allegation of hate speech or the interpretation of an act of speaking as hate speech with an allegation or interpretation built on a competing meaning of the term. In broadcast discourse about hate speech between 2003 and 2007, I found forty-four terms speakers used to explicate the meaning of hate speech. *Gyűlöletbeszéd* was discussed as "discrimination" (*kirekesztés*) and "stigmatization" (*megbélyegzés*), as "speech filled with hatred" (*gyűlölettel teli beszéd*), as "a derogatory remark about a group" (*leértékelő kijelentés csoport ellen*), and as "saying outrageous things about Hungarians" (*magyarokról felháborító dolgokat mondani*). These terms were connected by a network of family resemblances, but these resemblances did not bring about any widespread consensus about the meaning of hate speech. Hungarian public speakers agreed about one thing only: hate speech was despicable, and Hungarians needed to do something about it. There was no agreement, however, about exactly why hate speech was so despicable. The term was used to point to a variety of impending social catastrophes that appeared catastrophic only to those who voiced concern about them. Some said hate speech was hurting historically disadvantaged minorities; others maintained that it rendered Hungarian public discourse toxic; yet others complained that accusations of hate speech were a political ploy to silence the Hungarian radical Right.

There were some on the political Left, especially among Hungarian Socialists, who made multiple attempts to pass legislation outlawing hate speech as a category of criminal conduct. Champions of the "hate law" (*gyűlölettörvény*) found their vision of social catastrophe being contested by representatives of competing visions. First, not everyone was willing to accept the definition of hate speech as a type of public expression that violated the human dignity of its targets and therefore fell outside the boundaries of free speech. Hungarian free speech advocates saw the hate law as a pernicious attack on civil rights. Second, there was the issue of wildly variable interpretations of what forms of public expression constituted hate speech. A small but vocal group on the Far Right denied the very existence of hate speech as an observable form of expression and worried instead about their own right to uninhibited political expression. Third, the sentiment that some forms of talk constituted criminal behavior conjured up specters of dark national history. Since the late 1800s, most Hungarian political regimes found it necessary to outlaw speech they deemed contrary to their interests (Györgyi 2003). The Habsburg monarchy outlawed public expression challenging the legitimacy of the throne and the royal succession. After the 1919 Communist uprising, which temporarily brought Hungary into Bolshevik Russia's domain of influence, the Kingdom of Hungary outlawed all "slander against the [Hungarian] nation" (*nemzetrágalmazás*). When in the wake of the Vienna Awards Hungary annexed parts of present-day Ukraine, Slovakia, and Romania, a 1941 law ruled against derogatory public expression directed at ethnic minorities. After World War II, a variety of laws prohibited public criticism of the Socialist state. Proponents of the hate law tried to cultivate an alternative, but equally sinister, history of hate speech legislation. Such legislation, they argued, would acknowledge one of the most important historical lessons from the Holocaust, namely, that hateful expression is the harbinger of crimes against humanity. This alternative history, however, did not manage to mute its competitor.

## Language Use as Context: The Rhetorical Strategy of Invoking a Dilemma

After the demise of state socialism, Hungary's turn toward the European Union and the growing influence of the human rights discourse permeating EU social policy reinvigorated the Hungarian Left's quest for the hate law. The three excerpts discussed in this section are all concerned with, in one way or another, the possibility of legal sanctions against *gyűlöletbeszéd*.

In 2005, Péter Bárándy, a former Socialist minister of justice and one of the most prominent advocates of the hate law, was interviewed on the influential political television program *Nap-Kelte* (Sunrise). Toward the end of the interview, Bárándy (PB) brought up one of hate law advocates' most widely used arguments: those who value absolute freedom of speech over the protection of human dignity fail to appreciate that the Holocaust began with the public expression of hatred. Starting on line 14, the interviewer (IR) resisted the implicit argument that passing the hate law was a matter of legal or moral necessity. (Note that references to line numbers refer to the Hungarian original. All translations are the author's own.)

Excerpt 1, *Nap-Kelte* (*Vendégasztal*), 9 August 2005, 06:08

| | | | |
|---|---|---|---|
| 1 | PB | a jog is és az erkölcs is | Law and morality both reach |
| 2 | | elérkezik | |
| 3 | IR | Mhm | Mhm |
| 4 | PB | saját határához ennél a | their own limits with regard to |
| 5 | | kérdéskörnél és a viták | this issue, and the debates |
| 6 | | azok akkor ö | seem to be decided |
| 7 | | látszanak úgy eldőlni hogy inkább | in favor of |
| 8 | | a szólásszabadság mintsem az | freedom of speech rather than |
| 9 | | emberi méltóság amikor az emberi | human dignity when human |
| 10 | | feledékenység eljut arra a határra | forgetfulness reaches a point |
| 11 | | amikor már nem emlékszik | where it can no longer recall |
| 12 | | arra hogy minden a szavakkal | that everything begins with |
| 13 | | kezdődik. ((smiles)) | words. |
| 14 | IR | Én tökéletesen értem sokan | I understand perfectly, many |
| 15 | | értik ami ön mond de akkor | understand what you are saying |
| 16 | | amikor a szavakkal kezdődtek a | but when things started with |
| 17 | | dolgok és csak toporgott a jog | words the law just hesitated, and |
| 18 | | később amikor már a | later when forgetting, as you |
| 19 | | ö feledés ahogy ön mondta be | said, had hidden these beginning |
| 20 | | ö fedte ezeket a kezdeti időket | times from view, the law only |
| 21 | | akkor is tétován toporog a jog | hesitated. |
| 22 | | és lehet hogy ezt egyszerűen | And it is possible that even if |
| 23 | | a jog eszközeivel még ha | this ought to be solved by |
| 24 | | kellene sem lehet megoldani. | legal means it cannot be done. |
| 25 | PB | Nézze ez | Look, this |
| 26 | IR | Nem tudom, kérdezem | I don't know this, I'm just |
| 27 | | | asking. |
| 28 | PB | Az emberölés | The prohibition of murder |
| 29 | | tilalmazását sem lehet csak a jog | cannot be solved solely |

| | | | |
|---|---|---|---|
| 30 | | eszközeivel megodani. Semmit sem | by legal means. Nothing can be |
| 31 | | lehet csak a jog eszközeivel | solved solely by legal means, |
| 32 | | megoldani, a jog egy | the law is a |
| 33 | | eszköz. ön is így fogalmazott, | tool, as you put it as well |
| 34 | IR | Így van. | That's correct. |
| 35 | PB | én is mindig így fogalmazok. | and I always say so myself. |
| 36 | IR | Igen. | Yes. |
| 37 | PB | Egy fajta szerszámkészlettel | It is equipped with a certain set |
| 38 | | rendelkezik ami mindennek a | of tools that cannot be |
| 39 | | megoldására nem alkalmas. Nincs | used to solve everything. There |
| 40 | | olyan bűncselekmény kategória amit | is no category of criminal acts |
| 41 | | csak a jog eszközével | that can be prevented solely |
| 42 | | tudunk elhárítani mondom a | by legal means, as I said |
| 43 | | legsúlyosabb emberöléstől | including the gravest murder |
| 44 | IR | Jó csak | Okay, but |
| 45 | PB | a becsületsértésen keresztül | including libel |
| 46 | IR | bocsásson meg a ortodox jogászok | I'm sorry, among orthodox lawyers |
| 47 | PB | a lopásig. | all the way to theft. |
| 48 | IR | ortodox jogászok között ezt most | among orthodox lawyers, and I say |
| 49 | | leíró értelemben használom | this in a descriptive, not an |
| 50 | | nem minősítve azért látszik | evaluative way, I can see |
| 51 | | egy olyanfajta törekvés hogy egy | an attempt to squeeze |
| 52 | | véges rendszerbe belegyömöszöljük | infinite reality into a finite |
| 53 | | a végtelen valóságot. | system. |
| 54 | PB | ((smiles)) Igen azt hiszem hogy ez | Yes, I don't believe that this is |
| 55 | | nem egy helyes ö jogászi | an appropriate attitude among |
| 56 | | felfogás | lawyers. |
| 57 | IR | Ö ezt azért vetem föl mert | I am raising this [issue] because |
| 58 | | miután az erkölcsnek is és a | both morality and law must face |
| 59 | | jognak is ö valóságos | actual dilemmas here |
| 60 | | dilemmákkal kell itt szembenézni | |
| 61 | | és valóságos értékek | and actual values exist in a |
| 62 | | feszülnek egybe. Ezenközbe azt | relationship of tension, however |
| 63 | | tapasztalom hogy a | what I'm noticing is that the |
| 64 | | gyűlölettörvényről szóló beszéd | recycling of talk about the hate |
| 65 | | ö időnként ö történő | law from time to time serves as a |
| 66 | | elővétele politikai | vehicle for political |
| 67 | | manipulációkra ad alkalmat. | manipulation. |
| 68 | | Ezt olykor mintha | It seems that this [law] |
| 69 | | tudatosan dobnák be akkor amikor | is placed on the agenda when |
| 70 | | lehet hogy másról kellene beszélni | perhaps we should be talking |

| | | | |
|---|---|---|---|
| 71 | | olykor provokációszámba megy | about something else, and |
| 72 | | a másik oldalról ennek a | sometimes the other side seems to |
| 73 | | nagyon durva ö azt mondanám | provoke [the former] by denying |
| 74 | | hogy inkább ö intellektuálisan | [the legitimacy of the law] in an |
| 75 | | vagy erkölcsileg érzéketlen | intellectually or morally |
| 76 | | tagadása. Mindenesetre mind a | insensitive manner. In any event, |
| 77 | | két oldal számára lehetővé teszi | this gives both sides a chance to |
| 78 | | hogy olyan politikai | play such political games under |
| 79 | | játszmákat játszanak le ennek | this pretense |
| 80 | | örvén aminek se jogi se | that otherwise have neither legal |
| 81 | | erkölcsi alapja egyébként nem | nor moral |
| 82 | | lehetne. | foundations. |
| 83 | PB | Ez így van de sajnos azt kell | This is true, but unfortunately we |
| 84 | | látni hogy minden valamirevaló | have to recognize that all |
| 85 | | kérdést azt föl lehet | worthwhile issues can be used in |
| 86 | | használni demagóg | the service of demagogic |
| 87 | | politikai érdekek | political interests, which |
| 88 | | érvényesítésére ettől még az a | does not mean that a worthwhile |
| 89 | | valamirevaló kérdés valamirevaló | issue is no longer a worthwhile |
| 90 | | kérdés marad csak legfeljebb | issue, it only becomes smeared in |
| 91 | | besározódik hogyha a pártok | the hands of political parties. |
| 92 | | kezére kerül. De az egy | But it's interesting how [views |
| 93 | | érdekes dolog egyébként ez a | on] hate speech versus freedom of |
| 94 | | gyűlöletbeszéd szólásszabadság ez | speech become something like |
| 95 | | szinte ilyen hitkérdéssé | articles of faith. |
| 96 | | vált. Pont a múltkor egy e | Just the other day I was sitting |
| 97 | | témakörben nagyon sokszor | next to a public figure who had |
| 89 | | megnyilvánult közszereplővel | voiced an opinion on this matter |
| 99 | | ültünk egymás mellett ő az | numerous times, whose views on |
| 100 | | ellentétes póluson helyezkedik | this issue are located at the |
| 101 | | el ebben a kérdésben és | pole opposite to mine, and we |
| 102 | | végigvettük hogy tulajdonképpen | realized that we agreed on almost |
| 103 | | majdnem mindenben vagy mindenben | everything, everything actually, |
| 104 | | egyetértünk ebben viszont | but our convictions about this |
| 105 | | meggyőzhetetlenek vagyunk | are completely resistant to |
| 106 | | egymással szemben. | persuasion. |
| 107 | IR | A hitet ez ügyben is | We respect faith in this case as |
| 108 | | tiszteljük az eredményt meg | in any other, and we are looking |
| 109 | | várjuk köszönöm szépen. | forward to the outcome, thank you |
| 110 | | | very much [for the interview]. |

In what sense is this exchange political? We can point to some aspects of the conversation's context to make the case that what we see here is an example of political expression. *Nap-Kelte* was a political television program widely recognized for its political influence. The interviewee is a former politician advocating the political agenda of the Hungarian Socialist Party. The interview's conversational structure does in no way deviate from the widely accepted political interview format. A central topic of the exchange is the "political games" Hungarian politicians play with one another instead of tackling "worthwhile issues."

However, there is more "politics" to this exchange than immediately meets the eye. Notice that at the beginning of the excerpt (lines 1, 4–13) the interviewee adopts a critical stance toward those who deny that "everything begins with words." In the context of an ongoing, fierce political debate with no end in sight—such as the Hungarian hate law debate—to claim that one side is right and the other is wrong is a move that introduces an absolute normative standard against which the conduct and positions of participants can be evaluated. To "forget" about the role of public words in genocide, Bárándy suggests, is a sign not only of historical amnesia but also of irresponsible lawmaking.

The interviewer challenges the validity of this stance on two fronts after acknowledging that the stance is recognized and shared by "many" (line 15). The first challenge is a technical one: the law is not a panacea. It sometimes "hesitates" when it should act (line 21), and it cannot by itself eradicate the social evils it was designed to address (lines 22–24). Bárándy concedes that "[n]othing can be solved solely by legal means" (lines 30–31). The interviewer's second challenge targets "orthodox lawyers" who seek to "squeeze infinite reality into a finite system" (lines 48–53). It is possible to interpret this somewhat cryptic comment as a synopsis of the interviewer's technical challenge (i.e., that the law has limited efficacy in response to complex social ills), and it is likely that Bárándy's agreement on lines 54–56 draws on this interpretation. The interviewer's "I'm raising this because" (line 57) clarifies that he is moving past the technical challenge to a related but different issue and challenge. The interviewer suggests that the "actual dilemmas" (line 59) and "tension" between "values" (lines 61–62) must not be overlooked, but that is exactly what Hungarian politicians are doing as they play their "political games" (line 78) with the hate law. This second challenge targets Bárándy's position in two ways. First, it calls into question the existence of the legal and moral absolutes Bárándy invoked at the beginning of the excerpt; second, it implicates Bárándy, a former politician, in morally objectionable "political games."

The interviewer's invocation of "actual dilemmas" (*valóságos dilemmák*) merits closer examination. It is not immediately clear what the interviewer means by "dilemmas." We learn that this is a dilemma that morality and the law must face. We also learn that the dilemma is related, in one way or another, to "actual values exist[ing] in a relationship of tension" (lines 61–62). It is clear that the dilemma discussed here is different from ideological and interactional dilemmas discussed in the discourse analytic and ethnography of communication literature. These lines of scholarship are primarily concerned with dilemmas that *individual* social actors face in moments of negotiating contradictions in their system of values and beliefs and ideologies (Billig et al. 1988; Carbaugh 1988; Fitch 1998), when they face a difficult choice between socially consequential communicative goals, acts, or strategies (Tracy 1997, 2010; Tracy and Ashcraft 2001; Tracy and Baratz 1993), or when they feel that they cannot satisfactorily match their ideals to their communicative practices (e.g., Aakhus 2001; Guttman 2007). The interviewer's dilemma invocation, however, suggests that the agent negotiating a dilemma-ridden situation is not any particular individual, but a collective comprising all lawmakers involved in the political debates surrounding the hate law. (Morality and the law do not "face dilemmas"—humans arguing over them do.) This reading of a dilemma implies competing political and normative positions within the collective and a social necessity to choose between such positions. Cultural analysis may of course reveal that a dilemma carries within it ideological dilemmas, inconsistencies, or contradictions, but the dilemmas the interviewer brings into view highlight moral and legal rather than ideological tensions.

The meaning of a term is its function in interaction (Sanders 2005). The invocation of "actual dilemmas" prompts Bárándy to tell a story (lines 96–106) that "is responsive to both the immediate local context and the social projects that participants are engaged in" (Goodwin 1990/91: 263): "Just the other day I was sitting next to a public figure who had voiced an opinion on this matter numerous times, whose views on this issue are located at the pole opposite to mine, and we realized that we agreed on almost everything, everything actually, but our convictions about this are completely resistant to persuasion." This story serves as the illustration of the claim that "[views on] hate speech versus freedom of speech become something like articles of faith" (lines 92–95). In this we see the story responding to the immediate context. The larger social project is one that the interviewer initiated by challenging Bárándy's absolutist position. Bárándy completes this social project by accepting that his position on the hate law is but one position staunchly contested by those who wish to honor freedom of speech by opposing the law against hate speech. Bárándy and the interviewer thus collaborate on maneuvering a speaker, Bárándy, into a political position.

It is important to note that before Bárándy accepts the political positioning of himself and his agenda, he preempts the conclusion that, as an advocate of the hate law, he is just another politician playing "political games." To the interviewer's charge that both the proposed hate law and opposition to it tend to be vehicles of political games, Bárándy responds that "unfortunately we have to recognize that all worthwhile issues can be used in the service of demagogic political interests, which does not mean that a worthwhile issue is no longer a worthwhile issue, it only becomes smeared in the hands of political parties" (lines 83–91). Bárándy signals that he locates himself and his position on the hate law outside the realm of political parties and their ongoing "games," and that he represents an authentic political view.

Using the language of frame analysis, we can say that by line 106 Bárándy and the interviewer successfully align their definitions of the situation. The interviewer initiated a political framing of Bárándy's position by invoking "actual dilemmas," and Bárándy accepted the frame under the condition that his political stance would be understood to fall beyond the grime of party politics. On lines 107–110 the interviewer ceases his challenges and pledges to "respect faith in this case as in any other." The frame alignment is thus complete.

The analysis so far illustrates that one important function of invoking a communal dilemma in Hungarian public expression is that it can be used to place the ongoing interaction into a political frame. As a result, participants' political relations are discursively highlighted. Let us see another example of such an invocation. Excerpt 2 was taken from the transcript of a talk show on a state-sponsored radio station. The host of the talk show invited two expert guests, political scientist János Simon and sociologist András Kovács, to answer his own and callers' questions about hate speech. Throughout the program, Simon and Kovács were in disagreement about the defining features of hate speech. Kovács argued for a minimalist definition according to which only particular types of content constituted hate speech; Simon advocated for a broader definition. The following excerpt shows Simon (JS) responding to one of Kovács's (AK) principal arguments—that defamatory public expression directed at one's political opponent should not count as hate speech—and invoking a communal dilemma (line 43).

Excerpt 2, *Szóljon hozzá!*, 24 September 2003, part 1, 14:12

| 1 | AK | Azt gondolom hogy a az | *I think that political speech* |
|---|----|------------------------|-----|
| 2 | | emóciókra öö apelláló | *appealing to the emotions* |
| 3 | | politikai beszéd az nem tartozik | *does not belong to the category* |
| 4 | | a gyűlöletbeszéd kategóriájába, | *of hate speech,* |
| 5 | | akkor sem tartozik ha | *not even when politicians say* |
| 6 | | kemény dolgot mondanak egymásról | *really rough things about one* |
| 7 | | a politikusok hogyha az egyik | *another, when one* |
| 8 | | azt mondja a másikról hogy | *says that the other* |
| 9 | | hazudott vagy ha azt mondja | *lied or is leading the country* |

| | | | |
|---|---|---|---|
| 10 | | hogy ö ö romlásba dönti az | into destruction. |
| 11 | | országot. Lehet hogy ez nem igaz | It is possible that this is not |
| 12 | | nem hazudott és nem dönti | true, that the other is not |
| 13 | | romlásba de ez akor sem | lying and is not leading the |
| 14 | | gyűlöletbeszéd. Ha valaki azt | country into destruction, but |
| 15 | | mondja hogy ne | it's still not hate speech. When |
| 16 | | szavazzál ikszre mert az egy | someone says, don't vote for X |
| 17 | | szőröstalpú móc akkor ez | because [he or she] is a hairy- |
| 18 | | már a gyűlöletbeszéd | healed Móc [ethnic slur |
| 19 | | kategóriájába tartozik. | targeting Romanians], that |
| | | | belongs to the category of hate |
| | | | speech. |
| 20 | | ((9 turns omitted)) | |
| 21 | JS | Így hirtelen az jutott eszembe | So this reminds me of the time |
| 22 | | hogy a nyolcvanas évek | when in the mid-eighties I was |
| 23 | | közepén egy évig Mexikóban voltam | studying in Mexico for a year, |
| 24 | | az egyetemen, és amikor | and two or three days after I |
| 25 | | megérkeztem ö második vagy | arrived in the country I got |
| 26 | | harmadik napon egy Volkswagen | into a Volkswagen cab, a little |
| 27 | | taxiba, kis bogárba | Beetle, |
| 28 | | ültem, ö leintettem az úton | I flagged it down and I got in, |
| 29 | | és beültem és horogkereszt lógott | and a swastika was hanging there |
| 30 | | a taxiban meg fasiszta jelképek | and other Fascist symbols, and I |
| 31 | | voltak. S elkezdtem félni. | started to feel fear, |
| 32 | | Szó szerint fizikailag félni, | literally, physical fear, |
| 33 | | ömert alapvetően számomra | because basically this is what |
| 34 | | ilyen dolgot gerjesztett ez a, | it generated, very bad memories, |
| 35 | | nagyon rossz emlékeket és | and I could hardly wait for the |
| 36 | | alig vártam hogy vége legyen az | trip to be over. |
| 37 | | útnak. Ö s önmagában a | So symbols themselves can |
| 38 | | jelképek is ö gerjeszthetnek | generate |
| 39 | | félelmet. Tehát nem | fear, I mean |
| 40 | | feltétlen kell ahhoz hogy valaki | it is not necessary to give a |
| 41 | | mondjon beszédet de a | speech, symbols themselves can |
| 42 | | jelképek önmagukban gerjeszetenek | generate fear. |
| 43 | | félelmet. Egy nagy dilemma | It is a big dilemma |
| 44 | | nemzetközileg hogy engedélyezzék- | internationally whether [such |
| 45 | | e vagy se, hol van a határa a | symbols] should be allowed, |
| 46 | | szólásszabadságnak és a | where the boundaries of freedom |
| 47 | | véleménynyilvánításnak | of speech and freedom of opinion |
| 48 | | | are. |

Here, the invocation of the communal dilemma has a somewhat different meaning-in-use than in excerpt 1. Simon's dilemma invocation on line 43 places his disagreement with Kovács into the context of a "big international dilemma" about the "boundaries of freedom of speech and freedom of opinion" and about how drawing those boundaries shapes related legislation. This dilemma is not an individual dilemma—it is one negotiated by those representing various positions on the boundaries of free speech. The invocation of the dilemma depersonalizes the disagreement: the focus shifts from the disagreement to the dilemma, and thus the invocation allows Simon to preemptively protect his own solidarity face—the positive image of oneself as a likable person (Lim and Bowers 1991)—from the charge that he is personally attacking Kovács for his views. This disagreement is not "about" Simon, Kovács, and their interpersonal relationship, Simon seems to suggest. Rather, their disagreement is an enactment of the international dilemma that existed prior to the talk show and will continue to exist after the show is over.

But there is more facework performed here. By invoking the dilemma, Simon activates a political frame within which he enters into a political relationship with Kovács. In such a relationship, it is permissible for conversational partners equally concerned about hate speech to become advocates of two horns of the same dilemma and to represent irreconcilable positions. The dilemma thus levels the intellectual playing field between the opponents. This move is designed to protect Simon's competence face (the positive image of oneself as a competent person), as his stubborn opposition to Kovács's position is rendered plausible by the presence of the dilemma.

The political frame Simon introduces is ratified by the host, who, immediately after the end of excerpt 2, adds that some would even argue that the very debate about the legality of certain political symbols can generate fear in some audiences. Dilemmas exist, and sometimes dilemmas are but one horn of a related but different dilemma, suggests the host. The host's contribution affirms that the formation of complex political relations is an inevitable outcome of advocacy organized around these dilemmas.

Concerns about hate speech in Hungarian society and related dilemma invocations are observable in other processes of Hungarian public communication, notably in journalism. On 20 August 2001, the Calvinist pastor and then member of Parliament Lóránt Hegedűs Jr. published a highly controversial article in a district newsletter of his political party MIÉP (Hungarian Justice and Life Party). The article warned Hungarians that unless they exclude Jews from Hungarian society, Jews would exclude them. The open call for the exclusion of one of the most prominent ethnic groups in Hungary resulted in a firestorm of criticism and a lawsuit against Hegedűs for incitement against a community. In the context of Hungarian hate speech debates, the Hegedűs affair developed into the archetypal example of *gyűlöletbeszéd*.

On 6 September the daily newspaper *Magyar Hírlap* published the article in its entirety. The following day, the online edition of the paper published an editorial justifying the decision to publish the controversial text.

Excerpt 3, "A harag papja," *Magyar Hírlap*, 7 September 2001

| | | |
|---|---|---|
| 1 | Örök dilemma, hogy valamely helyi | *It is an eternal dilemma whether it* |
| 2 | orgánumban vagy a zugsajtóban | *is justifiable to give greater* |
| 3 | megjelent szöveget, bármennyire | *publicity to a revolting and* |
| 4 | fölháborító és tűrhetetlen, szabad- | *intolerable text published in the* |
| 5 | e beemelni a nagy nyilvánosságba, | *local or the gutter press, even* |
| 6 | egyértelmű elítélése mellett is | *while signaling the unequivocal* |
| 7 | növelve annak publicitását. Tegnapi | *rejection of its contents. In* |
| 8 | számunkban a közlés mellett | *yesterday's edition we decided to do* |
| 9 | döntöttünk, mert az üzenet minden | *so because the message is more* |
| 10 | eddiginél fertelmesebb—mert | *heinous than ever: it incites* |
| 11 | nyíltan uszító —, és mert egy | *openly, and it was signed by the* |
| 12 | parlamenti párt alelnöke írta, név | *vice chairman of a political party,* |
| 13 | szerint ifjabb Hegedűs Lóránt. | *notably Lóránt Hegedűs Jr.* |
| 14 | ((discussion of article's | |
| 15 | discriminatory contents)) | |
| 16 | Meggyőződésünk, hogy ebben az | *We believe that in a case like this* |
| 17 | esetben már a politikai | *the political stigmatization of and* |
| 18 | megbélyegzés és elhatárolódás is | *distancing oneself from the* |
| 19 | kevés. Itt a lelkész-képviselő | *perpetrator are not enough. The next* |
| 21 | büntetőjogi felelősségre vonásának | *step is to press criminal charges* |
| 22 | kell következnie. | *against the pastor-MP must follow.* |
| 23 | Ifjabb Hegedűs Lórántot—nem | *Lóránt Hegedűs Jr. ought to face an* |
| 24 | nézeteiért, hanem írásban | *independent court, not for his views* |
| 25 | elkövetett tettéért—kell a | *but for acts committed in writing.* |
| 26 | független bíróság elé állítani. | |

It is not clear from this excerpt or the full editorial whether it was written in response to critical voices objecting to the publication of the Hegedűs text or in anticipation of such critical comments. In either case, the dilemma invocation paints the picture of a moral and political battlefield where selecting sides and politically committed action are not only meaningful and appropriate acts, but also urgent necessities. The necessity derives from the "heinousness" (line 10) of what Hegedűs committed to paper. In the context of the dilemma, any response to the "heinous" act is likely to scandalize those who respond on the basis of contrary moral convictions, particularly those who believe that republishing a controversial text places it in the journalistic echo chamber and multiplies not only the size of its audience but also its potential impact on that audience. The editorial casts the publication of the Hegedűs text as an act of marshaling evidence for Hegedűs's culpability. Again, the irresolvable ("eternal," line 1) tension between relevant values and related political positions may be informed by ideological dilemma, but such dilemmas are not of concern to the author (or authors) of this editorial. The dilemma they invoke is communal; its invocation is designed to render the public criticism of the paper's choice a political act that invites a political response.

In sum, dilemma invocations accomplish a political definition of the situation by positing three types of tensions participants of dilemma-ridden situations are forced to negotiate: no absolute normative standards for action exist, yet action to prevent the catastrophic consequences of hate speech is a must; positions from which recommended courses of action are formulated stand in opposition, but both of those positions are equally principled and coherent; relevant participants represent conflicting political positions, but their disagreement is not only appropriate but inevitable in the context of the dilemma.

## Extrasituational Context:
## The Cultural Meaning of the Dilemma

In itself, the discourse analysis of frames cannot take us close enough to the widely shared and deeply felt cultural norms and premises that lend rhetorical force to political frames. It is possible to gain a deeper understanding of what a dilemma means in the context of this interaction by looking beyond the immediately available exchange to the extrasituational context. In the limited space provided, I can merely illustrate the significance of such meanings.

Let us return to excerpt 1. It is not clear from the interviewer's talk what particular dilemmas he had in mind in the moment. We can, however, investigate what dilemma Bárándy *understood* as the one the interviewer had in mind. From an interactional perspective, Bárándy's inference constitutes *the* relevant meaning of the dilemma. The dilemma Bárándy addressed is the one that pitted advocates of the hate law against free speech absolutists. In a cultural discourse analysis of the 2003 debates of the hate law in Hungarian parliamentary committee meetings (Boromisza-Habashi 2007), I established that arguments on constitutional grounds for and against the hate law placed lawmakers into irreconcilable political and moral positions. The language of the pre-2011 Hungarian Constitution was ambiguous about the relationship between two fundamental human rights: "human dignity" (*emberi méltóság*) and freedom of speech or, in the language of Hungarian constitutional law, the "freedom of expressing opinions" (*véleménynyilvánítás szabadsága*). Lawmakers agreed that hate speech constituted a violation of human dignity, but they remained divided about whether or not that violation was adequate grounds for declaring hate speech to be a form of public expression beyond the boundaries of free speech. The disagreement could be boiled down to two similar but competing positions:

> 1. Hate speech violates the human dignity of others. Human dignity is protected by the constitution. The freedom of expression is also protected by the constitution. Since the right to human dignity and the right to free expression are both within the constitution, one can serve as the limit to the other. ... Therefore, hate speech is a mode of expression not protected by the constitution.
>
> 2. Hate speech violates the human dignity of others. Human dignity is protected by the constitution. The freedom of expression is also protected by the constitution. Since the right to human dignity and the right to free expression are both within the constitution, one cannot be compromised for the sake of the other. Therefore, hate speech is a mode of expression protected by the constitution.

These positions led lawmakers to reach contrasting conclusions about the proper course of action against hate speech in Hungarian society. Proponents of the argument that hate speech did not deserve constitutional protection argued for placing additional constraints on the freedom of speech, whereas the critics of this argument argued against the expansion of constraints. None of the lawmakers expressed any uncertainty about which side of the argument they supported. The cultural analysis of their arguments showed that members of Parliament argued on the basis of deeply held cultural beliefs about the status of persons as "citizens." Those who endorsed the first proposition talked about the citizen as a communal member with responsibilities toward other communal members. Advocates of the second proposition saw the citizen as an individual endowed with individual rights. As a collective, however, lawmakers were concerned that the resolution of the dilemma might not be possible. Indeed, a paradox at the heart of the debate precluded any possible resolution: imposing legal restrictions on the freedom of speech to prevent hate speech would have led to curtailing citizens' fundamental human rights, as would have not doing so.

To summarize, the dilemma in excerpt 1 and among Hungarian lawmakers was a dilemma only from the collective's perspective; pitted different interpretations of the constitution against one another; generated competing recommendations for an ideal course of action; was informed by deeply held cultural beliefs about personhood; and derived its poignancy from a cultural paradox. By referring to such dilemmas as communal I wish to emphasize not only that they appeared to be dilemmas from the collective's perspective, but also that they are informed by cultural, communal meanings. It is possible that the communal dilemmas invoked in excerpts 2 and 3 share some cultural meanings with the one discussed here, but this cannot be taken as a given.

## Retexturing Communicative Action

The dilemma invocation as a rhetorical strategy in Hungarian public discourse about hate speech (*gyűlöletbeszéd*) draws on cultural communicative resources to respond to what speakers see as impending social catastrophe: the prospect of injustice and violence engendered by hate speech. The strategy entails defining the ongoing communicative situation as political and exposing relevant, recalcitrant moral positions to contestation. Public speakers who suggest (or concede) that interpretations of, and moral or legal responses to, hate speech are dilemma-ridden activate a definition of the situation in which no morally informed social or political position can be treated as absolute. The positions themselves remain valid, but they are presented as choices available to public actors against the background of conflict and deep cultural difference.

To pick up on a unifying theme of this volume, dilemma invocations are designed to alter the texture of ongoing interaction by attempting to braid the thread of political engagement to more dominant, thicker threads, such as moral and legal absolutes and the political identities associated with the act of professing those absolutes. The context-bound, strategic retexturing of communicative action thus involves more than interactional framing in Goffman's sense of the term. In addition to imposing a political definition on ongoing social interaction, a speaker invoking a dilemma taps into contested cultural meanings and paradoxes that have existed prior to the exchange and will continue to exist once the exchange is concluded. The speaker also conjures up the history of heated exchanges about hate speech and visions of social catastrophe that have lent, and will continue to lend, a sense of urgency to the related tasks of defining and responding to hate speech.

A cultural approach to the political retexturing of ongoing interaction suggests interpreting communal dilemma invocations as attempts to foster a politics of discursive space (Fischer 2006). Treating political, moral, and legal positions on an issue as open to contestation is itself a microlevel political move. In the excerpts discussed in this chapter, Hungarian public speakers strive to open up spaces for continued political engagement relative to a different discursive space populated by moral or legal positions that are presented as uncontestable and absolute. The interviewer and Bárándy (excerpt 1) collaborate on undermining an absolute position Bárándy expressed earlier. In excerpt 2, Simon presents his position and his opponent's as two horns of a dilemma. The editors of *Magyar Hírlap* in excerpt 3 acknowledge that their decision to publish a highly controversial text is contestable in the context of a communal dilemma. These speakers seek to carve out a space for political discourse in which more than one position can be meaningfully and defensibly claimed by Hungarian public speakers who feel compelled to join the national debate about what hate speech is and what can be done about it. A discursive space that recognizes the inevitability of contestation realizes a deliberative minimum in the sense that contestation sustains social issues and concerns about them (Fraser 1990), denies the legitimacy of absolute points of view (Benhabib 1996), and floats the possibility of communicative engagement among representatives of competing viewpoints (Dryzek 2000).

We have no reason to believe, however, that the retexturing of interaction in the hope of cultivating a political discursive space will inevitably accomplish a deliberative minimum. Three types of constraints temper the rhetorical force of dilemma invocations: the sheer recalcitrance of ideological positions, the lack of a unified terrain for political engagement, and the failure of political liberalism in contemporary Hungary. First, many Hungarian political actors are quick to unbraid the thread of political engagement from the texture of the hate speech debates. There are those deeply invested in one ideological position as opposed to another they see as misinformed or malicious (Boromisza-Habashi 2010, 2013); others call into question the impending social catastrophe itself (Boromisza-Habashi 2011).

Second, positing a communal dilemma seeks to reduce the number of available political positions on hate speech to two. The attempt to reduce Hungarian hate speech debates to a single, community-wide debate, and to define that debate as *the* terrain of political engagement, disregards the sociopolitical complexity of those debates. While some contested an opponent's interpretation of what forms of expression counted as hate speech, others debated the identity of the targets of hate speech or the value of legal sanctions. Additionally, for some, "joining the hate speech debate" did not mean commitment to sustained participation in the debate, but rather an opportunity to call attention to what they saw as moral panic over a contrived issue. Yet others suggested that, far from being an issue of national importance, hate speech was the concern of particular interest groups such as minorities, political bodies such as the European Union and particular Hungarian political parties, or journalists desperate to fill the news cycle. On the Hungarian political scene, "debating" hate speech can only mean joining one debate and not joining others. Hence, the rhetoric of positing a single debate that organizes the whole community into a coherent polity conflicts with Hungarian political reality.

Third, political liberalism, the ideological source of the belief in the value of discursive political engagement as a means of social progress, is virtually absent from the contemporary Hungarian political scene. The country experienced a brief moment of liberal political euphoria around the time of the fall of state socialism. All political actors of any consequence spoke the language of freedoms, equal rights, and engagement (Hegedűs 2005). However, by the end of the 1990s it became clear that new democratic institutions could not bring about immediate, radical, and lasting social transformation. Successive governments focused virtually all of their efforts on economic reform and attracting foreign investment (Fabry 2011). Economic "structural adjustment" ravaged standards of living, and institutionalized politics devolved into a competition for power between various factions of the ruling class (Tamás 2008). In the current political context, calls for engagement in the name of social progress are drowned out by calls for order in the name of economic progress.

Gauging the efficacy of the dilemma invocation as microlevel political action is beyond the scope of this study. The present chapter responds to the call issued by the editors of this volume to study the surface or texture of political action as a rich source of insight into sociocultural and historical context. I analyzed and interpreted a Hungarian communicative resource for locally meaningful rhetorical strategy and political action, the dilemma invocation. This work reveals that sometimes speakers—motivated by a sense of social catastrophe—tap into cultural resources to lend a political texture to ongoing communication. Designed to accomplish a deliberative minimum and to plant the seed of political engagement between political actors who represent incompatible political or moral positions, such retexturing is best seen as a micropolitics of hope.

**David Boromisza-Habashi** is an assistant professor in the Department of Communication at the University of Colorado–Boulder. He uses the ethnography of communication approach to investigate cultural resources for public participation. His first book, *Speaking Hatefully: Culture, Communication, and Political Action in Hungary* (Penn State University Press, 2013), is an ethnographic study of public debates surrounding hate speech in Hungary during the first decade of the twenty-first century.

## Bibliography

Aakhus, Mark. 2001. "Technocratic and Design Stances Toward Communication Expertise: How GDSS Facilitators Understand Their Work." *Journal of Applied Communication Research* 29, no. 4: 341–71.

Agar, Michael. 1994. *Language Shock: Understanding the Culture of Conversation*. New York: William Morrow.

Albert, Ethel M. 1972. "Culture Patterning of Speech Behavior in Burundi." In *Directions in Sociolinguistics: The Ethnography of Communication*, ed. John J. Gumperz and Dell Hymes, 72–105. New York: Basil Blackwell.

Bailey, Benjamin. 2007. "Heteroglossia and Boundaries: Process of Linguistic and Social Distinction." In *Bilingualism: A Social Approach*, ed. Monica Heller, 57–74. Basingstoke, UK, and New York: Palgrave Macmillan.

Bauman, Richard, and Charles L. Briggs. 2003. *Voices of Modernity: Language Ideologies and the Politics of Inequality*. Cambridge: Cambridge University Press.

Bauman, Zygmunt. 1999. *Culture as Praxis*. Thousand Oaks, CA: Sage.

Benhabib, Seyla. 1996. "Toward a Deliberative Model of Democratic Legitimacy." In *Democracy and Difference: Contesting the Boundaries of the Political*, ed. Seyla Benhabib, 67–94. Princeton, NJ: Princeton University Press.

Billig, Michael, Susan Condor, Derek Edwards, Michael Gane, David Middleton, and Alan Radley. 1988. *Ideological Dilemmas: A Social Psychology of Everyday Thinking*. London: Sage.

Bloch, Linda-Renée, and Dafna Lemish. 2005. "'I Know I'm a *Freierit*, But . . .': How a Key Cultural Frame (En)genders a Discourse of Inequality." *Journal of Communication* 55, no. 1: 38–55.

Boromisza-Habashi, David. 2007. "Freedom of Expression, Hate Speech, and Models of Personhood in Hungarian Political Discourse." *Communication Law Review* 7, no. 1: 54–74.

———. 2010. "How Are Political Concepts 'Essentially' Contested?" *Language & Communication* 30, no. 4: 276–84.

———. 2011. "Dismantling the Antiracist 'Hate Speech' Agenda in Hungary: An Ethno-Rhetorical Analysis." *Text & Talk* 31, no. 1: 1–19.

———. 2013. *Speaking Hatefully: Culture, Communication, and Political Action in Hungary*. University Park: Penn State University Press.

Cameron, Deborah. 2001. *Working with Spoken Discourse*. London and Thousand Oaks, CA: Sage.

Carbaugh, Donal. 1988. *Talking American: Cultural Discourses on Donahue*. Norwood, NJ: Ablex.

———. 1996. *Situating Selves: The Communication of Social Identities in American Scenes*. Albany: State University of New York Press.

———. 2002. "Some Distinctive Features of US American Conversation." In *The Changing Nature of Conversation in America: Essays from the Smithsonian*, ed. William F. Eadie and Paul E. Nelson, 1–75. Thousand Oaks, CA: Sage.

———. 2007. "Cultural Discourse Analysis: Communication Practices and Intercultural Encounters." *Journal of Intercultural Communication Research* 36, no. 3: 167–82.

———. 2008. "Ethnography of Communication." In *International Encyclopedia of Communication*, vol. 4, ed. Wolfgang Donsbach, 1592–98. Malden, MA: Blackwell.

———. 2011. "Situating Cultural Studies in Communication: Cultural Discourse Theory."

In *Hybrids, Differences, Visions: On the Study of Culture,* ed. Claudio Baraldi, Andrea Borsari and Augusto Carli, 97–112. Aurora, CO: The Davies Group.
Carbaugh, Donal, and David Boromisza-Habashi. 2011. "Discourse Beyond Language: Cultural Rhetoric, Revelatory Insight, and Nature." In *The Rhetorical Emergence of Culture,* ed. Christian Meyer and Felix Girke, 101–18. Oxford and New York: Berghahn Books.
Carbaugh, Donal, and Sally O. Hastings. 1992. "A Role for Communication in Ethnography and Cultural Analysis." *Communication Theory* 2, no. 2: 156–65.
Dryzek, John S. 2000. *Deliberative Democracy and Beyond: Liberals, Critics, Contestations.* Oxford and New York: Oxford University Press.
Fabry, Adam. 2011. "From Poster Boy of Neoliberal Transformation to Basket Case: Hungary and the Global Economic Crisis." In *First the Transformation, Then the Crash: Eastern Europe in the 2000s,* ed. Gareth Dale, 03–28. London: Pluto Press.
Fischer, Frank. 2006. "Participatory Governance as Deliberative Empowerment: The Cultural Politics of Discursive Space." *American Review of Public Administration* 36, no. 1: 19–40.
Fitch, Kristine. 1998. *Speaking Relationally: Culture, Communication, and Interpersonal Connection.* New York: Guilford Press.
Fraser, Nancy. 1990. "Rethinking the Public Sphere: A Contribution to the Critique of Actually Existing Democracy." *Social Text* 25/26: 56–80.
Gal, Susan. 1991. "Bartók's Funeral: Representations of Europe in Hungarian Political Rhetoric." *American Ethnologist* 18, no. 3: 440–58.
Goffman, Erving. 1974. *Frame Analysis: An Essay on the Organization of Experience.* Cambridge, MA: Harvard University Press.
———. 1981. *Forms of Talk.* Philadelphia: University of Pennsylvania Press.
Goodwin, Charles, and Alessandro Duranti. 1992. "Rethinking Context: An Introduction." In *Rethinking Context: Language as an Interactive Phenomenon,* ed. Alessandro Duranti and Charles Goodwin, 1–42. Cambridge: Cambridge University Press.
Goodwin, Marjorie H. 1990/91. "Retellings, Pretellings, and Hypothetical Stories." *Research on Language and Social Interaction* 24, nos. 1–4: 263–76.
Guttman, Nurit. 2007. "Bringing the Mountain to the Public: Dilemmas and Contradictions in the Procedures of Public Deliberation Initiatives That Aim to Get 'Ordinary Citizens' to Deliberate Policy Issues." *Communication Theory* 17, no. 4: 411–38.
Györgyi, Kálmán. 2003. "A gyűlöletbeszéd és a véleményszabadság jogi értékelése" [A legal assessment of hate speech and freedom of expression]. In *Aktuelle Aspekte des christlich-jüdischen Verhältnisses: A keresztény-zsidó viszony aktuális aspektusai— nemzetközi szakmai tanácskozás Budapesten, 2003. január.,* 69–83. Budapest: Konrad-Adenauer-Stiftung.
Hegedűs, István. 2005. "Politikai kommunikáció Magyarországon: Mítoszok és túlzások" [Political communication in Hungary: Myths and excesses]. *Médiakutató* (Spring). http://www.mediakutato.hu/cikk/2005_01_tavasz/02_politikai_kommunikacio_2004 (accessed 12 October 2014).
Huspek, Michael, and Kathleen E. Kendall. 1991. "On Withholding Political Voice: An Analysis of the Political Vocabulary of a 'Nonpolitical' Speech Community." *Quarterly Journal of Speech* 77, no. 1: 1–19.
Hymes, Dell. 1972. "Models of the Interaction of Language and Social Life." In *Directions in Sociolinguistics: The Ethnography of Communication,* ed. John J. Gumperz and Dell Hymes., 35–71. New York: Holt, Rinehart and Winston.

Lim, Tae-Seop, and John W. Bowers. 1991. "Facework, Solidarity, Approbation, and Tact." *Human Communication Research* 17, no. 3: 415–50.

Lippi-Green, Rosina. 1997. *English with an Accent: Language, Ideology, and Discrimination in the United States.* London and New York: Routledge.

Magyar Hírlap. 2001. "A harag papja (MH-álláspont)" [The priest of ire (MH-position)]. 7 September. http://www.magyarhirlap.hu/velemeny/a_harag_papja_mhallaspont.html (accessed 12 February 2012).

Philipsen, Gerry. 1992. *Speaking Culturally: Explorations in Social Communication.* Albany: State University of New York Press.

Sanders, Robert E. 2005. "Introduction: LSI as a Subject Matter and as Multidisciplinary Confederation." In *Handbook of Language and Social Interaction*, ed. Kristine L. Fitch and Robert E. Sanders, 1–14. Mahwah, NJ: Lawrence Erlbaum Associates.

Saville-Troike, Muriel. 2003. *The Ethnography of Communication: An Introduction.* 3rd ed. Malden, MA: Blackwell.

Tamás, Gáspár M. 2008. "A Capitalism Pure and Simple." *Left Curve* 32: 66–75. http://www.leftcurve.org/LC32WebPages/CapitalismPure.GMTamás.pdf (accessed 12 October 2014).

Tracy, Karen. 1997. *Colloquium: Dilemmas of Academic Discourse.* Norwood, NJ: Ablex.

———. 2010. *The Challenges of Ordinary Democracy: A Case Study in Deliberation and Dissent.* University Park: Penn State University Press.

Tracy, Karen, and Catherine Ashcraft. 2001. "Crafting Policies about Controversial Values: How Wording Disputes Manage a Group Dilemma." *Journal of Applied Communication Research* 29, no. 4: 297–316.

Tracy, Karen, and Sheryl Baratz. 1993. "Intellectual Discussion in the Academy as Situated Discourse." *Communication Monographs* 60, no. 4: 300–20.

Tyler, Stephen, and Ivo Strecker. 2009. "The Rhetoric Culture Project." In *Culture and Rhetoric,* ed. Ivo Strecker and Stephen Tyler. New York and Oxford: Berghahn Books.

Urla, Jacqueline. 1995. "Outlaw Language: Creating Alternative Public Spheres in Basque Free Radio." *Pragmatics* 5, no. 2: 145–261.

Witteborn, Saskia. 2004. "On Being an Arab Woman Before and After September 11: The Enactment of Communal Identities in Talk." *Howard Journal of Communications* 15, no. 2: 83–98.

CHAPTER 2

# Chronotopes of the Political
## Public Discourse, News Media, and Mass Action in Postconflict Macedonia

*Andrew Graan*

■ ■ ■ ■ ■ ■

An underexamined category has crept its way into fields of cultural study: public discourse. Across analyses of contemporary cultural phenomena, one inevitably encounters a reference to a public discourse on some topic. For example, studies might refer to public discourses on race, religion, celebrity, the suburbs, the Third World, lifestyle, taxation, George Washington's sexuality, and so on. In some cases, scholarly uses of the concept of public discourse draw on broader understandings of discourse itself, whether from Foucauldian, Bakhtinian, or sociolinguistic traditions (cf. Blommaert 2005). Oftentimes, however, the term is presented as self-evident and goes unanalyzed. In these cases, the concept is used to capture some regular way of speaking on or thinking about some subject matter, found among some distribution of people. But the epistemological status, institutional moorings, and social efficacy of such discourses are left opaque. In this unelaborated state, the default characterization of public discourse is that of an ideological miasma that haunts the ether, vaguely reflecting and affecting popular thought and action.

This chapter responds to the muddled station of public discourse in cultural analysis. Rather than treating public discourse as a categorical primary, I consider the social processes and semiotic forms that produce and reproduce the transcontextual narratives that scholars typically understand as public discourses. I develop these arguments by examining one specific case, a 2004 protest movement that arose in the Republic of Macedonia and that was directed against the Council of Europe in reaction to a perceived slight against the country. Via this analysis, I offer a conceptualization of public discourse that speaks to the manifest, if contingent, sedimentation of socially available narratives on society and their impact on political action.

This approach to public discourses and their social efficacy draws on Mikhail Bakhtin's concept of the chronotope. According to Bakhtin, the term "chronotope" refers to "the intrinsic connectedness of temporal and spatial relationships that are artistically expressed in literature" (1981: 84), although he suggests that the concept extends to social and cultural representation in general. Such time-space (i.e., chrono-topic) relationships do not merely constitute narrative settings. Rather, the conventional qualities of socially recognized time-space frames presuppose specific character types and logics of action. To take an example from Bakhtin, the adventure time setting of an ancient Greek romance and the social realist setting of a bildungsroman are not only different contexts in which a story unfolds, but furthermore these settings imply (and also exclude) particular sorts of characters, actions, and events. The concept of the chronotope thus provides us with a tool to reckon with the qualitative thickness of social narratives.

Harnessing this insight, I examine how key genres of public and mass-mediated discourse in postconflict Macedonia presupposed stock chronotopes of the political, which in turn grounded narratives of everyday politics. Insofar as these chronotopes implied certain typical forms of action and agents, they supported second-order cultural stereotypes about the political field and its key characters, ones that affected how social actors understood and experienced the agencies that animated political life. I thus explore how particular chronotopes that came to frame some of Macedonia's key political events in 2004 contributed to how actors responded to these happenings—or whether they responded at all. Attention to such chronotopes of the political, I submit, can not only enrich scholarly understandings of public discourse, but also constitutes one way of analyzing the textures of political action (Hariman, this volume) that animate contemporary lifeworlds.

## Chronotopes and Everyday Life

> What is the significance of all these chronotopes? What is most obvious is their meaning for *narrative*. They are the organizing centers for the fundamental narrative events of the novel. The chronotope is the place where the knots of narrative are tied and untied.
> 
> —Mikhail Bakhtin, "Forms of Time and of the Chronotope in the Novel"

The concept of the chronotope was originally formulated by Mikhail Bakhtin in his 1937 essay "Forms of Time and of the Chronotope in the Novel" to describe the way that particular literary genres represent time and space and how such time-space representations shape the possibilities of narrative development. Through his analysis of specific literary genres, Bakhtin argues that the chronotopic matrix or frames of a narrative influence the very quality and character of action in the narrative itself. As Bakhtin scholars Gary Morson and Caryl Emerson expound, the concept of the chronotope captures "a way of understanding experience; it is a specific *form-shaping ideology* for understanding the nature of events and actions" (Morson and Emerson 1990: 367; emphasis added).

The category of the chronotope thus constitutes a useful tool with which to analyze the relationship between conventional representations of time-space and social understandings of agency and eventhood. Although Bakhtin focused on literary narratives, a growing number of scholars from the field of linguistic anthropology (e.g., Basso 1996; Silverstein 2000; Agha 2007; Lemon 2009; Dick 2010; Stasch 2011) have applied the concept in studies of social interaction. On the one hand, these scholars have demonstrated that particular narrative and discourse genres from a variety of ethnographic contexts display conventional representations of time-space, that is, chronotopic frames, that impinge on how actions and characters are presented in specific narratives.

On the other hand, these scholars have theorized how social interaction itself can be understood as a dynamic process mediated by participants' acts of narration. According to this view, social interactions consist of participants collaborating (to degrees) on the production of some social narrative to which participants variously align in their contemporaneous interaction. Analysts therefore examine the emergent and dynamic alignments between the narrated events and the event of narration as a means to uncover the social effects and achievements of particular interactions (see Jakobson [1957] 1971; Silverstein 1999). Significantly, both the narrated event and the event of narration can be approached through the chronotopic representations on which they depend. At times, the chronotopic conventions of the narrated events can be signaled to mark off the events narrated as taking place according to a distinct logic when compared to the event of narration (e.g., "once upon a time" in fairy tales). At other times, the chronotopic frames of the narrated events may be aligned with the event of narration to produce, for example, narrative realism (see Silverstein 2000). How participants align or contrast the chronotopic frames of narrated events to those of events of narration thus constitute a central dimension of everyday interactions and their social outcomes.

While the category of the chronotope can be useful for the analysis of specific interaction, it is important to highlight the generic and conventional character of most socially recognizable and productive chronotopes. Indeed, depending on the breadth of their discursive circulation and the nature of their uptake, certain chronotopic models act as commonsense representations of the world, while others (or the same ones in a different context) arrive as controversial representations subject to critique and parody. In either case, however, as Asif Agha stated,

> whether or not a chronotopic model is widely known, is felt to be legitimate, is uniformly accepted by those acquainted with it, or whether it fractionates into positionally entrenched variants, the processes as a whole proceeds *as a social process* through modes and moments of participatory access to the model itself ... and through forms of alignment to *that* model (or variant) to which participants orient in some modality of response ... through their own semiotic activities. (2007: 322; emphasis in original)

Hence, while always contingent and subject to contestation and revision, chronotopes provide ideological matrices through which (or against which) social actors implicitly or explicitly make sense of their social world and respond within it.

In Macedonia, I contend, there were two major chronotopic models that regularly organized narrated worlds during the period of my research in 2003 and 2004. First, there was a chronotope of "transition." This chronotope represented a Macedonian here and now defined by the country's secession from Yugoslavia, the fall of state socialism, and the social instabilities that accompanied these political changes. Historically speaking, the years that followed Macedonia's 1991 independence were marked by hardship and turmoil. War flared in other ex-Yugoslav states, most tragically in Bosnia, and the Macedonian economy plummeted. Exacerbating the situation, Macedonia's neighbor to the south, the more powerful Greece, refused to recognize Macedonia by its constitutional name, claiming a historical monopoly on the toponym "Macedonia." Following a nineteen-month Greek embargo in 1994 and 1995, Macedonia was forced to accept the infamous designation "the former Yugoslav Republic of Macedonia," or FYROM, as a temporary name in the United Nations pending future negotiations. The naming dispute continues to this day. Then, in 2001, Macedonia experienced its own armed conflict, in which ethnic Albanian insurgents and ethnic Macedonian-dominated security forces clashed. Fortunately, a peace agreement, negotiated with the oversight of EU and US diplomats, ended the violence and mapped out a series of political reforms to stabilize and democratize the country. In the years following the armistice, European and American officials continued to play an active but unofficial political role in the country. This historical period, typically glossed as Macedonia's "transition," was experienced by many as a difficult time.

Reflecting such experiences of instability and hardship, the chronotope of Macedonia's transition represented a present in which time moved in a nonprogressive manner. Populated by social types such as corrupt politicians, meddling foreigners, and weary everypersons, the chronotope of transition was, ironically, one in which "nothing ever changes," where characters' actions reproduced a dreary status quo. (It thus differed from the nostalgic narrative on Yugoslavia, which presupposed that time-space's modernity, stability, and opportunity.) Accordingly, the actions represented through the chronotope of transition abided by a logic of deceit and intrigue.

Second, and in contrast to "transition," a chronotopic model of efficient and prosperous "Europe" also achieved widespread traction in Macedonia (cf. Gal 1991, 2005). Within the "European" chronotope, political actors were characterized as responsible and responsive: it was a time-place of consummate modernity and reason. The chronotopes of "transitional Macedonia" and "modern Europe" proliferated across the mediascape of fin de siècle Macedonia.[1] They routinely grounded report and commentary on current events by imbuing news stories with narrative conventions that contrasted the two imagined time-spaces.

The following vignette illustrates how these chronotopes would be called upon in the narration and construal of everyday experience. One Saturday evening in Skopje during June 2004, a friend invited me over to his family's home to join a number of others in watching a movie. *American Pie 2* was the film on the bill. Such an event—a group of friends gathered to chat and watch a move on a weekend night—would not likely warrant untoward suspicion. However, my own inclusion in this plan, and hence the appearance of an American anthropologist in a Macedonian living room, transformed the narrative that at least one participant constructed for that warm night. The participant in question was my friend Petar's fifteen-year-old sister, Maja.

Arriving at Petar's family's apartment, I met Maja for the first time that night, and I politely greeted her according to the informal Macedonian custom, shaking her hand while saying hello and offering my first name: a simple, "Zdravo, Endi." Alarmed by the peculiarity of my name and my accented Macedonian, instead of reciprocating my greeting, the teenager turned to her brother, asking, "Otkaj e?" (Where's he from?). I answered first and responded, "Amerikanec sum" (I'm an American). Listening to me but still refusing to acknowledge me, Maja spoke again to her brother: "Sram da ti e, Brate!" (Shame on you, brother!). Bewildered by this unfolding interaction, I again intervened before Petar had a chance: "Što?" (What?) I asked. With this question, Maja finally addressed me, with an intense certainty: "Pa, sigurno ste špijun!" (Well, surely you're a spy!).

With these words, Maja broke the building suspense and Petar and I broke into laughter. Petar chastised his sister for what he considered her rude conduct toward his guest while assuring her that I was in fact not a spy, but a researcher, an anthropologist interested in the news media in Macedonia, and a friend. In my own defense, I reasoned to her that most spies would probably not spend a precious weekend evening watching B-grade comedy movies in company that included teenagers. I have no idea whether we managed to alter Maja's prejudice, and she quickly left us to spend the remainder of the evening with her own friends in her room on the other side of the apartment. However, in Maja's initial reaction, one can discern the significance that chronotopes have on how people make sense of the happenings that constitute everyday life. What could have been an unexceptional (even banal) narrative—a group of friends in their midtwenties hanging out on a Saturday, watching a silly movie—instead became one filled with scandal and intrigue. Was this guest a spy? Was her brother an accomplice?

Grounding Maja's representation of and participation in the unfolding interaction was a chronotopic model of transition and its figure of the meddlesome foreigner with obscure intentions. The general salience of this chronotope as a narrative ground for talking politics in postconflict Macedonia enabled Maja to impart a meaning to the plans Petar and I shared that night, even if it was one that at first puzzled and then amused the two of us. Our sense of utter normalcy of "hanging out" (which implies its own chronotopy) on a Saturday evening was ruptured by Maja's sense of alarm over the foreign spy that she surely had in her midst. Her reframing of our plans (and our identities) as she aligned our encounter within the transition chronotope displaced our implicit self-understandings and ultimately produced our laughter.

Bakhtin (1981: 250) expressed this aptly: "[T]he chronotope makes the narrative events concrete, makes them take on flesh, causes blood to flow in their veins." As with the case of my interaction with Maja and her brother, social actors can be shown to presuppose and operate within socially available chronotopic models when figuring their own narrative understandings of even everyday encounters. Socially available chronotopes thus constitute a central semiotic material, grounding models of the world that, contingent on the nature of actors' alignment to them, inform subjects' experience of the everyday and their own place within social worlds.

## Media Chronotopes of the Political

Socially available and familiar chronotopes do not only affect small-scale social interactions; as we shall see, they also impact mass-mediated construals of the social world (see Agha 2007). While this point could extend to any number of mass media forms, it is exemplified by the narrative regularities found in cultures of news media and journalism. It is perhaps a truism within media studies that news reports do not merely describe a situation, but construct "events" through narrativization (cf. Hall 1980). Inherently, then, news media narratives depend on an array of chronotopes in producing such events via description. Insofar as particular chronotopes become dominant within and across news media, they yield commonplace public discourses on the nature of social and political reality.

In this section, I illustrate this point by examining the characteristics of political scandals within the Macedonian news media. Although in principle a many varied thing can be described as a scandal, as I demonstrate for the Macedonian case, the narrative making of a scandal emerged through and reproduced particular stock chronotopes of Macedonia's postconflict political culture. The result was that a narrow set of themes came to be common to most media scandals. It is this character of chronotopes, their role in bringing media scandals "to life" in narrative and to connect stories in a shared experiential framework, that I explore here.

In postconflict Macedonia, it was in fact common practice for journalists to break stories as scandals (*skandali*) that, contingent on their subsequent development, could earn the epithets *slučaj* or *afera* (i.e., the X incident or the X affair) that marked stories off as tokens of the scandal type. To give but a small indication of the range included within the category of the scandal, during the course of my research examples included the National Bank's failure to note the liquidation of an Irish bank in which it had holdings, an alleged plot by the interior minister that resulted in the murder of seven South Asian migrants, poll rigging on a popular news discussion television show, baby selling, and a government minister's shady real estate deal.

However, while many news reports would initially frame a story as an example of a scandal, only very few would take on a social life in which they emerged as perduring and socially robust topics of scandal. What, then, made a news story felicitous as a scandal in the postconflict Macedonian context? What made a scandal compelling to audiences? What enabled scandals to take off? In examining these questions, I reflect on the social processes by which public discourses take shape, circulate, and come to have tangible social effects.

As is the case with news in Macedonia more generally, stories about scandals developed through an intertextual process tied to the temporalities of news publishing. That is, news stories necessarily developed as socially significant events in a piecemeal fashion that spanned (a series of) published reports, public reactions, and public commentary that mutually alluded to and anticipated one another. Unlike basic examples of news reports, however, scandals advanced a moral narrative for the happenings framed as the news event. Grounding the scandal genre was thus a particular chronotopic frame, a here and now marked by moral crisis and demanding remedy. Articles on news scandals implicitly or explicitly called upon audiences to align themselves to the subject position of outrage within this chronotope: something happened, and "we," an implied public audience, should be angered by it. Furthermore, in the Macedonian context, the alleged violation of public morality at the center of a scandal narrative typically also relied on chronotopic contrast that made sense of this violation in terms of Macedonian and European difference. Scandals regularly drew on contrasts between "transitional Macedonia" and "modern Europe" to articulate and authorize statements expressing how "our" leaders disappoint "us," "the public" presumed to understand and value "European" ways.

An example of this can be found in a 2004 news story over milk quality in Macedonia. In this story, the publicization of a government report about the illegal and unhealthy presence of powdered milk in Macedonian milk supplies developed into a scandal over the government's allegedly insufficient commitment to food safety. A quick review of three news articles from different moments in the story's social life will reflect the social process through which the story's changing moral frames emerged.

The first report on the story—published in news daily *Dnevnik*—was presented as a synopsis of a scholarly study from the state's veterinary institute on milk quality in Macedonia. The government study stated that excessive amounts of powdered milk had been discovered in the ultra-high-temperature pasteurized milk produced by Macedonian dairies. Since the powdered milk supplement would have gone through the pasteurization process twice, the report explained, the nutritional content of the milk would be substandard. Common to the genre of unmarked news report, the title of this first article read as a dry statement of fact: "Powdered Milk Used Illegally" (*Dnevnik* 2004a). Indeed, from a linguistic perspective, the Macedonian-language verbal forms used in the article and the headline underscore its matter-of-factness. The preferred verbal tense locates the article's narrative in an isolatable, recent past, indicating that this happened and sources confirm it.

Several days later, once the study had been submitted to the appropriate government ministries for review, another *Dnevnik* report foregrounded the illegality and danger of powdered milk supplements to "the public" and also quoted demands that the implicated dairies be held accountable. In the title of this report, one detects the emergent moral frame of a scandal and the interpellation of a concerned public: "We Drink Dangerous, White Water Instead of Milk" (*Dnevnik* 2004b). While this report still locates events in an isolatable, recent past, through the inclusion of the calls for justice, the narrative also projects an imperative for a future time in which the issue has been resolved.

The story's "scandalousness" became even more pronounced in later news articles. Illustratively, one week after the second report, in an op-ed commentary entitled "Powdered Responsibility," *Dnevnik* columnist Todor Pendarov vociferously criticized both Economy Minister Stevče Jakimovski and Agriculture Minister Slavko Petrov for their handling of the milk issue and called for their resignations (Pendarov 2004). To do so, Pendarov contrasted a recent past of misdeed with an uncertain present demanding resolution. Thus, Pendarov's piece begins, "The milk quality affair has already continued two weeks, and *until now* no one has taken responsibility for it. Approximately twenty dairies use unapproved amounts of powdered milk in the milk they produce, but *it is still not* clear whether they will be punished nor by whom" (Pendarov 2004; emphasis added).[2] From this temporal frame, Pendarov then gave his moralized take on what was now referred to as the Powdered Milk Affair by linking the alleged misdeed to a chronic pattern. He wrote, "The contested milk remains in stores, *and Macedonia is once again confirmed as a state which cannot secure its citizens' most basic rights and give them protection to consume healthy food*" (Pendarov 2004; emphasis added).[3] By this time, the scandal had come to roost, and the implicated parties publically traded blame with the hope of minimizing their portion of the scandal's fallout.

The success of this scandal in achieving popular traction—as indicated by the public figures it animated and by its cycle of report and commentary—becomes understandable when we examine how it relied on oppositions between a chronotope of transition and one of Europe. In ways both implicit and explicit, the piecemeal development of this scandal came to turn on a commonsensical contrast between the popularly perceived inadequacies of a Macedonian here and now and an idealized Europe. Thus, in Todor Pendarov's commentary on the Powdered Milk Affair, he punctuated the failure of Macedonian officials by stating, "Didn't [Agricultural Minister Petrov] hear that we applied to the EU, where there are over 6,000 standards, laws, and regulations which control agriculture and the food industry" (Pendarov 2004).[4] In doing so, he highlighted the contrast between Macedonia and the EU in a manner that echoed their differing chronotopic representations. Evidence of substandard milk production was eventually framed within a narrative about Macedonia's intolerable backwardness compared to Europe. The anger that came to be directed at the state officials held responsible for the milk was not only anchored in concerns about public health, but also in perceptions of the typicality of such backward behavior on the part of the government officials. The scandalousness of the narrative thereby emerged as the "public" voice was embedded within a chronotope of European modernity that contrasted Macedonian hopes and expectations for the future with a state hopelessly mired in an unchanging, backward past.

While chronotopes of transitional Macedonia and modern Europe were broadly distributed across genres of social interaction in postconflict Macedonia, the media form of news scandals was a privileged and potent site in which this chronotopic distinction regularly emerged. In this regard, the regular manifestation of such chronotopic contrasts in reportage and commentary on scandals constituted a social process in which persons (in the form of journalists, news makers, and, crucially, audiences) routinely participated in mass-mediated interactions that took these chronotopes for granted. In doing so, a scandal functioned by breathing characterological qualities into the agents depicted in its narrative, from a "public" subject of outrage to the various other agencies with which it came into contact, for example, the state and foreigners. Consequently, a typology of social personae became widely available to Macedonian audiences and actors.

## Chronotopes and Agency

In the preceding analysis, I examined how chronotopic representation of time-spaces and the characters who populate them contributed to the social development of political scandals in Macedonia. It is worth highlighting that in these cases chronotopy functions on two levels. First, the news narratives produced within and across reports rely on particular chronotopic conventions and contrasts. In complement, the consumption of and reaction to these narratives (e.g., by individuals following the story or by news makers caught in the story's spotlight) presupposed their own chronotopic conventions that to degrees aligned with those in the narrated event. Thus, in the social emergence of any one scandal, mass-mediated narratives spurred on social action both on the level of the news makers implicated in a story and among the general audience of the news narrative.

Attention to chronotopy thus provides a novel perspective on an age-old problem of the social sciences: the structure versus agency debate. In a review essay on the subject, Laura Ahearn argued that, although the concept of agency remains ill defined in the social sciences, any definition should minimally conceive of agency as "the socioculturally mediated capacity to act" (2001: 112; see also Ortner 2006). Within this framework of mediation, an actor's agency (regardless of whether the actor in question consists of an individual or a collectivity) can be shaped by various degrees of sociocultural determination: from large-scale social structures to the participation frameworks of real-time social interaction.

I argue that socially manifested chronotopic models also provide one crucial level of mediation in on-the-ground reckonings of agentive capacity precisely due to their representational and characterological qualities. As Asif Agha argues, chronotopic representations "include figurements of social persons of many different kinds—historical actors, abstract agents of colonial history, fictional characters, sketches of political subjectivity—that become available to persons in semiotic encounters with mass-mediated representations and play a critical role in encounters with others oriented to the same representations" (2007: 326). In short, the logics of action and characterologies that define particular chronotopes constitute semiotic resources that can shape the nature and quality of social action.

Thinking about chronotopes in this way can highlight the semiotic and social processes by which collective dispositions toward action emerge and dissipate. For instance, in writing about hope, Vincent Crapanzano makes the point that, "[e]xcept where it is used as an equivalent to desire, hope depends on some other agency—a god, fate, chance, an other—for its fulfillment. Its evaluation rests on the characterization—the moral characterization—of that agency. You can do all you can to realize your hopes, but ultimately they depend on the fates—on someone else" (2003: 6). Reading this insight in terms of the concept of the chronotope, hope—whether an individual or collective disposition—arguably depends on a chronotopic representation of social agencies, while it also projects a field of possible action populated by these diverse agencies. It is within this projection, the chronotope, as it were, that the ego's own course of (in)action can take place.

So too can attention to chronotopy inform the analysis that both Hariman (this volume) and Citron (this volume) offer on the eclipse of the trope of revolution by that of catastrophe within recent political movements. As they each argue, the formulations of revolution that dominated in the nineteenth and twentieth centuries were organized according to a temporal logic of progressive stages. That is, revolution implied a chronotope defined by particular possibilities of action that oriented how individuals and groups acted under the mantle of revolution. The logics of action presupposed by the chronotope of catastrophe are markedly different. Whereas revolution conjures figures of popular uprising and, in its Marxist iteration, a progression of state forms, catastrophe instead projects unexpected and exogenous forces as agents of change that demand response. As Hariman and Citron both emphasize, the differences in how catastrophe figures agency compared to revolution reflects a profound shift in contemporary political culture.

The circulation of chronotopic models thereby bear on actors' reflexive sense of their own capacity to act. In some cases, the notion that "things never change" or that "change will eventually come"—when achieved in a discursive interaction—can ground a projection of a field of agency in which individual social actors feel little compulsion, or capacity, to act, in which their stance can be characterized as resigned (cf. Riskedahl 2007). In other contexts, political chronotopes, including those that figure revolution and catastrophe, can presuppose a collective agent at the center of social change to which individuals can align. Similarly, chronotopic models of activism exist that portray everyday social actors whose interventions do count (e.g., see Keck and Sikkink 1998). Broadly circulating chronotopes thus occupy a central role in anchoring expressions of social personhood and intersubjectivity and in setting the scene for the myriad social practices that form the material of everyday life. Such chronotopes overlap, complement, and conflict, but nonetheless they emerge and mediate action in the world when taken up within and across discursive interactions.

From this perspective, the conventionality of chronotopic models within Macedonian discourses of the scandal is very significant. Via scandals, chronotopes circulated that allowed people to make sense of everyday Macedonian political dynamics, but also to "tie the narrative threads together" when reflecting on their own position within the chronotope, whether it be one of backward Macedonia or progressive Europe. I often encountered people doing just this during my fieldwork: criticizing, complaining, explaining, defending, and rationalizing, all predicated on chronotopic representations of the Macedonian present. In doing so, they would constantly, if implicitly, evaluate their own agentive capacity in relation to those other agencies projected within the chronotope. Ergo, in postconflict Macedonia, as Agha observes, "[c]hronotopic representations enlarge the 'historical present' of their audiences by creating chronotopic displacements and cross-chronotope alignments between persons here-and-now and persons altogether elsewhere, transposing selves across discrete zones of cultural spacetime through communicative practices that have immediate consequences for how social actors in the public sphere are mobilized to think, feel, and act" (2007: 324).

## Say Macedonia!

My contention, then, is that analytic attention to the emergence and achievement of chronotopic framings of the political can illustrate not only how actors understand political experience, but also how they understand their own agency within a given social context. To demonstrate this, I offer an example that focuses on one news scandal that crossed the publicity threshold in Macedonia and resulted in many ordinary citizens rallying to public action. The scandal itself centered on the discovery of a Council of Europe document that stipulated terms of address for Macedonia and its residents that went further than the norms that had resulted from the country's name dispute with Greece. By exploring the emergence of particular chronotopes and chronotopic contrasts in the scandal's narrative development, I show how a mass mobilization in protest of the document became felicitious.

On 15 March 2004, journalist Zoran Andonovski broke a story in the now defunct Macedonia-language news daily *Vreme* about a Council of Europe (COE) document that outlined terms of address for Macedonia and its residents for use in communications within the office of the Secretary General (Andonovski 2004d). The Council of Europe, founded in 1949, is an interstate body that fosters European coordination and cooperation on matters related to human rights and the rule of law. According to Andonovski's article, the document, dated 2 March, prescribed that the dominant language and culture of Macedonia should be referred to as "(Slav) Macedonian"; that citizens of the country should not be called "Macedonians" but rather "citizens of the Former Yugoslav Republic of Macedonia"; and finally, that members of the Macedonian diaspora should be referred to as "individuals who identify themselves as (Slav) Macedonians." These guidelines were in addition to, but went well beyond, the use of "the former Yugoslav Republic of Macedonia," or FYROM, to refer to the country itself as set out by the United Nations. In the fashion of the news scandal genre, Andonovski's article blended a chronotope of factual report with one implying crisis and the need for remedial action.

Given the widespread resentment most ethnic Macedonians have toward the naming dispute that foisted the designation FYROM upon the country in the first place—it was perceived as a direct Greek attack on the Macedonian nation and national identity—this story was likely to draw popular attention. But, since the Macedonian press regularly churned out reports about perceived regressive or progressive steps taken by foreign governments and international organizations regarding the naming dispute, the story's uptake as a scandal was by no means guaranteed. Indeed, in its first rendition, the story, although mentioned on *Vreme*'s front page, was not highlighted as the lead story nor accompanied by a photograph. The story might have ended here.

The next day, 16 March, however, saw the story's acceleration. *Vreme* again highlighted the story, featuring a follow-up report on its front page. This time, however, the story had expanded. With a picture of Minister of Foreign Affairs Ilinka Mitreva, the headline read, "The Ministry Comforts Us; The Ambassador Protests" (Andonovski 2004c). In the report, a statement made by the Ministry of Foreign Affairs (MFA), which emphasized the unofficial status (and thus relative insignificance) of the document, is contrasted with the strong criticism that the Macedonian ambassador to the COE, Zvonimir Jakuloski, leveled toward COE Secretary General Walter Schwimmer. As *Vreme*'s coverage of the story continued, the developing narrative about injustice toward Macedonia at the COE was complemented with one that also cast doubt on the appropriateness of the government's reaction. Macedonia's other news dailies also picked up the story on 16 March and published reports that mirrored the narrative threads introduced by the *Vreme* coverage.

In addition, 16 March also saw two articles of published commentary on the emerging COE scandal: an editorial in *Vreme* by none other than Zoran Andonovski (2004a), and an op-ed piece in the newspaper *Dnevnik* by Ljubomir Frčkovski (2004), a former politician and one of Macedonia's leading public intellectuals. Each author highlighted the hypocrisy of the COE—an organization ostensibly with a mission to increase harmony and unity between its member states—for unilaterally taking sides on the Greek-Macedonian naming dispute and, in effect, subordinating all its constituent members to the will of one, Greece. Both of the articles, however, concluded with a call for a public response to the document: Andonovski called on citizens to "remind foreigners what [Macedonia's] name is," and Frčkovski asked readers to prove that Macedonia "will not acquiesce."

Already on this second day of news coverage, then, one can discern how the emergent news narrative on the COE scandal relied on distinct chronotopes that represented and contrasted "Macedonia" and "Europe." However, unlike the valences more typical of this contrast, in this instance, "Macedonia" was portrayed as a truthful and upright center (despite its government's ineptness) against a hypocritical "Europe." Furthermore, in line with the chronotopy of the scandal genre, this contrast supported the "outraged persona" (voiced both by Andonovski and Frčkovski) who demanded urgent action in response to the incident.

The next day, on 17 March, coverage of the COE scandal continued, but the play of chronotopes became more complicated. Reports in the newspapers *Vreme, Dnevnik,* and *Utrinski Vesnik* all focused on the MFA's new demand that the COE document be immediately withdrawn (e.g., Andonovski 2004b). This reproduced a chronotope of urgent action in which Macedonian justice countered European hypocrisy, and signaled government attempts to place itself at the heroic center of the emerging narrative. At the same time, however, the newspapers continued to question the MFA's conduct prior to the discovery of the document, suggesting a diplomatic failure on the part of the ministry.

In addition, the coverage of 17 March also elaborated on the unresponsiveness of the COE. The *Utrinski Vesnik* report, entitled "Strasbourg Is Silent about the Scandal around the Name," highlighted that Walter Schwimmer had not made himself available for questioning by Macedonian journalists. The *Utrinski Vesnik* article also intimated that, unofficially, it was known that

Schwimmer was more outraged at the leak than at the offense caused to the Macedonian public, and that the document had been the outcome of Schwimmer's efforts to recruit Greek votes to support his candidacy for a second term as COE Secretary General. Through this narrative trajectory, "Europe" further emerged as a place of intrigue, of backroom politics, and of nontransparent and unresponsive officials. In effect, it was assimilated to a chronotopic model of transitional Macedonia.

The narrative of the scandal thus developed across both reportage and commentary in two complementary directions: one direction highlighted the hypocrisy of "Europe," the perpetrator in a characterology derived from the chronotopic model of scandal, while the other direction questioned the lack of action on the part of the MFA. This strain of report constituted, as it were, a subscandal. Within this subscandal, the narrative represented the Macedonian state as an impotent entity that failed to confront the secret, hidden agencies of "Europe."

Over the next few days, further reports and commentary continued the narrative trend of the story and the growing diplomatic ripples caused by the Macedonian protest to the document. Notably, however, other social actors were getting involved. In particular, a consortium of nongovernmental organizations (NGOs) banded together to spearhead a mass postcard protest of the COE. As part of a "Say Macedonia!" campaign, the NGOs designed and printed a large amount of postcards that proclaimed slogans such as "Don't You FYROM ME" or "Call Me By My Name" (figure 2.1). The postcards' backs offered senders blank space to express their displeasure to the COE.

Figure 2.1. One of the postcard designs used to protest the Council of Europe's stringent guidelines on how to refer to Macedonia within the organization's documents.

The mass mobilization achieved by the postcard campaign was unparalleled when compared to other postconflict scandals that projected public outrage but rarely succeeded in mounting full-scale popular action. As I contend, the scandal's ability to effect mass action was hinged on the chronotopic contrasts that came to be employed in the dominant narrative that emerged around the news story. In particular, the effort to inundate the office of the Secretary General with postcards of protest operated in a chronotopic model opened up by central themes of reportage and commentary, that is, Schwimmer's (non)reaction to the issue, the MFA's inadequacy in handling the situation, and the expression of popular protest to the situation. Such themes contrasted a nonresponsive and unforthcoming outside power (i.e., the primary scandal) and an ineffectual state (i.e., the subscandal) with "the people," who had to stand up and act as their own advocates within the framework of the scandal narrative's chronotope of urgent action. Further animating this chronotopic model was a contrast between "Europe" and "Macedonia," but one in which their typical valuations and associations were reversed. Unlike previous moments of outrage over the name dispute, the postcard campaign, enlivened by chronotopic contrasts, projected a space for popular agency that could bring about concrete results. Mass action became felicitous.

The advance of the postcard campaign also resulted in further representations of Macedonian popular agency against hypocritical "Europe" and despite perceived state inactivity. Significantly, these reports all quoted the NGO coalition's statement saying that because the MFA had been so passive, this citizens' action must continue until the document is withdrawn and "responsibility is taken." Such rhetoric appeared in news reports over the subsequent days as the news narrative and participants' statements continued to align with the emergent chronotopic model of the scandal.

Beyond the framing of the postcard campaign and its news coverage, the emerging sense of popular action also had a palpable effect on daily life in Skopje. The postcard booth in Skopje's central square was well visited, and other "Say Macedonia!" paraphernalia (e.g., T-shirts, baseball caps) cropped up across the city. Many friends and neighbors also seemed revitalized by their sense of participation in the collective stand against "Europe's" hypocrisy, and many of them specifically urged me to participate in the postcard protest, which I did.

As the postcard campaign continued and expanded to other Macedonian cities, there was, however, only limited news coverage, until Tuesday, 6 April, when the "Say Macedonia!" campaign came to a close. Both *Vreme* and *Utrinski* each had stories on that day about the reception of the postcards in Strasbourg (Stojanovska 2004a; Jovanovska 2004). Finally, to punctuate the end of the campaign, the organizers of "Say Macedonia!" held a press conference on Thursday, 8 April, that was covered in all three papers. The media coverage highlighted the organizers' central claim that the initiative "united" government and citizens and even the government and the opposition ("The Battle for the Name Links Citizens and Politicians"; "Say Macedonia Unites Government and Opposition") (Stojanovska 2004b; *Utrinski Vesnik* 2004). In the end, the scandal concluded on a happy middle ground. COE Secretary General Walter Schwimmer admitted some responsibility for the incident and suffered embarrassment, which may have contributed to his failure to win reelection as COE Secretary General. The MFA declared a victory due to its role in holding the COE responsible for the document. The NGO coalition celebrated their remarkable organizational feat and the "citizens' action" that it precipitated.

In the case of "Say Macedonia!," the story's initial traction was in no small part due to its being cast within the scandal genre, with its characteristic chronotopic contrasts, resulting in a representation of pernicious "foreign intervention" in Macedonian politics. European actors within the chronotope of transitional Macedonia often took on undesirable characteristics, as two-faced agencies with unclear motivations and agendas. Insofar as the COE Secretary General was seemingly caught red-handed in his perceived defamation of Macedonia, he was easily construed as a glaring example of that character type. Reports and commentary foregrounded this viewpoint by echoing statements about the COE's—and, by extension, "Europe's"—hypocrisy. This narrative thrust, therefore, came into direct conflict with the other dominant chronotope of Europe, in which Europe constituted the realm of normalcy par excellence. By contrasting these chronotopes, the COE scandal showed not only a "European" bureaucracy plagued by petty politicking, but also one that held sinister motives toward Macedonia that threatened the integrity of the Macedonian national identity. The combination was powerful, or better said, empowering: the mischievous foreigners in Macedonia had typically been imagined as behind-the-scenes and therefore unable to be addressed. However, now materialized in "Europe" and embedded in scandal logic, European justice and efficiency could be used against "them."

Significantly, within this emergent, major chronotope, the appropriate delegate of the Macedonian state, Foreign Minister Ilinka Mitreva, developed as a character of impotence, that is, as one without initiative. In news coverage and commentary, the MFA could only respond—and ineffectually at that—following press and popular pressure. Thus, as the narrative paired a malicious Europe with an impotent Macedonian state where at stake was the integrity of the Macedonian identity itself, the conditions were ripe for a mass mobilization. Journalists and commentators seized on this in dually criticizing the COE and the government, as well as in urging citizens to action.

However, whereas most postconflict scandals either projected an impotent and intractable Macedonian state or the hidden power of foreigners against which public cries would fall silent, the "Say Macedonia!" scandal proved different. By revealing the hidden machinations of a European power not inside Macedonia but in the "heart of Europe" and guaranteed by "European" standards, the scandal produced a villain amenable to effective response. If the words of Macedonian politicians were empty and those of foreigners in Macedonia duplicitous, the COE by virtue of its history and moral authority not only could, but also needed to, answer Macedonian alarm in a form deemed substantive. Not coincidentally, in presenting the issue in terms of a contrast between a manipulative "Europe" bound by vested interests (e.g., of Greece, of Schwimmer and his campaign for reelection) and a just and honest "Macedonia," conditions were created for the mass demonstration of a collective national voice that at least momentarily reversed the moral underpinnings of the dominant chronotopic framings of the role taken by internationals vis-à-vis Macedonia.

This particular confluence of chronotopes that emerged in the unfolding scandal was instrumental in founding a situation in which the "Say Macedonia!" campaign could take off. The chronotopic model organizing the news narrative cast the *foreign* Council of Europe as an antagonistic but vulnerable agent and the Macedonian government as an ineffectual one, and so an NGO-led "people's action" appeared possible and necessary. The socially achieved chronotope of the COE scandal was crucial to the felicity of the NGO action: by capturing "Europe" as simultaneously secretive and transparent, a field of agency was projected upon which people could act.

## Conclusion

The "Say Macedonia!" scandal illustrates how salient chronotopes ground the social production of public narratives on the political. On one level, the availability and familiarity of particular chronotopic representations (e.g., of Europe and of transitional Macedonia) shaped the news story that emerged on the scandal across media outlets and a cycle of reports, follow-ups, and commentaries. On another level, insofar as public actors (e.g., the NGO coalition) aligned to the chronotopy of the scandal, mass public action became felicitous in the "Say Macedonia!" case. Attention to chronotopes in news narratives thus provides one lens through which to view the formal qualities of public discourses, the way such discourses frame social responsibility and agency, and their form-shaping relevance for political action.

The approach to public discourse outlined here privileges the analysis of both the textual qualities of public narrative as well as the institutional settings and social processes that function to (re)produce public narratives as a regular discourse. Indeed, the view on chronotopy described and applied here theorizes the relationship between the textual and the social-institutional. The salience of particular chronotopes impacts narrative conventions (e.g., genres of news report and news scandal) that define the political institution of professional journalism but that also shape public readings of political agency. In a dialectical fashion, public discourses at once depend on their uptake within and across social institutions and social contexts, and they also shape the practices found in these locations.

Ultimately, then, I argue that this chronotope-focused approach to public discourse amounts to a powerful conceptualization of political culture. The chronotopes of the political that circulate broadly within a society—including those that circulate via social technologies such as the political scandal—are not only central to the imaginations of political agency, but also become instrumental to social actors' reflexive evaluations of their own capacity for action in concrete cases. Through chronotopic models we can trace the representations of state power that are characteristic of a particular time and place, and also the relationship of these representations to the ways in which people negotiate their encounters with the state. In the chronotope as a major, social manifestation, then, one finds a practical notion of historical consciousness and historicity, not as abstract objects that are the outcome of analysis, but as orienting devices that are achieved in lived moments. Attention to chronotopes, their interdiscursive emergence in particular contexts, and their mediation of actors' representation of and action in a social field facilitates both an understanding of overarching regularities of a political culture, but also of the heterodox forms of praxis that inevitably emerge within social life.

**Andrew Graan** is assistant director of the Center for International Studies at the University of Chicago. He has previously taught at the University of Virginia, Wake Forest University, Columbia College Chicago, and the University of Chicago. His research in the Republic of Macedonia develops a sociocultural and linguistic anthropological approach to the study of political communication and contemporary forms of transnational governance. His research interests include mass media, political language and performance, public culture, international intervention, global governance, and nation branding in Macedonia, the Balkans, and the European Union.

## Notes

1. The narrative opposition between Europe and the Balkans has a long history within literary traditions of both Western Europe and the Balkans, as does a Balkan narrative about malicious foreign powers (see Todorova 1997; Wolff 1994; Bakić-Hayden 1995; Bakić-Hayden and Hayden 1992; Neofotistos 2008).
2. "Vekje dve nedeli trae aferata za kvalitetot na mlekoto, a dosega nikoj ne ponese odgovornost za toa. Dvaesetina mlekarnici koristele nedozvoleni količestva mleko vo

prav vo mlekoto što go proizveduvaat, no se ušte e nejasno koj i dali kje gi kazni." All translations are the author's unless otherwise noted.
3. "Vo prodavnicite ostana spornoto mleko, a Makedonija ušte ednaš se potvrdi kako država koja na svoite gragjani ne može da im obezbedi najosnovi prava i zaštita za da komsumiraat zdrava hrana."
4. "Dali ministerot slušnal deka apliciravme za členstvo vo EU, a tamu ima nad 6.000 standardi, zakoni, i propisi koi go ureduvaat zemjodelstvoto i prehranbenata industrija."

## Bibliography

Agha, Asif. 2007. "Recombinant Selves in Mass Mediated Space-Time." *Language and Communication* 27: 320–35.
Ahearn, Laura M. 2001. "Language and Agency." *Annual Review of Anthropology* 30: 109–37.
Andonovski, Zoran. 2004a. "Duhot na Lisabon vleze vo Strazbur." *Vreme* (Skopje), 16 March 2004.
———. 2004b. "MNR ostro protestira do Sovetot na Evropa: Vednaš da se povleče dokumentot što go negira identitetot na zemjava." *Vreme* (Skopje), 17 March.
———. 2004c. "Po preimenuvanjeto na Makedonija vo Strazbur: MNR ne teši, ambasadorot protestira." *Vreme* (Skopje), 16 March.
———. 2004d. "Upatstvo za 'upotreba na Makedonija' od Sovetot na Evropa: Em bivša, em slovenska Makedonija." *Vreme* (Skopje), 15 March.
Bakhtin, Mikhail. 1981. "Forms of Time and of the Chronotope in the Novel." In *The Dialogic Imagination* Ed. Michael Holquist. Trans. Caryl Emerson and Michael Holquist, 84–258. Austin: University of Texas Press.
Bakić-Hayden, Milica. 1995. "Nesting Orientalism: The Case of Former Yugoslavia." *Slavic Review* 54, no. 4: 917–31.
Bakić-Hayden, Milica, and Robert M. Hayden. 1992. "Orientalist Variations on the Theme 'Balkans': Symbolic Geography in Contemporary Yugoslav Politics." *Slavic Review* 51, no. 1: 1–15.
Basso, Keith. 1996. *Wisdom Sits in Places: Language and Landscape Among the Western Apache*. Santa Fe: University of New Mexico Press.
Blommaert, Jan. 2005. *Discourse: A Critical Introduction*. New York: Cambridge University Press.
Crapanzano, Vincent. 2003. "Reflections on Hope as a Category of Social and Psychological Analysis." *Cultural Anthropology* 18, no. 1: 3–32.
Dick, Hilary Parsons. 2010. "Imagined Lives and Modernist Chronotopes in Mexican Nonmigrant Discourse." *American Ethnologist* 37, no. 2: 275–90.
Dnevnik (Skopje). 2004a. "Mleko vo prav se koristi nezakonski." 28 April. http://star.dnevnik.com.mk/?pBroj=2441&stID=32855 (accessed 19 January 2012).
Dnevnik (Skopje). 2004b. "Pieme opasna bela voda namesto mleko!" 7 May. http://star.dnevnik.com.mk/default.aspx?pbroj=2448&stID=33243&pdate=20040507 (accessed 19 January 2012).
Frčkovski, Ljubomir. 2004. "Dolna zemja." *Dnevnik* (Skopje), 16 March.
Gal, Susan. 1991. "Bartok's Funeral: Representations of Europe in Hungarian Political Rhetoric." *American Ethnologist* 18, no. 3: 440–58.

———. 2005. "Language Ideologies Compared: Metaphors and Circulations of Public and Private." *Journal of Linguistic Anthropology* 15, no. 1: 23–37.
Hall, Stuart. 1980. "Encoding/Decoding." In *Culture, Media, Language,* ed. Stuart Hall, Dorothy Hobson, Andrew Lowe, and Paul Willis, 128–38. London: Hutchinson.
Jakobson, Roman. (1957) 1971. "Shifters, Verbal Categories, and the Russian Verb." In *Selected Writings*, vol. 2, 130–47. The Hague: Mouton.
Jovanovska, Slobodanka. 2004. "Od Sovetot na Evropa odbivaat da preciziraat kolku kartički stignale na nivna adresa: Strazbur gi oceni porakite od razglednicite kako učtivi." *Utrinski Vesnik* (Skopje), 6 April.
Keck, Margaret E., and Kathryn Sikkink. 1998. *Activists Beyond Borders: Advocacy Networks in International Politics*. Ithaca, NY: Cornell University Press.
Lemon, Alaina. 2009. "Sympathy of the Weary State? Cold War Chronotopes and Moscow Others." *Comparative Studies in Society and History* 51, no. 4: 832–64.
Morson, Gary Saul and Caryl Emerson. 1990. *Mikhail Bakhtin: The Creation of a Prosaics*. Stanford, CA: Stanford University Press.
Neofotistos, Vasiliki. 2008. "'The Balkans' Other Within': Imaginings of the West in the Republic of Macedonia." *History and Anthropology* 19, no. 1: 17–36.
Ortner, Sherry B. 2006. "Power and Projects: Reflections on Agency." In *Anthropology and Social Theory*, 129–53. Durham, NC: Duke University Press.
Pendarov, Todor. 2004. "Komentar: Odgovornost vo prav." *Dnevnik* (Skopje), 14 May. http://star.dnevnik.com.mk/default.aspx?pbroj=2454&stID=33497&pdate=20040514 (accessed 19 January 2012).
Riskedahl, Diane. 2007. "A Sign of War: The Strategic Use of Violent Imagery in Contemporary Lebanese Political Rhetoric." *Language and Communication* 27, no. 3: 307–19.
Silverstein, Michael. 1999. "NIMBY Goes Linguistic: Conflicted 'Voicings' from the Culture of Local Language Communities." In *CLS 35: The Panels—Language, Identity and the Other*, ed. Sabrina J. Billings, John P. Boyle, and Aaron M. Griffin, 101–23. Chicago: Chicago Linguistic Society.
———. 2000. "Whorfianism and the Linguistic Imagination of Nationality." In *Regimes of Language*, ed. Paul V. Kroskrity, 85–138. Santa Fe, NM: School of American Research Press.
Stasch, Rupert. 2011. "Textual Iconicity and the Primitivist Cosmos: Chronotopes of Desire in Travel Writing about Korowai of West Papua." *Journal of Linguistic Anthropology* 21, no. 1: 1–21.
Stojanovska, Sunčica. 2004a. "Kampanja: 'Kaži: Makedonija!'—Porakata stigna do Strazbur." *Vreme* (Skopje), 6 April.
———. 2004b. "Masoven oddsiv vo akcijata 'Kaži Makedonija!': Borbata za imeto gi sploti gragjanite i političarite." *Vreme* (Skopje), 8 April.
Todorova, Maria. 1997. *Imagining the Balkans*. New York: Oxford University Press.
*Utrinski Vesnik* (Skopje). 2004. "Akcijata 'Kaži Makedonija' ja obedini vlasta i opozicijata." 8 April.
Wolff, Larry. 1994. *Inventing Eastern Europe*. Stanford, CA: Stanford University Press.

CHAPTER 3

# THE IN-BETWEEN STATES
## ENDURING CATASTROPHES AS SOURCES OF DEMOCRACY'S DEADLOCKS IN KOSOVO

*Naser Miftari*

■ ■ ■ ■ ■ ■

In December 2012 the lackluster political landscape of Kosovo, the newest independent state of Europe, with a population of 1.8 million, became the center of attention when a number of leaked conversations between Kosovo high-ranking officials, wiretapped by European Union Rule of Law Mission in Kosovo (EULEX) as part of ongoing investigations into organized crime in Kosovo, found their way into social media channels and thereafter became breaking news in mainstream media.[1] It appeared as if a small dose of the WikiLeaks global virus that had stirred up the global audience earlier that year had been injected into Kosovo's politics in a contextualized version. The recordings, initially dubbed as big scandals, became a media hit and cheered up the apathetic public for a few weeks. In the absence of strong reactions from the main segments of Kosovo's political spectrum—one opposition party partially excluded—the scandals naturally moved back to social network forums for a while and were abandoned altogether a few weeks later. By January 2013 the recorded conversations ceased to be a topic. No one was fired, no official resigned, no one called for extraordinary elections, and nothing unusual happened after all.[2]

In conditions where elected officials are subordinate to the will of an informed public and a tradition of checks and balances, the resignations of politicians involved in alleged scandals are expected, if not a foregone conclusion. On formal grounds, Kosovo politicians, as in all supposedly democratic polities, are bound by such norms. In other circumstances, the recordings that surfaced could have taken down a government. Yet, that did not happen in Kosovo. It turned out the recordings were nothing more than a reflection of how politics really works, no matter how bizarre. Reactions died down. Case closed.

Remaining critical of the assumptions of the transition studies that see the realization of liberal democracy in transition countries as a matter of correct political choices and good timing, social anthropologists argue that in processes of democratization we can expect to observe variable degrees of resistance to or support for institutional change and state building (Hayoz 2010). To them, how the extent of support or resistance manifests itself depends on and must take into account important contextual factors that transition studies scholars seem to overlook. How politics operates contextually and with what ends, seems to puzzle social anthropologists more, and this is the question that is central to this chapter. What if the stakes in a given context are such that they tend to preclude development in favor of the status quo? What if resistance and support have to go hand in hand and the drive to maintain the status quo tends to be greater than the drive to consolidate the political order?

The main goal of this chapter is to reflect on how developing democracies like Kosovo experience, negotiate, and resist change while on their path toward the liberalization of their political and economic systems. The analysis takes into account important background considerations about how Kosovo's political structure was established in the first place; the unique internal and external circumstances that conditioned the emergence of the political elite; the context in which Kosovo was established as a state; and how the need to sustain political stability outweighs the drive for important principles of democratic governance—checks and balances—to take hold. In important ways, all of the above make Kosovo seem like some kind of giant laboratory of social engineering where the concepts of state, sovereignty, nation, politics, and so on are somehow detached from their essentialist characteristics and are seen as "work in progress." Exploring and articulating them in greater detail is the main task of this analysis. While the chapter explores both social-political structures and collective actors' motives and interests, by delineating between what is considered the political and politics (Kurtz 2001),[3] particular attention is given to the concept of *political ambiguity* (Connolly 1983, Alesina and Cukierman 1987:2),[4] while illustrating through practical examples how it guides the multiple relations in the cohort of the political and of politics in the case of Kosovo, and with what implications.

Seven years after it proclaimed its independence in coordination with the main Western powers, Kosovo's situation is as follows. The majority of its inhabitants (90 percent Albanian) believe Kosovo is independent, given that the main Western powers, including the United States, recognize Kosovo as a state. At the same time, the Serb minority, around 7–8 percent of the total population, look to Russia and China and draw their own line of argument that Kosovo is a contested state and as such is still part of Serbia, not an independent state. Then there is the international community presence—the United Nations Interim Administration Mission in Kosovo (UNMIK) and EULEX—which operate "as if" Kosovo is independent in their transactions with Kosovo authorities and "as if" Kosovo is part of Serbia when it comes to addressing transactions with local Serbs or Serbian politicians. In the diplomatic terms that provide the rationale for the operation of the international community in Kosovo, EULEX is seen as operating as a status-neutral mandate. In such circumstances, the political elites from Kosovo and Serbia remain engaged in continuous negotiations on issues of mutual practical interest carried on under the banner of creative ambiguity, as it is sometimes referred to, while falling short of mutual recognition.[5]

This analysis considers the role of the international community and its presence in Kosovo (the EU, the United States, and other relevant actors) and puts the emphasis on conditionality (EU accession prospects), used here as a trade-off in exchange for regional peace and stability. It also explores the role of Kosovo's political parties and their leaders as self-interested actors that help nurture the system of partitocracy. Closely linked to them is the engaged or quasi-clientelist electorate (which has a direct stake in the electoral outcomes and is engaged in direct/indirect transactions with politicians) and the remainder of the population (voters and nonvoters alike) with little or marginal interest in the electoral outcomes, those who stand to gain the least from politics, yet collectively remain hooked on the idea of and hopes for a better, brighter future in a normal state. To explain better the role of each of the aforementioned, the analysis brings to attention narrative episodes to illustrate how politics and the political intersect and complement each other in Kosovo, helping to sustain interchangeable cycles of long-term political catastrophe.

## The Argument

The main argument in this chapter is that modernity (Latour 1993),[6] used here to identify liberal democracies and liberalized markets brings with it a deep, abiding sense of order and the need to chip away at sources of disorder. But as the planetary project of modernity expands, it keeps running into specific localities that resist its expansion, or it runs into versions of modernity that have collapsed and have to be remade into what has become the standard model of modernity, that is, liberal democracies with free markets. The western Balkans and Kosovo specifically seem to be wedged somewhere in the latter category. The polities in this part of the world have successfully terminated the old regimes and have put in place, at least formally, democratic institutions necessary for the consolidation of the state. However, because the western Balkans remains a place of unfinished peace and of unfinished states, political catastrophe here endures, due to the ways in which peace was achieved, due to the ways in which postwar democratization has proceeded, and due to the ways in which agents look upon the structure. The international community in charge of remaking the western Balkans has found itself driven by the need to improvise and advance ambiguous propositions and platforms as substitute solutions in order to report success stories and progress.

The ambiguity that characterizes political transactions is much emphasized throughout the newly independent Balkan states, and the case of Kosovo is a good example to illustrate the larger point. It needs be stated here, however, that one great misfortune of the western Balkans is the fact that the introduction of political pluralism in 1989—following more than four decades of Communist one-party rule—and the immediate and unconditional promotion of freedom of debate left little breathing space or time for a critical understanding to emerge around political pluralism itself, nationalism, religion, and other pathologies of democratization (Snyder and Ballentine 1996). In Kosovo, almost overnight the old regime was substituted with a movement for liberation and pluralism (Clark 2000).[7] Still, the logic and legacy of monism continued to prevail. The transformation here occurred in form, but not in substance. Also, Kosovo is recognized as the state that has been traditionally less developed and more prone to corruption of all of the former Yugoslavia due to problematic embrace of the Yugoslav communist regime and inability of the state to reach out to all segments of society. (Binder 1981, 1987).

So even after the bloody conflicts of the 1990s given the peculiar conditions of the region and the proximity of the western Balkans to the EU, and before any of these states were able to feel and breathe their true independence in authentic ways, each one of them became submerged—albeit first and foremost rhetorically—into a larger process of interdependence due to their stated goals and aspirations to become part of the larger family of the EU, a family that brought with it rules, norms, conditions, and criteria that were quite abstract and unknown to the western Balkan states previously.

In such circumstances, democracy, in its contextual versions a container of anxieties in all Balkan states to a greater or lesser degree, gets filled massively with politicized versions of the recent and distant past and loosely coordinated efforts to connect these pieces into one coherent whole while also holding hopes for a better, prosperous future. It becomes a container that sustains the clash between traditionalism and modernism as culturally hybrid masses look forward and backward at the same time. Therefore, hopes and dreams for a better future are somehow overshadowed by a sense of incompleteness. It is this notion of incompleteness, that "we are still far from normal," that prevails across the board as the western Balkans remains hooked on an uncertain path to political and economic liberalism, which represents both an opportunity for change and consolidation and an opportunity for the maintenance of the status quo. Hence, this chapter refers to these "in-between states" and to catastrophe as a trope for social change in countries undergoing complex democratization processes.

The problem of vagueness or political ambiguity to which the international community has subscribed in the Western Balkans is common in the political behavior of all the countries that seem located somewhere in between the democratization debate—Bosnia, Serbia, Montenegro, Macedonia, Albania, and Kosovo. So how it is played out in reality is an important matter to elucidate. In the case of Kosovo, its political elite—like elsewhere in the Balkans—while swimming in nationalist ethos at home, is pressed to imitate cosmopolitanism abroad.[8]

In the case of Kosovo, the elite is seen as an important partner in advancing the prospects for peace between Kosovo and Serbia, since its commitment to peace means assurance for broader political stability, which the EU strives to ensure for the whole region. But its potential to offer and deliver on guarantees at the peace negotiations table does not make it automatically fit for the EU's integration agenda, which requires higher standards as benchmarks to be met and there EU uses different metrics.

The recipe for success applied in the former context is an unlikely recipe in the latter. Thus, on one hand the EU is pressed to work with radicals and conservatives to achieve peace, and on the other it strives to improvise a dialogue with the moderate forces in the society in an attempt to work toward EU integration. Here we observe the contradicting ideologies that guide the agents on both sides—the Kosovo political elite driven by the principles of ultra-politics and the EU bureaucracy guided by the principles of post-politics (Ingimundarson 2007; Sharpe and Boucher 2010),[9] unlikely to find common ground due to the metrics that each side uses. Therefore, the EU finds itself improvising to the point that the transactions become a model of political ambiguity.[10] Although progress toward peace in the Balkans—specifically between Kosovo and Serbia—and the road toward the EU are two different tracks, the circumstances make them seem relevant to one another, and so the political elites at home continue to sell them as one integral whole. In parallel to their work on the peace process, the political elite in Kosovo uses slogans to point out that the road to the EU is getting closer and to highlight EU membership as a strategic goal, when in reality the state is not even close to meeting the benchmarks. Because the EU is interested in long-term political stability in this part of the world and Kosovo's political elites are interested in short-term gains, this makes the political catastrophe enduring. Domestically, these elites hold captive publics, feeding them with empty spoons. The publics—embroiled in misery and unemployment—dream on about the Balkans becoming a part of the EU. The EU, of course, is aware of the contradiction, but it seems to lack a clear formula for narrowing, let alone closing, the gap between *historical dilemmas* that puzzle Balkans leaders such as Kosovo's political elite and the *economic determinism* that dictates the EU's expansion. In turn, then, the EU sometimes even offers romantic scenarios connected to historicism that do nothing but further the hopelessness.[11]

Because the strategy of the political elites in the Balkans is two-tiered—on one side oriented to convincing the international community that the Balkans is becoming normal by acting cosmopolitan abroad, and on the other to maintaining the support among the electoral base at home, proclaiming that "we are the true reformers" and the path to EU is assured through us—this approach to politics seems somewhat delusional. It is an attempt by the political parties to hit back at the impact of modernity while trying to freeze time. It nurtures the status quo while paying lip service to change. In each of the Balkan states, such ambiguity is played out in the public discourse—nurturing populism at home (to sustain their electoral base) and imitating cosmopolitanism abroad.

What this does is leave the region stagnant and captured by political parties' interests while favoring the strengthening of clan politics and consolidating a de facto system of partitocracy. It furthers the sense of hopelessness among ordinary people and plants the seeds for radicalization and deeper polarizations within society, as the gap between the haves and have-nots widens and ordinary people grow ever more alienated from politics and the complex bargaining that it entails. The alienation in turn only makes them vulnerable, a breeding ground for extremism and fanaticism of all sorts.

## COLLECTIVE ACTORS AND THEIR STAKES

Before elaborating further on the background conditions that make Kosovo what it is, it is worth highlighting in greater detail what each collective actor represents, and what their interests and goals are.

### *International Community*

The international actors in the case of Kosovo are ambiguous. There is, on one hand, the imperative to move places like Kosovo toward the rule of law and the trappings of the modernist state. Here, an international regime—EULEX, led by the EU and facilitated by US engagement—bears down rather forcefully. It can be observed in some of the resolute actions that it tries to take against corrupt officials, war crimes, and so on. Its goal is to establish conditions for a firm "rule of law" in Kosovo. At the same time, it has to work with Kosovo politicians accused of various crimes of corruption and war crimes, all while continuing the process of finding a lasting peace and a solution for the Serbia-Kosovo conflict. So when it comes to bringing Kosovo closer to the EU, Brussels officials shrug their shoulders and offer excuses and criteria for Kosovo that are model examples of political ambiguity.

## Political Parties

Kosovo still remains de facto under some broader umbrella of international management, but the day to day management of Kosovo is left in the hands of local institutions of self-government. At the center of attention here is the role of political parties as the most durable structures in the process of Balkan transformation. Their central focus is the struggle to establish dominance among an ill-informed, often confused electorate.

Kosovo is a partitocracy, a system that gives a strong and central position to the political parties that are present in and control almost all aspects of policy making (Matuschek 2003). What makes partitocracy function in the case of Kosovo is that its political parties are heavily centralized and hierarchical. In conditions where such political party interests occupy all public institutions—from schools to public enterprises and independent institutions—pursuing an individual political career becomes virtually impossible without passing through political parties as the predominant gatekeepers (Gashi and Emerson 2013).

A quick overview of the political party structure and recommendations made by the National Democratic Institute (NDI) in 1999 regarding Kosovo—how political parties should develop in the future and what some of the barriers in their future development are—shows that the NDI recommendations have been completely disregarded (CRPM 2012). A case in point is the election of the party leaders. In the past fifteen years, most of the elections within the parties for their leadership were held without a contender, and leaders were elected by acclamation, or at best, even when a contender entered the race, it was for the purposes of attending formally to the statutes of the parties, not to contest the leader (Krasniqi and Shala 2012). Such a centralization of political power in the hands of few political parties and their leaders captures societies and forges a culture according to which all social, political, and economic relations are perceived as a zero-sum game and the decision making is left in the hands of a few leaders.

## Engaged Electorate

Given its small size, most of the traditional political parties in Kosovo have a standard percentage of the electorate that votes for them. Few voters ever remain up for grabs. Among the engaged electorate fall all voters that are in one form or another connected to the anticipation of a job or a post in a public enterprise or government office in the aftermath of the elections. The same goes for business owners, many of them the owners of small enterprises struggling to survive in a precarious market. The mobilization of this engaged electorate does not necessarily happen along ideological cleavages. Rather, it occurs based on regional identification and clan affiliation, with the predisposition to push forward the clan's uncontested leader. It is appropriate to note that at the center of the divide, in particular with business owners emerge material interests. The mainstream political parties in Kosovo have more than a good guess about who will vote for whom in the elections. In addition, the patriarchal system that still prevails in rural areas of Kosovo gives parties greater leverage in obtaining the votes of the heads of households and, through them, of their larger families. It is a public secret that through emissaries, the political parties go knocking from door-to-door with employment lists, using open or discrete threats to the heads of households to ensure that large families, which in rural settings determine the electoral outcomes, will vote for their party.

## Disengaged Electorate

Who are these people? That section of the public that is indirectly affected by, or in other words, their immediate professional or social standing does not yet necessarily depend on the outcome of the elections, even if their perspective (the desire to live in a democratic, corrupt-free, and prosperous state) is otherwise affected short or long term. These people often do not even vote. Their absenteeism is supposed to reflect their dissatisfaction. Yet in a system such as Kosovo, it hardly does. Based on some accounts, it is largely the young people (aged up to twenty-five), often semi-independent, who feel that Kosovo needs change but feel powerless to do anything. These are the people who remain disengaged and unable to channel their input or contributions into a system that is organized around political parties and patriarchies.

At times, parts of this disengaged electorate become actively involved in the election process. We also see movements from the disengaged electorate in the model of Partia e Fortë, who enter the political contest not with the goal to compete, but rather with the goal to discredit the whole concept of politics through satire. In such conditions an "as if" engagement, in the best circumstances, might serve as a wake-up call to mainstream politicians to change but is unlikely to do much more. However, in conditions when such movements' influence is overshadowed by the omnipresent core of political parties, it just adds to the confusion and leads to further alienation of the apathetic electorate.

In fact, this category of the public knows very well the practices of the political and economic elites (Hayoz 2010). Its distrust toward authorities shows that it is aware of the instrumentalization of public positions for private purposes or profit—almost the classic definition of corruption—as well as the use of private resources for political power. In opinion polls, distrust toward political parties is heavily emphasized, and issues such as corruption and government abuse of power top the lists.[12] What this tells us is that there are Kosovars who want a prosperous, safe, and developed Kosovo. But the move toward prosperity, safety, and development is to be carried out by those who EULEX and the international community have to monitor at the same time for election theft, corruption, nepotism, and all other forms of administrative corruption and crime. It is through those same officials that Kosovo is supposed to advance on its path toward the EU.

## The Background: Politics and the Political in Kosovo

Going back to the basic question, how did Kosovo emerge as a political entity and as an aspiring democratic state, and what were the background conditions that made it what it is? It is argued that the transition toward liberal or, rather, illiberal democracies or even the development of dictatorships is path-dependent and points to the experience with and vicinity to democracy, rule of law, and the market economy (Hayoz 2010). Consequently, it is argued that such a path-dependent outcome can also be gleaned from the ways the old regime broke down, how the regime changed, and the processes of legitimation and delegitimation. In other words, the problem points to historical experience with what Hayoz (2010) calls the "arm's-length principle," and he sees it as related to the ability of each country to undergo its own Europeanization process to adapt to the new rules imposed by the EU enlargement.[13] Further, it is likewise argued that in such circumstances, specific institutions, the structures of the political system, or specific cultural patterns can become catalysts of change or obstacles to democracy. With reference to post-Communist states, Hayoz (2010) observes the existence of a gap between democratic structures and mentalities and argues that the extent of the gap is reflected in the ways in which political elites and their parties act, communicate, and deal with others, such as citizens or other parties.

Kosovo used to be part of the state of Yugoslavia, and following Yugoslavia's demise it was placed under Serbia's tutelage. Such a step led to the increase of resistance among Kosovo's majority population, and in 1999, Kosovo was liberated from Serbia's control following a three-month-long air campaign undertaken by the North Atlantic Treaty Organization (NATO) that aimed to force the Serbian forces to withdraw from Kosovo and give up control. Once the Serbian forces withdrew, a UN administration took over, making Kosovo a de facto protectorate until it proclaimed its independence in 2008. The decade of life in Kosovo under UN administration was marked by efforts to build democratic institutions and instill the democratic mind-set in the public discourse. But what it actually did was sideline the liberal and moderate forces in society and gave a prominent role to the former combatants, turning them into the de facto rulers of Kosovo, and since 2008 also the de jure rulers while seeking to channel the influence of the moderate forces by placing them at best in roles as advisors to the former combatants. The outcome of the experiment is a mixture politics, offering halfway solutions and adding pressure toward maintenance of the status quo.

What seems largely left unaddressed when it comes to the analysis of Kosovo society and its political system is the notion of regionalism that prevails in politics. Such regionalism is manifested in the form of multiple strongholds (geographically distinct regions) where political parties are organized around tribal/clan politics identified through powerful figures that vie for influence. Whatever its size, a region is always an entity "in between" and the concept of the region itself is an "in-between" concept (Roth 2007).[14]

Kosovo is divided into several such regions and subregions. While such divisions are not relevant to the outside world (due to Kosovo being geographically small), their subjectivity is heavily emphasized internally in the local political and socioeconomic contexts and transactions. The larger point about regionalism in Kosovo is that regions to a great extent function along the lines of clan politics, as studied thoroughly in sociology and anthropology, and this has a direct impact on how the democratic structures are put in place. Reflecting on the politics of clans, some authors emphasize that while the regime is formally institutionalized, clans can pervade, transform, and undermine the regime through their informal rules of the game (Collins 2005). It is then further argued that in institutionalizing such rules, the clans exercise kin-based patronage, where jobs and goods are given out on the basis of kinship, not merit; clan elites steal state assets and direct them to their network. Whole assets are distributed based on a clan's power, and clans engage in "crowding out," a process by which they participate politically through their networks, crowding out nonclan forms of association or participation (Collins 2005).

In the case of Kosovo, what this clan-based politics does is exclude the arm's-length principle, which is recognized as a devise in modern society that protects the autonomy of the different social spheres against "alien" interference, be it politics with its specific interests, economic interests, or interests related to clientelism, familism, or other forms of favoritism.[15] The problem, then, is more than it seems on the surface. One of the ironies of the democratic modernity is that it asks us to separate ourselves from our deepest attachments and adopt a kind of abstract fairness toward everyone. In this sense, democratic modernity interrupts some of our most basic, natural feelings. All that now becomes corruption or nepotism. The word "transparency" is another term for abstracted fairness. In new democracies, it is argued that it may be unavoidable to nourish a portfolio of friends, networks, connections, and so forth in order to get things done. But what seems to be a survival strategy on the individual level takes the form of a power-keeping strategy on the level of the rulers (Hayoz 2010). It is further acknowledged that power networks and friends in the right positions are important resources in a country where elections on the national level as well as in most cases on the local level are not about transferring power but about maintaining power. This comes at a very large price, since it widens the already existing gap between the rulers and the ruled (Hayoz 2010). Furthermore, in conditions such as Kosovo's it can lead to interlocking democracy deadlocks, as it did most recently in 2014 following a general election.

Elections are one indicator that helps elucidate the broader point about the intersection between the political and politics in Kosovo. As a manifestation of ritual politics, however, elections cannot be singled out from the broader context. Such ritual politics—emphasized especially during elections—have taken place over the last decade. Kosovo and Serbia are engaged in a political dialogue that should determine the future of the state of Kosovo, and much is at stake—the future of a functional versus failed Kosovo state, the future of a Serbian minority in Kosovo, the potential for a better life for the majority of Kosovo's citizens, the potential for the crisis to involve other states in the Balkans. So, when elections take place, much is at stake. Change is desired, but the need to preserve the political stability is perhaps even more crucial.

The international community, engaged in many fronts in Kosovo and the wider region—to facilitate the peace process, to ensure political stability and regional stability—all while dealing with other crisis points elsewhere in Europe, pays lip service to the need for change and to allow new leaders to come to the forefront—a standard cliché in a democratic race—but in reality, it feels more safe with leaders it knows, in this case the "old leaders." When political parties rally on Election Day, they all count on their clientelist voters to cast the ballot in their favor. In their campaigns, they likewise pay lip service to change through cliché slogans such as the True Road, the Road to the Future, the New Mission, the New Way, the New Direction, and so on. Ironically, only the word "New" is new in them. Their true intention, as becomes clear after the elections, is to continue doing more of the same, that is, maintain the status quo and sustain their clientelist electorate. When casting the vote, the engaged electorate is much more mobilized, as it counts the potential for future transactions and takes into account past benefits. The disengaged electorate cast votes for change as well or refrain from voting. Yet, paradoxically they are the ones that fear most what the future might hold. Therefore, their anxieties and fears about what a vote for change might bring are more likely to play out in favor of the status quo. Their distrust in the prospects for change is firmly rooted in experience. There have been, in the past decade, a few failed attempts to make good on the promise of bringing about "real" change, each time when new political parties or initiatives have emerged on the promise of delivering change. The result each time was disastrous for those new initiatives. Therefore, for the undecided or the disengaged electorate, change is desired but not at any cost. In other words, the disengaged electorate will not favor change if it means wondering towards uncertainty. So in short, everyone wants change, but no one really wants change, because change can only happen by subscribing to radical approaches.

## Election Outcome Stories as a Narrative

A case in point here is the election process. It was a difficult process in 2010, when Kosovo held an extraordinary national election due to the crisis that brought down the existing government. Better said, the government decided to overthrow itself so as to drop a coalition partner and select another. There was much talk of vote rigging right after the polls closed. The day after the elections, some representatives of the international community started to talk about "industrial vote theft" in Kosovo the night before. Yet, as the day progressed, their criticism died down, and their official statements went back to the usual/normal "ambiguous political language" that stresses the voting irregularities but places the emphasis on the fact that the process went well and congratulates Kosovo citizens for another successful round of elections. Once again, it appears that the deadlock was bypassed without much complaint. No matter that in the coming weeks and months it was reported that overall problems were noticed in almost all polling stations during the election process. In 80 percent of cases (712 polling stations), the number of votes cast for the candidates did not match the votes that were given to the parties. (In Kosovo's election system, voters cast votes for the candidate and the political party at the same time.) In other words, not only did the votes determine the outcome of the winning political party, but local political activists filled in the ballots on behalf of their favorites to manipulate not just the outcome in terms of rankings of different political parties, but the outcome and rank order of candidates within the parties themselves. Each polling station had seven commissioners in charge of the proper running of the whole voting process, including vote counting and the collating of information for the forms handed over to the Central Elections Commission. It turned out that the 4,984 commissioners engaged in 712 polling stations out of 900 throughout Kosovo, or 80 percent of the total polling stations, were involved in vote rigging, and criminal proceedings were initiated against them (KIPRED 2011). In the remainder 20 percent of cases (178 polling stations), mathematical errors were registered. This was a collective attempt at vote manipulation. It was a political catastrophe, but the outcome was not surprising. If no one was murdered, the elections were successful! So, then, what does political catastrophe mean in certain contexts such as Kosovo? Elections are frequent in this part of the world. Although the vote-casting and vote-counting rituals are marred by major irregularities and contestations, the major political actors in the end acknowledge the outcome and politics moves on as usual. In other words, elections are nothing but a ritual, because political parties and their uncontested leaders in the end determine not just the rank and order of the parties in the government, but also the ranking of the candidates within the parties themselves.

This seems unlikely to change soon. Fast-forward to 2014, and a new extraordinary election recently came to a close. It was largely an uncontested process, and the voting was free and fair with few, irregularities reported. Yet, because of how the electoral system works in Kosovo, even a free and fair election process, fails to produce a majority winner, as it did in 2014, and this leads Kosovo to a new stage of political impasse. Once again, political parties defending positions rather than principles, becomes the main point of contestation, producing long and nerve-wrecking democratic deadlocks.

The larger point here is that in such a political environment, characterized by a fluidity of rules, what sets a precedent is hard to establish. For example, in one election, despite allegations of massive fraud, the outcome might be broadly recognized, and the business of politics moves on as usual. In another election, even in the absence of election fraud, the ballot becomes contested on somewhat irrational grounds and largely as a result of political parties adhering to positions rather than principles, all the while producing a political spectacle of a sort, which keeps people tuned in to see the outcome of yet another election which in the end gets decided "under the table." Meanwhile, clan politics continues to successfully nurture the polarization within society, and the system of partitocracy, unlikely to yield stable institutions and a sustainable governing system, is further consolidated in Kosovo.

## Conclusions

This chapter represents an attempt to get closer to the pulse of the present political moment in the Balkans and specifically Kosovo. It attempts to reflect on how narrow political interests are pegged to suit the wider interests of the structure—in the sense that structure is equated sometimes with the political parties themselves, sometimes with the clan and region, sometimes with the state, and sometimes with something larger than the state: the EU integration process or strategic interests of big powers such as the United States.

The chapter tries to highlight how the notion of politics is perverted due to the above-mentioned constellations and how catastrophe is enduring in large part because of the fluctuating interests of domestic actors and the strategic interests of the international community—the need of the domestic actors to keep afloat in the political waters and the need of the international community to tell stories of success.

So, what does the Kosovo case tell us? The texture of political action, understood here as the form and organization of politics, becomes an ephemera, a spectacle of a sort—in that no platform is durable in a sense. What is relevant in one moment might become irrelevant in the next, and the political culture is similar to an aquarium in which fish-like actors swim while being associated with no particular ideology or political leaning, or tend to remain associated with several mainstream ideologies at the same time, none of which is central to them or represents a proper identification. In one moment you are on the Left, because that ensures that you get into power; in the next moment you might be on the Right, because that is where power is … and next you might be on the Left and on the Right at the same time, because that is what sustains your political capital. You do everything just to avoid being in opposition, which in the Balkans context is next to nothing; you are that dog chained behind the house that barks but does not bite. Meanwhile, those in power are in the position to control not just wealth and power but another strategic asset, and that is the making of history. If you are in power, you are on the producing end of history. If you are in opposition, you are not.

The "texture" of political action that the volume seeks to address then, becomes an interesting way to capture the ambiguity that is played out in the case of in-between states. There is the forceful modernity trying to do right according to the internationalist regime, there are the resistant political parties seeking power and wealth for themselves by manipulating the peasantry, and there are the peasants, rather overwhelmed by all the changes but savvy enough to know how to secure some stability for themselves until the next round of politicians comes around.

The lack of meaningful opposition in societies undergoing the early stages of transition to democracy can become a bottleneck for the viable development of such societies. This, in turn, leads to a gradual decline of those societies and of the grounds on which states base their raison d'être, after a while privatizing the state for the interests of one group, and hardly anything can distinguish such states from criminal enterprises. As noted, the implications of this are wide—political, social, and economic. Major concessions are granted, state enterprises are privatized at ridiculously cheap prices, nonviable economic platforms and projects are disguised under the curtain of nationalism and populism.[16]

In this case, the political culture of a given polity such as Kosovo's, driven by narrow political interests, fails to establish new values and diminishes the prospects for national unity and cohesion, keeping the states captive for private profits and overlooking checks and balances. Usually, the only place where solutions against such ills end up being sought in the streets—not in the institutions. So, we come to observe that both state and statelessness are played out interchangeably in the Balkans; peace does not feel like peace, compromise does not feel like compromise, and solutions offered leave everyone with a sense of being diminished.

In other words, "modernity" can come swooping down on Kosovo officials, and it does not bode well for their future. Granted, the public is in a situation in which it is made a pawn of political parties and the political structures striving to privatize the state for their own interests and poised to win at all costs, but if the other part of modernity (the economy) is a wreck, there is no other option left on the table for them. So, the question this comes down to is if the international regime should be so pure about its modernist values. Can modernity really accommodate all of their needs? What solutions can it offer that could ameliorate the polarization and at the same time offer ordinary people a sense of real hope and a better tomorrow?

For ordinary people in places such as Kosovo, formally there seems to be little reason to protest, because the claim is made constantly that their grievances are being addressed through the "independent" and "democratic institutions." However, those democratic institutions are nothing but extensions of private interests of political parties—too personalized and too politically biased—and contain a whole reservoir of distress and dissatisfaction of a depressed and disillusioned general electorate. Conventional channels of communication fail to highlight the whole dimension of catastrophe, which brings with it the sense among ordinary people (sidelined in politics) that risk is all-encompassing and that there is not much reason to expect a better tomorrow.

**Naser Miftari** earned his PhD from the University of Nebraska–Lincoln. Over the last decade, he has taught undergraduate and graduate courses in media and political science at various institutes, colleges, and universities in the Balkans and the United States, including the Kosovo Institute of Journalism, the Southeast Europe University in Macedonia, the University of Nebraska, and the University of Mississippi. His dissertation explores the relationship between the processes of democratization and the political economy of media. His main areas of interest are comparative media development and democratization, political culture, discourse analysis, and public opinion.

## Notes

1. See, for example, KohaNet (2012).
2. Some media commentators raised eyebrows at the matter, wondering how a number of simultaneous full-blown scandals could not bring down the government. At the center of the wiretapping scandals were Kosovo's prime minister and senior ruling political party and governmental officials discussing inner politics, mutual distrust, nepotism, cronyism, and patronage in government institutions, reflecting a gross disregard for checks and balances in the legislative and executive branches of the Kosovo government. For the broader public what the wiretapped conversations revealed was something of a public secret. The public is aware that the politicians are crooked but is powerless to do anything to change that due to the political setup in Kosovo and how politics operates. This is explained in greater detail further in this chapter.
3. Anthropologists who analyze problems associated with the idea of the political focus on social-political structures, such as lineages and age groups, or political systems, such as chiefdoms or the state. Human political agents are usually passive elements in these analyses, subject to forces beyond their control. The idea of politics, on the other hand, refers to the practices of agents who either operate within political structures and systems or are somehow related to them. In this context, anthropologists explore how political agents, usually leaders, use skill, power, cunning, wisdom, and numerous strategies to pursue goals and attain ends (Kurtz 2001: 9–10). In the case of the Balkans, exploring both the agents and the structure seems relevant.
4. Alesina and Cukierman (1987) define ambiguity in a more narrow sense as the "noise between the policy outcome observed by voters and the policy instrument chosen by the policymaker." Connolly (1983, 1987) offers a much broader philosophical definition of the term. It is political vagueness, or political ambiguity, that characterizes all sorts of political transactions in Kosovo. As a central component of the ritual politics in Kosovo, such political vagueness keeps things moving, or at least makes them seem as if they are moving, without much understanding as per the direction—whether forward or backward, positive or negative.
5. The political vagueness/ambiguity is attributed primarily to the plan drafted by Martti Ahtisaari in 2007. The plan entails a conditionally independent Kosovo with special rights for the Serbian minority in an asymmetrical state (if all works out in the end as designed). How the efforts to introduce the features of such a state impacts the realities

on the ground, how the international community works with it, how political parties operate within it, and how the electorate reacts toward it are big unknowns. There has been much concern to date that the asymmetric state of Kosovo as envisaged in the Ahtisaari Plan is bound to lead to a dysfunctional state. The point here is that for Serbs and Albanians, everything is history, whereas a solution can be found through an ahistorical approach. In other words, an ahistorical approach might be required to address Kosovo's issues. See http://www.unosek.org/docref/Comprehensive_proposal-english.pdf.

6. Latour notes that "modernity" comes in as many versions as there are thinkers or journalists, yet all its definitions point, in one way or another, to the passage of time. He sees the term "modern" as being asymmetrical and designates a break in the regular passage of time, and a combat in which there are victors and vanquished (Latour 1993: 10). While it is impossible to come up with an exact definition of "modernity," the term "modernity" is used here to signal a set of practices, habits of thinking, institutionalized beliefs, and so on. Actors act in the name of modernity, and most times without even the name—they just do their policy making, lawmaking, and so on because those have become the prescribed ways of managing society. For example, "best practices" is one of the international community's favorite terms used in Kosovo.

7. In the 1990s the opposition parties in Kosovo were introduced as décor, just to impress the international community and convince them that some oppositional voices exist in Kosovo. In the first elections held in Kosovo in 1992, LDK won approximately 77 percent of the total votes. In fact, on a number of occasions the leader of LDK has come out in support of opposition parties, asking them to be more assertive. Despite this, the opposition could never gain traction until the latter part of the 1990s, and even then selectively and cautiously.

8. For example, a Kosovo head of Parliamentary Group traveled with a delegation to Brussels trying to impress EU representatives with ideas about democratization, multiculturalism, cosmopolitanism, and tolerance, which are supposedly being forged in Kosovo. The MP then bragged about the visit in a phone conversation with the prime minister about how "our delegation made up of representatives of different ethnic groups from Kosovo" (i.e., speaks in derogatory terms about the representatives from other ethnic groups) has "impressed the EU parliamentarians." The phone conversation was, in turn, wiretapped by the EU mission in charge of facilitating the roadmap of Kosovo's move toward the EU, EULEX, and the conversation ended up in public.

9. While the public discourse in Kosovo, just as elsewhere in the Balkans, explores politics based on the strategic positioning that was lost about two centuries ago—in the 1880s—as described in historical narratives, the EU technocrats seek to test Kosovo's capacities based on how it has performed in the first decade of the twenty-first century and eventually based on how it might do in the next decades. Ingimundarson (2007), in an analysis of Kosovo's political elite, captures all too well this dilemma, noting that Kosovo's elite is caught between the nationalist discourses of the previous two centuries and the supranational identification with Euro-Atlantic structures.

10. For example, in the European Commission (EC) Progress Reports of 2013 and 2014, the process of dialogue for peace received positive notes. The same was not true for other matters, such as governance, freedom of expression, and rule of law, where slow progress was noted.

11. To some degree, even the EU reciprocates by raising false hopes, allowing later entrants such as Greece to connect important historical references with possible acces-

sion dates. We should recall here the romantic side of the EU narrative pushed forward by Greek Prime Minister Andreas Papandreou and how he tried to build on the momentum of the Thessaloniki Statement in 2003 by including a goal to have the western Balkans enter the EU in 2014 because that marked one hundred years after the Balkan Wars.
12. See, for example, Gallup (2013). According to the Gallup poll, Kosovo is ranked among the world's top countries where the public expressed the highest perception of government corruption.
13. Hayoz (2010) defines the arm's-length principle as the independence and equal footing the parties of a transaction should be guaranteed. Equitable agreements should be possible despite the existence of shared interests, for example, between employer and employee or of familial ties. As a public policy principle applied in the political, economic, or legal system, the arm's-length principle has to do with the checks and balances between the different constitutional powers.
14. Roth (2008) points out that Yugoslavia was one of the few exceptions in the former Communist bloc to have allowed regional autonomy of some kind to thrive. Yet, what he leaves out of the equation is that regional autonomy was allowed only at the higher levels of political administration. In other words, autonomy was granted to political entities reflecting linguistic, cultural, ethnic, or similar features, yet within such regions further differences—recognized within the in-group, such as dialectical or other and stemming from tribal belonging—were disregarded.
15. A few years ago, when a Kosovo minister of finance was accused of nepotism for giving favorable access to a tender to his nephew, his response was, "Kosovo is small. We are all uncles and nephews."
16. See, for example, Lorenzo Capussela (2012).

## Bibliography

Alesina, Alberto, and Alex Cukierman. 1987. *Working Paper No. 2468*. National Bureau of Economic Research.
Binder, David. 1981. "One Storm Has Passed but Others Are Gathering in Yugoslavia." *New York Times,* 19 April. http://www.nytimes.com/1981/04/19/weekinreview/one-storm-has-passed-but-others-are-gathering-in-yugoslavia.html (accessed 2 May 2015).
———. 1987. "In Yugoslavia, Rising Ethnic Strife Brings Fears of Worse Civil Conflict." *New York Times,* 1 November. http://www.nytimes.com/1987/11/01/world/in-yugoslavia-rising-ethnic-strife-brings-fears-of-worse-civil-conflict.html?pagewanted=all&src=pm.
CRPM (Center for Research and Policy Making). 2012. *Internal Party Democracy in Kosovo*. Konrad Adenauer Stiftung. Pristina, Kosovo. http://www.kas.de/wf/doc/kas_32753-1522-1-30.pdf?130116163406 (accessed 13 June 2015).
Clark, Howard. 2000. *Civil Resistance in Kosovo*. London: Pluto Press.
Collins, Kathleen. 2009. *Clan Politics and Regime Transition in Central Asia*. Cambridge: Cambridge University Press.
Connolly, William E. 1983. "Discipline, Politics, and Ambiguity." *Political Theory* 11: 325–41.
———. 1987. *Politics and Ambiguity*. Madison: University of Wisconsin Press.
European Commission, Commission *Staff Working Document, Kosovo Progress Report,* Doc, SWD, (2013) 416 final, 16 October 2013.

European Commission, Commission *Staff Working Document, Kosovo Progress Report*, SWD(2014) 306 final, 8 October 2014.
Gallup. 2013. "Corruption Is Pervasive Worldwide." http://www.gallup.com/poll/165476/government-corruption-viewed-pervasive-worldwide.aspx. (accessed 26 June 2015).
Gashi, Drilon, and Shoghi Emerson. 2013. "A Class of Its Own Patronage and Its Impact on Social Mobility in Kosovo." Democracy for Development. Research Paper, http://rs.boell.org/sites/default/files/d4d_pi_2_eng_inside_print_2.pdf (accessed 13 June 2015).
Hayoz, Nicolas. 2010. "Power, Democracy and Informality in Eastern Europe: On the Persistence of Old Power Structures in Politics." In *From Palermo to Penang/A Journey into Political Anthropology*, ed. Francois Ruegg and Andrea Boscoboinik, 223–42. Vienna: Lit Verlag.
Ingimundarson, Valur. 2007. "The Politics of Memory and the Reconstruction of Albanian National Identity in Postwar Kosovo." *History & Memory* 19: 95–123.
KIPRED (Instituti Kosovar për Kërkime dhe Zhvillime të Politikave). 2011. "Election Crimes: An Analysis of the Criminal Prosecution and Trial of the Cases of Election Crimes in Kosovo." Prishtina. http://www.kipred.org/advCms/documents/15928_election_crimes.pdf (accessed 26 June 2015).
KohaNet. 2012. "Afera 'Pronto'—Thaci hesht, BE s'ka koment, EULEX heton" [The affair "Pronto"—PM Thaci silent, EU has no comment and EULEX continues investigations]. 4 December. http://www.koha.net/?page=1,13,125848. (accessed 26 June 2015).
Krasniqi, Albert, and Krenar Shala. 2012. "Strengthening the Statehood of Kosovo through the Democratization of Political Parties." Policy Paper Series 2012/04. Prishtina, Kosovo.
Kurtz, Donald. V. 2001. *Political Anthropology: Paradigms and Power*. Boulder, CO: Westview Press.
Latour. Bruno. 1993. *We Have Never Been Modern*. Cambridge, MA: Harvard University Press.
Lorenzo Capussela, Andrea. 2012. "Road to Ruin—An Unnecessary Highway in Kosovo Could Bankrupt Europe's Poorest State." *Transitions Online*, 13 January. http://www.tol.org/client/article/22939-albania-kosovo-hig. (accessed 26 June 2015).
Matuschek, Peter. 2003. "Spain: A Textbook Case of Partitocracy. "In *The Political Class in Advanced Democracies*, ed. Jens Borchert and Jurgen Zeiss, 336–51. Oxford: Oxford University Press.
Sharpe, Matthew, and Geoff Boucher. 2010. *Žižek and Politics: A Critical Introduction*. Edinburgh: Edinburgh University Press.
Snyder, Jack, and Karen Ballentine. 1996. "Nationalism and the Marketplace of Ideas." *International Security* 21: 5–40.
Roth, Klaus. 2007. "What's in Region? Southeast European Regions between Globalization, EU-Integration and Marginalization." In "Region, Regional Identity and Regionalism in Southeastern Europe," ed. Klaus Roth and Ulf Brunnauer, special issue, *Ethnologia Balkanika* 11: 17–42.
United Nations Office of the Special Envoy for Kosovo (2007): The Comprehensive proposal for Kosovo Status Settlement. S/2007/168/Add.1, March 26, 2007. http://www.unosek.org/docref/Comprehensive_proposal-english.pdf (accessed 13 June 2015).

CHAPTER 4

# Occupy Wall Street as Rhetorical Citizenship
## The Ongoing Relevance of Pragmatism for Deliberative Democracy

*Robert Danisch*

■ ■ ■ ■ ■ ■

The General Assembly of NYC circulated a poster in early August 2011 announcing a meeting to organize an occupation of Wall Street on the following 17 September. The poster claimed: "We are the General Assembly of NYC—We are building a horizontal collective open to anyone, we are recovering the political dimensions of our lives ('politics' in the sense of organizing our lives with others), which has been kidnapped by the elites in power—We are part of a global network of assemblies functioning in the same way. The General Assembly of NYC is here to stay, it's [sic] life will go beyond a particular action" ("General Assembly Poster" 2012). The meeting that this poster promoted was held on 13 August in Tompkins Square Park. A photograph of that meeting, taken by Bob Arihood, shows about forty people sitting in a circle engaged in an argument about whether the photographer has a right to take their picture ("Bob Arihood Photo" n.d.). In the months that followed, the meetings grew larger and larger, as did public awareness of this new movement. On 29 September 2011, the General Assembly of NYC accepted the "Declaration of the Occupation of New York City" at Zuccotti Park in lower Manhattan ("Declaration of Occupation of NYC" n.d.). This six-hundred-word declaration is mostly a list of grievances and an assertion of the importance of process in democratic decision making. Documents like the poster and the declaration, along with the structure of the General Assembly meetings, demonstrate the ways in which Occupy Wall Street (OWS) tried to embody a texture of political action.

The specific texture of political action embodied by the General Assembly has a history. It is not a radical new invention. Moreover, it advances a specific argument about democratic life and responds to the failures of specific forms of citizenship and political theory in American history. This chapter argues that the texture of the Occupy movement has its roots in American pragmatism. Furthermore, I argue that the movement updates some of the basic commitments of pragmatism by enacting a specific form of rhetorical citizenship. This form of rhetorical citizenship employs reasoning in response to problems and uncertainties instead of reasoning based on propositions. Because of this, the small group structure of the movement and the ambiguity of its goals allow Occupy Wall Street to practice a unique brand of rhetorical citizenship that advances what the pragmatists called "social democracy." At the core of a social democracy is the belief that technical, policy solutions are less relevant than the deliberative process and the formation of democratic communities that embody specific communicative practices. In addition, a social democracy looks to supplement traditional social contract theory by founding citizenship on something other than rights. Occupy Wall Street, narrowly, and pragmatism, broadly, have a tolerance for uncertainty that is generative of rhetorical citizenship as a small group encounter.

In the first section of this chapter, I describe and interpret the "Declaration of the Occupation of New York City" and the processes employed by the occupiers. Second, I show that the beliefs and processes advanced by OWS have their roots in the American pragmatist tradition. Furthermore, I argue that these roots align OWS with specific prescriptive arguments about what democracy ought to be. Third, I use the concept of the "rhetorical citizen" to illustrate one of the most important entailments of the prescriptive arguments about democracy. One of those entailments is that "rights" are not sufficient for promoting equality within large-scale, multicultural democracies. In terms of the history of political theory, rights-based politics has actually failed to promote equality. This is precisely what the occupiers are responding to—the presence of massive inequality and the ways in which that inequality stands in opposition to, and prevents the flourishing of, democratic life. As the poster advertising for the General Assembly meeting clearly states, politics is a matter of "organizing our lives with others," and this should be a "horizontal" form of organization. This is another way of suggesting that the social dimensions of democracy are just as important as laws and policies. What the occupiers seek is a form of social democracy in which the process of communication between citizens is a starting point for the promotion of equality and in which those processes are horizontal and not vertical. This, I argue, was also a central concern of first-generation pragmatism as it was developed at the beginning of the twentieth century. And it is also grounds for the articulation of a specific form of rhetorical citizenship in which the act of talking with others is more important than the possession of abstract rights. Analyzing the political texture of the Occupy movement can make this clear.

## Rights, Processes, and Radical Democracy

The "Declaration of the Occupation of New York City" begins with the following phrase: "As we gather together in solidarity to express a feeling of mass injustice." Two critical words of this opening phrase immediately highlight the texture of OWS as a political movement. First, "solidarity" signals the extent to which the occupiers are committed to the social dimension of politics. Second, "feeling" signals that the solidarity of which the occupiers speak is not derived from an abstract, rational, theoretical proposition about the world. Instead, solidarity is founded on an affective state generated by a series of problems. The rest of the document is mostly devoted to an explanation of what the occupiers "feel" "mass injustice" means. This explanation ranges from an "illegal foreclosure process" to "colonialism," "torture," "outsourced labor," and the sale of "privacy as a commodity." In other words, the feeling of "mass injustice" is the grounds for the feeling of "solidarity" and makes possible a form of cooperation capable of uniting "as one people" a "formerly divided" group. Solidarity and cooperation, therefore, are driven by the felt presence of injustice and inequality, mostly caused by corruption at the hands of "economic power."

The title of the declaration obviously pays homage to the Declaration of Independence, but a stark contrast between these two documents promotes different forms of politics. The Declaration of Independence also describes a list of grievances and the existence of a kind of injustice. However, it stipulates the existence of "inalienable rights." The preamble promotes a general theory of government that is used as a justification for rebellion against the king. This general theory of government is different in kind than the one promoted by the Occupy Wall Street movement. The beginning of the Declaration of Independence does not announce the existence of a feeling, but rather the existence of a set of "self-evident" truths. A system of government founded on preserving the rights of its citizens becomes, in light of these "inalienable rights," the basic mode of political life. "Inalienable rights" have a minor role in the "Declaration of the Occupation of New York City." Rights are not mentioned until the seventh line. At that point, the authors claim that "our system must protect our rights, and upon corruption of that system, it is up to the individual to protect their own rights." This is a startling denunciation of American government. The occupiers are arguing that corruption has prevented the US government from doing just the thing it was implemented to do after the Declaration of Independence—secure its citizens' rights. When "corporations ... run our government," then "true democracy" is not attainable, or so say the occupiers. The most important right for the occupiers to assert, therefore, is the right to "peaceably assemble." The only other mention of rights in this declaration refers to the right to assembly. Note that the occupiers do not cite their right to free expression or life, liberty, and the pursuit of happiness, but instead they have faith in the right to assemble, for it might hold the potential to counter the forces of corruption led by corporations.

The "Declaration of the Occupation of Wall Street," therefore, does not assert or really use human rights as either a cause or a motivating factor for the kinds of political action that issue from it. This is not a rights-based politics, to put it simply. It is a politics with faith in assembly as an antidote to corruption and a key to equality. This is why OWS has put so much effort into thinking about the structure and format of their General Assembly meetings. These meetings are, so the occupiers claim, based on Athenian direct democracy and the Roman Republic, both examples of instances in which citizens had the power to act, create, and work on laws. At the General Assembly, everyone is heard, and equal opportunities for speech are made possible. The goal of the General Assembly is "modified consent," which simply means that "everyone is in agreement when we come to a decision.... What we want, and what we're hoping to achieve, is an agreement by everyone. So that way no one is excluded and no one is stepped on." If that kind of consensus cannot be reached, "then we [the General Assembly] have to move to a nine-tenths vote. We don't want to have to do this. We're fighting against a system that oppresses people like voting. Voting means that some people are ignored, they're completely forgotten about. So that way the majority can enact something, so we want consensus. The reason it's nine-tenths is because that's almost impossible to get. That's an insurance policy to ensure something that conflicts with the group isn't being put through" ("General Assembly Training Video" 2012).

The commitment to, and faith in, assembly is one of the reasons that OWS was illegible or incoherent in the eyes of the mainstream press (see, e.g., Denning 2011). Some argued that OWS was not a proper social movement or form of political dissent because it did not have a clear, definitive goal or policy solution that it sought. But OWS was intentionally violating discourse conventions around typical forms of political dissent because it sought to make claims about the very texture of political life. What OWS calls "process" (the methods of meetings, facilitating discussions, and making decisions) reflects the movement's values and advances an argument about what democracy ought to look like. In other words, the processes employed to cultivate a specific texture of political life sought to perform or enact democracy in a different manner from other, more traditional modes of political action. Further, the meetings themselves (and any meeting that uses consensus) were long, often frustrating, and deeply ethical. The experiential side of the meetings held the potential for the personal transformation of the participants and cannot be captured in more basic forms of political analyses. To understand how these meetings worked as a kind of texture of political action is to understand the prescriptive and political arguments that OWS advanced.

Although OWS employed many different kinds of meetings, the working group meetings and the General Assembly meetings stand out as the two most important. The General Assembly meetings were typically larger and more formal, while the working group meetings were smaller and more informal. But both typically included facilitators, a note taker, the use of hand gestures, a speaking stack, and the need for consensus. These functional characteristics of the meetings have probably become the central identifying feature of OWS, more than any particular policy goal or political proposition. While the political agenda of OWS may have been illegible to the mainstream press, the hand gestures, as the most visible form of the process employed at the meetings, were perhaps the clearest representative feature of the kind of politics preferred by the occupiers ("General Assembly Hand Gestures Guide" n.d.). There were seven specific hand gestures used during the meetings. First, holding one's hand up, with the palm open, and fanning one's fingers back and forth signaled that the person agreed with the proposal or liked what he/she heard. Second, holding one's hand down and fanning one's fingers back and forth signaled disagreement with a proposal or dislike of what was being said. Third, holding one's hand flat while fanning one's fingers up and down signaled a neutral stance on a proposal. Fourth, curling one's hands and fingers into a C shape signaled either the need for clarification or that the person making the gesture had clarifying information. Fifth, raising one's index finger up signaled that the person had information pertinent to the discussion. Sixth, making a triangular shape with one's hand by joining one's index fingers and thumbs signaled that the process governing group discussion was not being followed properly. Seventh, crossing one's arms in front of one's chest to form an X signaled strong moral or ethical reservations about the proposal being considered. Collectively, these gestures insured that everyone at the meeting was physically incorporated into the communicative practices of the group and the decision-making process. These gestures ritualized participation and concretized the language from the declaration that insisted on the importance of the "horizontal" dimension of politics. As a set of communicative practices, these hand gestures helped to distribute the process of reaching consensus equally among all the participants in the meetings. Further, these hand gestures prevented the possibility of any vertical or hierarchical organization from emerging. In other words, privileging the communicative practices that belonged to everyone at the meetings maintained and reproduced the feeling of solidarity while at the same time barring any potential fractures between those who might attempt to assume more power or control to direct meetings.

The other practices in place at the meetings worked toward the same ends. The "stack taker's" job was to organize a list of people who wanted to speak. The stack taker was required to make a "progressive stack," which meant that people in minority groups were moved up to the top of the list to make sure that everyone had an opportunity to speak and to make certain that old and enduring forms of creating hierarchical divisions between people were not reproduced at the meetings. Members of the meetings were also encouraged to practice "step up, step back," which meant that those members of the group who had traditional advantages would step back to allow others to be heard. This was a form of acknowledging that some people have been suppressed in their lifetimes and have not been given as many opportunities as others to speak and be heard. The meetings also typically used "temperature checkers" who would deliberately interrupt meetings to gauge how the group was feeling about a particular proposal or idea. These "temperature checkers" were another mechanism of insuring that the horizontal structure of the meetings remained and that the group was working toward consensus. All meetings were run by "cofacilitators" who implemented the rules for the meetings and kept the meetings to the established agenda. This was a "leadership role," but the facilitators were not "leaders." The facilitators were trained to introduce themselves into the group as authoritative figures with no real direct power. Each meeting strived to achieve more diversity of cofacilitators instead of less. The combination of these practices was necessary to achieve consensus, the goal of the meetings. These practices were necessary for eradicating the notion that particular "leaders" ran democracies and were important for turning all participants into leaders.

The combination of these practices gave OWS a texture and embodied the shift from vertical to horizontal democracy called for in the "Declaration of the Occupation of New York City." These practices, in other words, represented the most important political claim advanced by OWS—that the best way to redress inequality is through organizing our lives together in a more egalitarian manner whereby everyone participates in decision making. The most fundamental entailment of both the meetings and the declaration was that democracy ought to be practiced differently if it is to produce something other than the massive inequality and injustice that plague present-day

American society. The means of democratic life ought to reflect the ends that democracy seeks to create. Present historical circumstances seem to indicate that the means of American democracy have created the ends of massive inequality and injustice. Therefore, the best available solution is to change the means of practicing democracy. If the occupiers wanted more representation in government and economic life, then the movement itself needed to practice greater representation within its own precincts. This means that the practices of the meetings were more important and valuable than the policy outcomes or recommendations that issued from those meetings. The process was slow, complicated, and frustrating, but it allowed everyone to be heard, and that was, in itself, a kind of political transformation.

In large-scale, multicultural democracies of the size and complexity of the United States, vertical forms of democracy are easier to identify, understand, and practice. By vertical forms of democracy, I mean systems of government whereby specific elected officials hold power, make decisions, offer justifications and support for particular policies, and persuade publics to vote for them. The public, from the perspective of a vertical democracy, is protected by rights granted by the government. These rights do not require positive participation in public decision making, and they do not redistribute power from elites to others. If a public is dissatisfied by a particular government policy, then that public can organize itself and apply pressure on those that hold power in order to effect specific material changes. In this way, possibilities for participation are open and available but not required or expected of everyone. Power is unequally distributed, but hypothetically answerable to a public willing to organize, challenge, or critique those with power. Rights like free speech hypothetically provide publics with the opportunity to critique or challenge those in power and transform government practices and policies. However, one of the main arguments advanced by OWS was that such a system failed to produce what it sought. The collusion between government and corporations allowed for a corrupting control of vertical democracy. Horizontal democracy, on the other hand, redistributes power, requires positive participation in decision making, and is generative of a deep, social equality.[1] If one views the American political process as a vertical democracy, one can identify a specific texture of political life, complete with forms of protest, modes of decision making, and systems of power. These features of American democracy are easily legible and can be easily analyzed or critiqued through standard forms of political science. However, OWS cannot be analyzed or critiqued with those same methods, because OWS argues that we ought to replace or supplement vertical democracy with a form of horizontal democracy. The texture of the meetings makes this argument clear. But this is not the first time in the history of American democracy that such an argument has been made.

## Pragmatism and the Roots of OWS

From the 1890s on, American pragmatism sought a kind of deliberative democracy similar in kind to what the occupiers sought—a kind of horizontal democracy that could complement the vertical democracy of rights and governments. Pragmatism's major innovation in political theory was to think about democracy as a way of life and not just a system of government. John Dewey was most responsible for this position, and his vision of a public supported by a great community of social inquirers was an attempt to counteract the massive inequalities of the early twentieth century. In addition, Jane Addams was perhaps the first to claim that it was time "to add a social ethic to democracy," and by doing so announced pragmatism's belief that the social was a prerequisite for successful and effective democratic decision making (Addams 1964: xii). In other words, pragmatism was committed to the proposition that American democracy needed a "social ethic" because that was the only way of providing a structure or organization through which many people could participate in politics. Addams founded a settlement house in order to develop this social ethic. Her essay "The Subjective Necessity for Social Settlements," a key piece of pragmatist political theory, identifies the importance of a social dimension in American democracy. According to Addams, the major function of the settlement house was "to make social intercourse express the growing sense of economic unity of society.... It [Hull House] was opened on the theory that the dependence of classes on each other is reciprocal" (Addams 2002: 14). Challenging the notion that "political equality alone would secure all good to all men," Addams traces a litany of political abuses that separate and alienate citizens from one another and fail to promote equality. She cites different forms of abuses and has a different set of grievances from the contemporary occupiers, but the shape of the argument remains the same: corruption alienates people from one another and causes massive inequality, and only a social ethic can change that. Pragmatism remains relevant today because of the argument that democracy is as much a way of life as it is a system of government. Occupy Wall Street brought this into sharp relief and showed what the texture of such an argument might look like in real time. A settlement house might not be a relevant twenty-first-century mechanism for promoting democracy as a way of life, but it shows the continued importance of thinking about politics in terms of how we organize our lives with each other.

The existence of massive corruption at the turn of the twentieth century led Addams to claim that the United States was entering a "second phase of democracy" (Addams 2002: 16). The "French philosophers" had entered the first phase by identifying the need for political equality and for natural rights (equality, liberty, and fraternity). However, the French philosophical system had clearly stalled on American soil, given the abuses that Addams witnessed. The second phase of democracy, she argued, must involve the social realization of the abstract French philosophical ideals. Furthermore, the first phase of democracy had established political institutions with a guiding constitution and the right to vote. Although this phase was crucial for the construction of democracy, it needed to be supplemented. The second phase needed to create a social organization capable of the following: demonstrating the interdependence of classes and people, disseminating and interpreting information openly and fairly to all people, educating citizens, and fostering a higher civic life through common social intercourse. This is Addams describing the goals of her work, but it could easily be a present-day occupier describing the goals of their own work. Addams understood politics as a way of "organizing our lives with each other," just as OWS did. Another way to describe the two phases that Addams identified is through the distinction between vertical and horizontal democracy that OWS made in their declaration. The first phase, vertical democracy, with systems of government and the constitutional protection of rights, cannot produce equality without the second phase, horizontal democracy, to develop a social ethic capable of generating solidarity and organizing people's lives with one another.

Generating the kinds of social conditions Addams thought necessary for horizontal democracy required a radically different set of rhetorical practices. In what Addams identified as the "first phase of democracy," rhetorical practices had remained much closer to the practice of public address. Ideally, professional politicians persuaded citizens to vote for them, and then those professional politicians engaged in deliberation over specific courses of action as an embodied voice of their constituents. These politicians could be kept in check by the rules agreed upon in a constitution. A constitution could secure the rights of citizens and provide equal protection to those without a literal voice in the decision-making process. Addams demonstrated that this system could not work in an efficient, open, or successful manner. Poverty, inequality, corruption, and class, race, and sex discrimination all worked to prevent the mass of citizens from genuine participation in deliberation and politics. The constitution and the right to vote were meant as theoretical protection from these problems, but such problems persisted. Again, this is exactly the claim advanced by the occupiers—corruption and inequality have bankrupted the entire political system. A vertical democracy does not produce the ends that it claims to produce, and in the process it excludes people from participation when participation in decision making is what ought to be required.

Instead of relying on politicians to represent citizens, and instead of relying on constitutional rights for protection, Addams advocated the development of social structures and organizations capable of supporting the economic and social unity of citizens. Citizens could then work within those social organizations to begin to exercise their voice in political deliberation—voting and constitutional protections were supplemented with more proactive methods. Traditional deliberative rhetoric, then, cannot aid in the operations of a democracy without first attending to a sense of social unity among citizens. The challenge of large-scale democracy, according to Addams, is to find mechanisms and organizations capable of bringing diverse people together. In addition, deliberative rhetoric was still needed in the "second phase of democracy" precisely because the French philosophical ideals of the first phase existed only in theory, not in practice. This deliberative rhetoric was different in kind than persuasion as public address. It required a sensitivity to difference; it sought solidarity; and it was practiced as face-to-face interaction. These were the same values orienting the General Assembly meetings.

The operations of the General Assembly, narrowly, and OWS, broadly, are clearly in line with Addams's concerns and preoccupations. In many ways, OWS updates and extends Addams's line of thinking by promoting new mechanisms and a new social organization that brings diverse people together into collective, social life. The similarities extend even further when one begins to analyze just what happens within diverse, collective encounters and what pragmatism hoped would happen. Much of John Dewey's philosophical work rests on a rejection of realist epistemology. The "spectator theory of knowledge" suggests that we ought to understand knowledge as the outcome of observation of an object by a subject. In *The Quest for Certainty*, Dewey attacks this epistemology and displaces it with a commitment to "inquiry," understood as a kind of struggle of human intelligence to solve problems and suggest provisional solutions to the practical problems that ignite thinking. Dewey's notion of inquiry lies at the heart of both his epistemology and his conception of democracy. Inquiry, for Dewey, becomes an idealized way for individuals within a community to be drawn together into deep, meaningful relationships with one another. Inquiry served this social end while also serving the practical end of being an intelligent method for solving problems. Thus, Dewey argues for the importance of "the great community" as a kind of realization of the social democracy that Addams describes, and then shows that social inquiry lies at the heart of the communicative process within the great community. At Hull House, the residents often participated in what Dewey would have recognized as social inquiry. Problems like the outbreak of various diseases in the city of Chicago brought citizens together at Hull House in an effort to find intelligent, melioristic solutions. Hull House was the realized ideal of Dewey's model of inquiry. Remarkably, the working group meetings that made up so much of OWS seem like a more contemporary realization of just this line of thinking, which I will show below.

Three features of Dewey's conception of inquiry clearly resonate with the texture of OWS. First, inquiry is an exercise in problem solving. We engage in inquiry as part of a struggle with a plural, uncertain, and ever changing environment. The goal of inquiry is not to change the beliefs of the inquirers, but to solve a particular problem in hopes of making incremental improvements to our environment (improvements that may only be temporary and may require new solutions in the future). The "Declaration of the Occupation of New York City" along with the invention of working groups that identified problems and recommended solutions are clearly organized from the same perspective. OWS was not a social movement that began with a particular policy proposition and then sought to persuade a mass audience to accept that proposition. It began with a set of problems and an open/provisional perspective on how those problems might be solved.

Second, inquiry is experimental, progressive, and historical. Solutions are understood as hypotheses that are invented, used, tested, and revised. New methods for the invention, use, testing, and revision of hypotheses are constantly being created, and so are new standards for evaluating hypotheses. In this way, modes of inquiry are not fixed but instead have a history and develop progressively in the light of new discoveries, new facts, new interpretations, and new inventions. The structure of the working group meetings allowed for constant revision, feedback, and incorporation of new ideas or facts. Outcomes of working groups were understood as provisional.

Third, inquiry is social or communal—its findings must be subject to scrutiny or testing by other inquirers. Or, as Dewey put it, "an inquirer in a given special field appeals to the experiences of the community of his fellow workers for confirmation and correction of results" (2008: 484). The idea and structure of the working group meetings highlighted the communal process, and the value of these meetings was understood to be just as much a matter of the communal process underpinning them as the outcomes that were recommended. Working group meetings were at the core of the OWS movement and were designed as communal, experimental processes of intelligent problem solving. Solutions were generated in the process of communication between members of working groups, not in advance by a set of ideological beliefs.

Much more can be said about Dewey's conception of inquiry and its role in generating social cohesion and solving problems in intelligent ways. Employing an experimental, provisional, and social logic was both instrumental in making good decisions and building communities in which freedom and equality could be realized, according to Dewey. For the purposes of this chapter, I want to pick out one feature of this process that is especially important. There is little question that Addams's notion of social democracy is close to the heart of Dewey's pragmatism, but Dewey is able to develop this notion of social democracy further through his commitment to both inquiry and communication. In several of his most important works, including *The Public and Its Problems* (1927), *Experience and Nature* (1925), *Democracy and Education* (1916), and *Art as Experience* (1934), communication plays a central role. Thus, from its inception, pragmatism has understood embodied communication to be a central practice for life in a democratic society and fundamental to social inquiry—this is also one of the major innovations of pragmatist political philosophy and one of the reasons this philosophy remains relevant today. From such a perspective, rights and national identity become secondary to figuring out what kinds of communicative practices will work to secure a better future and how communication ought to be conceptualized. Dewey's commitment to inquiry serves to highlight the importance of communication practices in the work of both making communities cohere and finding intelligent solutions to pressing problems.[2] By attending to the process of communication and inquiry instead of the outcomes of those processes, pragmatism attempts to describe what horizontal democracy might look like and how it might help improve our circumstances.

One of the most important features of Dewey's pragmatism is that it understands communication as a fundamentally social activity. *Democracy and Education* begins by stating the connections between communication and social communities: "Men live in a community by virtue of the things which they have in common; and communication is the way in which they come to possess things in common" (Dewey 1916: 4). Furthermore, "communication is a process of sharing experience till it becomes common possession. It modifies the disposition of both parties that partake in it" (Dewey 1916: 9). In *Art as Experience,* this position is elaborated even further: "Communication is the process of creating participation, of making common what has been isolated and singular" (Dewey 1934: 244). This commitment to communication underpins Dewey's epistemology: "[K]nowledge is a function of association and communication; it depends upon tradition, upon tools and methods socially transmitted, developed and sanctioned" (Dewey 1927: 158). Both communication and knowledge, then, serve to bring people into association—the meaning of the world they share is produced and regulated through communication as a practical activity. Dewey's notion of inquiry is meant to describe this process of communication working toward intelligent, deliberative ends. From this perspective, communication becomes the means by which the world is understood and organized: "[W]hen communication occurs, all natural events are subject to reconsideration and revision" (Dewey 1925: 166). Here is another version of the rejection of the spectator theory of knowledge and another reason that inquiry must be communal. Events are also capable of "immediate enhancement": "Communication is an exchange which procures something wanted; it involves a claim, appeal, order, direction or request, which realizes want at less cost than personal labor exacts, since it procures the cooperative assistance of others. Communication is also immediate enhancement of life, enjoyed for its own sake" (Dewey 1925: 183). Here is the transformative power of communication described eloquently. This is, in many ways, an abstract account of the communal process of inquiry aligned with an explanation of the value of this process—people and the world are changed through cooperative assistance. This is part of the radical philosophy of democracy that Dewey promoted and that OWS practiced.

For social cooperation to happen, persuasion must play a key role, and Dewey acknowledges this. In fact, *The Public and Its Problems* ends with a call for better methods of persuasion: "The essential need ... is the improvement of the methods and conditions of debate, discussion, and persuasion. That is the problem of the public. We have asserted that this improvement depends essentially upon freeing and perfecting the processes of inquiry and the dissemination of their conclusion" (Dewey 1927: 208). Methods of persuasion allow for the participation of the public in the process of democratic decision making. The problem of the public is essentially a problem of how we are to organize our lives together so as to perfect the process of inquiry and improve the ways in which we talk with one another. *The Public and Its Problems* also includes a vision for a "great community," a community whose success would rely on "the perfecting of the means and ways of communication of meanings so that genuinely shared interest in the consequences of interdependent activities may inform desire and effort and thereby direct action" (Dewey 1927: 124). Accordingly, pragmatism seeks methods of communication that would allow individuals in a democracy to participate in decision making and realize the interconnectedness of the community to which they belong. Pragmatism suggests a version of rhetorical citizenship as communion and reconciliation, oriented toward the common good. Politics, democracy, and community are all tied intimately together in American pragmatism. They are tied together by the belief that communication is the primary means by which the connections between politics, democracy, and community can be realized and the promise of each fulfilled: "The highest and most difficult kind of inquiry and a subtle, delicate, vivid, and responsive art of communication must take possession of the physical machinery of transmission and circulation and breath life into it. ... Democracy will come into its own, for democracy is the name for a life of free and enriching communion. ... It [democracy] will have its consummation when free social inquiry is indissolubly wedded to the art of full and moving communication" (Dewey 1927: 184).

Dewey is at his best when arguing for, and describing, a normative conception of democratic life with social inquiry, communication, and community as fundamental for equality and freedom. However, one of the limitations of Dewey's work is that he was not as clear about how these normative commitments ought to be realized in everyday life. This is the transformative power of OWS and why the texture of the movement matters more than its politics. The great innovation of pragmatism in political theory was to suggest that rights-based constitutions combined with elected, representational government was not sufficient for generating freedom and equality and thus not sufficient for democracy. Democracy required a social ethic. In the language of OWS, a horizontal way of organizing our lives together was necessary. OWS has understood their movement as a completely unique phenomenon, but it is not. Since 1890, pragmatism, as a minor key in American political philosophy, has consistently advanced that same argument. What is unique, however, is that OWS was able to add such fine-grained detail and texture to how the commitments to social inquiry, communication, and community were to be realized. The rules for the meetings demonstrate this in great detail. They are rules for communication practice intended to generate community and arrive at solutions to difficult problems. They are radical not for the political philosophy they represent but for how they are able to bring ideals to life and remake the ways in which we organize our lives together. Communication procedures can build horizontal democracy (or social democracy) because those procedures stitch a community of inquirers together. OWS was certainly not the only way this could be made real (just as Hull House was not the only way to do so in the early twentieth century), but it remains an important illustration of what democracy as a way of life, and not just a system of government, looks like.

## Rhetorical Citizenship within Public Culture

Clearly communication practices mattered for political engagement in the pragmatist tradition, and clearly they matter for OWS, because in both cases they point to the relationship between inquiry, community, and democracy. However, the argument that communication matters for citizenship is a larger, more ambitious claim. Much Enlightenment political philosophy, upon which contemporary democracies rely for justification and inspiration, rejected the role of rhetoric in political affairs. Thomas Hobbes is perhaps the foremost leader of the rejection of rhetoric. Eloquence and metaphor, so Hobbes thought, should be banned from the commonwealth and replaced with scientific methods of analyses (see Garsten 2006). This is because Hobbes totally distrusted citizens' capacities for exercising practical judgment, and he thought that public deliberations quickly devolved into wars. In some ways, documents like the US Constitution legally instantiate this distrust by placing the deliberative procedures of governance outside or beyond ordinary citizens. The very notion that the Senate rightfully deliberates on the issues of the day is an indication that rhetoric, in the hands of ordinary citizens, could not, and should not, be trusted. Here is the difference between vertical and horizontal democracy. A vertical democracy places rhetorical communication in the hands of elected officials and removes from ordinary citizens the responsibility of participating in deliberation. Horizontal democracy, of the kind advocated by pragmatism and OWS, argues that the proper place of deliberative communication is with everyday, ordinary citizens. At its deepest level, OWS challenges the traditional American answers to these two most basic questions: Who speaks? And why? The difference between vertical and horizontal democracy is most simply a matter of the difference in how those two questions are answered.

Enlightenment visions of the place of rhetoric in political affairs mimic a Platonic perspective on rhetoric. From both perspectives, distrust is the central value associated with rhetorical practice. It is against this tradition of distrust that natural rights and ethnic and national identities can be evaluated as pillars of modern and contemporary citizenship. If the very institutions of governance within which citizens reside distrust those citizens' participation in political affairs, then by what means are people considered citizens of a state? Rights and identity became the two basic mechanisms of granting an individual citizenship in Enlightenment-era democracies. Therefore, implicit in the idea of natural rights and national identity lies a distrust of the people granted those rights and that identity. That distrust amounts to a worry over the capacity of ordinary citizens to exercise practical judgment and engage in effective public deliberation about the issues of the day. Rights and identity produce equality and legal protection in abstract form. But rhetorical engagement is a different kind of equality. Rhetorical engagement only guarantees that each of us has an equal opportunity for participation. In such circumstances, citizens are not equal in terms of the advice they can offer or the knowledge that they possess (a doctor can comment on public health from a more authoritative position than a plumber). But all citizens know that they can and should participate in political affairs. This kind of equality is displaced by natural rights and national identity, which provide a different kind of equality (legal as opposed to deliberative). The hidden component of that act of displacement is the implied distrust in citizen participation. This distrust would have been inconceivable to an ancient Athenian democrat. The Athenians relied so heavily on the participation of all of the citizens of Athens in the affairs of the state that a distrust of the people would have amounted to the end of the institutions of governance. American pragmatism does not share the Enlightenment or the Platonic distrust of the ability of ordinary citizens to exercise practical judgment and engage in public deliberation. Instead, just as the Athenians did, pragmatists believed deeply in the vast potential that lies within the citizenry, and they sought methods capable of tapping into that potential for the betterment of American democracy. OWS advanced this same argument as well, putting emphasis on the transformative and ethical power of egalitarian deliberative systems like those represented by the General Assembly meetings.

Communication matters for citizenship because communicative practices are the means by which democratic societies can use the full resources of the communities that exist within those societies. It also matters because it alters the relationship between the state and the citizen by eliminating the distrust inherent in Enlightenment conceptions of democracy. In other words, it seeks the means of citizen participation in political affairs so as to prove the value and worth of citizens to the state instead of proving the danger of citizens to the state. But even more importantly, communication matters for citizenship because it is the means by which communities are bound together in solidarity, and it is capable of transforming participants. Carrying the pragmatist tradition forward requires that we continue to seek the best available means of incorporating the rhetorical performance of citizens into political deliberations. This is the lesson that we learn from Jane Addams, and it is what OWS has sought to demonstrate in carefully attending to the form and rules of its meetings. Horizontal democracy is capable of forming great communities in ways that vertical democracy is not, and that is the clearest meaning of the texture of OWS. Active communities of inquirers are transformed by the processes in which they participate—they are not ideologues intent on advancing an agenda. The outcome of structures like the General Assembly meetings is a specific kind of rhetorical citizenship capable of generating intelligent solutions to pressing problems and binding communities together in solidarity.

Put simply, rhetorical citizenship is the search for, and practice of, methods of communication capable of guiding public decisions and judgments. If a democracy is to be a government of, for, and by the people, then it must allow its citizens a voice in the affairs of the state. The question, however, becomes how one practices rhetoric in large-scale, multicultural democracies. Under what conditions? In what manner? Using what technologies? Toward what end? The ancient Greeks had simple and elegant answers to these questions, embodied in the notion of the orator-citizen, but our contemporary moment lacks such clarity. Instead, we have the responsibility of cultivating our own rhetorical practices suitable for our own moment. OWS recommends a way of developing a form of rhetorical citizenship fit for our contemporary moment, and that is perhaps its most important legacy. This way of developing rhetorical citizenship is indebted to the tradition of American pragmatism broadly and to Jane Addams specifically.

In most Enlightenment-era democracies, public address is perhaps the most standard and obvious form of political communication. Presidents make speeches, as do other elected officials. These speeches attempt to persuade a citizenry to believe or to act. If such a process can be described as rhetorical citizenship at all, then citizens are merely the receivers of rhetoric. Public address looks similar in kind to the manner in which rhetoric was practiced in ancient Athenian democracy, and so it commands the attention of rhetorical scholars, the media, and various publics. But this vertical process of persuasion should not be the only mode of communication within democratic societies. OWS recommends a form of rhetorical citizenship with five key features. First, rhetorical citizenship is practiced as a small group encounter. Second, it is embodied and requires presence. Third, it is aware of historical forms of power and oppression and how history has shaped opportunities for speech. Fourth, its goal is consensus, and it strives for mutual understanding of diverse perspectives. Fifth, small group encounters involve social inquiry and not the recitation of dogmatic ideology. The combination of these five factors recommends the cultivation of different kinds of communication practices (or at the least, does not require training in public address). Therefore, the central argument of OWS is that we ought to create the means for horizontal democracy and that people ought to participate as rhetorical citizens with those five attributes. To accomplish both ends would be to realize democratic life (and to make real the pragmatist normative argument for social democracy).

To argue for a model of rhetorical citizenship is also to hypothesize the existence of a deliberative ecology. Communication practices do not happen in a vacuum, but instead are made possible by a particular context. What Hobbes wrongly assumes is that rhetorical practice can be successfully banished from the commonwealth. This is not the case. Rhetorical practice is always present within political cultures. The question, however, is always a matter of the kinds of rhetorical practice that exist within specific political cultures.[3] For this reason, the notion of a deliberative ecology becomes a partner term in elucidating a theory of rhetorical citizenship. A deliberative ecology refers to the ways in which specific public cultures are organized and managed by the laws, institutions, spaces, policies, and people that inhabit that public culture. The ecology metaphor highlights the ways in which organisms interact with, and can change, the environment within which they live. Citizens live within, adapt to, and sometimes change the political environments within which they live. In democratic societies, the word "deliberative" properly describes a public ecology because any democracy relies on some form of collective, public decision making. Surely there are public ecologies within dictatorships or monarchies, but they need not necessarily be deliberative ecologies. The important point, however, is that different ecologies make different kinds of rhetorical practice possible, and if we alter the conditions of the deliberative ecology, we will also alter the kinds of rhetorical practice available to us. More important, the conditions of a deliberative ecology can change, and improve, the decision-making process. The texture of OWS attempted to build a deliberative ecology conducive to rhetorical citizenship as a small group encounter. The key word here is "attempted." Perhaps the conclusion of this volume gives some clue as to why this was merely an attempt and did not result in some revolution. At the very least, the occupiers posed the question: How do you produce revolutionary change against a democracy that has turned out to be entirely undemocratic (as the massive economic inequality and the catastrophe of the Great Recession have shown)?

We must continue to confront the question of whether Jane Addams was right in her understanding of the two phases of democracy. If she was, a form of rhetorical citizenship that focuses squarely on the first cannot solve the more pressing problems that stem from the second. Those pressing problems are often the result of inequality, corruption, and social isolation, and thus rhetorical education would be expected to take on the task of reconciliation and the promotion of social cohesion. OWS's slogan, "We Are the 99%," is an attempt to promote such social cohesion and weave a specific texture of political action out of the limits of modernist, managerial, vertical democracy. Addams and Dewey articulated an innovative American political philosophy that includes a unique perspective on the role of communication in sociopolitical life. OWS provides a fascinating case that illustrates what that political philosophy might look like and how it might work. OWS tapped into the resources of the community that makes up the state and showed how to trust the capacity of that community to exercise good, practical judgment, just as pragmatism had argued was necessary. This may seem like a risk, but it is, at the least, a way to move beyond the limitations of the Enlightenment to a place in which equality becomes something more than the possession of some rights or some legal document like a passport. Equality, along these lines, is in terms of practices and not possessions. The texture of OWS demonstrates what such equality looks like and why it is important.

**Robert Danisch** is an associate professor in the Department of Drama and Speech Communication at the University of Waterloo. His research interests concern rhetorical theory and public communication within democratic societies. He has published work on Richard Rorty, Stanley Fish, John Dewey, Jane Addams, and Barack Obama, and he is the author of *Pragmatism, Democracy, and the Necessity of Rhetoric* (University of South Carolina Press, 2007).

## Notes

1. It is important to note that the occupiers themselves refer to their movement consistently as a version of horizontal democracy and make a link between horizontal democracy and anarchy. In other words, I have not invented the distinction between horizontal and vertical democracy, but I am borrowing it from OWS to make a larger argument about political texture and democratic theory.
2. I should note that Dewey's focus on inquiry and community, alongside Addams's focus on social democracy and the OWS commitment to "solidarity," complicate more recent attempts to articulate deliberative democracy as a strictly rational mode of generating consensus. Some scholars, including Habermas and those influenced by Habermas, claim to advance a kind of pragmatism by focusing on deliberation as strictly a process of reasoning. In addition, some might argue that democratic agency is actually forestalled by attempts to build networks or communities. My aim in this chapter is not to quarrel with these opposing positions, but to articulate how and why a pragmatist conception of deliberation has a social dimension and cannot be reduced only to rational procedures that strive for consensus.
3. Hobbes wanted a version of rhetorical practice that left devices like metaphor and eloquence out and prevented ordinary citizens from participation.

## Bibliography

Addams, Jane. 1964. *Democracy and Social Ethics*. Cambridge, MA: Harvard University Press.

———. 2002. *The Jane Addams Reader*. Ed. Jean Bethke Elshtain. New York: Basic Books.

"Bob Arihood Photo—Occupy Meeting." n.d. Ev Grieve Blog. http://evgrieve.com/2012/01/bob-arihood-briefly-appears-in-february.html (accessed 15 September 2012).

"Declaration of Occupation of NYC." n.d. Occupy Wall Street. http://www.nycga.net/resources/documents/declaration/ (accessed 15 September 2012).

Denning, Steven. 2011. "What Do the Occupiers Want? Phase Change." *Forbes Magazine*, 25 October.

Dewey, John. 1916. *Democracy and Education: An Introduction to the Philosophy of Education*. New York: Free Press.

———. 1925. *Experience and Nature*. New York: Dover Publications.

———. 1927. *The Public and Its Problems*. Athens, OH: Swallow Press.

———. 1934. *Art as Experience*. New York: Perigree Books.

———. 2008. *The Later Works of John Dewey*. Vol. 12. Carbondale: Southern Illinois University Press.

Garsten, Bryan. 2006. *Saving Persuasion: A Defense of Rhetoric and Judgment*. Cambridge, MA: Harvard University Press.

"General Assembly Hand Gestures Guide." n.d. Occupy Wall Street. http://www.nycga.net/group-documents/intro-to-direct-democracy---facilitation-training/ (accessed 20 August 2012).

"General Assembly Poster." n.d. Occupy Wall Street. http://evgrieve.com/2011/11/3-months-ago-in-tompkins-square-park.html (accessed 15 September 2012).

"General Assembly Training Video." n.d. Occupy Wall Street. http://www.youtube.com/watch?v=WfTf2db6YfI (accessed 12 August 2012).

CHAPTER 5

# Contemporary Social Movements and the Emergent Nomadic Political Logic

*Peter N. Funke and Todd Wolfson*

■ ■ ■ ■ ■ ■

The ascendancy of neoliberal capitalism, with its tendencies toward extreme economic inequality as well as structural instability, has inspired an innovative cycle of protests and mobilizations around the globe.[1] The first wave in this cycle of protests included the "bread riots" against the austerity policies of the International Monetary Fund (IMF), the Zapatista rebellion in southern Mexico, and the Seattle anti–World Trade Organization (WTO) protests, among others. Building on the vision and strategies of this period, the more recent wave is characterized by the Arab Spring,[2] as well as the antiausterity protests of the 15-M movement in Spain or Greece and the Occupy-type protests and encampments from New York to Frankfurt and Hong Kong. These two interconnected waves of struggle exemplify the current broader epoch of contention (Funke 2014; Wolfson 2014).

In this chapter, we examine the underlying logic that informs these diverse and locally specific instantiations of the current movement epoch. This logic, we argue, is linked to the shifting nature of capital accumulation and transforming information and communication technologies. We label this movement logic "nomadic logic" to capture the distinct political and cultural fabric of contemporary movement politics. This "nomadic logic" finds expression in the diversity of mobilizations, protests, and demonstrations from the 1990s to today, and we argue that it is different from the previous cycles of resistance during the periods of the Old and New Left.

In this chapter, we first offer a set of theoretical interventions on the shifting dynamics of capitalism and movement politics as they intersect with the information revolution. We then outline our understanding of the currently dominant "nomadic movement logic." We argue that this "nomadic logic" is distinguishable from earlier movement axioms and practices. In particular, three dimensions of this new logic are discussed, which bring out its distinctiveness and illustrate the particular desire of contemporary activists for horizontality: first, the organizational model, which prioritizes networking structures ("flattening of forms"); second, the acceptance of the diversity of movement agents, celebrating the multiplicity and equality of struggles and actors ("flattening of fronts"); and third, the decision-making process, which embraces grassroots democracy and seeks out consensus decision making ("flattening of governance").

The second part of this chapter provides empirical illustrations of this nomadic movement logic, drawing on the Indymedia movement, the World Social Forum process, and Occupy-type protests and encampments. While the chapter has an empirical bent, we focus on developing the conceptual framework of the "nomadic logic" to suggest its fruitfulness for a fuller analytic understanding of the current movement cycle and the structural homology between the diversity of resistance and the contemporary movement politics surfacing around the globe.

Finally, while the focus of this chapter is on scrutinizing the main dimensions of the "nomadic movement logic," this emergent form of movement building is not without its challenges and shortcomings. In the conclusion of this chapter we examine some of these weaknesses and pitfalls in order to have a fuller analysis of the contemporary logic of resistance.

## From the Old Left to New Social Movements

Capitalism is a historical and dynamic phenomenon, changing over time and space (Boltanski and Chiapello 2005; Mandel 1978). And, as both David Harvey and Frederic Jameson note, transitions in the nature of capitalism have a critical role in refashioning the cultural logic of a given period (Harvey 1990; Jameson 1990). For Jameson, the shift toward a global, multinational form of capitalism and the material outcomes of this shift have led to a dominant logic of art, culture, and self that prioritizes fragmentation, individuation, flexibility, and decentralization—in short, the postmodern. Thus, while many theorists see the shift from the modern to the postmodern as a new cultural episteme, Jameson argues that the new postmodern logic is driven by the shifting nature of social life under late capitalism. Following Jameson's analysis, scholars have begun to argue that there is a transforming logic of social life under neoliberal capitalism (Ong 1999) and, correspondingly, a shift in the logic and practices of social movement activists (Funke 2012; Juris 2008; Wolfson 2013).

It is our contention that the shifts in capitalism have transformed the contours, logics, and trajectories of resistance in general and social movement politics in particular. When looking at social movement politics across the twentieth century, distinctions have generally been made between the Old Left and the New Left (e.g., Diggins 1992). The Old Left was dominant in the first half of the twentieth century and arguably privileged a class-based analysis, pitching the working class against the bourgeoisie. Following from this, the New Left emerged in the 1960s and 1970s, partially in reaction to the Old Left, thus shifting the struggle away from the realm of work to what Alain Touraine called "the setting of a way of life, forms of behavior and needs" (1988: 25).[3] These changes in strategy, structure, and governance of social movements, we argue, must be linked to shifts in the nature of the political economy in order to more fully understand the development, progression, and implications of social movements.

Succinctly put, the Old Left emerged and developed in the era of industrial capitalism, under the imperative of mass production and the goal of building economies of scale. This led to the development of massive factories and dockyards, inflexible production, stable work patterns, standardized mass consumption (structured along class lines), and seemingly fixed gender roles. This particular type of capital accumulation, and its intrinsically linked sociopolitical arrangements and regulations, dialectically generated a particular type of Left resistance.

Along these lines, the "Fordist" system was, at times unconsciously, mirrored by the Old Left, which forged mass parties and unions, hierarchical organizational structures, and comparatively rigid understandings of race, gender, and sexual orientation. Movement and party organizing was mostly done on the shop floor or in working-class neighborhoods, where the Old Left constituency tended to work and live together in similar conditions, leading to a physical and cognitive/cultural proximity that allowed workers to share experiences and build solidarity. Labor unions and political parties tended to use hierarchically organized governing structures to engage and negotiate with similarly organized owners and government officials or to mobilize their constituencies for protests and strikes.

The New Left emerged in the 1960s, during the growing crises within the Fordist system, brought about through changes to production, distribution, and consumption patterns as well as to its sociopolitical regulations. Patterns shifted from more standardized mass production and consumption to more individualized and flexible production and consumption. This in turn started to shift the nature of the workforce as Fordist "conveyor belt"–style work was replaced with more flexible arrangements typified by part-time, outsourced, and subcontracted forms of labor. This new flexible work experience has been characterized as informal and often precarious.

In this period—which is marked by the 1973 oil shock that spurred low growth rates, rising inflation, and increasing unemployment—employers faced rising national and international competition as liberalization and deregulation policies were implemented, and they advanced antiunion campaigns to increase productivity by driving down labor costs. While labor, and in particular rank-and-file workers, fought back (Brenner, Brenner, and Winslow 2010), Reagan's 1981 destruction of the Professional Air Traffic Controllers Organization (PATCO) and Thatcher's defeat of the long miner strike in 1983/84 are symbolic of the end of the "Fordist compromise." This meant an intensifying war on labor and the beginnings of large-scale neoliberal restructuring policies.

Along with the changing nature of production, distribution, and consumption came the emergence of what European scholars called new social movements. In the postwar "golden age of capital," in which material needs were met for many, nonmaterial issues emerged, and with them struggles related to questions around race, gender, and sexual equality, abortion rights, the antiwar movement, or environmentalism. Often in tension with Old Left concerns, these new social movements stressed the monotony and rigidity of social life. This vision of a stultifying, hierarchical society led movement activists to fight for what Anthony Giddens called "life politics ... issues which flow from processes of self-actualization in post-traditional contexts" (1991: 214) as opposed to "emancipatory politics," which address issues of economic inequality.

Through this transition to life politics, the New Left allegedly shifted the struggle for power away from the realm of work and toward questions of identity such as gender and race. In fact, many of the so-called New Left's concerns were aimed at the Old Left and the "Fordist compromise," making alliances between the Old and New Left challenging. While the Old Left was associated with, for example, somewhat outdated understandings of the family and gender roles, a disregard for the environment, organizational structures that emphasized more hierarchical party- and union-like structures, as well as a still predominately nation-state focus, the New Left sought novel organizational models beyond the labor movement and notions of class struggle.[4] Despite a "strategic strain" within the New Left (Breines 1989), the dominant tendency stressed more prefigurative politics and unconventional forms of political organizing. As such, the New Left was critical of representative structures and central authority and distrusted institutional politics writ large, embracing instead communitarianism and autonomism, spontaneity, and participatory and process-oriented movement politics.

## Nomadic Movements

With this historical view on the intersection between the Old and New Left in mind, we argue that novel resistance formations have been emerging since the end of the Cold War—fueled by the advancement of neoliberal capitalism, the "financialization of daily life," the emergence of the information revolution, and the perceived shortcomings of the Old and New Left. These movement-based formations, we hold, function on the basis of a distinct "nomadic logic" of movement politics, seeking to bridge Old and New Left concerns of anti-capitalism and identity politics.

We take the term "nomadic logic" from the joint work of Gilles Deleuze and Félix Guattari. Focusing on the philosophical interventions of Nietzsche, Deleuze and Guattari first mark the nomad as that which refuses to be defined, and therefore prioritizes becoming over being. This form of thought is characterized by a lack of stable hierarchies, fixed identities, and definitions. In this sense, nomadism seeks to capture the transgression of allegedly set codes and rules, stressing instead a form of being, thinking, and ultimately engaging the political that prioritizes search processes, uncertainty and multiplicity of approaches, struggles over blueprints, and assemblages instead of top-down hierarchical organizational structures. The lack of organization and structure allows nomadic formations to attract a variety of diverging elements and influences. Deleuze and Guattari detail this logic in an oft-quoted passage:

> The nomad has a territory; he follows customary paths; he goes from one point to another; he is not ignorant of points (water points, dwelling points, assembly points, etc.). But the question is what in nomad life is a principle and what is only a consequence. To begin with, although the points determine paths, they are strictly subordinated to the paths they determine, the reverse happens with the sedentary. The water point is reached only in order to be left behind; every point is a relay and exists only as a relay. A path is always between two points, but the in-between has taken on all the consistency and enjoys both an autonomy and a direction of its own. The life of the nomad is the intermezzo. (Deleuze and Guattari 1980: 380)

We suggest that this metaphor offers a fruitful perspective from which to conceptualize contemporary social movement dynamics. Like the nomad, movements today are "not ignorant of points," congregating at protests, encampments, and forums. These sites, however, are not primarily places to build, to stay, to ground politics, and to engage in long-term and sustained movement building. They are "reached only in order to be left behind." In this sense, then, the Seattle or Genoa protests, the World Social Forum sites in Mumbai or Porto Alegre, and the Occupy encampments at Plaza del Sol in

Madrid or Zuccotti Park in New York City are transient moments. The nomadic texture of in-betweenness, of swarming in and quickly detaching again, and the subsequent reluctance or inability to develop sustained—and sedentary—structures characterizes these spaces. This reluctance to build long-term structures makes it hard to organize and build powerful long-term social movements, a point that political theorist Slavoj Žižek makes as he criticizes the inability of contemporary social movements to author a real alternative to the status quo (Tsipras and Žižek 2013).

## The Zapatistas and Nomadic Beginnings

One of the first instantiations of this emerging nomadic logic was the Zapatista Army of National Liberation (EZLN) in Chiapas, Mexico. The EZLN emerged on the world stage on the eve of the North American Free Trade Agreement (NAFTA). Claiming NAFTA was a death sentence for the peasants of Chiapas, on 1 January 1994 members of the EZLN took over the capital of Chiapas (the poorest state in Mexico) along with multiple towns and called for a democratic revolution in Mexico. They chose NAFTA as a symbolic marker of neoliberal capitalism, and their military uprising set the stage for a new cycle of protests (Tilly 1986; Wolfson 2012, 2014) or epoch of contention (Funke 2014). Building on this analysis, we suggest that the emergence of the EZLN is emblematic of the beginnings of a new logic of movement organizing and a new texture of the political, which traveled through various channels and communication pathways to the global north. These developments were fueled by the emergence of new communication technologies and the realization that the "enemy" could no longer be located solely in the national government of Mexico, but was also in the global dynamics of neoliberal capitalism. In addition, the Zapatistas realized that linkages needed to be forged among the now splintered or splintering working class and various and ultimately related struggles against racism, gender inequality, environmental justice, and other fronts of struggle.

In this sense, one of the cornerstones of the nomadic logic of resistance has been an understanding that struggles can no longer challenge neoliberal capitalism on a strictly national basis, but must incorporate an international dimension as well as multiple fronts of struggle, from more classical material foci of the workers' movement to the identitarian concerns of indigenous or gender groups. This vision was exemplified by the global conference the Zapatistas organized in 1996 called the Intercontinental Encuentro for Humanity and Against Neoliberalism. During this conference, which brought together thousands of activists from across the world, members of the EZLN called for an international struggle against neoliberalism and, correspondingly, an international communication network of struggle (Wolfson 2012).

The other cornerstone of the EZLN and the corresponding nomadic logic is the reappropriation of new information and communication technologies. The EZLN emerged at a time when the Internet was in its infancy. Thus, when the EZLN declared war on the Mexican state in 1994, they were reliant on old media like radio, but they also harnessed the power of the Internet and new media. In fact, many scholars argue that through the power of online networks, the EZLN was able to successfully win an armistice and peace accords with the Mexican government (Wolfson 2012). The use of new media prompted scholars and commentators to argue that the Zapatista struggle was the first "netwar" and the first "postmodern revolutionary moment" (Ronfeldt et al. 1998).

Taking this moment of struggle as a beginning of sorts, we suggest that when looking at contemporary movement formations, from the Zapatistas to the "Battle of Seattle," Indymedia, the World Social Forum process, or the more recent Occupy-type protests, a distinct logic of current movement politics can be identified, which we suggest calling "nomadic logic." Based on shifts toward neoliberal capitalism and heavily reliant on the reappropriation of information and communication technologies as a central infrastructural dimension or nervous system for interlinking movements and groups resisting neoliberal capitalism, it is in particular three dimensions or characteristics of this logic that make it distinct and novel. First, the nomadic logic is defined by the network form ("flattening of forms"). Different from the hierarchical party- or union-type structures that dominated the Old Left and at least critically questioning the "structurelessness" of much New Left organizing, the network form seeks to allow for a diversity of organizational formations and for this diversity to be at least rudimentarily linked. Second, the nomadic logic no longer privileges one particular struggle or actor, but rather—through the network form—embraces multiple fronts ("flattening of fronts"), struggles, and actors as equals (Laclau and Mouffe 1985). While the New Left has accepted multiple fronts of struggle, the nomadic logic brings or seeks to bring labor back into the network without privileging its struggle as the Old Left did. Third, the nomadic logic embraces grassroots democracy and consensus-based decision making ("flattening of governance"), at times privileging the procedural aspect of prefiguration over strategic leadership and decision-making processes.

In looking at the current movement milieu through the lens of such a nomadic logic, we make two primary arguments. First, we argue that, when keyed to the particular dynamics of neoliberal capitalism, the nomadic logic of resistance offers a distinctive texture to the nature of political struggle in the twenty-first century, a texture that is brought to life by attempts to network multiple fronts of struggle, without prioritizing a particular front or actor, and a strong belief in grassroots and participatory democratic decision-making processes. Second, we suggest that many social movement scholars and movement activists have too uncritically embraced this nomadic logic. While there are important strengths in this new nomadic movement logic, it also entails serious limitations in its current configuration. In particular, its voluntaristic leanings and unease about institution building as well as its often dogmatic presumptions of the equidistance of the various struggles and radically participatory and often consensus-seeking decision-making procedures lead to challenges for sustained organizing. We will return to these critical aspects of this new texture of the political in the conclusion of this chapter. In the following, we look at each of the three characteristics of the nomadic logic, discussing its theoretical implications and providing illustrations of its workings in various contemporary movement formations.

## Flattening of Forms: Organizational Model

Lenin's insights into the organizational structure of mass parties and social movements has played a critical role in Left practice across the globe for much of the twentieth century. While Lenin was a fluid and flexible thinker (Mayer 1999), many of his insights, which were meant to be harnessed for a certain time and place (Lih 2008), were taken as universal dictates around organizational structure. Thus, some of the central insights of social and revolutionary movements that emerged from the Soviet experience were a hierarchical party structure or organizational structure, which placed emphasis on lines of command, authority, and power. This is exemplified by the Communist Party and many of the sectarian derivatives that emerged across the middle of the twentieth century, as well as the structure of organized labor in the United States and Europe and many of the social movement organizations of the New Left, including the Students for a Democratic Society (SDS) or the Black Panther Party.

However, with the rise of new communication technologies and other tools, movements have transformed away from the hierarchical party-based organizational form to decentralized all-channel network structures. Ronfeldt and Arquilla, researchers that have looked extensively at the growing dominance of networked structures, argue that there is an evolutionary progression toward the networked organizational form. The organizational form, as Ronfeldt argues,, is not merely about the institutional makeup of linkages, but "represents a distinctive system of beliefs, structures, and dynamics about how society should be organized—about who gets to achieve what, why and how." (Ronfeldt 1996: 2).

Perhaps the organization that best exemplifies this network structure is the Independent Media Center (IMC), or Indymedia. Indymedia emerged during the anti–World Trade Organization (WTO) protests in Seattle in 1999. While there were many factors that led to the development of Indymedia (Wolfson 2014), the greatest factor was the increasing consolidation of telecommunications, which has led to fewer voices and perspectives in the mainstream media. Activists began to recognize that the media consolidation was undermining social movement politics. With the emergence of the Internet, activists decided to establish their own alternative communications network, reappropriating these new information and communication technologies and linking them to older forms of media such as radio or television.

The first IMC emerged during the WTO meetings in Seattle, but the idea quickly caught on, and within four years there were over one hundred local IMCs creating news in multiple formats—from newspapers and radio shows to TV programs and online reporting—on six continents and in over thirty different languages. Within a few years, the Indymedia movement was the largest alternative noncorporate media infrastructure across the world.

As the movement grew, organizational structure became a key question. Over time, the Indymedia network developed as a multiscalar network structure. Specifically, the Indymedia network is made up of interconnected nodes—usually local IMCs, which are linked through a robust communications infrastructure with the goal of building an alternative media infrastructure and a set of doctrines or principles upon which the network rests. The Indymedia network is global, with local IMCs on all six continents, although the network is heavily skewed toward North and South America and Europe. Indymedia also has a multiscalar local, national, and global structure. By this we mean that there are local IMCs in particular cities, and many of these local IMCs directly relate to a national IMC, like IMC-US or IMC-Brazil, and the national IMCs all relate to the global Indymedia network. This nesting structure allows the network to focus on local politics while scaling up as a national and global formation.

The network organizational form embodies the nomadic logic of resistance as it repudiates hierarchical organizational forms and creates loose structures and processes. Moreover, much like the nomad and his or her customary paths, in the network each point is a relay within a bigger, undefined route, a mapping rather than a tracing.

## Flatting of Fronts: Celebration of Multiple Fronts of Struggle

In one of the most serious contributions to political theory in recent years, Laclau and Mouffe argued in 1986 that class was no longer (nor had it ever been) a privileged site of struggle. Building on the turn toward identitarian politics and following some of the criticisms of Marxism, they famously declared that class was one signifier in a chain of signifiers (Laclau and Mouffe 1986). Based on these new sociopolitical cleavages, new identities, carried forward by a cacophony of movements, from the civil rights movement to the feminist, environmentalist, or gay rights movements, emerged. Corroborating this point, activists and organizers began to broaden the fronts of struggle and argued for an approach that did not prioritize any specific front of struggle, actor, or strategy but rather stressed the equality of causes, actors, approaches, and visions, and thus embraced the lack of a unifying aim, identity, or one main adversary (Castells 1997; Touraine 1971).

What we thus suggest calling the dominance of "flattening of fronts" makes up a key dimension of the nomadic movement logic. It can readily be observed when looking at key protests and mobilizations of the last decades. From, for example, the anti-WTO protest in Seattle in 1999, to the massive Genoa anti-G8 mobilizations in 2001, the 2005 anti-WTO protests in Hong Kong, or the 2010 anti-G20 protests in Toronto, to the more recent antiausterity mobilizations in Spain or Greece and the Occupy-type protests and encampments, the celebration and acceptance of diversity describes a significant feature of the currently dominant nomadic movement logic.

Possibly the most illustrative example of embracing a diversity of actors and struggles is the World Social Forum (WSF) and the process it has generated. The WSF is an unprecedented, regularly organized global meeting of social movements, networks, nongovernmental organizations, and other civil society organizations opposed to neoliberalism that brings together roughly one hundred thousand activists and organizers from around the globe. The first WSF, which took place in 2001 in Porto Alegre (Brazil) as a counterevent to the World Economic Forum held in Davos (Switzerland), has spurred the production of countless autonomous regional, national, local, and thematic forums on all continents. Thriving on multiplicity and thus lacking a dominant core, center, or axis, what we called elsewhere the Global Social Forum Rhizome (Funke 2012) emphasizes the multiconnectivity and heterogeneity of this process. Mirroring the nomadic movement logic writ large, social forums lack or rather insist on the absence of a central actor, issue, strategy, or ideology beyond a broad opposition to neoliberalism. Dovetailing with the famous Zapatista slogan, "One no, many yeses," the World Social Forum process epitomizes this celebration of multiple fronts of struggle and acknowledges the diversity and plurality of alternatives, needs, aspirations, and tactics. The World Social Forum matrix thus allows

> for the diversity of constitutive groups and movements [to] come together and to do so without fear for their autonomy, without the need to agree on

any kind of programmatic and binding positions or submit to an overriding or superior struggle, actor or strategy. The core characteristics of the Global Social Forum Rhizome are aimed at protecting the independence of each group and movement and thus their diversity taken as a whole, while at the same time providing for a possibility to articulate and enact linkages, commonalities and convergences. (Funke 2012)

The World Social Forum process thus illustrates the "flattening of fronts" dimension of the currently dominant nomadic movement logic. Loosely connected through broad opposition to neoliberalism, no actor or struggle, no strategy or movement-building dynamic, is privileged. Since we revisit challenges to the nomadic movement logic in the concluding section of this chapter, suffice it to say here that the flattening of fronts also leads to a privileging of networking over movement building, which despite successful protest mobilizations tends to lead to transient linkages and difficulty in generating sustained movement building (Funke 2008).

## Flattening of Governance: Embrace of Grassroots Democratic Structures

The embrace of grassroots and participatory democratic structures and consensus decision making is the third characteristic of the nomadic movement logic. In many ways this horizontal decision making must be understood in contrast to the perceived authoritarian governing logics of state socialism and the Old Left, and the perceived inadequacy of the liberal representative democracy of Western societies. Antonio Negri captured the growing rejection of old democratic forms and the embrace of deep forms of democracy:

> Rarely has the corruption of political and administrative life been so deeply corrosive; rarely has there been such a crisis of representation; rarely has disillusionment with democracy been so radical. When people talk about a "crisis of politics," they are effectively saying that the democratic State no longer functions—and that in fact it has become irreversibly corrupt in all its principles and organs. (Negri 1996: 214; cited in Maeckelbergh 2009: 140)

Building on this sense of the complete corruption of democratic states, activists and organizers are similarly wary of organizations linked to the state apparatus such as unions or parties and the broader shared model of representative democracy. Arguably growing out of democratic experiences in the movements of the New Left, the nomadic logic today builds on these experiences, celebrating grassroots participatory democracy that shuns representative and permanent organizational or decision-making structures, including "officers" or any other positions of leadership. Participatory democracy has become the hallmark of current movements. This understanding of participatory democracy is intrinsically intertwined with the notion of prefigurative politics. While participatory democracy has, of course, been a core pillar of the New Left, it emerged forcefully again with the Zapatistas. Linking it to the flattening of fronts discussed earlier, subcommandante Marcos of the Zapatistas famously argued that

> [w]e feel that revolutionary change in Mexico will not be the product of only one kind of action. That is, it will not be, in the strict sense, either an armed or a pacific revolution. It will primarily be a revolution resulting from struggle on various fronts, using many methods, under various social forms, with various degrees of commitment and participation. And its result will not be the victory of a party, an organization or an alliance of triumphant organizations with their own specific social proposals, but rather a democratic space for resolving the confrontation of various political proposals. This democratic space will be based upon three fundamental, historically inseparable premises: democracy to define the dominant social proposal; freedom to endorse one proposal or another; and justice as a principle which must be respected by all proposals. (cited in Lorenzano 1998: 132)

While both the Indymedia movement and the World Social Forum were premised on prefigurative democracy, no movement has symbolized new forms of horizontal democracy like Occupy Wall Street and the subsequent Occupy movement. The essence of the Occupy movement has been the General Assembly, which is the decision-making apparatus within every Occupy encampment. Collective, consensus decision-making practices are deployed in the General Assembly, which consists of hundreds if not thousands of people. The logic and practice of the General Assembly, and the collective structure of Occupy more generally, offers a window onto the new direct participatory democratic forms that are dominant across social movements today. This model of movement practice is illustrative of nomadic thought. Much like Deleuze and Guattari's nomad, this form of direct democracy and horizontalism eschews hierarchies and prioritizes becoming over being. This is exemplified by the fact that the process of decision making in the General Assembly is seen as more important than the decision itself. It is through this nomadic democratic practice that activists believe they can structure new, open, equal social relations that are not premised on power and hierarchy.

## Conclusion

From the moment the EZLN declared war on the Mexican state to the recent upsurge of struggle from the Middle East and North Africa to Wall Street and Athens, we have seen the outlines of a new logic of resistance. In this chapter, we argue that this new logic is best understood through the metaphor of the nomad, first developed by Deleuze and Guattari as they tried to understand the psychological tendencies of contemporary society. Building on their concept, we suggest that there is a discernable pattern of action, with three identifiable characteristics: the flattening of forms, the flattening of struggles, and the flattening of governance. While each particular movement in the contemporary era is different and combines different aspects of these emergent characteristics, taken together they form the countenance of this new logic of resistance.

The main goal of this chapter is to point to this new logic and delineate how it is brought to life in movement principles and practices. That said, many scholars of contemporary social movements are laudatory of said movements without looking more analytically at the strengths and weaknesses of the prevailing nomadic logic. While it is beyond the bounds of this chapter to offer a thoroughgoing critical analysis of this new logic, we do want to point to some important blind spots or concerns we have with this new texture of social movements.

The flattening of forms and embracing of networked organizational forms has led to multiscalar organizational and movement structures, which have been able to flexibly challenge different forms of power. At the same time, however, this logic has often led to the prioritizing of such networking tactics over resilient movement building. While the network form might not necessarily prevent long-term movement building, in its current instantiations it presents challenges to stable movement-building structures.

The privileging of networking over movement building is further reinforced through the challenges that the flattening of fronts dimension presents. The supposition that all actors and concerns are similarly important, that no struggle or actor can be prioritized within the more general fight for emancipation and against exploitation, is highly problematic. For one, the capitalist structures forge the metamatrix within which all other forms of exploitation are linked and find themselves. Struggles over gender inequality, environmental degradation, or racism are critically part of capitalist dynamics and as such need to be centrally concerned with the forms of power and exploitation that emerge through the capitalist political economy. Moreover, in that capitalism, as an exploitive system, generates multiple intersectional forms of oppression, the fight against capitalism and its multiple forms of exploitation offers a critical strategic unity for interlinking and generating a more resilient and shared doctrine across multiple fronts of struggle. The realization of the centrality of capitalism to all other struggles would also provide relief for the often ungrounded nature of much movement politics. It would lead to the inclusion of those poor and working poor communities that are most disaffected by neoliberal capitalism and would allow activists to move beyond the often middle-class nature of much movements and groups today.

The final dimension of the dominant nomadic movement logic, the flattening of governance, also presents a potential challenge for successful movement building. The fetishization of form over function, of radically participatory democracy and the ideal of consensus decision making, has often led to a privileging of certain members that have the time and social capital to engage in these activities and functions. This becomes a problem as the dominance of communities with more social capital (read: the middle class) makes it hard for nomadic movements to merge with the mass of the working class, thus forging partial movements that cannot connect the social forces necessary for real change. Moreover, it allows for a politics of acceptance of diversity for diversity's sake instead of using democratic governance mechanisms to work through this diversity and to generate a new and shared synthesis—to "become other together," as Nunes (2006: 305) put it.

This chapter looked at the emergence of a new nomadic movement logic. As we argue, contemporary social movements are defined by this logic, which is composed of a desire to flatten politics and society, prioritizing horizontality over verticality. While this new logic has offered new forms of resistance and mobilizations, it is forged in dialectic tension with neoliberal capitalism, and therefore encounters challenges if it is to create a world where many worlds fit.

**Peter Funke** is an assistant professor of government at the University of South Florida, Tampa. His publications include "Building Rhizomatic Social Movements?" in *Studies in Social Justice* and "The Global Social Forum Rhizome" in *Globalizations*. With Todd Wolfson, he coauthored the articles "Class in Formation" and "Communication, Class and Concentric Media Practices," among others. Peter's work has been supported by the Social Science Research Council and the Miami-Florida European Union Center of Excellence at Florida International University. More information at http://www.peterfunke.net/.

**Todd Wolfson** is an assistant professor in the Department of Journalism and Media Studies at Rutgers University. His research focuses on the convergence of new media and social movements, and he is author of *Digital Rebellion: The Birth of the Cyber Left*. Todd is also cofounder of the Media Mobilizing Project (www.mediamobilizing.org), which uses media and communications as a strategy for building a movement of poor and working people in Philadelphia and beyond. Todd's work has been supported by the Knight Foundation, the Social Science Research Council, and the Dodge Foundation, among others.

## Notes

1. This chapter was written collaboratively by the two authors: there is no first author. The author's names therefore appear in alphabetical order.
2. As other scholars have argued (Joya et al. 2011), the Arab Spring was as much about economic inequality and poverty as it was about democracy.
3. We recognize that there are problems in thinking of periods, because they both elide continuity and paper over dissonance within a specific moment in time, but as Jameson (1990) argues, if we do not see patterns in history, then we are forced to argue that the contemporary moment is an anarchic jumble of phenomena with no sociohistorical link.
4. We do not suggest that questions of identity were irrelevant for the Old Left or that class issues were absent during the time of the New Left. We maintain, however, that changes in the capitalist system shifted the principle concerns and central foci of the respective movements and with them the commanding fronts and preeminent strategies of struggles in the transition from the Old to the New Left and onward to the current time.

## Bibliography

Boltanski, Luc, and Eve Chiapello. 2005. *The New Spirit of Capitalism*. New York: Verso Press.

Breines, Wini. 1989. *Community and Organization in the New Left, 1962–1968: The Great Refusal*. New Brunswick, NJ: Rutgers University Press.

Brenner, Aaron, Robert Brenner, and Cal Winslow, eds. 2010. *Rebel Rank and File: Labor Militancy and Revolution from Below During the Long 1970s*. New York: Verso Press.

Castells, Manuel. 1997. *The Information Age: Economy, Society and Culture*. Vol. 1, *The Rise of the Network Society*. Cambridge: Wiley-Blackwell.

Deleuze, Gilles, and Félix Guattari. 1980. *A Thousand Plateaus: Capitalism and Schizophrenia*. Paris: Minuit.

Diggins, John Patrick. 1992. *The Rise and Fall of the American Left*. New York: W. W. Norton.

Funke, Peter N. 2008. "The World Social Forum: Social Forums as Resistance Relays." *New Political Science: A Journal of Politics and Culture* 30: 449–74.

———. 2012. "The Global Social Forum Rhizome: A Theoretical Framework." *Globalizations* 9: 351–64.

———. 2014. "Building Rhizomatic Social Movements? Movement-Building Relays during the Current Epoch of Contention." *Studies in Social Justice* 8: 27–44.

Giddens, Anthony. 1991. *Modernity and Self Identity: Self and Society in the Late Modern Age*. Cambridge: Polity Press.

Harvey, David. 1990. *The Condition of Postmodernity: An Enquiry into the Origin of Cultural Change*. New York: Wiley-Blackwell.

Jameson, Frederic. 1990. *Postmodernism, or, The Cultural Logic of Late Capitalism.* Durham, NC: Duke University Press.
Joya, Angela, Patrick Bond, Rami El-Amine, Adam Hanieh, and Mostafa Henaway. 2011. *The Arab Revolt Against Neoliberalism.* Socialist Interventions Pamphlet Series. Toronto: Socialist Project.
Juris, Jeffrey S. 2008. *Networking Futures: The Movements Against Corporate Globalization.* Durham, NC: Duke University Press.
Laclau, Ernesto, and Chantall Mouffe. 1985. *Hegemony and Socialist Strategy: Towards a Radical Democratic Politics.* London: Verso Press.
Lih, Lih. 2008. *Lenin Rediscovered: "What Is To Be Done?" in Context.* Chicago: Haymarket Books.
Lorenzano, Luis. 1998. "Zapatismo: Recomposition of Labour, Radical Democracy and Revolutionary Project." In *Zapatista! Reinventing Revolution in Mexico,* ed. John Holloway and Eloina Pelaez, 126–58. London: Pluto Press.
Maeckelbergh, Marianne. 2009. *The Will of the Many: How the Alterglobalization Movement Is Changing the Face of Democracy.* London: Pluto.
Mandel, Erik. 1978. *Late Capitalism.* London: Verso Press.
Mayer, Robert. 1999. "Lenin and the Practice of Dialectical Thinking." *Science and Society* 63: 40–62.
Nunes, Rodrigo. 2006. "Nothing Is What Democracy Looks Like: Openness, Horizontality and The Movements of Movements." In *Shut Them Down! The G8, Gleneagles 2005 and the Movement of Movements,* ed. David Harvie, Keir Milburn, Ben Trott, and David Watts, 299–319. Leeds: Dissent!; New York: Autonomedia.
Ong, Aihwa. 1999. *Flexible Citizenship: The Cultural Logics of Transnationality.* Durham, NC: Duke University Press.
Ronfeldt, David. 1996. *Tribes Institutions, Markets and Networks: A Framework About Societal Evolution.* Santa Monica: RAND.
Tilly, Charles. 1986. *The Contentious French: Four Centuries of Popular Struggle.* Cambridge, MA: Belknap Press.
Touraine, Alain. 1988. *Return to the Actor: Social Theory in Postindustrial Society.* Minneapolis: University of Minnesota Press.
Tsipras, Alexis, and Slavoj Žižek. 2013. "The Role of the European Left." Moderated by Srećko Horvat. 6th Subversive Festival, Zagreb, Croatia, 15 May. https://www.youtube.com/watch?v=aUh96oXYt18 (accessed 14 April 2014).
Wolfson, Todd. 2012. "From the Zapatistas to Indymedia: Dialectics and Orthodoxy in Contemporary Social Movements." *Communication, Culture and Critique* 5: 149–70.
———. 2013. "Democracy or Autonomy? Indymedia and the Contradictions of Global Social Movement Networks." *Global Networks* 13: 410–24.
———. 2014. *Digital Rebellion: The Birth of the Cyber Left.* Urbana: University of Illinois Press.

CHAPTER 6

# "Project Heat" and Sensory Politics in Redeveloping Chicago Public Housing

*Catherine Fennell*

■ ■ ■ ■ ■ ■

On the second Sunday of every August, the Bud Billiken Day parade snakes through Chicago's South Side, thrilling over a million spectators. True to its mission to showcase the city's African American children, drum and bugle corps march in bright uniforms, flanked by dance troops and tumblers. Yet young musicians and acrobats are not the only people parting the thick blue barbeque smoke that curls through the parade route. The parade has long served as a venue for businesses and politicians to reach black Chicago. Waving from floats and cars, local businesspeople, representatives from community groups, city agencies, and unions, and a cast of national and local political luminaries woo the parade's tremendous crowd.

At the 2005 parade, public relations and marketing efforts met mixed reactions. The Chicago Housing Authority (CHA)—the agency spearheading the transformation of that city's public housing system—had festooned its float with balloons, smiling resident leaders, and children. As its float lumbered by, members of the crowd began to heckle, "Get me off the waiting list!" "The CHA wrecked my building!" or, more simply, "Boo!" Commonwealth Edison, the private company that electrifies the Chicagoland area, sent its float rolling not far behind. Led by a boisterous emcee, Com-Ed employees danced on the float and riled up the crowd. "Make some noise if you've got lights!" the emcee shouted, punctuating the crowd's cheers with arm pumps. "Make some noise if you've got AC!"[1]

Com-Ed's float soon met a fate similar to the CHA's, when members of the crowd began again to heckle: "We're hot!" "Give me back AC," and "Cut my lights back on!" The emcee paused from his dancing, laughed, wagged a finger at the hecklers, and sang, "Pay your bill, pay your bill, pay your bill!"

## Introduction

In Chicago, debates about public housing reform, utility use, physical comfort, and personal responsibility are more than a coincidence of parade order. Chicago's brand of economic and racial segregation can make summer cooling and winter heating matters of life and death for the city's poor (Klinenberg 2002). In this context, utility access has emerged as an especially serious concern for those low-income African Americans transitioning out of Chicago's public housing. This chapter examines the demise of subsidized home heating on Chicago's Near West Side, as the Henry Horner Homes housing complex (Horner), named after Depression-Era Illinois governor Henry Horner, is being demolished and redeveloped into the mixed-income neighborhood of Westhaven.[2] In this chapter, I use the term "project heat" in the same way my interlocutors did—to describe the very particular kind of heat one had access to while living in a Chicago public housing project. In their words, this was heat that was "hot," "free," and "blazing all the time." Before transitioning into Westhaven, the vast majority of my interlocutors had never paid a heat bill. Horner, like many Chicago Housing Authority (CHA) developments, had provided its tenants with heat generated on-site and included in rents.

In 1999, the CHA undertook the most ambitious experiment of its kind: the demolition of troubled public housing projects and their transformation into mixed-income, small-scale, neighborhood-based developments called "new communities." These lower-density redevelopments have been financed and managed through public-private partnerships, with federal funds leveraging private and nongovernmental commitments. Extended another five years in 2006, proponents of the CHA's Plan for Transformation argued that by 2015, Chicagoans would find their city a *changed* one, devoid of its vertical slums and their grinding poverty. To date, some twenty thousand units of public housing have been demolished, and some twenty-five thousand low-income households have been relocated, most headed by African American women.[3]

The process of demolition and redevelopment at Horner began in 1995, and has stood out among other Chicago public housing sites. Horner owes its somewhat unique redevelopment course to a consent decree that preceded the Chicago-wide Plan for Transformation by several years. This unique course has offered transitioning Horner residents several protections unavailable to their counterparts at other redeveloping sites. However, there are several mandates that all residents transitioning into Chicago's "new communities" must navigate. This chapter focuses on one such mandate. As a condition of lease compliance, a transitioning Horner resident must now assume financial and physical control of her domestic utilities, including her heating.[4]

Through an examination of transitioning Horner residents' changing sensory experiences of home heating, I show how mandates to control one's heat have also involved compulsions to manage subjective senses of comfort. I argue that such compulsions have transformed Horner residents from entitlement-bearing subjects to new kinds of risk-bearing subjects. I explore these compulsions through two avenues. The first concerns the effects of residents' ongoing attachments to Horner as a place that merged physical sensations of intense heat with subjective senses of security and comfort. The second avenue examines how new modes of heat provision in Westhaven are reconfiguring kinship obligations in risky ways. I show how approaching welfare reform as a kind of "sensory politics" allows us to interrogate the emerging conditions of formal political recognition available to transitioning Horner residents at a moment when their long-standing representational bodies (e.g., tenant councils) face obsolescence.[5] Finally, I argue that such an approach invites us to reconceptualize theories of contestation and survival within urban poor people's social movements in our "neoliberal" moment.

## Site and Methods

This chapter emerges from a multi-sited ethnographic and archival study that investigated how a rapidly changing urban built environment shapes a new ethics of social care as the American welfare state itself undergoes substantial restructuring. I started following Horner's redevelopment in earnest in 2003 as a graduate student of anthropology concerned with the politics of urban planning and poverty. Over the next decade, I ended up conducting some three years of full-time research tracking Horner's transformation into Westhaven. The most uninterrupted periods of this work fell between 2005 and 2007, the very years Westhaven moved deeper into its mixed income phases.

With respect to project heat's demise at Horner, research included archival analysis, observing operations at two CHA heat plants comparable to the ones that once stood at Horner, and observing social service programs designed to assist transitioning Horner residents with accessing heat. I also observed and participated in heat consumption and redistribution practices among transitioning Horner residents that took place both inside and outside of their homes. A myriad of institutions, agencies, and actors make heat possible in

Westhaven. Accordingly, I conducted interviews with heat plant engineers, gas company staff and officials, social service workers, and transitioning residents that touched on the particularities of providing, consuming, managing, and amplifying heat at Horner and Westhaven, and places like them. However, as I am interested here in the political subjectivity of residents, I limit my discussion mainly to their experiences with project heat's demise.

The Henry Horner Homes officially opened in 1957 two miles west of Chicago's downtown, in the heart of what was then the city's second-largest African American enclave. Horner stood at the forefront of the CHA's efforts to meet black Chicagoans' housing needs—needs exacerbated by severe housing shortages, a racially constrained housing market, and residential displacements related to early urban renewal initiatives on the city's South Side (Hirsch 1998; Seligman 2005). The Henry Horner Homes rose on an eighteen acre site and consisted of eleven mid- and high-rise buildings situated within carefully landscaped grounds. It formed the first part of plans for a substantial housing complex that would come to include two other subdevelopments. In 1961, the Horner Extension opened with 736 additional units, and the Horner Annex opened in 1969, bringing another 109 units to the complex. Budgetary problems, deferred maintenance, the exit of working-class families during the 1970s and early 1980s, and the ravages of drug epidemics hit Horner hard. By the late 1980s, the complex had fallen into severe decline. Combined with the devastating poverty of its residents, Horner's deteriorating physical conditions, its unusually high vacancy rates, and related crime problems led the CHA in 1991 to name it "the authority's most troubled development" and to count it among "the most distressed housing properties in the nation" (cited in Wilen 2005: 68).

Horner's deterioration formed the basis of a 1991 class action lawsuit brought by a group of its residents against both the CHA and the United States Department of Housing and Urban Development. A settlement in 1995 ushered in a consent decree that has since governed Horner's ongoing redevelopment. Unlike many of the CHA's "new communities," Horner's transformation has unfolded across multiple phases. This allowed many families to remain on-site and move around the complex's older buildings while they awaited the construction of their new homes. Over the past decade and a half, Westhaven has slowly taken shape as a neighborhood of town homes, walk-up apartment buildings, and one mid-rise building. During most of this time, two built environments—the gradually demolished architecture of the Keynesian welfare state and the gradually emerging architecture of a post-Keynesian urban communitarianism—have stood alongside each other. Each has offered its inhabitants radically different sensory and social dimensions. Each has also demanded radically different modes of engaging these dimensions.

## "Project Heat" in Historical Context

In the earliest phases of my research, I regularly barraged interlocutors with questions designed to elicit contrasts between life at Horner and Westhaven. Most lauded physical improvements in Westhaven while also lamenting that they no longer lived near their friends and family. As 33-year-old Mark, who had grown up at Horner and then stayed with his fiancée in Westhaven, emphasized, "It was easier to have a better time then with everyone closer together in the buildings. It was just love."[6] When I pressed to learn if such nostalgia extended to the physical dimensions of now demolished buildings, many would rattle off the decrepit conditions that they claimed nobody could ever miss: dark and dingy common spaces, vermin, broken elevators, the lists wound on. But many also closed such lists with variations on a curious caveat: "I don't miss anything," insisted Rhoada, a 50-year-old former resident of the Extension. "Well, OK," she added as an afterthought. "The only thing I *can* say that I *do* miss is the heat. It was the best heat we ever had. I can't even describe it. *That's* how good it was, toasty all the time."[7]

My first full winter in Westhaven fell in 2005–6, and was a mild one according to the books.[8] At this time, Horner's project heat had gone the way of the demolished buildings from which Rhoada hailed. Yet by no means did project heat's absence or the relative mildness of that winter diminish the attention that transitioning residents paid to heat. I quickly learned that musings about project heat were not limited to offhanded caveats. Residents obsessed over heat, with casual talk, jokes, and whispers among friends and neighbors incessantly turning toward the topic. Consider one of many similar conversations I documented between two middle-aged friends, both of whom had grown up in an Extension high-rise. They had been gossiping about a niece's relocation from Horner to a private rental apartment nearby. "I visited my niece in her new apartment on Sunday," gossiped Trisha. Her friend followed up: "Nice place?" Trisha leaned in, and I braced for the onslaught of questions I had begun to catalog in my notes as "the moving conversation"—questions that would dissect everything from room sizes to children's bunk beds and the landlord's integrity. Instead, Trisha and her friend embarked on an entirely different topic. "She has some good heat up in there," gushed Trisha. "Good heat." Her friend asked skeptically, "Good, like project heat?" "Yes," replied Trisha, and the two spent twenty minutes marveling at the niece's luck.

No longer physically part of Trisha's or Rhoada's life, project heat had nevertheless seized hold of their imaginations. In line with the CHA and Westhaven managers' general attempts to cultivate new habits among transitioning Horner residents, a Westhaven leaseholder was required to monitor and manage her heat and electricity usage as a condition of remaining on-site.

This meant that heat would no longer arrive at her unit on a preset schedule. Nor would it be included in her rent, as it had been at Horner. Chicago's private gas utility company now brokered winter warmth, which arrived at each unit through a forced air heat system gauged by an individual thermostat. A resident would need to control her own thermostat and pay for the heat she consumed. Through steady talk about project heat and its aftermath, I began tracing the extent to which residents registered Horner's ongoing transformation as a set of changing sensory qualities. How had project heat become such an ingrained part of everyday life at Horner, such that only the relatively recent loss of its particularly intense qualities has thrown its social significance into sharp relief?

By the 1980s and 1990s, popular media accounts examining CHA developments had begun to make passing mention of project heat, grouping it alongside the raft of problems that plagued Chicago's deteriorating housing projects. Several local news articles and evening television exposés marshaled fluctuations between public housing's intense heat and its periodic absence due to infrastructural breakdowns as further evidence of the careless planning and mismanagement that plagued the housing projects (e.g., Kamin 1999). Yet project heat should be attributed to more than a shortsighted accident or a general climate of mismanagement. Historical materials suggest that it emerged in the middle decades of the twentieth century as part of the many ambitious poverty programs and building projects associated with the then expanding American welfare state.

At the time of their construction between the late 1930s and the late 1960s, Chicago's housing projects featured some of the largest and most technically advanced heating infrastructures to be found in the country.[9] These sophisticated infrastructures allowed the CHA to provide its tenants with cheap and abundant heat. Significantly, this commitment did not just involve supplying the minimum level of heat necessary for survival. Rather, as a tenant handbook from the 1950s suggests, it spoke to something with much more subjective overtones—what I read as a comprehensive system of social care that treated sensory well-being qua ample heat as part of obligations to its charges' "comfort" and "happiness" (figure 6.1).

Discussions of subjective goods and heat appeared outside of historical materials. Many current and former heat engineers whom I located spoke of their jobs as providing "comfort" to tenants, as did Victor, a heat engineer working at a South Side plant that was still operating during my fieldwork: "In public housing, it's been traditional to make people comfortable. People in most cases like it warm. We obliged them for the forty years, and they've become accustomed to that. But as the systems got older and older, it got harder to maintain that type of comfort." Victor, a self-described "successful product

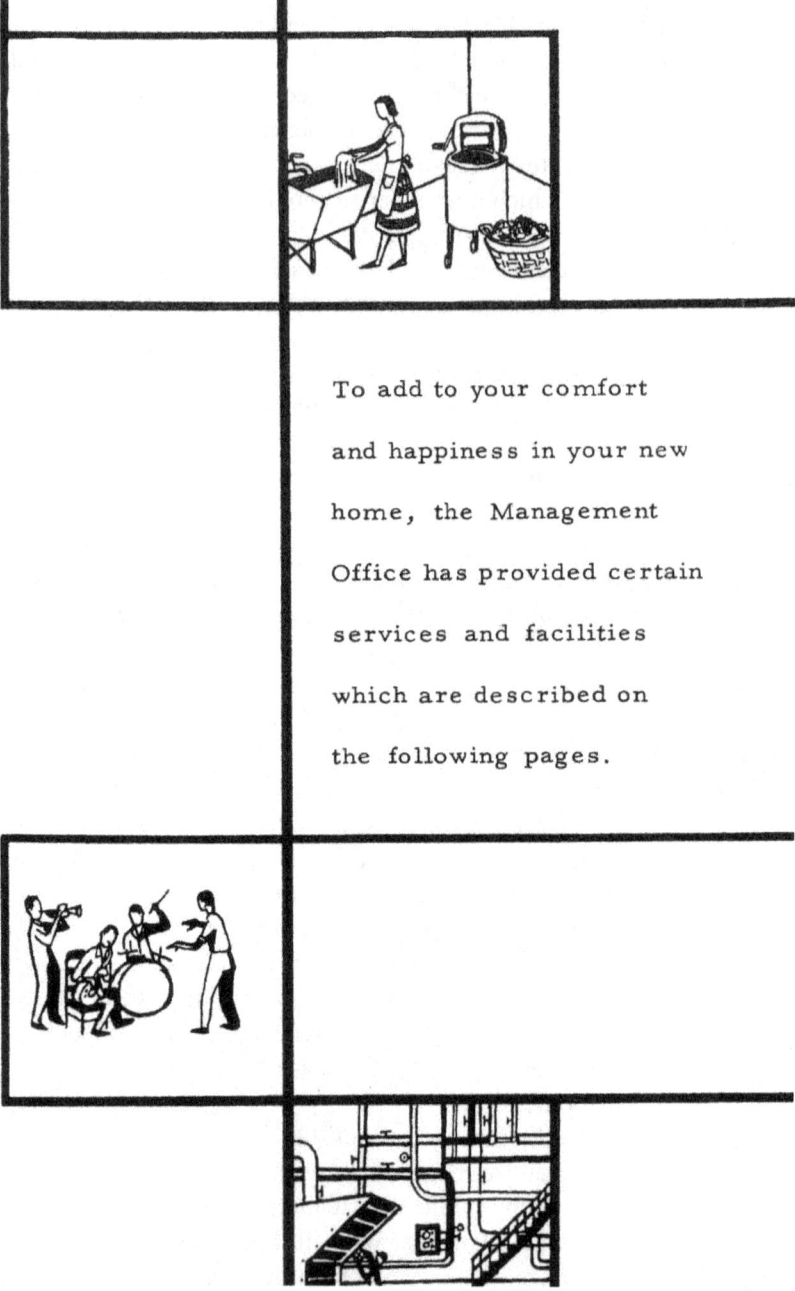

Figure 6.1. Laundry, recreation, and heat facilities promote "comfort" and "happiness," circa 1950 (CHA n.d.b). Image courtesy of the Chicago History Museum.

of [Chicago] public housing," understood his charges' taste for warmth to be rooted in their biological sensitivity to the cold. For instance, as evidence of this sensitivity, he often pointed out to me that black men in Chicago, himself included, broke out their winter hats much sooner than white men did. Most social scientists would now discredit Victor's correlation between racial categories and sensory thresholds. Significantly, though, Victor's folk theory intersected with his above assertion that the design and operation of the CHA's heat plants involved commitments to tenants' comfort that actually amplified their need for warmth. This commitment to tenant comfort involved pairing most developments with their own heat plant and including heat in most rents (figure 6.2).

The CHA heat plants varied significantly according to technologies available at the time of their construction. Across the authority, a network of boilers, coal berths, conveyors, radiators, radiant floors, pumps, oil tanks, miles of pipes, and a small legion of unionized engineers and pipe fitters delivered heat to tenants during the "heating season," which ran every year from 15 September through 1 June.[10] Several different heating technologies existed at Horner. A low-pressure heat plant pumped steam through a tangle of underground

Figure 6.2. Residential building and heat plant at Chicago's Stateway Gardens, January 2006. This plant was similar to the one that stood at The Henry Horner Homes.

pipes that fed Horner Homes' baseboard radiators. A second, high-pressure plant pumped hot water into the Extension's buildings, where it then passed through a system of pipes embedded directly in concrete slabs. Engineers had designed both plants to maintain indoor temperatures at roughly 70°F (21.1°C). Residents of Horner Homes could adjust heat via the valves on their unit's radiators, but the Extension's residents could not—their floors and ceilings simply radiated heat. The CHA had adopted then cutting-edge radiant heat technologies in the early 1960s in order to promote efficiency and eliminate the burn risks that radiators posed to children and the elderly. However, as then CHA chairman Charles Swibel conceded in a 1965 response to a newspaper series that criticized conditions at Robert Taylor Homes, radiant floor systems meant that "[h]omes are sometimes too warm because ceiling and floor slabs do not cool as quickly as rapidly rising outdoor temperatures would make desirable" (Swibel 1965: 2).

From an operations standpoint, Horner's plants placed enormous demands on the heat engineers, firemen, and pipe fitters who managed them. These men spent the heating season fixing pipes, boilers, radiators, and exchangers and gave summer over to full system checks, maintenance, and upgrades. Despite Horner's declining physical conditions, archival records confirm what its former residents recalled as generally smooth heating operations throughout the 1960s and 1970s. The systems did, however, have a major idiosyncrasy—units were heated well beyond 70°F (21.1°C).

Project heat did not only circulate within its elaborate physical infrastructures. As an idea, it also circulated within national and local concerns regarding municipal and federal obligations toward low-income citizens.[11] While the Housing Act of 1937, which first established a public housing program in the United States, required that public housing authorities manage local developments, it did not require that they cover utility services for tenants, let alone generate heat. The CHA's decision to do both emerged from arguments that centralized heating plants would allow for construction and operations savings. Yet it also emerged from nationally influential housing reformers' convictions that poor people should devote no more than a quarter of their income to housing and housing-related costs, like utilities (Hunt 2009). The heat plants would allow the CHA to provide heat at a cheaper rate than a utility company, with savings to be passed onto tenants.

Ample heat was an incredible novelty for low-income and black Chicagoans. As late as the 1940s, many black Chicagoans did not enjoy easy access to domestic basics. Regardless of their income, racially restrictive housing covenants crowded many into areas rife with substandard housing. Overcrowding rendered haphazardly divided residential units that lacked sufficient heat and hot water, a common feature of the housing stock in black enclaves (Hirsch

1998). Indeed, some of my elderly interlocutors recalled that before they moved into Horner in the late 1950s and early 1960s, they tapped fire hydrants for the water supply unavailable in their apartments. Others detailed life in "cold water flats." Such units lacked both hot water and a mechanical heating source, leading tenants to improvise. Insufficient or improvised heat courted dangers like illnesses and house fires. In the 1940s and 1950s, conditions around domestic utility access in black enclaves contributed to arguments for comprehensive urban renewal, slum clearance, and public housing construction that were increasingly influential on local and national levels.[12] Through project heat, municipal redevelopment initiatives and poverty relief discourses interfaced federal priorities in ways that made the sensory care of low-income Chicagoans thinkable and doable on a large scale. As I have suggested above, such care must be conceptualized as having exceeded basic survival needs by incorporating the more affective, indulgent, and subjective qualities of comfort.

## "Project Heat" in Ethnographic Contexts

The elaborate scale of heat operations and the breadth of ambitions that stood behind them were not what made project heat's demise ethnographically significant at Horner. My interlocutors paid neither attention. What, then, made heat's qualities central within residents' experiences and navigations of Horner's redevelopment? This section follows the charge that "[a]n inquiry into the senses directs us beyond the faculties of a subject to the transfers, exchanges and attachments that hinge a body to its environment" (Hirschkind 2006: 29). I detail how remembered sensations of abundant but now lost heat "hinge" residents to a demolished place. The "hinges" of particular interest to me include the nostalgia that anchors feelings of personal and collective comfort and security to a hot place, and the implication of such nostalgia for obligations toward kin. I should add that the empirical veracity of transitioning residents' narratives about project heat's bygone qualities concerns me less than the fact that these narratives constitute a set of arguments about one particular world, as well as shed light on practices of care and security necessary within that world. I suggest in the next section that it is precisely these arguments and practices that now shape the forms of political subjectivity available to transitioning Horner residents.

### *Comfort and Security as a Hot Place*

Anthropologists have long noted that landscapes and built environments can become repositories for meanings, identifications, and bodily orientations salient within a particular group (Bourdieu 1977; Basso 1996; Stewart 1996). Moreover, they have shown how the changing material and social dimensions of one group's physical environment can bring each to the fore in politically consequential ways (Munn 2004; Holston 1989; Cattelino 2006). As Westhaven emerges, these meanings, identifications, and orientations have become especially prominent through nostalgic narratives about project heat and efforts to replicate its qualities. These narratives and efforts mark project heat's former recipients as subjects of a special form of governmental care—subjects for whom embodied comfort and security was and continues to be anchored in the capacity to inhabit an especially hot place.

Horner's project heat owed its major idiosyncrasy—that it was extremely hot—to design miscalculations. Horner's designers had not accounted for concrete's heat-retaining capacities. Similar to other housing projects built during Chicago's postwar urban renewal, concrete abounded in Horner's building frames and slabs. Horner's heat engineers and firemen subsequently had a hard time calibrating interior temperatures against the fluctuating exterior temperatures of Chicago's temperamental winters. Thus, they pumped heat into buildings at abundant levels, making extreme heat a total sensory fact of everyday life at Horner.

My interlocutors recalled interior temperatures that soared between 85 and 95°F (29.4–35°C). Jean, who moved into the Extension in the late 1970s as a young adult, described the elegance and intensity of her radiant heat one morning while preparing breakfast: "You got real good heat … through the floor. You didn't have those big, ugly radiators like [in Horner Homes]. You could tell that it comes up through the floor because you'd be walking and [it] would be real hot—like that!" She delivered the last line while pointing at the skillet. Extension residents did not hold a monopoly on intensely embodied experiences of heat. Sylvia, who spent ten years at a Horner Homes high-rise, remarked, "I don't care how cold it was outside. Them bricks kept the heat in there. You sweat. Everyone sweat, even the walls, they sweat too!" Like other transitioning Horner residents, Sylvia and Jean focused on the material registration of intense heat. A winter at Horner scored one's body as much as it scored the built environment. Just as steam escaping from radiators wetted down walls and radiant heat flaked paint off of interior surfaces, relentless sweating and bared skin became the embodied marks of Horner's seasonal rhythms.

Residents' narratives about project heat also underscore its unusual relationship to time. Barring any systemic breakdowns in infrastructure or operations, winter was on permanent hold. As one senior man put it, "We had summertime in the wintertime." This summer wintertime demanded very particular practices of inhabiting the built environment. Residents slept blanketless or on mats rolled out onto radiating floors. Fans whirred around the clock, and winter wardrobes consisted of shorts, housecoats, T-shirts, and bare feet. When wearing light clothes or adjusting radiator valves gave no relief, Horner Homes residents would crack open their windows. Many Extension windows remained ajar all winter because it was the only way to throttle the heat. At both sites, the meeting of indoor heat with outdoor air made vapor drifting around buildings a common sight. Condensation formed along the edges of windows and froze them open. Horner's intense heat also allowed people to enjoy a pleasure unusual in Chicago—year-round, outdoor socializing. Steam flashing from deteriorating underground pipes melted snow and heated the area above to balmier levels. Another elderly man who had lived most of his adult life at Horner recalled how one could "go out and see the birds along the building, singing, because [there was] no snow! Everybody be standing over the pipes, talking because it's warm, standing out all winter long."

Physical and sensory conditions at such odds with seasonal rhythms struck outsiders as unbearable, but many of my interlocutors defied this interpretation. They could readily identify the risks posed by Horner's intense heat, including aggravated asthma, radiator burns, and nosebleeds.[13] Yet most did not waiver from their insistence that they longed for project heat's return, praising its sublimities in remarkably similar terms: "great heat," "the best heat in the world," and "the best heat we ever had." One might view this nostalgia as a longing for a "free" service whose costs residents must now bear. Yet my interlocutors disagreed with this view, like Samantha, a 32-year-old who had relocated to private rental housing.

Samantha: It was the best heat we'll ever have.

Author: Well, it was free.

Samantha: No. It was hot. They didn't just give you a little heat, and then you freeze. They gave us heat constantly.

Samantha's correction points to how the "freeness" of project heat cannot be separated from the largesse that colored the comfort it provided.

Project heat's demise made clear to its former recipients that it had been a boon for anyone on a fixed income, but their nostalgia cannot be reduced to the fact that it was "free heat." Nayna, a middle-aged woman who grew up in an Extension high-rise, reiterated this point when she mused, "People miss it, yes, because it's free. Now you have to pay. But also because now you have to turn your heat up high just to get comfortable." Concerns about comfort went beyond individual preferences, speaking instead to a group-level comfort, as suggested by one resident's distinction between his personal tastes and the collective benefits of project heat. P.B. had lived the entirety of twenty-one years at Horner, save for brief stints away at college and in jail. "Me, I don't miss it because I dig breezes. So I just opened the windows and let it out," P.B. claimed. "But it was pretty nice for *us*" (emphasis added).

Nostalgia for project heat's sensory pleasures intersects discourses that shaped comprehensive welfare reform in the 1990s in interesting ways. Scholars have noted within popular critiques of welfare programs that led up to these reforms a preoccupation with welfare recipients' unchecked allocations, excessive consumption habits, and general dependency upon outside institutions for basic sustenance and support (Fraser and Gordon 1994; Mink 1998; Schram 2000). Critiques of project heat made to me by various social advocates and heat plant staff shared striking parallels with these discourses. They suggested that the CHA's heat infrastructures conjoined wastefulness and neglect in ways that encouraged tenants' attachments to heat and, with respect to heat consumption, placed them permanently beyond practices of self-sufficiency. It would seem, then, that yearnings for heat so excessive that its recipients had to let it out the window are entirely consistent with discourses that drove welfare reform in the first place. Moreover, measures compelling leaseholders to manage their own heat speak well to what scholars have approached as the cultivation of self-management techniques within "neoliberal" welfare reforms (Cruickshank 1999; Rose 1999; Goode and Maskovsky 2001). Here, such techniques champion personal choice and self-sufficiency as both generally empowering and an antidote for the excesses of the Keynesian welfare state. However, rampant nostalgia for project heat poses certain challenges to analyses of a generalized neoliberal subjectivity. A closer consideration of this nostalgia offers a complementary avenue for charting how and with what specific effects sensory yearnings shape everyday social and political potentials in Westhaven.

In her approach to memory as material culture, Nadia Serematkis (1996) observes that as sensory memories mediate historical experience, they can also bring the past into the present in ways that produce a social and historical reflexivity capable of transforming that present. What kinds of materially imbued reflexivities might remembered sensory pleasures initiate in a context where the self-regulation of heat has recently become implicated in the self-management of sensory care? Mark and Sylvia shed light on this question in their separate comments on the sensory landscapes and certainties of the past.

> Mark: In the wintertime winds is shooting up through here because you're not far from the lake. Say you got to go to the store and walk through the fields with the snow up high. But you don't worry, because you come back to the heat. No heat can ever be like that again.
>
> Sylvia: Some radiators you control and some you couldn't. But that's OK. You knew you was going to be warm and not ever have to worry about being cold and about paying no bill.

By contrasting a place where one need not worry about adequate warmth with one where worries over its absence abound, Mark's and Sylvia's comments typify the individual anxieties that Nikolas Rose has discussed as central to "advanced liberal" political subjectivity—that is, a motivating internalization of policies, discourses, and practices that would "free" an individual to govern herself.

More than that, though, Mark's and Sylvia's comments are shot through with an awareness that project heat warded off the very seasonal worries that now bear down so strongly upon transitioning Horner residents. In other words, their comments suggest a recognition of both a unique and uniquely emplaced status among citizens that has now passed: that, despite its shortcomings (e.g., that it could not be controlled), project heat had located them in a system of care that mobilized the certainties of one particular built environment to mitigate the material exigencies of poverty. Moreover, Mark's and Sylvia's comments indicate an awareness that the passing of Horner has located them within a field of worries and risks already faced by nonpublicly housed Chicagoans. I read their comments as prefacing reflexive stances that mark a shift from a type of political subjectivity defined by an emplaced form of sensory well-being to an emerging one defined increasingly by the intensification of sensory and social risks. Below, I explore how reflexivity about this shift has shaped the actions taken and arguments mobilized by transitioning Horner residents to mitigate such risks.

## *The Intensification of Social and Sensory Risk*

Transitioning Horner residents' nostalgia for project heat went beyond personal yearnings for the sensory certainty it had provided to anxieties about how its loss complicated kin relationships. The prior system of care had made them beneficiaries of commitments to their personal comfort and happiness. Less formally, it had also obligated them to mitigate poverty's risks through redistribution. While Horner stood, residents redistributed project heat's comfort and security across their intimate networks in two ways.

The first mode of redistribution involved forecasting project heat's guarantees across a long horizon. Horner residents had no immediate need for private gas utility accounts, so they could loan or sell their names and social security numbers to nonpublicly housed relatives and friends who had difficulty maintaining such accounts. Banks of broken mailboxes in building lobbies and requirements that they wear identity badges during the late 1980s and early 1990s also made tenants' personal information available for the taking.[14] Many accounts opened through name loans, sales, and thefts fell delinquent. Martha, who lived at the Extension until the late 1990s, describes how this situation later complicated the process of opening utility accounts, a lease requirement in Westhaven.

> People noticed the problem [around 1998], after they started moving around. They go to open up their light or gas and learn that they can't because they names was burnt up. My cousin took my name and opened up accounts in Milwaukee. She thought I would never find out, that I would never need it because I stayed in the projects. I was raised with her like my sister, but she took my name anyway and burnt it up! At the time, I didn't know not to leave things around. She probably took that information right off my [ID] card.

As Martha suggests, precisely because project heat's reliable comfort and security were such a taken-for-granted fact of Horner's built environment, many residents and their relatives could not anticipate the day in which a loaned, stolen, or sold name would become a liability.

The second mode of redistributing project heat's comfort and security fell in line with more general obligations to kith and kin. Horner leaseholders had long opened their homes to friends and relatives in need of a place to stay, allowing everyone to pool resources, manage household tasks, and share shelter basics like heat. As they had at Horner, these "off-lease" arrangements violated lease conditions in Westhaven, but the practice remained common. Practical and ethical considerations barred many leaseholders from shunning the very networks critical to everyday survival.[15] At the same time, Westhaven's new heat provision context complicated these long-standing obligations. Leaseholders' own tastes for abundant heat already caused financial problems. Managing other household members' tastes amplified this dilemma, as illustrated by two middle-aged Westhaven leaseholders joking with friends about the sensory demands of their children, grandchildren, and other visitors.

> Henry: People is going to work now, and when they go, their kids turn the heat up to 90. When the kids hear that door open, baaam! They run to get that heat back down!

> Nayna: I know that when I get home, I turn it down to 70 because it be up there, 80, 90. I go in there and look right at that thermostat [everyone laughs]. Wait! They've got the oven and the heat on. I pay that!

The lighthearted tone with which Nayna and Henry traded stories about keeping visitors in check belied the seriousness of their situations. Nayna, for instance, struggled with the regular stays of siblings and an adult child who had all grown up at Horner, but who did not hold leases in Westhaven. Their attachments to Horner as a hot place persisted in ways that made Nayna's obligations to them serious liabilities. She tellingly addressed her visitors as "heat-suckers," and openly blamed them for the unmanageable heat bills that pushed her close to a lease violation. Nayna began to deny their visits, which caused tensions. Yet these risks did not diminish the enormous pride she took when she could finally again share abundant heat with her kin. In early 2007, high strains on her heating system put it out of commission for good. This led to her "emergency move" to one of the few buildings in the complex that still included heat in the rent. A few weeks after this move, she beamed, "I can have [my kin] over again. We sit riding the heat all day long." The mix of pleasure and risk that characterized project heat's demise in Westhaven did not so easily resolve itself for other transitioning residents. For them, the pursuit of adequate heat, let alone comfort, steadily intensified risks that were both sensory and social in nature.

By the winter of 2005, Westhaven's managers, developers, social service workers, and resident leaders had recognized the seriousness of heat issues. Chilly units and delinquent gas bills that ranged everywhere from $200 to $3,000 revealed the insufficiency of income-based utility allowances provided by the CHA to help residents adjust. The CHA had begun collaborating with social service subcontractors, private developers, and gas utility officials to stave off evictions. Collaborations included workshops, incorporating energy-saving measures in future building designs, transferring utility allowances directly to the utility company to guarantee the funds were applied to utility debt, and referring residents to federal and charity programs. If transitioning residents accessed these programs, they could mitigate some of the risks associated with the loss of project heat. Yet Westhaven's social service workers frequently complained to me that many residents chanced disconnection rather than reveal their utility problems and invite the kinds of scrutiny widely thought to lead to eviction.

Social service workers repeatedly reminded residents that it did not "make sense" to be cold when thermostats stood at recommended settings (69–72°F [20.5–22.2°C]). Many residents understood this, but nevertheless still felt cold. A young woman summarized this dilemma when she lamented, "Winter is [for] being sweaty, with the fan on. What do I do if 'warm' feels like 90? I have to have my heat on 80 just not to be cold." Residents thus supplemented formal heat assistance by trading tips and experimenting with methods designed to replicate project heat's sensory qualities. Some donned coats and hats indoors and swaddled children in thick blankets. Others huddled all winter long in one or two rooms sealed off by heavy blankets and plastic tarps. Keeping one's electricity bill current before all other accounts could guarantee that, barring other disconnections, one could still plug in an electric heater or boil water in the microwave. Some filled pots and bathtubs with steaming water to release humid heat slowly. Supplemental electric, kerosene, and butane heaters sent interior temperatures above recommended settings. Still others who preferred more intense blasts of heat than what could be coaxed out of thermostats, portable heaters, and pots fired up ovens and stove burners.

Chasing such habituated comforts not only led to delinquent utility accounts and tattered credit records. It also sent residents down the path of ever intensifying social and sensory risks. Unpaid heat bills would build up and result in disconnection. Disconnections were barred during certain parts of the year, but once that time was over, heat could legally remain off until an account holder resolved her debt. In such situations, residents who did not avail themselves of utility assistance programs or could not rely on kin undertook dangerous measures to secure adequate heat. A few admitted to tampering with their heat. The ones that did always situated this practice within obligations to their family, as one young woman does here: "Of course I did what it took to help my babies because nobody else cares. The [utility] companies won't help you out. On [local street] my mother-in-law showed me how to fix the gas so it could circulate through a rubber hose. It was really dangerous but it worked." My interlocutors would more readily, and hypothetically, walk me through the steps necessary to reconnect heat. I learned how makeshift connector hoses could carry gas from a neighbor's source to one's oven and how running extension cords from a neighbor's home or tripping their current could power portable heaters. Others explained how to remove locks from gas meters and grind down gears to slow registration. Still others relayed how to "borrow" someone else's account indefinitely by swapping one's gas meter with ones from vacant units.

Improvised heat involved risks that eclipsed the utility company's hefty tampering charges—it could cause fires that harmed household members and burned adjacent units. The aftermath of a house fire in Westhaven did not just involve a scramble to replace ruined basics like beds and clothes or to find temporary housing. It also involved avid speculations about the exact cause of the fire, the extent of damage beyond the originating unit, and who was to blame for a botched tampering job. Gossip flew about fire victims who meted out their own justice. A handyman with a reputation among my interlocutors as a go-to person for safe reconnections critiqued several recent botched heat cases: "You can go to prison. But worse, you can cause a death. The people that you did this to, the survivors, do you think they are not going to tell when they learn who set [the heat] up, and then [a fire] happened? Do you think their families won't come [for you]?" This man's comments reflect the most extreme situations that emerge when lingering sensory attachments to intense heat meet the material exigencies of everyday life in Westhaven. Nevertheless, when considered alongside the experiences of other residents, his comments reveal the extent to which place-based attachments saturate transitioning Horner residents, their kin, and neighbors in an ever intensifying field of physical and social risk.

## *The Formal Politicization of Risk*

In Westhaven, project heat's lingering qualities echoed beyond individual nostalgia and intimate social networks to constrain the forms of political recourse available to transitioning Horner residents. The ways in which some Westhaven residents have managed to politicize project heat's demise speak to longer-term dynamics on-site, but they also suggest changing conditions of political recognition for the poor in urban America.

At the most micropolitical level, Westhaven's resident leaders brokered access to home heat to shore up support among their constituency. When faced with intractable heat bills or disconnections, transitioning Horner residents could always petition members of their representational body, the Local Advisory Council (LAC). Resident leaders then on a case-by-case basis mobilized ties with on-site social service workers and managers to resolve disconnections and facilitate applications for utility assistance. Heat provision thus entered broader patron-client obligations that had long characterized relationships between tenant leaders and residents within Chicago public housing.[16] Much more was at stake, however, in the politicization of project heat's demise than micropolitical exchanges and the reproduction of local power.

Throughout my research, Westhaven's private developers wielded increasingly effective arguments about the LAC's obsolescence. They argued that a separate political body for transitioning residents thwarted efforts to integrate them into an emerging mixed-income neighborhood. Their push to deflate the LAC centered on assertions that its practice of mediating residents' access to critical resources, like heat, encouraged residents' continued dependency while simultaneously obstructing efforts to familiarize them with mainstream social and political channels. It was within this ongoing contestation of authority that LAC members politicized problems with heat to assert their relevance as both resident advocates and "stakeholders" in Horner's redevelopment.

During the 2005–2006 and 2006–2007 winters, leaders leveraged residents' preoccupation with heat to mobilize a series of disjointed critiques and actions. They dispatched allied residents to troll the development with clipboards in hand and instructions to note all the telltale signs of heat issues visible within Westhaven's built environment: shrink-wrapped windows, missing storm doors, and gaps yawning around window frames and doorjambs. Leaders followed up with informal audits that scrutinized the intensity of heat outputs and drafts and the condition of windows and doors. Through this work, leaders began suggesting to developers and external advocates that hasty construction had resulted in substandard weatherization, which had in turn adversely affected residents' capacity to manage their heat bills. They also documented cases in which crossed utility lines caused one unit to carry the heating loads of one or more others in a building. Residents and their leaders also began positioning heat problems within broader imaginaries of conspiracy. Here, they spun theories that the CHA had worked with architects or utility companies in decades past to fashion a built environment specifically designed to produce abnormal attachments to intense heat. Accordingly, such attachments would eventually compel residents to spend excessive sums on the private utility market while also facilitating future evictions from subsidized housing.

Despite their limited success, the flurry of formal critiques and actions cohering around project heat's demise in Westhaven could be seen as a form of political empowerment within a redevelopment process widely critiqued for disempowering Chicago public housing residents. In order to understand what kind of political empowerment these critiques and actions might engender, it is important to consider on what terms such empowerment unfolds and what these terms demand of transitioning Horner residents. In other words, I want to implicate these moves within a politics of recognition that, in the wake of entitlement-based welfare programs like public housing, I suggest now governs transitioning Horner residents' formal access to critical resources like heat.[17]

Arguments about heat problems in Westhaven took less conspiratorial bents, but nevertheless still interfaced broader genres of formal political recognition that conferred legitimacy and its resources through demonstrable risks and related harms—in this case, the kinds inflicted by the material conditions of an unsound built environment. In making such arguments, the LAC president herself drew on the legal trajectory of the class action lawsuit that had mobilized dangerous physical conditions on-site to win Horner residents unique protections in the redevelopment process. She repeatedly warned Westhaven's development team that crossed utility lines, insufficient weatherization, and the lack of adequate training to prepare transitioning residents for life without project heat could become the grounds for a "new lawsuit." The fact that this suit never materialized did not stop her and her allies from imagining a settlement large enough to wipe out all past utility debts and cancel all future utility payments on-site. Although it never happened, other LAC members toyed on and off with the idea of "going public" with heat troubles in Westhaven. In an instance particularly suggestive of the broader discourses of harm through which some residents were fashioning a post-Horner political subjectivity, an elderly LAC member proposed that residents make a "heat march" on city hall and CHA headquarters. She explained that the idea struck while watching a television documentary about the Warsaw ghetto. Footage of people wearing overcoats inside decrepit apartments, huddled around improvised fires, and standing by children wrapped in heavy blankets had leapt out at her. She insisted that these grainy images confirmed "how much they [the interned Jews] were like us."

## Conclusion

Transitioning Horner residents' experiences with heat and the related ambitions of their leaders touch on two strands of thought running through recent scholarship on the politics of neoliberal urbanism and urban citizenship movements. By way of conclusion, I would like to consider how the sensory politics of project heat's demise speak to both, as well as how it might push them in productive directions.

The first line of thought, emerging from urban geography, might situate project heat's demise within the overhaul of national, transnational, and municipal regulatory landscapes during the past several decades (Brenner and Theodore 2002; Harvey 2005). Here, project heat's demise provides a concrete example of the historic shift from the regulatory frameworks of Fordist and Keynesian development to "neoliberal" restructuring strategies. It exemplifies how a state project to care for its citizens through a large-scale intervention in the urban built environment, for instance, the pairing of heat plants with state-subsidized housing, now enters restructuring regimes that promote market deregulation alongside consumer discipline. In this vein, transitioning Horner residents compelled to both recalibrate and privately manage their own sensory comfort seem to be archetypes of a distinctly "neoliberal subjectivity" that "normalizes the logics of individualism and entrepreneurialism, equating individual freedom with self-interested choices, making individuals responsible for their own well-being, and redefining citizens as consumers and clients" (Leitner et al. 2007: 2).

Scholars working with the above approach have charted the lived effects of what Brenner and Theodore (2002) have called "actually existing neoliberalism" through case studies that show how urban residents have worked together to counter regulatory restructuring (Leitner, Peck, and Sheppard 2007). These cases resonate with project heat's demise. Transitioning Horner residents' experiences around heat emphasize the severity of social and physical risks posed by enduring sensory attachments to what we might call "Fordist" heat within a radically different built environment. These experiences also show how residents have developed alternative imaginaries and resourceful strategies that critique new forms of heat provision, all the while reaffirming a type of care that could attend adequately to sensory comfort. In many ways, then, residents' formal and informal mobilizations around heat can be approached as a grassroots contestation of assumptions that underwrite a neoliberal political subjectivity.

The above approach helpfully positions neoliberal restructuring as a fundamentally uneven and by no means inevitable process. Yet it can privilege acts of contestation at the expense of investigating the specific discursive and material conditions under which responses like mobilizations around heat become effective. Acts like utility piracy or a class action suit might well expand access to resources curtailed by neoliberal restructuring regimes, but exactly what kinds of belonging are they expanding?

A second strand of thought pertinent to analyzing the political subjectivity of transitioning Horner residents comes out of studies of what are sometimes called "quality of life" movements (Holston and Appadurai 1996; Caldeira 2000; Appadurai 2002). These studies have investigated urban contexts in which translocal or transnational flows of goods, populations, and ideas have upset regulatory structures associated with the nation-state in ways that complicate formal citizenship and its state-mediated guarantees. Drawing on theories of modern governance that emphasize the most mundane articulations of regulation and power, scholars have shown how urban dwellers mobilize the quality of everyday environments to achieve informal modes of social and political inclusion. Examples have included mobilizations around sanitation, housing, and public space.

We can recognize in transitioning Horner residents' preoccupations with project heat and practical responses to its loss concerns similar to those that have driven quality of life movements in other cities. Moreover, as some transitioning Horner residents leverage relationships with kin, neighbors, utility pirates, or external institutions to secure sensory comfort, the material exigencies they face have begun to gain broader political traction. In particular, the practices by which some have documented and publicized heat problems speak to what Arjun Appadurai has discussed in a very different context as a kind of "countergovernmentality": "animated by social relations of shared poverty, by the excitement of active participation in the politics of knowledge and by its own openness to correction through other forms of intimate knowledge and spontaneous everyday politics. This is government turned against itself" (Appadurai 2002: 36). As transitioning Horner residents push social service providers, housing agencies, and private developers to take notice of heat provision in Westhaven, they render its associated risks thinkable and visible beyond Westhaven.

We can also see how nascent organizing efforts around heat might renegotiate the benefits of substantive citizenship in a place impacted by comprehensive welfare reform. Federal grants and private charity programs have in fact emerged to ameliorate the risks associated with project heat's loss. At the same time, the social and physical risks that transitioning Horner residents now navigate alongside project heat's loss (e.g., kinship strains, house fires, credit problems, eviction threats) raise questions about the nature of a citizenship born out of severe material exigencies. If the politicization of these exigencies enables new forms of belonging, how and with what effects might it also constrain the political and social legitimacy afforded to transitioning public housing residents and groups like them? I want to suggest some preliminary inroads into this question by considering how the sensory politics of welfare reform in Westhaven circulate within a broader politics of recognition.

In recent years, scholars have asked how the moral sensitivities of liberal society have been implicated within contemporary arguments for political recognition (Kymlicka 1995; Povinelli 2002; Markell 2003). They have suggested that liberal society has distributed recognition based on a social group's ability to embody some set of acceptable differences (e.g., a sanctioned cultural identity), or alternately, how they embody a set of harms resulting from the failure of a society to recognize what has made them a distinct group. Such a politics holds out the promise of formal recognition to groups thought to have experienced some form of cultural, social, or economic marginalization, provided that harms attributed to such marginalization can be demonstrated. The stakes of such a politics are not insignificant. As others have shown, in contexts characterized by severe material want, demonstrations of sympathetic or reasonable differences have become tied to the distribution of resources that support social and physical well-being (e.g., Povinelli 2002).

The politics of recognition scholarship has centered on identity debates within the context of cultural pluralism. I want to expand this scope by examining arguments about how built environments born of American welfare programs rendered the people who inhabited or navigated them on an everyday basis distinct in consequential ways. I have shown above that the atypical sensory landscape of Chicago public housing rendered project heat's recipients distinct kinds of citizens in that they developed attachments to homes characterized by intense and abundant heat. It is precisely these attachments that many of my interlocutors credited with making their transition to the consumer-based forms of discipline that other Chicagoans must practice especially difficult. At the same time, this difficulty has also become a political resource in its own right.

In the past, Horner residents' political legitimacy—and thus their access to critical resources—rested on their ability to organize around public housing's myriad insecure conditions. It is perhaps not surprising, then, that the political struggles of residents transitioning into Westhaven still focus on residents' associations with the material qualities of a very particular place. Perhaps more surprising is how some residents have begun to formally politicize bygone and emerging sensory landscapes.

Sensory comfort qua intense heat is no longer an entitlement in Chicago public housing. Some transitioning Horner residents have adjusted to this new utility context by recalibrating their expectations about such comfort and adopting austerity measures. For them, winter will never again be the season for "being sweaty, with the fan on." Others have suggested that they have been negatively impacted by the faulty material conditions of their new homes—conditions that encourage or necessitate excessive utility consumption. On a case-by-case basis, they have benefited financially from increased assistance with utility debts or from repairs and designs that improve the energy efficiency of their units. In this way, some individual entrances into a neoliberal subjectivity that both valorizes and mandates self-regulation have been softened.

Yet many more transitioning Horner residents have not severed their attachments to public housing's disappearing sensory landscapes and in fact insist that it is impossible to do so. For them, attachments to abundant heat are indelibly ingrained across their skins, tastes, and perceptions. Some even argued that because these attachments were born of neglect by the very institutions charged with making state-subsidized, low-income housing safe for the poor, any dangers resulting from residents' efforts to approximate past sensory comforts warrant formal, if not also legal redress. For them, the compulsions and harms of a habituated comfort, especially as both complicate obligations to kith and kin, have become a risky political currency. This currency provides distinctions with which to petition for political recognition and its resources, but only while also requiring those wielding it to continue inhabiting ever intensifying fields of physical and social risk. In the context of American welfare state transformation, the relationship between the two substantive forms of political belonging I have touched upon in this chapter—what we might see as a consumer-inflected form of citizenship and a harm-based one—warrants further scrutiny.

**Catherine Fennell** is an associate professor in the Department of Anthropology and the Center for the Study of Ethnicity and Race at Columbia University. Her interests lie in the transformation of the American welfare state, particularly its subsidized housing programs, and the effects of that transformation on the politics of citizenship, social protection, and difference. Her ethnographic work has centered on housing reforms and demolitions in Chicago and Detroit. It follows how the affective and sensory qualities of everyday life within a changing built environment contribute to the cultivation of a "postwelfare" ethics of care and concern.

## Notes

Field and archival research for this chapter was supported by the National Science Foundation Graduate Research Fellowship, the Irving Horowitz Foundation for Social Policy Grant, and the United States Department of Housing and Urban Development Doctoral Dissertation Research Grant. Earlier versions of this chapter were presented at the Planners Network Conference at the University of Illinois at Chicago (2006), the Department of Anthropology at the University of Chicago (2007), the annual meeting of the American Anthropological Association (2007), and the annual meeting of the Social Science History Association (2007). Several people provided helpful feedback during these discussions, especially Kabir Tambar, Jessica Cattelino, Michael Silverstein, and Robert Fairbanks. I also thank Sarah Muir, Rocio Magaña, Joseph Hankins, Kelda Jamison, and four anonymous reviewers for their comments, as well as Megan Zutter for her editorial assistance. Finally, I am extremely indebted to all those in Chicago who taught me how to notice and appreciate the sublimities of project heat.
Originally published in:
Fennell, C., *Ethnography* 12(1)
p. 40–64, copyright © 2011 by SAGE Publications
Reprinted by Permission of SAGE.

1. "AC" is an abbreviation for "air conditioning."
2. Domestic electricity use is also very much an issue within redeveloping Chicago public housing. However, at Horner it was provided in a manner different enough from heat to warrant a separate discussion that is beyond the scope of this chapter.
3. In 1999, the CHA's housing stock consisted of approximately thirty-eight thousand units. The CHA reports that between 1999 and December 2014, 18,807 units were demolished under its Plan for transformation, including 12,914 high-rise units. It also reports that approximately another 3,000 units were demolished between 1995 and 1999, but not under the Plan (pers. email comm., CHA-Research, 16 December 2014). The overall goal of the Plan was 25,000 newly constructed or rehabilitated units. The total number of people displaced under the Plan is hard to reckon, but the CHA generally reports that twenty-five thousand households were eligible to return to redeveloped or rehabilitated housing under the Plan, the majority headed by African American women. The number given me by many tenant activists and policy analysts I worked with was at least seventy-five thousand persons displaced, assuming twenty-five thousand households, each averaging three persons. I stress that this is an estimate, and it would not account for people who resided in public housing in an unofficial capacity. I should also note that most official relocation figures provided by the CHA do not include relocations that occurred in the years leading up to the Plan. Horner's demolition and redevelopment began in 1995.
4. Women hold the majority of leases in Chicago public housing, which my use of the feminine pronoun form in this chapter is meant to reflect.
5. With respect to the politicization of project heat's demise, this chapter focuses on the formal representational politics of redeveloping public housing. Its demise has been politicized in other contexts that warrant more consideration, for instance, within more general discourses of market-based social liberation.
6. All personal names are pseudonyms, most of which were chosen by my interlocutors.
7. Unless otherwise noted, all emphases are original.

8. With a seasonal mean temperature of 29.1°F (-1.6°C), Chicago's 2005-6 winter stands on the warmer side of the record books. Since official records began in 1873, the average temperature in Chicago between December and February has registered at 25.5°F (-3.6°C). This reading does account for Chicago's "wind chill," that is, the temperature felt on any exposed skin when factoring in wind speeds and directions. Given Chicago's intense winter winds, temperatures feel much more frigid than average readings suggest. Local slang for this biting winter wind—"the hawk"—captures some of this feeling.
9. For instance, at the time of its construction, the South Side's Robert Taylor Homes featured an extremely sophisticated hydronic radiant floor system comparable to only one other site in the country—the Air Force Academy in Colorado Springs. Heat engineers and firemen who manned several CHA heat plants stressed repeatedly in interviews with me that in their day, the heating systems they operated stood at the vanguard of engineering technologies.
10. These details, as well as those below pertaining specifically to heat operations at Horner, come from archival reports, documents, and blueprints in the Chicago Housing Authority archive's Development Contract Files for Horner Homes and the Extension (CHA n.d.a).
11. An object moving through a network can help identify particular "cultures of circulation," that is, meaningful practices that emerge in conjunction with the flow of objects, ideas, and concepts. However, the everyday significance of such networks cannot be reduced to their objects (Povinelli and Gaonkar 2003). The heat that circulated within the Chicago Housing Authority developments must be situated within a broader system of meanings surrounding the care of citizens in New Deal and post–World War II urban America. With respect to domestic utilities, this era involved much larger-scale infrastructural commitments to the poor than heat provision in Chicago public housing. Consider, for example, the Tennessee Valley Authority, billed as an agency that would generate numerous jobs while also providing electricity to the rural poor.
12. For a discussion of how the circulation of photographs that visualized such conditions influenced arguments for urban renewal in Chicago and beyond, see Benjamin Lorch's treatment of Mildred Mead's domestic interiors (2005).
13. For a description of heat-related injuries common at Horner well into the late 1990s, see McRoberts (1996).
14. With varying degrees of success, the CHA attempted to rein in security problems at Horner during the late 1980s with mandatory ID badges, turnstiles, and the installation of a security station.
15. Such arrangements were not specific to Horner, nor were they limited to Chicago public housing. For a classic anthropological treatment of such networks and their practical and ethical demands, see Stack (1974).
16. For a discussion of such relationships, see Venkatesh (2000).
17. By "politics of recognition," I mean a process by which one group of social actors mobilizes a set of distinguishing indices that another group recognizes as legitimate, and thus worthy of political recognition, as well as any resources it affords (Taylor 1994). I follow others in approaching these indices not as inherent to any one group, but rather as marks achieved within specific historical contexts across social interactions (e.g., Povinelli 2002).

# Bibliography

Appadurai, Arjun. 2002. "Deep Democracy: Urban Governmentality and the Horizon of Politics." *Public Culture* 14, no. 1: 21–47.
Basso, Keith H. 1996. *Wisdom Sits in Places: Landscapes and Language among the Western Apache.* Albuquerque: University of New Mexico Press.
Bourdieu, Pierre. 1977. *Outline of a Theory of Practice.* Cambridge: Cambridge University Press.
Brenner, Neil, and Nik Theodore. 2002. "Cities and Geographies of 'Actually Existing' Neoliberalism." In *Spaces of Neoliberalism: Urban Restructuring in North America and Western Europe,* ed. Neil Brenner and Nik Theodore, 2–32. Malden, MA: Blackwell.
Caldeira, Teresa. 2000. *City of Walls: Crime, Segregation, and Citizenship in São Paulo.* Berkeley: University of California Press.
Cattelino, Jessica. 2006. "Florida Seminole Housing and the Social Meanings of Sovereignty." *Comparative Studies in Society and History* 48(3): 699–726.
Chicago Housing Authority (CHA). n.d.a. Development Contract Files. Chicago Housing Authority Archive, IL 2-19 and IL 2-35.
———. n.d.b [circa 1950]. "Your House, Your Home: Handbook for the Residents of Chicago Housing Authority Apartments." Books and Periodicals, Chicago History Museum Research Center.
Cruickshank, Barbara. 1999. *The Will to Empower: Democratic Citizens and Other Subjects.* Ithaca, NY: Cornell University Press.
Fraser, Nancy, and Linda Gordon. 1994. "A Genealogy of Dependency: Tracing a Keyword of the U.S Welfare State." *Signs: Journal of Women in Culture and Society* 19, no. 21: 309–36.
Goode, Judith, and Jeff Maskovsky. 2001. *The New Poverty Studies: The Ethnography of Power, Politics and Impoverished People in the United States.* New York: New York University Press.
Harvey, David. 2005. *A Brief History of Neoliberalism.* Oxford: Oxford University Press.
Hirsch, Arnold R. 1998. *Making the Second Ghetto: Race and Housing in Chicago 1940–1960.* Chicago: University of Chicago Press.
Hirschkind, Charles. 2006. *The Ethical Soundscape: Cassette Sermons and Islamic Counterpublics.* New York: Columbia University Press.
Holston, James. 1989. *The Modernist City: An Anthropological Critique of Brasília.* Chicago: University of Chicago Press.
Holston, James, and Arjun Appadurai. 1996. "Cities and Citizenship." *Public Culture* 8, no. 2: 187–205.
Hunt, D. Bradford. 2009. *Blueprint for Disaster: The Unraveling of Public Housing in Chicago.* Chicago: University of Chicago Press.
Kamin, Blair. 1999. "Out of Housing into Homes: Architecture of Normalcy Appears to Succeed at Weaving Henry Horner Residents into the Fabric of the City." *Chicago Tribune,* 31 March.
Klinenberg, Eric. 2002. *Heat Wave: A Social Autopsy of Disaster in Chicago.* Chicago: University of Chicago Press.
Kymlicka, William. 1995. *Multicultural Citizenship: A Liberal Theory of Minority Rights.* Oxford: Clarendon Press.

Leitner, Helga, Jamie Peck, and Eric S. Sheppard. 2007. *Contesting Neoliberalism: Urban Frontiers.* New York: Guilford Press.

Leitner, Hega, Eric S. Sheppard, Kristin Sziarto, and Anant Maringanti. 2007. "Contesting Urban Futures: Decentering Neoliberalism." In *Contesting Neoliberalism: Urban Frontiers,* ed. Helga Leitner, Jamie Peck, and Eric S. Sheppard, 1–25. New York: Guilford Press.

Lorch, Benjamin. 2005. "Vertical Reservations: Imagining Urban Blight and Renewal in Chicago." Master's thesis, University of Chicago.

Markell, Patchen. 2003. *Bound by Recognition.* Princeton, NJ: Princeton University Press.

McRoberts, Flynn 1996. "Doctor Cited for Finding Cause Why Many Children Suffer Burns." *Chicago Tribune,* 27 September.

Mink, Gwendolyn. 1998. *Welfare's End.* Ithaca, NY: Cornell University Press.

Munn, Nancy. 2004. "The 'Becoming-Past' of Place: Spacetime and Memory in 19th Century Pre-Civil War New York." *Suomen Anhtropologi: Journal of the Finnish Anthropological Society* 29, no. 1: 2–19.

Povinelli, Elizabeth. 2002. *The Cunning of Recognition: Indigenous Alterities and the Making of Australian Multiculturalism.* Durham, NC: Duke University Press.

Povinelli, Elizabeth, and Dilip Gaonkar. 2003. "Technologies of Public Forms: Circulation, Transfiguration, Recognition." *Public Culture* 15, no. 3: 385–96.

Rose, Nikolas S. 1999. *Powers of Freedom: Reframing Political Thought.* Cambridge: Cambridge University Press.

Schram, Sanford. 2000. *After Welfare: The Culture of Postindustrial Social Policy.* New York: New York University Press.

Seligman, Amanda I. 2005. *Block by Block: Neighborhoods and Social Policy on Chicago's West Side.* Chicago: University of Chicago Press.

Serematkis, Nadia. 1996. "The Memory of the Senses, Part 1: Marks of the Transitory." In *The Senses Still: Perception and Memory as Material Culture in Modernity,* ed. Nadia Serematkis, 1–18. Boulder, CO: Westview Press.

Stack, Carol. 1974. *All Our Kin: Strategies for Survival in a Black Community.* New York: Harper & Row.

Stewart, Kathleen. 1996. *A Space at the Side of the Road: Cultural Poetics in the "Other" America.* Princeton, NJ: Princeton University Press.

Swibel, Charles. 1965. Personal letter to editors of *Chicago Daily News* in response to series on Robert Taylor Homes. *Chicago Daily News* Scrapbooks, Chicago History Museum Research Center.

Taylor, Charles. 1994. "The Politics of Recognition." In *Multiculturalism,* ed. Amy Gutmann, 25–73. Princeton, NJ: Princeton University Press.

Venkatesh, Sudhir. 2000. *American Project: The Rise and Fall of a Modern Ghetto.* Cambridge, MA: Harvard University Press.

Wilen, William. 2005. "Horner as the Model: Successfully Redeveloping Public Housing." *Northwestern Journal of Law and Social Policy* 1, no. 1: 62–95.

CHAPTER 7

# READING BETWEEN THE DIGITAL LINES
## THE POLITICAL RHETORIC OF ETHICAL CONSUMPTION

*Eleftheria J. Lekakis*

■ ■ ■ ■ ■ ■

### CHANGING THE WORLD ONE CUP AT A TIME?

There is a simple story permeating the cause of fair trade and distributed in the global shibboleth: buy a fair trade product and you can ensure that its producer will be paid a fair price for it. The fair trade cause is primarily concerned with the promotion and practice of global trade in light of agendas of humanitarian development, environmental sustainability, and gender equality. Fair trade has become an integral part of ethical consumption[1] across the globe, most notably in the United Kingdom, the particular geography that this chapter explores. Coffee remains one of the most popular ethical commodities. So does this mean that by consuming fair trade coffee, we are changing the world one cup at a time? This chapter outlines an understanding of the transformation of political action through the transformation of the rhetoric and culture that define the historical trajectory of the popular cause of fair trade. What I argue is that the rhetoric of social change has become textured with a rhetoric of promotionalism.

Whether consumption can be a political action has been heavily debated.[2] Yet, the politics of consumption are part and parcel of a toolkit for global social change of which we are constantly reminded in the spaces of the market. As a product in the globalized free market, coffee has involved a network of intermediaries between producers and consumers. Coffee politics have been increasingly interwoven not just with consumer culture, but also with the economics of development and the contentious politics of trade justice. The interplay between these traditions has resulted in the coffee commodity becoming a powerful object for ethical consumerism. As consumer activism has grown more sophisticated since the late twentieth century, this chapter charts a history of interlaced narratives that pose an intricate texture of ethical consumption. At the heights of advanced consumer cultures, the market seems to be offering a "solution" to its business-as-usual model: buy fair trade products and some producers will be paid fairly. By analyzing the narratives of fair trade, I outline the digital rhetoric of mobilization, its variances according to the agencies articulating it, as well as its historical transformations.

This chapter also presents an exploration of different activist voices involved in fair trade. The framing of the cause through their rhetorical practices brings a certain culture into being; the political operation of the fair trade movement mobilizes citizens on the basis of this culture, a culture which that is inherently tied to the complex economics of globalization. At the outset, the trope of culture politicizes the capitalist marketplace through a neoliberal rhetoric of consumption for one's self. Fair trade rhetoric culture has developed narratives, allegories, and metaphors that bolster consideration toward "distant others" by promoting a culture of connection between consumers and producers. By placing human faces along the trade cycle from the field to the shop, fair trade rhetoric creates a certain culture that I explore with regard to its mediation. What is encouraged online is predominantly offline (ethical) consumption; support for the fair trade movement is to be demonstrated through the consumption of fair trade goods. Therefore, the politicization of consumption reshapes the notion of participation by directing it toward the market. There is, then, an interchangeable relationship between the rhetoric and promotional culture of fair trade. What constitutes action in the fair trade cause is evident in a gradual transformation of the rhetoric of participation in fair trade activism ranging from campaigning to consumption.

This chapter identifies the historical alterations in the narrative of fair trade activism in relation to broader changes in its definition and scope. I question the political rhetoric of ethical consumption as informed by specific case studies.[3] The reading and interpretation of this rhetoric is primarily explored through the perceptions and practices of an assorted array of activists. These narratives conveying the cause have been increasingly overtaken by corporate communication, as the logic of promotionalism and branding has permeated the rhetoric of fair trade (Lekakis 2012). While activists' concerns vary in terms of the potential "silencing" of the radical culture of the movement, literature on fair trade has tended to celebrate the sovereignty of consumers in making ethical decisions and breaking unethical corporate practices (Andorfer and Liebe 2012). The tensions inherent in a politics of consumption are located at the heart of the convoluted relationship between fair and free trade. This relationship exists within a broader framework of operations; the market-driven model of fair trade (Nicholls and Opal 2005) fits well with the market-driven politics of the UK (Leys 2001). In the case of fair trade, there appears to be an instant association in the sense of and equation between ethical consumption and political action.

The relationship between rhetoric and action when it comes to fair trade cannot be explicated through a binary perspective of the free market versus fair trade, as fair trade and free trade are deeply textured together. Here, the concept of texture as both noun and verb is employed to illustrate the complexities of a politics of consumption. As a noun, texture is used to define an interwoven material composed of threads that belong to other threads. For instance, when referring to ethical consumption as a political action, the texture of that action would include both a claim to justice and a tool of market participation. As a verb, texture is used to describe the process of incorporating different material to already existing fabrics. For example, the process of making fair trade competitive with free trade has caused a rearticulation of the rhetorical and organizational culture of free trade and its incorporation in the free market. The rhetoric culture of fair trade that manifests through market and political narratives is particularly discernible within the context of the UK (Wild 2004; Lekakis 2013). There is a durable tradition of support for the fair trade market and grassroots politics centered on the official structures of the movement, evident in the establishment and expansion of the Fairtrade Foundation. These structures formulate the common perception of fair trade among British publics.

## Methodological Note

Through an analysis of the digital rhetoric of fair trade in the UK, the particular traits, implications, and interpretations of narratives of participation in this idiosyncratic market and movement (Jaffee 2007) are outlined. An analysis of the mediation of fair trade activism online foregrounds the "power of a communicating text" (McQuail 2002). The term "digital rhetoric" is employed to signify and interrogate the shape and substance of political narratives online. An important aspect of storytelling is that it becomes public in various ways; from posters and leaflets to e-mails and forums, narratives that mediate fair trade activism in particular ways are created, printed, attached, forwarded, or disseminated to a potentially global audience. In order to capture some of the changes on the websites examined, the period of data gathering for this stage of analysis was six months.[4]

The main themes and architectures as well as the social, economic, and political ideologies of the websites were explored through narrative analysis. Drawing from the information available on activists' websites regarding their involvement in the field, I identified and analyzed information pertaining to the self-definition of those actors, as well as information they offer about the fair trade cause. Outlining the digital rhetoric of fair trade would present an incomplete picture if it did not include the readings of and reflections on these narratives and the cultural transformations of fair trade by those who articulate them. The analysis presents both the digital rhetoric of mobilization for action on fair trade, as well as key concerns of activists.

## Kaleidoscopic Narratives: The Digital Consumer and the Political Rhetoric of Fair Trade

In the case of the highly mainstreamed fair trade movement in the UK, digital media burgeon with stories about the cause. Storytelling in activist politics is based on the need for different people to reach a common understanding about what that politics is (cf. Polletta 2006). In fair trade activism, this has resulted in the creation of heterogeneous narratives. These primarily revolve around solidarity and social justice as well as development and lifestyle, corresponding with the splitting of the fair trade movement into "a 'development' strain and a 'solidarity' strain" (Jaffee 2007: 12). The development strain is almost exclusively the business of churches and charity organizations, while the solidarity strain includes politically radical groups. Correspondingly, these two aforementioned types of stories are narrated among fair trade activists. The data from their websites exhibits gradations between the two stories. There is interplay between official and unofficial types of diverse groups and organizations that shape various political roles that the citizen is expected to assume with regard to the issue of coffee trade.

On the whole, the rhetoric culture of fair trade can be summarized in the form of a continuum of narratives within which the variance of fair trade activists resides. On one side, there is the "social justice through solidarity" narrative, aligned with a political rhetoric of participation, while, on the other side of the continuum, there is a "lifestyle through development" narrative, which resonates with a consumer-oriented rhetoric of mobilization. The "social justice through solidarity" story is overtly political and highlights solidarity and social justice as the bases for involvement for both activists and consumers in fair trade activism. Altogether, this story is rooted in a historical political process of support for a cause or against an injustice, and thus highlights the negative aspects of the global coffee trade. For instance, the Nicaragua Solidarity Campaign (NSC) has been campaigning for solidarity with Nicaragua since the late 1980s, and its involvement in fair trade activism directly corresponds to its political work in the region: "We work with organizations and coalitions ... highlighting Nicaragua as an example of the devastating consequence of trade injustice on the majority of the population, and the benefits of fair trade."[5] This is echoed among the websites of small and medium-sized organizations. The Active Distribution Network (ADN), the NSC, the Reading International Solidarity Centre (RISC), and the Trade Justice Movement (TJM) are groups that emphasize such a narrative in their online environments and their offline action. One of the core elements of this type of narrative is support for a specific political cause where fair trade is employed as a tool to convey this type of support: "We have no doubts about the value this coffee plays in supporting the revolutionary struggle both in Mexico and worldwide."[6] Attention to details about the places of production, cooperatives, and political work are emphasized in this story, although this is not necessarily an indicator of this type of story when the element of direct political action is projected: "We are campaigning for trade justice—not free trade—with the rules weighted to benefit poor people and the environment."[7] A question arises here concerning the degree to which activist rhetoric embeds solidarity in their narratives and represents the subjugated; this language denotes keenness on revolutionary struggle, resonating with the struggle of farmers in renegotiating trade relations. Therefore, the rhetoric of solidarity-oriented activists textures the polarities of capitalism by joining the struggles of distant coffee-producing communities in the representational repertoires of organizations.

The role of the consumer in fair trade activism is a crucial element of this narrative. RISC points out the power of the citizen consumer: "By changing our patterns of consumption we can help to change the unsustainable system of world trade which increases inequality, destroys the environment and threatens our future. ... Consumer power can bring about change."[8] Yet, there are alternate reasons as to why consumer power is recurrently advocated. For instance, funding is one of the most significant obstacles for nongovernmental groups and organizations. Oftentimes, the aim of the articulators of such stories is to generate income in order to achieve their political goals. Groups such as NSC and RISC depend on their shops in order to keep on campaigning and promoting solidarity and awareness. Beatrice from RISC suggests that "you could say that fair trade saves us so that we can continue to campaign." This does not mean that fair trade becomes a profit-making tool for aspiring "fair" enterprises, but rather that it can provide a solution for those activists who do not possess the necessary means to set up an organization to campaign for a cause. Therefore, by "capitalizing" on the success of the market side of the movement, smaller groups can promote their presence. RISC is such an example, as they started their fair trade shop in the late 1990s and have within a decade expanded to an organization receiving various forms of funding from UK organizations such as the Department for International Development (DFID) and the Big Lottery Fund of the National Lottery (BIG).[9] Thereby, fair trade remains deeply textured with the free trade marketplace, since the logic that drives activists to survive is one that has to comply with capital accumulation prior to embarking on their journey.

As a movement of eighty groups and organizations, TJM is a slightly different case, as it is explicitly concerned with campaigning for trade justice. Fine (2006) argues that consumer politics mainly addresses the marketplace and its limitations and does not necessarily engage in social or political change. However, the link between active political campaigning and ethical consumption can be seen as the only viable form of consumer politics. This has been a key concern of fair trade activists. As encapsulated in John's (RISC) description, fair trade is "a useful way of mobilizing opinion." The "social justice through solidarity" story line underlines the necessity for a combination of political action and market-based action. Therefore, an interpretation of textured market-based action and political action is regarded as the target when activists are narrating a fair trade story based on justice and solidarity.

On the other hand, "lifestyle through development" communicates a simple and normative story as to what constitutes action in fair trade activism. There is a portrayal of coffee farmers' stories, which keenly makes visual connections between producers and consumers and accentuates the positive effects of fair trade by highlighting its effects on the biographies of individual farmers and their families. It is evident in cases such as Ecocoffee (EC), the Fairtrade Foundation (FTF), and the European Fair Trade Association (EFTA). This type of story is typically bound in official information and adopts an organizational narrative. However, it is also the most popular, as it has extensive reach in supermarkets and is carried through very simple story lines such as "Hatch Yourself a Fairer Easter," "Tell Your Mum You Love Her with Fairtrade Flowers," or "Fairtrade Has All the Ingredients for a Very Merry Christmas." Within this narrative, the mobilized concerned consumer exists within branded "lifestyle politics" (Bennett 2004). In this sense, the narrative is addressed toward the citizen at the consumer level and does not necessarily make the link between politics and consumption. Bennett and colleagues (2007) argue that from the consumer viewpoint, narratives can either be purely consumer-driven at the entry level or involved in social justice at a higher level. The consumer story is the "entry level" into fair trade activism and merely requires the purchase of ethical goods for participation in a wider phenomenon.

The Fairtrade Foundation's website is a good example of how an elaborate story that includes a variety of elements ranging from trade injustice, environmental responsibility, and development to consumer action can be summarized and visualized in a single picture. Two smiling people form one of the most common visual representations of fair trade activism. One of them is male and quite likely a coffee farmer, as he holds a coffee plant, while the other is female, holding a cup of coffee. This image corresponds to the general fair trade concept of bridging the gap between producer and consumer. Here, the smiles on the faces of the people depicted connote the positive effects of the cause. This also suggests a cherished connection between human beings, thus amplifying the rhetoric culture of fair trade as outlined in the introduction of this chapter. In the background, there is a coffee plantation, denoting environmental consciousness, while trade justice is more latent. Consumer action is symbolically summarized in the coffee cup the woman is holding. In other words, action, according to this image, is seen as thriving in the marketplace.

Elaborate storytelling about the effects of fair trade characterizes the "lifestyle/development" story; in contrast with the more action-oriented "solidarity/social justice" version, this type of story tends to publicize research on the personal benefits of fair trade. Activists from the "social justice through solidarity" narrative are deeply concerned with these "lifestyle/development" stories. For instance, Jon (RISC) makes the following point:

> It's easy to get the message that [if] you buy fair trade and these happy families will benefit, they can send their kid to school.... That's a relatively easy message to sell and people buy into that, because it doesn't really hit them in the pocket. But if you're saying that you need to go beyond that, it's a much more difficult message and requires you to spend time at the very least, you know, writing letters to your MP, or … having a much more campaigning role as a consumer, most people just aren't interested.

Once again, storytelling about coffee farmers concludes with the same impression as the picture analyzed above: buy fair trade and you are helping farmers live a better life. This appeals to individuals and personalizes one's sense of political involvement. Furthermore, in terms of finances, organizations engaged with this rhetorical framing of fair trade are more likely to enjoy a more stable financial situation. A clear illustration of this is that FTF has established a secure income from the license fees paid by companies who use the Fairtrade Mark on their products. FTF also receives grant income from governing bodies and organizations such as the European Commission, the DFID, British charities (Oxfam, Comic Relief, Shared Interest Foundation), as well as an organization involved in venture philanthropy (Impetus Trust). Some of these funding relationships are more stable than others. Paradigmatic is the defined-term partnership between Impetus Trust, the co-investor Charities Aid Foundation, and the Fairtrade Foundation. Venture philanthropy borrows concepts and practices from venture capital finance and applies them to organizations campaigning for good causes. In this sense, the market logic of financing is further textured in the logic of fair trade financing.

While it might appear feasible to separate two distinct types of narratives, in reality, the two stories intertwine and hardly exist in their pure form. With the exception of TJM, the organizations portray either more "trade justice through solidarity" elements or more "development through lifestyle" elements. A more grounded way of designating the selected organizational structures in a continuum is depicted in Table 7.1. In this continuum, TJM is on the very left edge, more focused on trade justice than any other aspect of fair trade. ADN follows closely after, as its reason for involvement in fair trade activism is declared to be solidarity with the Zapatista cause, while NSC is next, as it is quite similar in its campaigning for solidarity with Nicaragua. RISC is next, as is FTF; both are somewhere in the middle of the continuum. FTF has a rich "Get Involved" webpage that includes soft types of action (awareness and consumption-oriented activities) for fair trade, but it leans more toward the "development through lifestyle" story. EFTA also tends to project "development" rather than "trade justice," while EC is clearly the most "lifestyle"-oriented.

Table 7.1. A continuum of stories in fair trade activism.

| ← Trade Justice through Solidarity → | | | | ← Development through Lifestyle → | | |
|---|---|---|---|---|---|---|
| TJM | ADN | NSC | RISC | FTF | EFTA | EC |

In conclusion, fair trade activism is either perceived as a side issue, an entry point into causes that are at the heart of activist organizations, or a core issue that prioritizes awareness-raising. As outlined above, in the first case, consumption of ethical commodities is accepted as a mode of finance, while in the second case, it is political action. Large-scale organizations (such as EFTA and TJM) tend to either be quite proactive and in line with a political agenda, or more professional and leaning toward a "development" agenda. There are many groups and small businesses, such as Ecocoffee, that lightly touch upon the injustices behind coffee but heavily focus on ethical consumption as a personal experience of indulgence (Soper 2007). FTF exhibits an intricate story line that includes both narratives. However, because of its organizational culture and the foundation of the consumer label that it is responsible for, it tends to lean toward the "development through lifestyle" narrative. As for the rest of the fair trade activists, all of which are medium-sized organizations, they are mostly found nearer to the solidarity-based narrative. This is why the idea of separate stories is often not useful, whereas the continuum suggested above can be applied to any case. Recognizing the textured narratives further asserts the point that the relationship between consumption and activism cannot be directly identified, and that the correlation of the consumer with politics is strong. Moreover, there are different approaches to the parameters for participation in fair trade activism. The "trade justice through solidarity" story perceives meaningful participation in the movement as a combination of political and consumer action, while the "development through lifestyle" story assumes faith in consumer power and equates ethical consumption with political action.

## *Textured Rhetoric and Promotional Culture: Perceptions of Political Action in Market-Driven Social Change*

In typical urban settings, narratives of coffee attempt to bring out multidimensional aesthetic aspects of the beverage through sensual art, advertising, and the interplay between the two. The chains of coffee shops around the high streets—the main shopping streets—of the United Kingdom cover their walls in opulent black and white or vibrantly colored traditional or modern pictures of coffee beans and coffee drinks. While coffee is promoted in the mainstream market as an experience of the senses, fair trade activists offer more elaborate frames of the act of consuming coffee. These types of stories center on the origin, production, and processing of the product, thus touching upon all stages of its trade chain. However, the sensual consumption of coffee is becoming intrinsically linked with ethical consumption, which is, in its turn, becoming the most common type of action in fair trade activism. This relates to Soper's (2007: 211) notion of the "good life" as a result of the realization that "previously unquestioned forms of gratification such as driving, or air flight, or eating certain foods, or using certain materials are becoming tainted by their side-effects." Extensively, the rhetoric of a commodity-centered lifestyle and the combination of gourmet quality and sustainability ethics has permeated the politics of fair trade activism. While there appear to be two traditions in the rhetorical framing of fair trade, as analyzed previously, the most prevailing type of narrative remains that of the Fairtrade Foundation, the official organization for the certification and licensing of products, support to producers, and awareness raising among the British public. There thus appears to be a distancing from the need to link political action with ethical consumption.

The shift from mobilization of politics to consumption is evident in the digital repertoires of fair trade activism. Furthermore, where it is especially evident is in digital calls for mobilization. There is an abundance of forms of engagement in fair trade activism that range from direct involvement in a borough campaigning group, a local faith group, or a university, to attendance at fair trade events, to ethical consumption. Mobilization concerns a range of actions, from "soft" practices such as awareness and market practices like ethical consumption to "hard" (but less frequently observed) calls for participation in protest politics such as demonstrations and marches. In the websites examined, the majority of online mobilization calls equally concern increasing awareness, volunteering, donations, and participation in events, as well as, crucially, ethical consumption, which follows closely. The types of mobilization practices advocated online appear to suggest both online and offline action. The most widespread calls for action typically concern ethical consumption and participation in fair trade events, such as coffee mornings, bazaars, and fêtes.

The majority of appeals for participation in fair trade activism involve "fun" events, which allow fair trade politics to engage citizens through entertaining activities (cf. Scott and Street 2001; Van Zoonen 2005). The Fairtrade Foundation launched its first public event (Fairtrade Fairground) in 2008, and an interviewee from the organization explains the motivation behind it:

> We wanted it to be fun, because people walk along the South Bank to kind of divert themselves on a Saturday or a Sunday and ... we wanted to have something that would engage people, so it wasn't just straight sampling but there was kind of a variety of things people could do. So that's the Fairground. We wanted people to have fun, so we set a challenge for our NGO [nongovernmental organization] and licensing partners who wanted to book a stall. You have to think of some device that's more interesting than handing people leaflets or samples. (Olivia, FTF)

There is a clear insistence on the accessibility of fair trade through engagement in fair trade events. The Fairtrade Fairground can be regarded as a carnival; Scott and Street suggest that "carnival now appears to have been taken as a paradigmatic model for many recent social movement campaigns" (2001: 42). The Fairtrade Fairground resembles more of a consumer carnival, as mobilization revolves around the promotion of ethical consumption. The poster call for the Fairtrade Fairground as the first big public event in 2008 put forward by the foundation read: "Come and enjoy a traditional helter skelter, tea cup rides, Fairtrade coconut shy and candyfloss using Fairtrade sugar. Visit market stalls, competitions and crafting. Talk to a farmer involved in Fairtrade and visit the Choose Fairtrade Bus before it leaves on its tour of the UK." This call for mobilization places a leisurely dimension at the forefront: helter skelters and tea cup rides are exciting playground-type activities for the entire family, the same as enjoying coconut shy and candyfloss. Market stalls are engaging, competitions are thrilling, and crafting is creative. Talking to a farmer from the global south who participates in the fair trade scheme is a more intense activity and makes it directly evident to the ethical consumer why buying fair trade is important. This suggested interaction between fair trade consumers and producers further illustrates the typicality of the rhetorical culture of fair trade. Visiting the bus is another way of becoming further informed about the cause. These cultural activities do not threaten our comfort zone, but rather invite us to a warm and wholesome environment where we are welcomed to partake in enjoyable activities.

Meanwhile, the political repertoires and targets of fair trade activism appear to be waning. There has been a minimization of the traditional political types of action that are called for, which relates to the major tendencies of the mainstream fair trade movement. The escalating absence of more political events on a macro scale and the presence of more market-type events on a micro scale is an observation that demands more exploration. TJM has been organizing political events such as rallies since 2001. However, since then the calls for action have been decreasing. In 2001, eight thousand trade justice campaigners rallied in London for trade justice at the World Trade Organization. Then, in 2002, over twelve thousand campaigners put trade justice high on the political agenda when they converged on Westminster for "the biggest ever mass lobby of Parliament."[10] In 2005, there was a series of cross-national events during the "global week of action for trade justice" (10–16 April),[11] "with over 25,000 trade justice campaigners descending overnight on Whitehall and Westminster on 15 April."[12] Finally, in 2007, campaigners staged the first ever simultaneous lobby of all European Union embassies during the "Global Day of Action against Europe's Unfair Trade Deals" in London.[13] In parallel to the limited organization of trade justice events, there appear to be increasingly more calls for local fair trade events, such as bazaars and coffee mornings. The rise and frequency of micro level commercial events correspond to arguments concerning the growth of forms of participation, which are increasingly taking place in the market arena in light of the transformation of political participation (Micheletti, Follesdal, and Stolle 2004; Micheletti and McFarland 2011; Stolle and Micheletti, 2013). The increasing equation of political action and ethical consumption is evident in the case of fair trade activism. When it comes to encouraging action, activists tend to prioritize the increase in awareness and the preference for ethically produced and traded goods by providing the relevant structures and calls on their websites.

Moreover, the proliferation of ethical consumption and the gradual processes of mainstreaming fair trade have reconfigured the notion of participation in fair trade activism. Only two fair trade activist groups (ADN and TJM) call for alternative political action; needless to say, these are articulators of the "social justice through solidarity" narrative. The anarchist ADN, infused by a culture of punk and do-it-yourself (DIY), sells fair trade coffee in support of the Zapatista movement; the coffee is produced by autonomous collectives of coffee growers in conjunction with the social and community projects of the

Zapatista Army of National Liberation (EZLN). ADN encourages participation in events in a section of its website titled "DIY, Politics and Action." These types of events include helping at a volunteer-run café, getting involved in the local Infoshop, or participating in gigs or book fairs; these calls are indicative of a deep political commitment, although they are not very closely linked to trade justice activism. As for TJM, which campaigns for exactly that issue, there have been calls for protest marches almost every two years. A reason for this specific frequency was offered by a member of the Fairtrade Foundation:

> Yes, the Trade Justice Movement had big demos and there are still big demos. I think ... you [need to] look politically at where trade negotiations have gone to and the NGOs are saying "What can we do? The trade negotiations have collapsed. What's the point of marching in the streets? We need to be in the corridors of where these deals are negotiated. Let's get in there." But there's nothing to hook on to hardly at the moment. But I'll tell you something; when they call a demo, it's the people that buy the fair trade products who are on those demos. (Olivia, FTF)

The political efficacy of mobilization calls closely tied to entertainment is a sound argument, according to which social action transforms alongside the political needs of societies. However, the fact that social action is currently limited to the realm of the market questions the ability of that action to adapt to a political reality outside the market. For example, the growing replacement of the movement's rhetoric with "fair" rather than "alternative" trade signifies the appropriation of fair trade activism by a more free trade friendly movement. The official structures of the fair trade movement in the UK re-create popular consumer-driven suggestions for involvement in fair trade activism, which provoke action as attendance at fair trade events and as ethical consumption. Actual participation in fair trade events is, in turn, more indicative of consumer-based engagement. As Corner (2007: 669) points out, "politics is conducted as, in part, a business of publicity and mediation, in the broader social and cultural settings of a routine promotionalism." Publicity has become the cornerstone of fair trade rhetoric in the same way that publicity functions as the cornerstone of commodification—both must promote. In fair trade activism, the politics of popular culture come into play at the texturing of consumer culture and political action; in doing so, publicity entwines the motivations for action, but also the activations for personal gladness and participation in the cause. In other words, the emphasis on individual gratification can make dissent fade away. The shift toward individually oriented promotionalism can further the distance between fair trade action and fair trade consumption and is embedded in the history of mainstreaming fair trade activism in the UK.

## Historical Framings of Fair Trade Rhetoric

The evolution of the fair trade market and movement from a niche to the mainstream has been quite spectacular. There are several milestones that can be identified in the success story of fair trade in the mainstream marketplace; these include the agreement of big supermarkets such as Sainsbury's and Tesco's to include fair trade products on their shelves, the massive percentage of awareness of and trust in the fair trade label (Fairtrade Mark) among the British population (96 percent of consumers in the UK are aware of the label and 91 percent of those consumers trust it[14]), and, significantly, the agreement of Starbucks to only sell fair trade espresso-based coffee drinks in the UK. Indeed, Howard Schultz, the founding father of Starbucks, visited London in 26 November 2008 to announce that 100 percent of their espresso-based drinks sold in the United Kingdom and Ireland would become Fairtrade Mark certified by the end of 2009.[15] Prior to this, Starbucks had one space in its menu of "flowery prose" (Holt 2005) for Café Estima, a fair trade blend in the form of freshly brewed coffee. Throughout its history of campaigning, the fair trade movement has grown in significance and impact. However, there have been significant alterations to its activist communication and consumerist promotion that have coincided with its mainstreaming.

One such alteration has been evident in the change in the rhetoric of fair trade. The original term for fair trade was "alternative trade"; this was then changed to the politically milder term "fair trade" (Moore, Gibbon, and Slack 2006). Fair trade has been promoted under this very phrase in an attempt to highlight the positively charged term "fair." Thus, in this type of rhetoric, a political narrative is not directly evident in the mainstream promotion of fair trade. This transformation is a result of the compromises necessitated by mass marketing. While the movement was characterized by the term "alternative," contemporary discourse in the 1990s brought the replacement of this term with the term "fair" in the movement's popular discourse. "Fair" is certainly a politically milder word than "alternative" or "campaign." This change in the narrative is not total. Rob of ADN does not classify the coffee he trades as "fair trade" but "rebel trade" and highlights that "it is actually supporting something that is proactive." This distinction between "rebel trade" and "fair trade" concerns the political charge of the first term as opposed to the politically exhausted term "fair." This perspective is characteristic of the radical politics of fair trade activism that was more evident in the 1980s. This distinction resonates with the pervasive narratives of textured promotionalism; although "rebel trade" is rhetorically more contested than "fair trade," ideologically these claims belong on the topoi of the greater good, where sharing the same vocabulary with the struggles of destitute communities allows activists to proclaim these struggles through their own textured frames.

The rhetorical medium for this texturing is sometimes a distinction between the variances of fair trade activism that interplay in the transformation of the movement in the course of its mainstreaming (Lekakis 2013). The process of mainstreaming fair trade has been aided by the promotional synergy between NGOs and businesses and has been particularly escalated through the consumer label and brand. Before the adoption of the Fairtrade Mark and the macroscopic promotion of fair trade across the UK, the term "campaign coffee" had been used to describe ethically produced and traded coffee during the 1980s.[16] This type of terminology, however, has been disappearing, as the cause has now been streamlined into the brand of "fair trade." The also fading "rebel trade" is an anti-brand that is contested both in terms of rhetoric and structures of trade. Although this is lost in the dominant lifestyle repertoires of the fair trade movement, it in essence offers a contentious representation of the cause that speaks for the subjugated. In contrast, the mainstream brand of "fair trade" does not inject the politicization of the cause into its narrative; it rather highlights and promotes a less contentious form of trade, which exists as a powerful well-meaning alter ego to the free market. It can be argued that "rebel trade" and "campaign coffee" are etymologically synonymous with political support of fair trade activism, while "fair trade" is synchronous to the beat of consumerism with a conscience. The question of whether such transformations have resulted in further and more serious compromises at the core of the movement is often asked (Moore, Gibbon, and Slack 2006).

While "campaign coffee" remains a beverage of choice for a few, "fair trade coffee" reaches a wider caffeine-thirsty audience. In this case, consumer satisfaction and ethical coffee consumption are tantamount. There are seemingly striking differences in product quality between "campaign coffee" and "fair trade coffee." The persistence in emphasizing quality over politics has been understood as another symbolic compromise of the process of mainstreaming fair trade (Raynolds 2009). Campaign coffee has been described by interviewed ethically consuming citizens as being of low quality but perhaps "high politics," whereas fair trade coffee today is of high quality but "low politics" (Lekakis 2013). By the latter I mean that the motivations for consumption are not evident, and neither is further involvement in the political campaigning of the fair trade movement. In this capacity, the shift from niche to mainstream has resulted in the gradual moving away from the radical culture of the movement. This presents an example of how structural changes of fair trade activism have influenced the ways in which people understand and experience fair trade in their daily lives. The infiltration of promotional narratives in fair trade activism has further commercialized the political narratives of consumerism.

## Conclusion: Texture, Rhetoric, and the Politics of Fair Trade

The adjective "fair" has permeated all levels of society, including its political and economic organization, as it has become both institutionalized and imagined. On the level of imagination, there appears to be a commonsensical appeal to fair politics, particularly during and after the financial crisis of the late 2000s (Hutton 2010). On the level of institutionalization, there have been attempts to define trade and commerce on a global scale, evident in the intensification of fair trade initiatives and networks. The imagination of fairness has clear consequences for the politics of ethical consumerism. The rhetoric of mobilization is centered on positive, normative interpretations of what political action means in terms of dealing with trade injustice. The rhetoric framing the issue has been increasingly simplifying political action and directing it to the market. The growing replacement of the rhetoric of "alternative" with that of "fair" trade signifies the commandeering of fair trade by a more free trade friendly movement. The very term "fair" serves to complicate things even further: "fair" lies in the eye of the beholder. For advocates of free trade, fair is free; for advocates of fair trade, fair is fair; for advocates of rebel trade, rebel is fair. The definition of activism poses rhetorical traps in the conceptualization of the nature of activism. Thereby, while these transformations denote the gaining of distance from contentious narratives toward more broadly acceptable framings, the repertoires of fair trade activism need to be cross-examined with the targets of the movement. This is not to suggest that the growth of the movement has not been successful, but rather that the orientation of the movement is based on the following statement: "If Fairtrade didn't deliver commercially, it wouldn't survive. We're not interested in a bit of charity. This is about transformative business models" (Harriet Lamb, cited in Flintoff 2012: 79). The commercial success of fair trade lies in the repackaging of its narratives from more to less contentious ones. At the same time, by adopting and adapting ethical narratives, businesses can promote brands that draw legitimacy from the authenticity of a cause (Boyle 2003; Banet-Weiser, 2012). The rhetoric of branded commodity lifestyle, product quality, and ethics has permeated the politics of fair trade. In the grid of the case studies examined, diverse activists demonstrate diverse positioning with regard to the involvement of powerful economic actors in global social justice. Among those who advocate solidarity trade over fair trade, the infiltration of economic organizations that advocate free trade in the fair trade movement is viewed with more skepticism. There is, therefore, an uneasy relationship between the brand, rhetoric, and the cause of fair trade.

Ethical consumption is promoted through online market structures in some activist websites and throughout fair trade narratives. The most common calls for action typically concern ethical consumption and participation in fair trade events. The increasing absence of more political events on a macro scale and the presence of more market-type events on a micro scale can be related to the mainstreaming of fair trade. There is both apprehension and optimism toward the use of online commercial spaces among the interviewed activists; there are those who view the dominant rhetoric of fair trade as threatening their politics, and there are others who view participation in the marketplace as easily transformed into mass-scale action should the need arise. Two corresponding types of stories narrated by coffee activists can be identified: the "trade justice through solidarity" story and the "development through lifestyle" story. While in the first story ethical consumerism is regarded as essentially complementing political campaigning, in the second story ethical consumerism is seen as empowering and equal to political participation in a mainstream market arena. There is an overwhelming tendency to celebrate ethical consumerism at the expense of further political engagement. A notable increase in ethical consumption has been observed, while a relevant increase in political action has not. The flourishing of the fair trade market and movement seems to be uneven.

Evidently, no binary is able to deal with the variances and intricacies in the case of consumer politics; what we may discern is the usefulness of the concept of texture. There has been a textured culture of fair trade as both a lifestyle consumer choice and a committed political cause, woven by diverse rhetorical devices and practices. Fair trade consumption cannot be completely disregarded as apolitical and a futile consumer act, since the effectiveness of the movement relies on the success of the market. At the same time, it cannot be regarded as a contentious political act, since that would radicalize the market and hinder its mainstream reception. Fair trade consumption is, rather, a textured type of political action that involves a strong market dependency both in rhetorical (narrative) and practical (structural and financial) terms and a strong political claim to justice. This texturing emerges from the rhetorical devices and practices of fair trade activists and follows a series of historical transformations parallel to and depending on the advancement and crisis of neoliberal capitalism.

**Eleftheria J. Lekakis** is a lecturer in global communications at the School of Media, Film, and Music at the University of Sussex. She has been a research fellow at the Centre for the Study of Global Media and Democracy at Goldsmiths College, University of London, and a visiting scholar at the Annenberg School for Communication, University of Pennsylvania. She is the author of the book *Coffee Activism and the Politics of Fair Trade and Ethical Consumption in the Global North: Political Consumerism and Cultural Citizenship* (Palgrave, 2013) and researches contemporary issues at the intersection of promotional culture and everyday politics.

## Notes

1. Here, I use the term "ethical consumption" to encompass all theorizations of politically progressive conscious consumption, inclusive of "ethical" (Barnett et al. 2011) and "radical" (Littler 2009) consumption and "political consumerism" (Micheletti, Follesdal, and Stolle 2004).
2. This debate has recently been captured in Mukherjee and Banet-Weiser's (2012) volume on commodity activism, which, according to the editors, presents a potential case of the transformation of activism into a branded commodity. For the authors, the dismissal of or cynicism about the incorporation or appropriation of activism within a neoliberal or consumerist fold is not viable. Their argument is one that proclaims that understanding a politics of consumption is more important than dismissing it from the outset.
3. Seven case studies account for the bulk of this analysis. These reflect the diversity of the population in terms of localities, scales, and types of actors, and include six groups and organizations based and operating in the UK as well as a transnational organization operating in Europe. These are the Active Distribution Network, the Nicaragua Solidarity Campaign, the Reading International Solidarity Centre, Ecocoffee, the Fairtrade Foundation, the Trade Justice Movement, and the European Fair Trade Association.
4. The data collection period included two significant moments during which information was likely to be updated more frequently: Christmas and the Fairtrade Fortnight. The Christmas period is a considerably commercialized period in advanced consumer economies (cf. Nissenbaum 1997; Waldfogel 2009). The second period covers a fortnight that typically spans February and March and has been celebrated by the Fairtrade Foundation since 1997 as the Fairtrade Fortnight. The events that take place during the fortnight are organized by local fair trade grassroots groups with the aim of promoting awareness of fair trade and are advertised on FTF's website. Events typically organized throughout the Fairtrade Fortnight include coffee mornings, fair trade breakfasts, church events, school events, bazaars, stalls, sales events, fashion shows, art shows, talks, campaigns, craft fairs, and fun days, among others. The period of December–May appear more vibrant than the June–November period, during which there are hardly any events directly connected to fair trade. The complete websites of the case studies were downloaded and processed throughout a period of six months (December 2008–May 2009), during which I monitored the websites on a daily basis and obtained six different snapshots of the webpages of each website on a monthly basis.
5. http://www.nicaraguasc.org.uk/campaigns/index.htm (accessed 10 May 2013).
6. http://www.activedistributionshop.org/shop/content/6-zapatistacoffee (accessed 1 August 2014).
7. http://www.tjm.org.uk/about.shtml (accessed 26 April 2010). By September 2014, TJM had replaced the phrase "we are campaigning for" with "we call for," which is a term textured with a different set of assumptions.
8. http://www.risc.org.uk/ethicalcon.html (accessed 9 April 2013).

9. The Big Lottery Fund (BIG) is a nondepartmental public body sponsored by the Cabinet Office that delivers 40 percent of all funds raised for good causes.
10. http://www.tjm.org.uk/masslobby/index.shtml (accessed 15 April 2010).
11. http://www.tjm.org.uk/wakeup/gwabackground.shtml (accessed 15 April 2010).
12. http://www.tjm.org.uk/wakeup/index.shtml (accessed 15 April 2010).
13. http://www.tjm.org.uk/event2007.shtml (accessed 15 April 2010).
14. http://www.fairtrade.net/fileadmin/user_upload/content/2009/news/releases_statements/2013-09-03_ConsumersFavourFairtrade_Media_release_FairtradeIntl.pdf (accessed 30 May 2015).
15. http://www.fairtrade.org.uk/press_office/press_releases_and_statements/november_2008/starbucks_uk_and_fairtrade_foundation_announce_industry_leading_2.aspx (accessed 30 May 2013).
16. Equal Exchange dates "campaign coffee" back to the late 1970s; "the origins of Equal Exchange stretch back to 1979 when three voluntary workers returned to Edinburgh after working on aid projects in various parts of Africa. Along with a sister organisation in London, Campaign Co-op, they started buying instant coffee from Bukoba on Lake Victoria in Tanzania. As a result, Campaign Coffee was born." See http://www.equalexchange.co.uk/about/index.asp (accessed 30 May 2012).

## Bibliography

Andorfer, Veronika A., and Ulf Liebe. 2012. "Research on Fair Trade Consumption—a Review." *Journal of Business Ethics* 106, no. 4: 415–35.

Banet-Weiser, Sarah. 2012. *Authentic™: The Politics of Ambivalence in a Brand Culture*. New York: New York University Press.

Barnett, Clive, Paul Cloke, Nick Clarke, and Alice Malpass. 2011. *Globalizing Responsibility: The Political Rationalities of Ethical Consumption*. Oxford: Blackwell.

Bennett, W. Lance. 2004. "Branded Political Communication: Lifestyle Politics, Logo Campaigns, and the Rise of Global Citizenship." In *Politics, Products, and Markets: Exploring Political Consumerism Past and Present*, ed. Michelle Micheletti, Andreas Follesdal, and Dietlind Stolle, 101–25. New Brunswick, NJ: Transaction Press.

Bennett, W. Lance, Kirsten Foot, Lea Werbel, and Michael Xenos. 2007. "Strategic Conflicts in Advocacy Networks: How Narrative Frames Shape Relations among U.S. and UK Fair Trade Organizations." Paper presented at the International Communication Association, 24–28 May, San Francisco.

Boyle, David. 2003. *Authenticity: Brands, Fakes and the Lust for Real Life*. London: Harper Perennial.

Corner, John. 2007. "Mediated Politics, Promotional Culture and the Idea of 'Propaganda.'" *Media, Culture & Society* 29, no. 4: 669–77.

Fine, Ben. 2006. "Addressing the Consumer." In *The Making of the Consumer: Knowledge, Power and Identity in the Modern World*, ed. Frank Trentmann, 291–311. Oxford: Berg.

Flintoff, John-Paul. 2012. "When Good Deeds Pay Dividends." *CNBC Business*, January/February.

Holt, Douglas B. 2005. "Brand Hypocrisy at Starbucks." http://poorfarmer.blogspot.co.uk/2006/11/brand-hypocrisy-at-starbucks.html. (accessed 1 June 2015)

Hutton, Will. 2010. *Them And Us: Changing Britain - Why We Need a Fair Society*. London: Little, Brown.

Jaffee, Daniel. 2007. *Brewing Justice: Fair Trade Coffee, Sustainability, and Survival*. Berkeley: University of California Press.

Lekakis, Eleftheria J. 2012. "Will the Fair Trade Revolution Be Marketised? Commodification, Decommodification and the Political Intensity of Consumer Politics." *Culture and Organization* 18, no. 5: 345–58.

———. 2013. *Coffee Activism and the Politics of Fair Trade and Ethical Consumption in the Global North: Political Consumerism and Cultural Citizenship*. Basingstoke, UK: Palgrave Macmillan.

Leys, Colin. 2001. *Market-Driven Politics: Neoliberal Democracy and the Public Interest*. London: Verso.

Littler, Jo. 2009. *Radical Consumption: Shopping for Change in Contemporary Culture*. Berkshire, UK: Open University Press.

McQuail, Denis, ed. 2002. *McQuail's Reader in Mass Communication Theory*. London: Sage.

Micheletti, Michele, Andreas Follesdal, and Dietlind Stolle, eds. 2004. *Politics, Products, and Markets: Exploring Political Consumerism Past and Present*. New Brunswick, NJ: Transaction Press.

Micheletti, Michelle, and Andrew McFarland, eds. 2011. *Creative Participation: Responsibility Taking in the Political World*. Colorado: Paradigm.

Moore, Geoff, Jane Gibbon, and Richard Slack. 2006. "The Mainstreaming of Fair Trade: A Macromarketing Perspective." *Journal of Strategic Marketing* 14, no. 4: 329–52.

Mukherjee, Roopali, and Sarah Banet-Weiser, eds. 2012. *Commodity Activism: Cultural Resistance in Neoliberal Times*. New York: New York University Press.

Nicholls, Alex, and Charlotte Opal. 2005. *Fair Trade: Market-Driven Ethical Consumption*. London: Sage.

Nissenbaum, Stephen. 1997. *The Battle for Christmas: A Cultural History of America's Most Cherished Holiday*. New York: Knopf.

Polletta, Francesca. 2006. *It Was Like a Fever: Storytelling in Protest and Politics*. Chicago: University of Chicago Press.

Raynolds, Laura T. 2009. "Mainstreaming Fair Trade Coffee: From Partnership to Traceability." *World Development* 37, no. 6: 1083–93.

Scott, Alan, and John Street. 2001. "From Media Politics to E-protest? The Use of Popular Culture and New Media in Parties and Social Movements." In *Culture and Politics in the Information Age: A New Politics?*, ed. Frank. Webster, 32–51. London: Routledge.

Soper, Kate. 2007. "Re-thinking the 'Good Life': The Citizenship Dimension of Consumer Disaffection with Consumerism." *Journal of Consumer Culture* 7, no. 2: 205–29.

Stolle, D. and Micheletti, M. (2013) *Political Consumerism Global Responsibility in Action*, Cambridge: Cambridge University Press.

Van Zoonen, Liesbeth. 2005. *Entertaining the Citizen: When Politics and Popular Culture Converge*. New York: Rowman and Littlefield.

Waldfogel, Joel. 2009. *Scroogenomics: Why You Shouldn't Buy Presents for the Holidays*. Princeton, NJ: Princeton University Press.

Wild, Anthony. 2004. *Black Gold: A Dark History of Coffee*. London: Harper Perennial.

CHAPTER 8

# The Uncertainty of Power and the Certainty of Irony
## Encountering the State in Kara, Southern Ethiopia

*Felix Girke*

■ ■ ■ ■ ■ ■

> Irony and humour preserve a potential for social criticism, because they reinforce the scepticism that makes us see everything as less divine and more human. Therefore there is no enduring evil and all empires must fall.
> —Gabriel Torres, *The Force of Irony*

More than a century after the troops of Emperor Menelik descended from the Abyssinian highlands in his conquest of the southern marches of what is today Ethiopia,[1] the incomplete integration of the inhabitants of the south (and east, and west) has remained a thorn in the flesh of nation building. The divide between the dominant "highlanders" and the subordinate "lowlanders" still has political, economic, and ideological weight. Areas such as the South Omo region constitute "tribal zones" (Ferguson and Whitehead 2000), sporting a patchwork of small to minuscule territorially bounded populations (figure 8.1), often not entirely pacified and little integrated into civil society or transformed by development efforts ("capacity building" in the local diction), and not coincidentally well-loved by tourists. Within the African colonial exception that is Ethiopia, the conquered south has never been decolonialized.

Research among the Kara (pop. 1,400) has shown that they routinely conflate "state," "government," and "the highlanders": these are the Other, by categorical definition, and this felt difference is often acted out both internally and in the encounter with highlander representatives, but less in terms of submis-

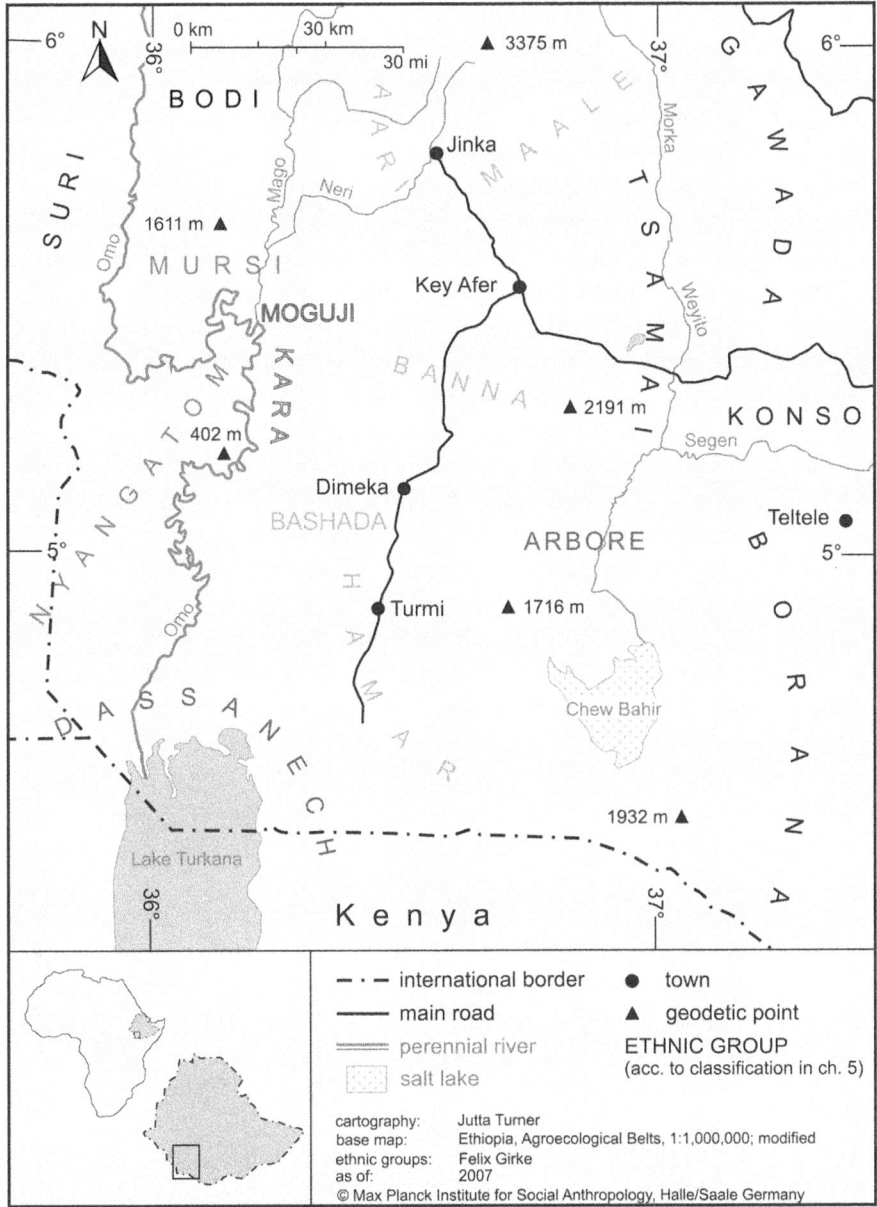

Figure 8.1. Local populations in South Omo.

sion or resistance than in gentle mockery and ironic reversals. Thus, the Kara reciprocate the "view from above," the long-standing attempts to define them as marginal and uncouth, by in turn applying their own definition of the situation. Data collected from 2003 to 2008 reveals the degree of reflection among the actors involved in this encounter, who are skeptical of official claims that they see as illegitimate impositions on their autonomy, or, in the case of development driven by modernist optimism, as implausible hyperbole: too many promises of a bright future, fueled by high modern narratives of progress, have gone unfulfilled; too often has the gap between the rhetoric of civil society and the extant discriminatory hegemony not been bridged.

I argue that the incongruence of the situation is not lost on the participants: they are aware—at some level—that they are often enough enacting an ancient, repetitive, and global play, with its dramatic, situational, and verbal ironies. Center stage is awarded to the question of power: while the Ethiopian government certainly claims dominion over the remote South Omo region, and has (by right of imperial conquest, no less) a historical claim to rule, there is little hands-on governing going on, and material representations of central state power are equally lacking. As a result, the political culture under consideration is stunted and formalized, and yet at times humorous and flamboyant: this very encounter, between the awkward official, eager to get back to the city, and the confident Kara, on their home turf, serves to illustrate the uncertainty of power at the periphery of empire. That this situation is rather abruptly changing today does not invalidate an analysis of the status quo maintained for so long, but rather underlines the importance of looking clearly at the textures of the political encounter, as they reveal relevant values, cultivated practices, and even long-term strategies.

## Ethiopian History, Geography, and Culture

> The history of humanity in the last few thousand years has been a history of expansion and conquest. The centrally organized societies have absorbed others that did not have sufficient means of defense and that were not organized hierarchically, equipped with armies, infrastructure, and centralized resource management.
> —Peter Skalnik, "Outwitting the State"

The particularities of how the Ethiopian empire incorporated the surrounding lowlands have been discussed elsewhere (for critical views, see Holcomb and Ibssa 1990; Strecker 1994); here, I only wish to highlight the bare necessities in terms of history, geography, and culture needed to make sense of what is to follow.

Ethiopia has always been governed from the highlands, in the north and center of today's national territory: it is there that the great kingdoms, petty princes, and upstart pretenders wrestled for supremacy. The periphery has always been the imaginary land of the savages, the uncultivated, barbarian frontier—as such, this was where the Amhara, who long were the dominant group, could first raid for grain, livestock, and slaves, and to where at a later time the consolidated Ethiopian empire could expand its influence and, still later, colonialize: "The Ethiopian empire was formed during the same period that the British and French African empires were, and with many of the same means: through a series of conquests, some of them quite brutal. … Following the conquest came domination of the new subjects by an alien and exploitative elite, who through the first half-century, at least, took whatever of value they could and gave virtually nothing in return" (Lewis 1993: 160–61). It is not surprising that many of the groups on the edge of empire still maintain their narratives of trauma and grievance (e.g., Naty 2002). One of the central concepts from this historical dynamic that survives into today's Ethiopia is the polar and highly stereotyped dichotomy between the Habesha, the civilized, (Orthodox) Christian, "red" (from their somewhat lighter skin) highlanders, and the Shankilla, the illiterate, pagan, "black" potential slaves, much maligned and little respected. The claims to Ethiopian nationhood ("Greater Ethiopia"), the attempts to legitimize the existence of this political structure, as well as the demands on all inhabitants to subscribe to this idea are confronted with this dark history, and there seem to be very few interests that the "elites" in the upland regions of Amhara or Tigre (Tigray) and the descendants of the subjugated peoples of the south (or west, or east) genuinely have in common.

The ecological conditions in Ethiopia allowed for the emergence of a pattern that presents a total reverse to what the political scientist James Scott has recently propagated for Southeast Asia: there, the political and economic centers were in the lowlands, and ever tried to expand upward, to subjugate and integrate the so-called hill tribes found all over the region. All centralization was made possible by paddy rice cultivation, and (to simplify things) groups that sought to evade control simply had to flee to higher altitudes, where they were too difficult to pursue for the longest time, as the center could never adapt to gain permanent footholds in the hills (Scott 2009). In Ethiopia, instead, to escape imperial control (or any other attempts at centralization) meant to move downhill, away from the high plateaus so very useful for grain agriculture and into the inhospitable savannahs, the desert, marsh, and swamp regions. It is no surprise either that many of these groups still today resort to pastoralism or swidden cultivation, both forms of subsistence production qualifying as "escape" practices (see Strecker 1976 on the Hamar example)—if one is encroached upon too severely, usually the opportunity costs for just picking up and leaving for elsewhere are low.

Lacking historical sources, one can only surmise how the polity known today as Kara emerged during the eighteenth, nineteenth, and twentieth centuries (and I have done so elsewhere; see Girke 2011; cf. Bassi 2011); here, it is relevant to know that the Kara represent a pioneering spearhead of a larger Omotic-speaking population that has been thrust downhill and west from the Hamar hill range.[2] The Kara came to occupy a highly beneficial ecological niche, a stretch along the perennial Omo River that is heavily inundated by the yearly floods and fertilized through deposits of silt. These conditions allow flood-retreat agriculture of high productivity (Matsuda 1996), just as they (due to the unpredictable flooding involved) prohibit industrial irrigation. Even though certainly vulnerable to freak meteorological events, the Kara by and large can sustain themselves by a little over half a year of work: the Omo River starts receding in August, exposing its inundated banks, which are eminently suited for sorghum and maize, along with some side crops such as beans. Many Kara also maintain herds of small stock, which play a minor role in subsistence. There is a distinct lack of central leadership among the Kara, who by and large oscillate between anarchic individualism, stubborn factionalism, and at times surprising political unity. Much value is placed on accountability, enterprise, cleverness, watchfulness, endurance, and eloquence, all traits that are directly helpful in the standard economic tasks (herding, agriculture), in surviving as a small group among much larger polities, and in the highly communal face-to-face village life (Girke 2008, 2011). In terms of Scott's approach, they have (intentionally or not) adopted social structures that are particularly intractable to direct or even indirect rule.

Not surprisingly, the Kara's economic practices count as backward in Ethiopia, and the fact that there are considerable numbers of people at the edge of empire still practicing subsistence production is an embarrassment to the highland centers, as well as annoying, as no taxable surplus is produced. While the lands of the periphery are in general assumed to be disease-ridden and full of dangerous wildlife, the Lower Omo has always been especially malaria-prone and hot—all in all rather illegible for bureaucracies and difficult to govern for the succession of state bodies from Menelik until today.[3] While there are numerous haphazard attempts to mainstream local culture(s), a policy often called Amharization, which centrally includes stimulating Christianization (whether Orthodox or some kind of Protestant), the Amharic language, peasant ethics, and an adherence to the state, there is little reason for people at the periphery to feel gratitude to their state and to develop a sense of belonging to the Ethiopian nation. Responses to such moves toward integration vary—from defiant attempts to maintain autonomy to enlightened self-interest in exploiting the state-offered opportunities of education and development. Many southerners know well that it will never be easy to become accepted members of civil society, and to tangibly profit from modernization, capacity building, and the grand Millennium Development Goals of the United Nations (Epple and Thubauville 2012).

The defining feature of the arrangement up until very recently was that it simply did not pay for the Ethiopian state to assert itself: "complete control" would not have "produce[d] results justifying the costs" (Claessen 1989: vii). The Omo Valley is peripheral—taking the Kara as an extreme case, it is not on the way to anywhere; it is seasonally inaccessible, inhospitable, and lacking in the most basic infrastructure such as sanitation, electricity, and so forth. It also appears unsafe: adult males and even adolescents commonly carry assault rifles wherever they go to protect their herds. There is no permanent police presence, and many affairs that would count as criminal matters are regulated locally (see Girke 2011), as the Kara find themselves left to their own devices most of the time. Obviously, lacking material incentive, the determination of states to actually govern hands-on every place they are supposed to or claim to cannot be taken for granted.[4] Hence, the power relations between state representatives and members of encapsulated polities at the margins of the state are not always clear. This lack of determination in governance creates spaces to be creatively appropriated, and in the case of the Kara, it has over the last decades led to the emergence of a very specific, richly textured political relationship between the local (and somewhat immobile) inhabitants and the encompassing colonial state.

Rather than simply "resisting" the state, many Kara put their massive experience in public speaking and in manipulating social relations to work to shape the encounter between them and the state according to their own ideas. People in general aim to be free from imposition; while the Kara know they probably could not make the state leave them alone forever, they have found, at the very least, some options for turning the relation into something more bearable and entertaining. In Skalnik's terms, one might say they are engaged in "outwitting the state" by "applying strikingly different models of 'power'" (1989: 3); and while this is view is acceptable, I will argue for a different terminology below. Still, the question of power remains central, not just for the analyst, but for the participants in the encounter themselves. The relation between them, which combines colonial features with assertions of equality and citizenship as issued by a modern state, is fundamentally incongruous, I argue, as claims and visible social facts diverge in a rather pointedly obvious way. This incongruity is enhanced by the fact that not even the defining feature of the Weberian state, the monopoly on violence, is being enforced in South Omo. Accordingly, the matter of domination and subordination is far from resolved, and much interaction between the Kara and the Habesha is marked by constant negotiations of power, specifically the power to define.

## Textures of Encounter

I experienced, or rather felt, the texture of the encounter between the Kara and state representatives largely during events that were known by the term *gubai*, from the Amharic *gubaye*—assemblies. One could distinguish between meetings in the market towns and meetings in people's home villages, as the contents and style of the debates varied somewhat, but this is not a central point in the argument. In all cases, meetings were headed by members of the district (*woreda*) administration, often in direct cooperation with nongovernmental organization (NGO) personnel. Town meetings often as not were aimed at members of several of the local polities, especially in the case of tribal warfare or larger development interventions. For such meetings outside Kara country, it has been common over the last years for cars to be sent to the villages to collect a set number of elders, and some token women. Often, per diems are paid. There are some people who always seem to be at meetings, and a look at a list of delegates reveals much about recent social dynamics in Kara. The material setup is also telling: usually, the conveners will be placed at some sort of table, while the attending Shankilla will be sitting on their small stools/headrests or on school benches, more or less looking up to the chairmen and minute takers. The procedural rules are familiar to all participants: the officials first hold forth about the purpose of the meeting and about current events, and then basically spell out what they want the outcome of the joint debate to be. Then, elders are called up to give a speech and express their group's hopes, expectations, worries, and concerns, but also to justify recent conduct. These speeches, in the respective vernaculars, are constantly interrupted for translation into Amharic or any other languages required.

The topics of the meetings range from peacemaking over health and education to rangeland management and wildlife protection. Note that the structure of such meetings presumes that the Kara delegates can and do represent "the Kara," a fundamentally problematic assumption: the delegates are better seen as emissaries allowed to speak their own mind, but who can in no way commit "the Kara" to a given course of action. But even where there is nothing they can decide, the Shankilla who have been called to a meeting can hardly afford to ignore the summons, for fear of being stigmatized as uncooperative by the conveners, along with their entire community. They also know from experience that it is often detrimental to one's position to speak too frankly: either one is branded a liar or accused of being contentious. A confrontational stance should in general be avoided; righteous indignation works better.

When attending *gubai*, it becomes painfully obvious that it is not only the Shankilla who are under a lot of constraints: the administrators who run the meetings have usually been sent on these errands by their higher-ups, closer to the center, and strive at all cost to avoid having to report bad news, unresolved complaints, or fresh worries. The hierarchies involved extend invisibly far beyond the storehouses, schoolrooms, or shade trees where the meetings are commonly held, and it is apparent that the local (or at best regional) officials simply do not have the capacity for resolving major issues, much less to enforce a verdict at that scale. This is why in several meetings that I attended, the Habesha conveners stated explicitly that "we do not want to talk about the grievances of the past today, just about what we can do to avoid such problems in the future." The only option that is reliably available to them is to stall voiced grievances in an attempt to wear down the petitioners. People are quite aware that for many meetings it is rather likely that whatever is being debated will never be implemented, or that its eventual implementation will be wholly independent of whatever was debated. The Kara have learned not to invest too much stock in delayed gratification, and recognize the nature of such events well: *gubai* meetings are mostly epiphenomenal effects of processes taking place elsewhere, and not so much goal-oriented projects in themselves. Ripples of a splash far away, it is unsurprising that the meetings rarely have well-defined outcomes. As a result, personal style comes to hold the audience's attention better than substance, so to speak. In Robert Hariman's terms, "political experience, skill, and result often involve conventions of persuasive composition that depend on aesthetic reactions" (1995: 3). If they feel they cannot achieve tangible results in a meeting, speakers see it as a priority to leave an impression, either by behaving exactly as they are supposed to, or by subverting the occasion through multivocal talk. Rhetorically, this comes out in the pattern that statements aiming to persuade, to be Habermasian "superior arguments" to the question under discussion, are complemented by sophistry in the negative sense, by phatic jokes and aggressive provocations, intended to unsettle the competition, with speakers scoring points either against some specific (if absent) opponent or by untargeted displays of cleverness and wittiness. Additionally, as if mentally marking off well-memorized boxes, a Shankilla speaker to an at least part Habesha audience will often try to hit certain buzzwords, commonplaces that elicit satisfied nods and encouraging scribbles of pencils on paper. Consider these examples, nearly inevitably uttered at peace conferences:

- "Do we have one father, or two?" (The reference is to the government, which through its administration is seen to act biased and unfairly, even though it claims not to.)
- "We should marry one another, and then we shall have peace!" (While anthropologically threadbare, this is a standard element in conflict analysis.)

- "We took the words from the last meeting and brought them home, telling everybody what had been decided. But they, they did nothing of the sort, and this is why the trouble started again!" (Officials are aware, to a degree, of the problems of delegation, authority, and dissemination of information; to proclaim one's efforts in this regard indicates that it is the others who have invalidated the results of previous meetings, wasting everybody's time.)

Other such modular utterances could be listed. These phrases are remarkable in that each reflects some official values that are eternally propagated by the Habesha representing the state in any interaction with the Shankilla: equality and citizenship, solidarity and cooperation, and accountability and responsibility. It is not far-fetched to assume that the speakers who use these arguments are aware from whence they came, and while I cannot say for certain that this "echoic" function[5] is always at the forefront of people's minds, the predictable manner in which these statements are uttered is striking.

It is not surprising that this situation has given rise to its very own speech genre, with its own commonplaces, such as the ones above, its own metaphors, and its own presenting style—a feature of which has become to speak in thirty-second increments, and then wait for the translators to catch up, all the while holding the latest pose. There is a specific aesthetic to these meetings, which some people cannot stomach at all and some seem to cherish, well evidenced by the energy they invest in these social performances for little tangible gain.

Beyond the aforementioned commonplaces, what is also repetitive are the concrete interventions connected to such meetings. I myself have—over the years—born witness as NGO staff members or administrators have loudly proclaimed a "new way" of doing things, which in fact had been announced quite similarly the year before. The center also reveals itself as unreliable: one year, there are funds to pay villagers to start cutting a road through the bush; the next year, the dedicated funds are exhausted and the road is not maintained and quickly deteriorates (also contributing to soil erosion, alas!); another year, a water pump is brought to set up a small irrigation site, then the fuel runs out or the pump malfunctions, and nothing is done to fix it. A schoolhouse is built, and with great ceremony inaugurated—but soon, despite stringent admonishment to all families to send their children (especially girls) to school, it becomes apparent that the teachers are unmotivated, that materials are lacking, and that nobody feels responsible to maintain even the building.[6] The high rotation among personnel sent to the periphery—Schlee's "ever-new officials" (1989: 399)—as well as the systemic and seemingly cyclical emphases in NGO work contribute to the effect that again and again, people seeking to develop (or pacify) the Lower Omo start from scratch—as if they were truly involved in a first contact situation and were dealing with actual savages, inexperienced in the ways of bureaucracy and progress. Of course, they are not, and awareness of this is the lever needed to dislodge any assumptions (or pretensions) that the power imbalance is as clear-cut as the administrators, after all representing the mighty center, would proclaim.

One of the most problematic Kara practices, infanticide for ritual reasons, is another issue that is again and again tackled by various governmental or NGO intervention programs. But even as each attempt starts afresh—specifically, the personnel involved being unaware of any intervention even from the last year—one of the few things that the historical record about Kara-Habesha relations reveals is that this debate has been going on for over one hundred years: the hunter and traveler Stigand ([1910] 1969) reports that even at the time of his journey "To Abyssinia through an Unknown Land" in 1908/9, the local garrison was urging the Kara to abandon this custom. All these very material instances of repetitive rather than cumulative attempts at development are rather incongruous when one considers the earnestness with which each "innovation" is announced during the meetings. It is this dynamic that has strongly shaped what the Kara expect from the state to which they so haphazardly belong.

*Gubai,* then, have come to be one of the most important performative sites of Kara-Habesha interaction. They always embody the key feature of the relation between the peripheral lowlanders and the highlanders: a display of power imbalance, already visible in the material setup, well manifested in the procedural order, and constantly implied by verbal acts. At the same time, the lack of correspondence between claim and implementation paints a very different picture: the administrators are far from home, seriously understaffed, uninformed, badly equipped, unable to understand the Kara if the latter use their own language; they are uncomfortable, sweaty, worried about mosquitos every minute of their stay in Kara; and they are faced with these lean, well-armed men (many of whom wear—with varying degrees of pride—the marks of a killer) who, especially on their home turf, cut an imposing image.

## Peripheral Wisdom and Irony

In this imperial encounter, both sides engage in mutual face-saving practices, allowing pretensions of the respective Other to stand, even as they are mutually contradictory and at cross-purposes. This tension, that hapless and often frustrated individuals need to embody the state while not controlling the resources to enforce anything, and that their locally formidable counterparts should be docile but are elusive and unruly, as if they were in control of the situation, is resolved by tacit collusion, and challenges are rarely met head-on. There is little outright hostility when administrators announce hardly applicable policy or make far-fetched requests—instead, like Rortyan ironists, the Kara engage in this encounter at the edge of the state with both outrageous dismissiveness of the imperial claim and the "final vocabularies" that are the narratives of development and nationalism, and yet a certain gentle solidarity with the individual administrator, who—as they realize in their "peripheral wisdom" (Fernandez 2000)—is in his own perspective just as marginalized as they are. My data, mostly drawn from public debates and informal conversations, illuminate a situation in time and space where the haplessness of the imperial agent in the face of recalcitrance and shiftiness at the periphery has not led to radicalization or violence from one side or the other. "Resistance" is not an apt characterization. Instead, these inequalities in power, or, which is more accurate for the Kara case, these unresolved, antagonistic claims to power, provide a fertile ground for irony. Where such incongruous languages of claims as entailed by the Habesha-Shankilla opposition are involved, it is unsurprising when either or both sides take recourse to irony to better bear the contradictions and tensions of the extended situation (cf. Capurro 1990 on Schlegel; Hutcheon 1994: 7 on Canada). The essence of irony, in Kenneth Burke's words, lies just in such awareness that "the greater the *absolutism* of the statements, the greater the *subjectivity* and *relativity* in the position of the agent making the statements" (1945: 512; emphasis in original)—and what is more absolute than the narratives of progress and statehood? To embrace their own relativity and contingency frees actors from (self-)imposed constraints, especially from having to believe their own basic lies. In this, irony is "possibly the most powerful trope" (Friedrich 1989: 305).

As has been argued by James Fernandez, and as is well familiar to anthropologists who often seem to find "marginal men" as main informants, the view from the periphery may be much clearer than the one from the center, what with its pretensions and entanglements. The present case supports this by emphasizing that the Kara have all attended numerous such meetings, year after year after year, while the officials at each meeting are so often new to their job and unaware of the history of the encounter and the resulting genre. Lending political speech an ironic texture presents a safe haven in this constellation, and while its "edge" (Linda Hutcheon's metaphor) does cut, it opens no wounds: it just cuts the strings that would otherwise make the participants dance across the stage, simple enactors of the lifeless play of master and slave. As it is, it helps both sides deal with the fundamental uncertainty of who has power over whom, as it allows postponing a resolution of contesting claims, which would likely involve violence, the ultimate determinant. In a resonant discussion of structural violence, David Graeber speaks of the "imaginative wall" (2007: 405–6), the autopersuasive way in which the powerful prevent themselves from identifying with their subordinates. "Structural violence always seems to create extremely lopsided structures of imagination.... The victims of structural violence invariably end up spending a lot of time imagining what it is like for those who benefit from it; the opposite rarely occurs" (Graeber 2007: 405). For my case, I suggest that the barrage of more or less gentle mockery from the Kara can at times breach or simply cross the imaginative wall, leading officials to relativize their own positions and presumptions of superiority. An example illustrates this.

A young official of the Hamar *woreda*, the administrative district to which the Kara belong, arrived in Dus (the main village) on 1 February 2007 and had the elders and some select women assemble. He had come to bring some news about recent policy, and to assess the local moods and attitudes. The policy news, it turned out, came not from the district administration only, but from the all over Ethiopia customarily conflated chimera of government and ruling party (EPRDF), simply known as *mengist,* or "government." At some point, the meeting turned into an admonishment to order, civility, and loyalty. The visitor sternly inquired whether anybody had been criticizing the EPRDF government, colloquially known as Ihaddik in Ethiopia: "And when you heard somebody speak badly of the Ihaddik, and when you heard him praise the Derg government [the old junta that ruled the country from 1974 until 1991], did you call him to order and show him the right way again?" In reaction, a Kara elder (whom I will call Gui-Imba throughout this chapter, the father of Gui) languorously got up from his little stool and announced with considered gestures and a firm voice: "No, no, we don't have anything of that sort here in our land. Such problems only exist up there in the mountains. When the Ihaddik came into power, we all welcomed it." That was all; Gui-Imba sat down again. The official nodded somewhat grimly, did not reply, and proceeded with the meeting.

This tiniest of snippets reveals much. As a first layer, Gui-Imba displays some astute cleverness in the self-assured and well-chosen reply that rendered the official speechless: he asserted the closed ranks of the Kara to this outsider, who had hoped to find (and presumably exploit, or even aggravate) latent factionalism. The reversal in the situation achieved by Gui-Imba is obvious. The visitor, attempting to speak from authority, ended up confounded. His charge that some of the Kara, backward Shankilla to him, were harboring dissident thoughts was turned right back not at him personally, but at the imperial center he represented and that had sent him forth. The Kara know that the main opposition to the current government and to the ruling party comes from other groups that are also Habesha, groups that belong to the distant center as well. They also know that they themselves by a huge majority did in fact vote for the EPRDF in the last election. Even though in other places there had been accounts of rigged ballots and the like, most Kara do appreciate that despite all its shortcomings, the current administration has done more for them than any other before. There is also a more basic message here, about the nature of Kara and Habesha sociality: while Kara often engage in internal factionalism, theirs is a face-to-face community, in which authority always needs to be earned; here, consensus rather than conflict mark the political process.

In effect, Gui-Imba, when giving his reply, revealed the duplicity of the official paternalistic discourse: "Before you go and try to shame us, or try to divide us, look, it's your own house that is divided." This is what I understood him as saying, and the official could hardly escape considering this interpretation as well. He did not have an answer to that, so he passed on this chance to turn the tables again and, in the way the game is played, had to concede the point. As Bailey has stated, this sort of "[c]ombative irony challenges the victims to look at what is being done to them and to acknowledge that they are helpless.... To challenge ironic mockery with anything but a counterirony is exactly that—an admission of defeat" (2003: 167). Likely, in the official's admonishment he had simply reproduced what he (and countless other officials just like him) had been trained to say on visits to the outlying districts. Instead of being accorded sincere deference, though, he had been shown in no unclear terms that the Kara were not willing to let the administration maneuver them into the receiving end of a conversation on morality (cf. Abbink 2006: 162–63).

The Kara, in terms of my methodology, were able to define the situation through the reply by Gui-Imba so that their loyalty became quite unassailable. They rejected the insinuations with which the official's question had been so ripe, and imposed some of their own on the visitor, which he could not refute: they were uncomfortable truths in the face of his "saving lie" (Bailey 2003), the God-given and seemingly evident superiority of the Habesha over the Shankilla. Already here the similarity of Gui-Imba's action to the self-deprecating ways of Socratic irony can be noted: Socrates too underplayed his perspicacity in order to let his interlocutors deconstruct their erroneous discursive positions themselves. If we follow Lambek's contention that "[w]e think of irony as a stance that gives ambiguity, perspective, plurality, contradiction, and uncertainty their due" (2004: 3), it is quite apparent how Gui-Imba's statement is fruitfully understood as ironic.[7] While we cannot know what he thought, we do know that he is a competent elder well-versed in oratory, and must have fine control over the space he left for ambiguity in interpretation. While definitions of irony that hold water when applied outside formal speech situations are hard to come by, this would fit most of those that are on offer.[8] Of course, to call some instance of behavior "irony" does not explain it. But to recognize the aspect of irony provides a richer context for the interpretation of the corresponding sequences of behavior (Torres 1997: 21). To diagnose such behavior as ironic is an attempt to do justice to the ambiguity of actions, rather than eliminating it from the ethnographic record, or trying to flush out the "real meaning" behind some hidden transcript, to use James Scott's terminology (1990). Linda Hutcheon's (2004) cogent suggestion that irony comes into being less through a speaker's intention and more through a hearer's internal unfolding of a statement provides the methodological argument. This is in line with a general audience-centered approach to the analysis of interaction, and with other inferential models of communication (Sperber and Wilson 1995: 24; see also Strecker 1988). A speaker might try to mark their stance as ironic, but we can never be certain that our interpretation matches their intention. What we do know is that we find ourselves seduced by suspicion, turning a statement over in our heads, unfolding it, looking for the "unsaid" behind the "said." The ironic effect occurs not when we unveil "what somebody really means," but emerges in our mental oscillation between what is said and what remains unsaid.

The young official, then, might have understood the elder Gui-Imba to be telling him something along these lines: "Come on, what do you expect? We will play your little games as far as necessary, but spare us these silly inquiries that we would never answer truthfully anyway. And you could not make us either. You know that, really; you poor guy, they sent you here and made you ask such pointless questions. Now, I have provided you with a straight (if barbed) answer that you can take home to your superiors who know even less of us than you do." Writing this in such a linear form, making legible what was wholly intended to remain illegible, imposes order and structure where there are only inchoate hints, allusions, and evocation, and the offered translation above should be considered only one of several readings available to the actors (and us). But I think the official could not but realize that people found his attempt presumptuous, to define the situation in terms that would put the Kara on the defensive. He was not lecturing schoolchildren but savvy elders who had seen many people just like him come and go before. At any rate, to paraphrase Scott, where "humility and deference" are not convincingly performed, the display of "haughtiness and mastery" required for domination is hard to sustain (1990: 11). At the same time, Gui-Imba's little speech presents a good instance of the echoic function mentioned above: he knew exactly the way to return the ball, confronting the young official with a definition of the situation that entailed that the standards demanded from people on the periphery were hardly fulfilled by the center itself. Irony thrives where discrepancies between a claim and its substantiation obtain; the case of the Kara-state encounter shows how people manage very ambiguous power relations through irony so as to sustain a stable condition of uncertainty, basically stalling systemic change.[9] The state has grown and encompassed them, and it demands their allegiance and civility, but the Kara act in a way that denies the inevitability of their subordination. Below, I will present a number of ethnographic examples of where Kara more or less subtly acted in disregard of the demands made by state agents. The argument is that only attention to the interaction between the Kara and the Habesha can give any indication of how the Kara, in their peripheral wisdom, perceive of and deal with what is for them "the state." For such a constellation, as suggested by Fernandez and Huber, irony is the applicable frame, since "irony can be expected in situations of unequal power when discourses, interests, or cultures clash" (2001: 4), and more generally, since "ironies have to do with contacts between peoples greatly unequal in power and wherewithal: people in the center and margins of history" (Fernandez 2001: 85; Friedrich 2001: 229).

A Kara youth one day surprised me with the news that near the ferry crossing the Omo, some men had intercepted a truck bound for the Kara's neighbors, the Nyangatom, loaded with coffee. Inquiring further, I got confirmation and further details: the truck had been ambushed, and armed Kara had made the driver turn around and head to a local safari camp. There, they had deposited the owner of the coffee, a Nyangatom man. Then, they directed the truck to the southernmost Kara village, unloaded the coffee (purportedly one hundred sacks), and let the driver go. The Kara who told me this were laughing slyly, and when I asked about the police, they just shrugged their shoulders. Discussing this with a Habesha who at the time oversaw the Kara irrigation site, he shook his head and said that this was sure to get a response from the feared Federal Police. So, Kara country waited and wondered about what sort of reaction was to be expected. Only a number of weeks later the owner of the sacks of coffee came to the village, accompanied by some district policemen. I was not present, but this is the story I was told: when the police asked around for the coffee, the Kara said they would not return it. After all, had not the Nyangatom stolen last year's harvest from the fields of the western bank of the Omo? They had, in a way: in a much-appreciated bout of cooperation, Kara and Nyangatom had been jointly cultivating the Kara's farms. Then, one day, a young Kara had shot two Nyangatom herding boys on the western bank, thus taking revenge for the killing of his wife some years before by a Nyangatom sniper. Immediately, all the Kara withdrew from the western banks of the river. With bated breath, people waited to see whether the event would escalate into a hot war. Eventually, the Nyangatom collected the ripe grains from the fields and carried them off, and the Kara had to resign themselves to the harvest from the eastern bank. This is what the Kara told the police, and, so the narrative proceeded, the police agreed, and returned to whence they had come. The trader was left a pauper, and the southern part of Kara country drank *bume bunno* (Nyangatom coffee) for months.

The deed itself was audacious. Not only did it disrupt trade and involve Habesha (the driver of the truck), but it also sent a clear message to the Nyangatom and the regional administration: Kangaten, the entry point into Nyangatom territory, the one site where everybody and everything has to cross the river, could be cut off from outside access by the Kara if they waylaid cars on the single feeder road. While no physical violence occurred, this act necessitated an official response—but when it came, it was too little, too late. The policemen who did come were merely from the local district. The coffee was nowhere and everywhere, and no individual perpetrators could be identified. Instead of attempting the impossible, the policemen accepted the Kara justification, and so could go home without an even more spectacular loss of face.

Another case concerns the individual mentioned above, who took revenge for the death of his wife. His identity was known from the moment of the deed onward. All Kara and certainly all Nyangatom knew who he was, and what his motives were. For this occasion as well, eventually the police had to come to Kara country. He, however, had taken his rifle and disappeared into the forest as soon as the nature of the visitors became clear. When again policemen came and demanded his surrender, the assembled elders washed their hands of the affair: "He will shoot us too if we try to catch him. If you want him, you will have to get him yourself." The police departed. Over the next months, I could observe the man drifting away from the village whenever cars came into sight, and returning once it was safe to do so. Some time has gone by since, and the Kara estimate that in a few years, this will blow over too, so that he can even go to town again.

The list could be continued. No case can be considered a separate incident. Each one contributes to the dossier on the actual power of the police and, concomitantly, the state administration. In an ironic twist, the hesitation of individual police and their superiors in the district to escalate such a conflict is not discursively praised as restraint. Instead, it offers an occasion for people to reaffirm the old saw that "the Habesha are all liars." To first loudly impose a number of rules and then to not enforce adherence to them sends a clear message about agency and power. I have encountered only a very few incidents where justice was meted out in the way prescribed by laws and regulations.

The Kara, aware of the predicaments of police, who hardly feel secure in pressing an issue in the face of the well-armed Shankilla, and of the low- to midlevel administrators, who (as I said above) cannot make far-reaching decisions, understand that they can get away with a lot (see Abbink 2006). How far can they push it? This, of course, is contingent and unknowable, but every case in which they manage to escape retribution with their transgressions sets yet another precedent. It is clear that too blatant a humiliation of the administration, or too gory an act of violence, would be crossing the line, Scott's "cordon sanitaire" (1990: 19). But this line had not been drawn very clearly in recent times. What does this say about power relations? In these situations on the internal periphery of the Ethiopian state, power is not only analytically more a potential than an actual faculty; the actors themselves are aware that they are negotiating claims. All sides involved are thus trying to get at least a little bit of what they demand, and thus avoid losing face over being unable to follow through with an exaggerated claim. It is not that their elusive performances make the subordinates "opaque to elites" (Scott 1990: 132). The main effect of Kara displays of cleverness and ironic reversals is that the "elites" have to realize that they are not as superior as they wish. "If someone misbehaves, send him to Gamo-Gofa," today's South Omo, goes an old Amharic saying (cited in Naty 2002: 61). Nobody voluntarily transfers to South Omo, and it must not be assumed that this common Habesha dislike of the lowlands has remained obscure to the Shankilla.

Established hierarchies work best for the assumed dominant powers if their sway is not publicly challenged—but the texture of this political encounter in Kara country is so dripping in slippery irony, so eel-like in its evasiveness and exasperating in its ambiguity, that up until today, representatives of the state could hardly ever feel they were in control of the situation, or could bend people to the will they embodied against those people's own wills. In Kara country, I met people who constantly took on distanced positions that allowed them to ironize, and who then cast doubt on the "final vocabularies" (Rorty 1989: 73–74) with which they were confronted. To me, this seemed most prominent in arenas where power was at stake, where claims to equality met crass hierarchy, and where the mantle of authority was regularly worn by the most undeserving individuals. This is, then, an aspective description of the Kara-Habesha relationship, which precisely focuses on irony and power, offering a methodological counterdiscourse to approaches that assume that domination and resistance are necessarily clear-cut issues. Irony denies this; ironists realize their implicatedness in the situations they comment upon, and even where they are in a subordinate, marginal position, they realize that their rulers are entrapped in demanding roles and constraining discourses just as much, if not more.

Fundamental to the Kara attitude is the explicit recognition of their peripheral location. While in the mythic past the entire Lower Omo valley might have shaken in fear of the mighty Kara (Girke 2008), it is quite obvious today that their position demographically and geographically, as well as in terms of the administrative space of the Ethiopian state, could hardly be more marginal. Their response to this recognition, though, is far from simple. The a priori negative connotation of "periphery" is denied from a Kara perspective, and their peripheral location is instead revalued in positive terms. As a first aspect, the distance from the Ethiopian center is relativized: if even the tourists come despite the long and arduous journey, they really must want to see South Omo (and especially the Kara) very badly, goes the local understanding. The desires and opinions of some white Ferenji (foreigners), though just tourists rather than officials or professionals, are praised as a surer guide to significance than merely national(ist) discourses. Second, there is at least by now a clear awareness that Ethiopia itself is peripheral in a wider context. "Why is it," an elder asked me once, "why is it that all these others [polities within the greater region, but significantly not limited to Ethiopia], the Dassanech, the Turkana, even the Toposa, that all of them speak English and we don't?" I told him what I knew about the colonial history of the Sudan and Kenya, assuming he actually had wanted an answer—he might have, but he was also making a subtle statement that the Habesha did not speak any English either, and so could not teach the Shankilla like him. Finally, the attraction of the center comes to be denied. The *katama*, the "city," a term applied to the local market villages as well as to larger, more distant towns, is described as a dirty, violent, immoral place, where "everything costs money, no-one will give you anything for free." The fact that in return their own lowlands are seen as highly inimical by highlanders is also known well. How could it not: most Habesha who come to Kara country make no secret of it that they seek to depart as quickly as possible.

These three factors combine in the reimagination of the peripheral location of the Kara and of South Omo within Greater Ethiopia. The Kara claim that they could live happily and autonomously in the land of their forefathers. While people will travel when expedient, and while it even is a stereotypical inclination of young men to roam widely, it appears that there is little need for a shift toward the center: numerous others, tourists, organizations, researchers, all come to the Kara out of their own accord; most Kara students who go and seek higher education maintain very close ties to home. Anthony Cohen and James Fernandez call such an awareness "peripheral wisdom," a "mode of knowledge on the periphery" that inverts the given imbalance by conceptualizing "itself as central, and the putative centre as remote, inept, peripheral to its own essential value." They explicitly highlight the tropological structure of such a reversal (Cohen 2000: 12).[10] An additional, less spatial aspect of the Kara attitude vis-à-vis the Habesha is that there exists, in stark contrast to other groups of the region, no dominant narrative about the trauma of the conquest. I could elicit little of the history of the conquest beyond the plain and unembellished accounts of how they had fled from their lands and spent some time hiding in a dense forest up north. While certain elders would put names to people and places, most younger Kara were unclear about where, when, and for how long this had been. This in itself is telling. When I prompted them explicitly, people would agree that there had been slavery and abuse and unfair taxation, but this topic had no conversational relevance today. Instead, my interlocutors preferred to turn to exciting narratives of the late 1930s, of how their parents' generation, in alliance with fugitive Ethiopian loyalists, adventurously ambushed Italian forces.

## A Megastructural Solution to a Historical Struggle

The Kara, well aware that they are expected to be subordinate to the Habesha, and not supposed to be able to assert their autonomy, presented this situation to themselves (and to me, and to any other audience) as contingent rather than necessary. The question of the power differential between them and the Habesha is apparently not considered closed by the Kara, but kept unresolved. One would assume that the 1,400 Kara cannot possibly think that they could assert themselves militarily vis-à-vis state authorities; but they act as if they did think just that. Staying on the fence, as it were, by ironizing situations (each situation being a metonymic or rather iconic instance of the larger relation) allows people to *not* resolve the situation in one final way or another, when to do so would be individually problematic or even dangerous. The same is true for the administrators in contact with the Kara—they are satisfied when they can achieve some of their goals, and when the surface appearance of the hierarchy is not challenged. While they know that the state could certainly crush Kara resistance in a heartbeat when sufficiently provoked (which it has not been), they know that their own lives could very quickly become much more difficult if they confronted the Kara's duplicity head-on.

Kirsten Hastrup suggests that "[i]rony treats the world as inherently contingent, and it therefore comes closer to experience than those categories that are normally used to describe it" (2007: 203). This statement serves to reduce any reservations one might initially hold toward interpreting ethnographic material in these terms. For the user of irony, an acceptance of contingency is enabling, as it offers "ways of dealing with the prospect of living without radical alternatives and coping with only partially improving conditions" (Torres 1997: 19). This need not lead to surrender of ideals, of the hope for change, to giving in to blatant cynicism, but preserves "a potential for social criticism, because [irony and humor] reinforce the skepticism that makes us see everything as less divine and more human. Therefore there is no enduring evil and all empires must fall" (Torres 1997: 188)—but of course, they must not. In fact, it is likely that very soon, a cataclysm will reach the Kara, as a development far away threatens their existence, preeminently as a somewhat autonomous polity, but just as much as socialized beings with bodies and hopes and desires.

Construction of the Gilgel Gibe III Dam (often shortened to "Gibe 3"), located several hundred kilometers upstream, has finished at the time of writing. Without getting too technical here, I just want to state the main effect that critics expect for the Lower Omo valley: as the reservoir of this massive structure, at some point the largest dam planned for all of Africa, is slowly filling, the Omo floods will be reduced or even stop (see Abbink 2012 for a useful and current overview). Just this is enough to destroy the entire basis of the Kara subsistence production, and along with it their system of landholding, and the local calculus of exchange and status, and, as I argue, their pretensions—so far successfully if ironically upheld—to a degree of political autonomy. It used to be that a man who owned many plots along the river (and therefore could insure his household's autonomy) was a desirable son-in-law. When they were growing old, men used to exchange some of their goats, or a gun, or even money for some plots to leave to their sons. No more. Already in 2008, years before the dam would be completed, people stopped buying plots. "It is just going to be soil, not a field—why should I buy it?" said one Kara man to another with whom he had been in negotiations over the purchase of a field for a long time. Without the Omo floods that make the Kara system of cultivation sustainable, everything will change. The Kara have no way of compensating for the loss of the natural river fluctuations. To add two other moments, one cynical and one of cosmic irony: the very boon of the Omo flood has, over the last years, been denigrated by official sources as a destructive, deadly natural force that requires taming in order to protect the inhabitants of the area. Additionally, large tracts of Kara country were earmarked as feasible sites for industrial irrigation once the unpredictable and sometimes massive Omo floods stop. Surveyors have already been sent out, and maps showing the demarcation of huge farms along the river are freely available on the Internet, some having already been established today. The consequences of this megascale intervention, which simply skips the local political arena that the Kara had been able to manage so well over the last decades, will completely alter the Kara lifeworld. If both the dam project and the industrial irrigation are fully implemented, it is not clear what choice the Kara will have other than seeking unskilled, low-wage employment and hope for access to some plots to work for themselves—and even for this, they would require outside help, because without the natural river inundation, they would depend on a pump scheme. Alternatively, always a possibility given Ethiopia's record (e.g., Gebre 2002; Pankhurst 1990), they might simply be resettled elsewhere.

Elsewhere along the Omo, the bulldozers arrived much earlier than in Kara country. Protests have been attempted, battles have been fought, and critics are still intimidated and arrested. At the same time, international observers lead campaigns against the land leases,[11] against the dam, and against resettlement, a movement that has inadvertently served to transform the issue: in the eyes of many Ethiopians, national pride has come to be at stake. The dam has achieved a symbolic status for the nation's uplift into electrical autonomy, and the international protesters (among them most prominently Richard Leakey) are deftly recast as neocolonialists who would prefer to keep Africans undeveloped and in the dark. But the dam will mark the end of history for the Kara. As I have argued at length elsewhere (Girke 2008), they only became who they are by migrating to the river in the first place. Kara identity is intrinsically bound up with their occupation of these riverlands. It is not even that the Kara have no concept of "alienable rights to land": according to their own oral history, their ancestors took the land on the Omo River from the alleged autochthones by guile when they came to the river, so in principle, there is no inhibition to an understanding that people can rightfully lose their control over land. The myth is couched in terms of ritual and productivity—the original owners (again, according to myth) never cultivated, and it was basically the Kara's arrival (with their extensive knowledge of agriculture) that made the river valley into "proper" land in the first place. This is, of course, analogous to the *terra nullius* argument used by the central state in developing the area—it is not productive (enough), the local inhabitants (i.e., today's Kara) are not doing anything with it, and in the end, everybody (including the Kara) profits from the developments. The Kara understandably do not see this reasoning as applicable today, because the scale of this massive transformation transcends their horizon of experience and robs them of a vision of their future. Legally, this is entirely moot—in Ethiopia, all land belongs to the state, period; there are precedent cases where expropriation occurred.

But it never pays to discount people's creativity when faced with such extremely dire prospects—as cynical as it sounds, often catastrophe can enable action and rhetoric, and not merely constrain it, as it forces people to engage with the world anew. But the Kara do not seem to have an alternative, non-cataclysmic vision of their future. Not that they could voice it openly in the meetings they so masterfully attended before: with the importance placed by the regime on the dam, the exportable hydropower generated, and the farm leases offered to international investors, the relationship between the Kara and the police and administration seems to have taken a turn for the worse.

With this obliteration of indeterminacy, with this clear display of what the state can do once it finds it worthwhile to turn its attention to the periphery, for the Kara the fun has gone out of their attempts to outwit the state. The deferral discussed above is faltering; it could only really emerge from a situation of governmental negligence and a largely disinvested administration, along with the perpetual experience of the Kara that they could get away, literally, with murder. Obviously, the stakes have been raised. Suddenly, the region is of tremendous economic potential, with the pleasant side effect that the long frustrated "civilizing mission" in the Lower Omo valley will be advanced by turning subsistence farmers into dependent laborers. The Kara were never persuaded by the brand of civilization urged on them by their state (see Tronvoll 2012 for the current dynamics); after over a hundred years of integration, there are very few cultural elements that they seem to have adapted after recognizing them as worthwhile. The dam, however, sidesteps persuasion and conviction.

Mega dams and agricultural schemes make previous subsistence-based autonomy impossible, and it is not clear how the Kara will deal with the experience of catastrophe, globalization, and hegemony so typical for the outgoing twentieth and early twenty-first centuries. What are the options open to the Kara? What will happen to their view from the margins? This remains an open question, as it has to. But the shift in national priorities and interest, as evidenced by the new attention to South Omo and its inhabitants, has radically changed the texture of the political encounter in the region. The very real threat of having one's lifeline turned off when the river is dammed, and the incipient resettlement or "sedentarization" schemes, with the concomitant brutality and surveillance, have realigned the realities of power for all the actors involved. Current reports from the Kara leave no doubt that most individuals are markedly cowed and hardly dare speak about the dam, the irrigation schemes, and other recent developments. In terms of my argument, Kara country is threatened by a complete ideological turnabout—the certainty of always finding, at the end of the day, refuge in shiftiness and evasion, and the long decades of experience that the most ambitious schemes of the state will go awry, could well be shattered very soon.

The way the Kara will react when the looming events do come to pass, whether with a surrender to the stronger God (for example, giving in to Amharization for good), by engaging in coping mechanisms, or by attempting an interpretive twist that yet again allows them to feel clever and agentic, will tell us much about the resilience of a people's take on political culture, and its dependence on the political economy. I expect the cleverness of the Kara to linger and find new applications. If the Kara have to reassess their relationship to the state, there are still their neighbors to be outfoxed in the ongoing struggle for resources and recognition. While in the face of the total transformation of their lives and lands they might well be rendered speechless at first, the rhetorical process of invention can begin again, maybe even with a shift back to welcome uncertainty at the periphery.

**Felix Girke** is an anthropologist working at the Center of Excellence: Cultural Foundations of Social Integration at the University of Konstanz. Previously, he held positions at the Universities of Mainz, Bielefeld, and Halle-Wittenberg, as well as at the Max Planck Institute for Social Anthropology in Halle. His publications include edited books on rhetoric culture theory, tourism, and stereotypes in Ethiopia, as well as several articles and book chapters on the Kara of South Omo. Currently, he is researching the political use of cultural heritage in contemporary Myanmar.

## Notes

Fieldwork in Kara country, southern Ethiopia, was financed by the SFB 295 of Mainz University up until 2005, and by the Max Planck Institute for Social Anthropology (Dept. 1, "Integration and Conflict," Director: Günther Schlee) in Halle/Saale afterward. It was a pleasure to present this material at a conference in Evanston, and I thank the organizers and all other presenters and attendants for a very stimulating event. I profited especially from commentary by the editors as well as Dilip Gaonkar, Christian Meyer, and Ivo Strecker.

1. See Lewis (1993: 160) for a useful overview, and the chapters in Donham and James ([1986] 2002) for more in-depth studies.
2. Ivo Strecker and Jean Lydall have been working with the Hamar since 1970, and have greatly aided my research in numerous ways.
3. Holcomb and Ibssa (1990) provide the argument that despite repeated regime change, there has never been a real revolution in Ethiopia.
4. Regarding the state: for the purposes of this chapter, the government and its bureaucracy are summed up as "the state," which reflects the Kara's point of view.
5. Note that Dan Sperber and Deirdre Wilson see such "echoing" as a defining feature of irony (1995: 240).
6. Zitelmann has bitterly analyzed these tendencies for the Ethiopian case, emphasizing how thinking in terms of "projects" limits temporal perspectives for development (2005: 141).
7. That in the Kara language there is probably no word that directly corresponds to our notion of irony should not be off-putting: Odysseus himself was being ironic before *eironeia* became a staple of Sophistic rhetoric. Fernandez has suggested that as irony is fairly common in our lifeworlds, "how much more common must [it] be in the societies studied by anthropologists which are proverbially reliant upon indirection and analogy rather than upon direct analysis" (1977: 101).
8. As a response to criticism involving definitions of irony, I want to refer to the web comic *The Oatmeal* (http://theoatmeal.com/comics/irony; accessed 22 September 2014), which makes the point about its essential contestedness well.
9. Audience members at the conference in Evanston have suggested that one could interpret the Kara stance not as constructive, revolutionary engagement, but as mere coping—raucous energy does not a political momentum make. Are the Kara so good in just dealing with the status quo that they lose their capacity for transformative work or for linking up to a wider discourse? Such questions are difficult to answer empirically; I address the issue in the conclusion, when I look at the future prospects of the Kara.

10. Arguably, in the denial of the centrality of the center and the peripheral nature of the periphery and the implicit inversion, a chiasmic relation looms. For the role of chiasmus in culture, see the contributions in Paul and Wiseman (2014). The general chiasmic ambiguity of peripheral/border regions is indicated by Wilson and Donnan (2005). An inverted parallel to this ironizing peripheral wisdom is found in W. E. B. Dubois's notion of the "double consciousness"—while it would be understandable if they did, the Kara do not seem to look "at one's self through the eyes of others, of measuring one's soul by the tape of a world that looks on in amused contempt and pity" (DuBois 1903; cited in Lukes 2005: 120).
11. Academics have also begun drawing the line, with some actually seeking to offer alternatives to the currently pursued policies in the Horn of Africa. Abbink and colleagues (2014) is a strong example.

## Bibliography

Abbink, Jon. 2006. "Ethnicity and Conflict Generation in Ethiopia: Some Problems and Prospects of Ethno-regional Federalism." *Journal of Contemporary African Studies* 24, no. 3: 389–413.

———. 2012. "Dam Controversies: Contested Governance and Developmental Discourse on the Ethiopian Omo River Dam." *Social Anthropology/Anthropologie Sociale* 20, no. 2: 125–44.

Abbink, Jon, Kelly Askew, Dereje Feyissa Dori, Elliot Fratkin, Echi Christina Gabbert, John Galaty, Shauna LaTosky, et al. 2014. *Lands of the Future: Transforming Pastoral Lands and Livelihoods in Eastern Africa*. Max Planck Institute of Social Anthropology Working Papers 154. Halle: Max Planck Institute for Social Anthropology.

Bailey, F. G. 2003. *The Saving Lie: Truth and Method in the Social Sciences*. Philadelphia: University of Pennsylvania Press.

Bassi, Marco. 2011. "Primary Identities in the Lower Omo Valley: Migration, Cataclysm, Conflict and Amalgamation, 1750–1910." *Journal of Eastern African Studies* 5, no. 1: 129–57.

Burke, Kenneth. 1945. *A Grammar of Motives*. New York: Prentice-Hall.

Capurro, Rafael. 1990. "Ironie: Begriffsgeschichtliche Erörterung einer menschlichen Grundstimmung." Unpublished manuscript, no pagination. http://www.capurro.de/ironie.html (accessed 22 September 2014).

Claessen, Henri J.M. 1989. "Preface." In *Outwitting the State*, ed. Peter Skalnik, vii–xi. New Brunswick: Transaction.

Cohen, Anthony P. 2000. "Introduction: Discriminating Relations—Identity, Boundary and Authenticity." In *Signifying Identities: Anthropological Perspectives on Boundaries and Contested Identities,* ed. Anthony Cohen, 1–14. London: Routledge.

Donham, Donald, and Wendy James, eds. (1986) 2002. *The Southern Marches of Imperial Ethiopia: Essays in History and Social Anthropology*. Oxford: James Currey.

Epple, Susanne, and Sophia Thubauville. 2012. "Cultural Diversity in Ethiopia between Appreciation and Suppression." *Paideuma* 58: 153–66.

Ferguson, R. Brian, and Neil L. Whitehead, eds. 2000. *War in the Tribal Zone: Expanding States and Indigenous Warfare*. Santa Fe: School of American Research Press.

Fernandez, James W. 1977. "The Performance of Ritual Metaphors." In *The Social Use of Metaphor,* ed. David Sapir and J. Christopher Crocker, 100–131. Philadelphia: University of Pennsylvania Press.

———. 2000. "Peripheral Wisdom." In *Signifying Identities: Anthropological Perspectives on Boundaries and Contested Identities,* ed. Anthony Cohen, 117–144. London: Routledge.

———. 2001. "The Irony of Complicity and the Complicity of Irony." In *Irony in Action: Anthropology, Practice, and the Moral Imagination,* ed. James W. Fernandez and Mary Taylor Huber, 84–102. Chicago: University of Chicago Press.

Fernandez, James W. and Mary Taylor Huber. 2001. "Introduction. The Anthropology of Irony." In *Irony in Action: Anthropology, Practice, and the Moral Imagination,* ed. James W. Fernandez and Mary Taylor Huber, 1–40. Chicago: University of Chicago Press.

Friedrich, Paul. 1989. "Language, Ideology, and Political Economy." *American Anthropologist* N.S. 91, no. 2: 295–312.

———. 2001. "Ironic Irony." In *Irony in Action: Anthropology, Practice, and the Moral Imagination,* ed. James W. Fernandez and Mary Taylor Huber, 224–252. Chicago: University of Chicago Press.

Gebre Yntiso. 2002. "Contextual Determination of Migration Behaviours: The Ethiopian Resettlement in Light of Conceptual Constructs." *Journal of Refugee Studies* 15, no. 3: 265–82.

Girke, Felix. 2008. "The Ädamo of the Kara: Rhetoric in Social Relations on the Lower Omo." PhD dissertation, MLU Halle-Wittenberg.

———. 2011. "Plato on the Omo: Reflections on Decision-Making among the Kara of Southern Ethiopia." *Journal of Eastern African Studies* 5, no. 1: 177–94.

Graeber, David. 2007. "On the Phenomenology of Giant Puppets: Broken Windows, Imaginary Jars of Urine, and the Cosmological Role of the Police in American Culture." In *Possibilities: Essays on Hierarchy, Rebellion, and Desire,* ed. David Graeber, 375–418. Oakland, CA, and Edinburgh: AK Press.

Hariman, Robert. 1995. *Political Style: The Artistry of Power.* Chicago and London: University of Chicago Press.

Hastrup, Kirsten. 2007. "Performing the World. Agency, Anticipation and Creativity". In *Creativity and Cultural Improvisation,* ed. Elizabeth Hallam and Tim Ingold, 193–206. Oxford, New York: Berg.

Holcomb, Bonny K., and Sisai Ibssa. 1990. *The Invention of Ethiopia: The Making of a Dependent Colonial State in Northeast Africa.* Trenton, NJ: Red Sea Press.

Hutcheon, Linda. 1994. *Irony's Edge: The Theory and Politics of Irony.* London and New York: Routledge.

Lambek, Michael. 2004. "Introduction: Irony and Illness—Recognition and Refusal." In *Illness and Irony: On the Ambiguity of Suffering in Culture,* ed. Michael Lambek and Paul Antze, 1–19. Oxford and New York: Berghahn Books.

Lewis, Herbert. 1993. "Ethnicity in Ethiopia: The View from Below (and from the South, East, and West)." In *The Rising Tide of Cultural Pluralism: The Nation-State at Bay?,* ed. Crawford Young, 158–178. Madison: University of Wisconsin Press.

Lukes, Steven. 2005. *Power: A Radical View.* 2nd ed. Houndmills, UK, and New York: Palgrave.

Matsuda, Hiroshi. 1996. "Riverbank Cultivation in the Lower Omo Valley: The Intensive Farming System of the Kara, Southwestern Ethiopia." In *Essays in Northeast African Studies,* ed. Shun Sato and Eisei Kurimoto, 1–28. Osaka: National Museum.

Naty, Alexander. 2002. "Memory and the Humiliation of Men: The Revolution in Aari." In *Remapping Ethiopia: Socialism and After,* ed. Wendy James, Eisei Kurimoto, Donald L. Donham, and Alessandro Triulzi, 59–73. Oxford: James Currey.

Pankhurst, Alula. 1990. "Resettlement: Policy and Practice." In *Ethiopia: Rural Development Options,* ed. Siegfried Pausewang, Fantu Cheru, Stefan Brune, and Eshetu Chole, 121–134 London: Zed Books.

Rorty, Richard. 1989. *Contingency, Irony, and Solidarity.* Cambridge: Cambridge University Press.

Schlee, Günther. 1989. "The Orientation of Progress: Conflicting Aims and Strategies of Pastoral Nomads and Development Agents in East Africa—A Problem Survey." In *Transition and Continuity in East Africa and Beyond: In Memoriam David Miller,* ed. Elisabeth Linnebuhr, 397–450. Bayreuth African Studies Series. Bayreuth: E. Breitinger.

Scott, James C. 1990. *Domination and the Arts of Resistance: Hidden Transcripts.* New Haven, CT: Yale University Press.

———. 2009. *The Art of Not Being Governed: An Anarchist History of Upland Southeast Asia.* New Haven, CT: Yale University Press.

Skalnik, Peter. 1989. "Outwitting the State: An Introduction." In *Outwitting the State,* ed. Peter Skalnik, with a foreword by H. J. M. Claessen, 1–22. New Brunswick, NJ: Transaction.

Sperber, Dan, and Deirdre Wilson. 1995. *Relevance: Communication and Cognition.* 2nd ed. Oxford: Blackwell.

Stigand, C. H. (1910) 1969. *To Abyssinia through an Unknown Land: An Account of a Journey through Unexplored Regions of British East Africa by Lake Rudolf to the Kingdom of Menelik.* New York: Negro Universities Press.

Strecker, Ivo. 1976. "Traditional Life and Prospects for Socio-economic Development in the Hamar Administrative District of Southern Gamu Gofa: A Report to the Relief and Rehabilitation Commission of the Provisional Military Government of Ethiopia." Unpublished manuscript.

———. 1988. *The Social Practice of Symbolization: An Anthropological Analysis.* London: Athlone.

———. 1994. "Glories and Agonies of the Ethiopian Past." Review Article of *A History of Modern Ethiopia* (Bahru Zewde) and *The Invention of Ethiopia: The Making of a Dependent Colonial State of Northeast Africa* (Sisai Ibssa and Bonnie Holcomb). *Social Anthropology* 2, no. 3: 303–12.

Torres, Gabriel. 1997. *The Force of Irony: Power in the Everyday Life of Mexican Tomato Workers.* Oxford and New York: Berg.

Tronvoll, Kjetil. 2012. "The 'New' Ethiopia: Changing Discourses of Democracy." In *Contested Power in Ethiopia: Traditional Authorities and Multi-party Elections,* ed. Kjetil Tronvoll and Tobias Hagmann, 269–287. Leiden, Boston: Brill.

Wilson, Thomas, and Hastings Donnan, eds. 2005. *Culture and Power at the Edges of the State. National Support and Subversion in European Border Regions.* Münster: LIT.

Zitelmann, Thomas. 2005: "Blühende Landschaften in Äthiopien: Entwicklung als Versprechen, Macht und Mythus." In *Bewegliche Horizonte: Festschrift zum 60. Geburtstag von Bernhard Streck,* ed. Katja Geisenhainer and Katharina Lange, 139–152. Leipzig: Universitätsverlag.

CHAPTER 9

# Grassroots Rhetorics in Times of Scarcity
## Debating the 2004 Locust Plague in Northwestern Senegal and the World

*Christian Meyer*

■ ■ ■ ■ ■ ■ ■

The realms of rhetoric—as we know at least since Aristotle—are uncertainty and contingency. The greatest domain of uncertainty, of course, is the future. None of us is able to foresee what will happen in the future—which kind of contingencies will affect us and which kind of uncertainties we will be confronted with. Thanks to its open character, the future has always been one of the favored subjects of rhetoric—joint decisions have to be made with respect to preparations, provisions, and measures to be taken, and these decisions are often the outcome of long deliberative discussions in which the only measure is persuasiveness.

With what sociologist Ulrich Beck has called the world risk society and even more so with the ubiquitous presence of disasters in the global media, we should therefore expect another and enriched blooming of rhetorical theory and practice in the twenty-first century (cf. Danisch 2010; Sauer 2003). As Ralph Cintron puts it, disasters, being the dark side of modernity—the "setback in the tale of ascension"—have become "reminders of the work to be done" if the "planetary project" of modernity is to be made right (in this volume, p.359, 354). The self-selected and self-addressed representatives of this planetary project are the Western discourses in the media, but also in science and politics, all of which are bound to the enlightenment ideal, assuming a constant progress achieved through the rationalization of knowledge and the domestication of nature.

However, given the global landscape of multiple modernities, the question appears appropriate of whether in all the regions of the world, people adhere to the same imaginations of modernity as are advocated by Western discourses. Do we really have only one project of modernity? Or do we have a plurality of projects according to the local textures and repertoires of social practice? This question will be discussed in this chapter. To do so I will compare globally spread discourses about a major catastrophic event of 2004, the West African locust plague, with local discussions of Wolof farmers of northwestern Senegal about the same event. Before I do so, however, let me first introduce some thoughts about disaster and disaster communication.

## Disaster and Disaster Communication

Disaster is, under the perspective developed in this book, a constant thorn in the flesh, as it permanently reminds us of the incompleteness of the projects of modernity. What, then, is a disaster? The definitions of disaster and catastrophe are inextricable, and discussions are ongoing (see Quarantelli 1988; Perry and Quarantelli 2005). The editors of this volume have made clear that disasters are unthinkable without some social or cultural domain that takes damage; consequently, they are not purely natural. A tsunami on Mars is not a disaster, since there are no human beings concerned. Even a volcanic eruption in the subsea is mostly just a geological event, uninteresting for most human beings. Additionally, a disaster is conceptualized by cultural standards in some way: it only becomes a disaster because it is interpreted as such by some cultural and social standards of meaning.[1]

Clausen (1992) has identified three fundamental properties that distinguish a disaster from, say, a misfortune, a calamity, or a trouble. These are, first, rapidity: a disaster is distinguished by its temporal character. It is fast, it is overpowering, and it is unstoppable. It entails accelerated social change. Second is radicality: a disaster produces a deep impact upon the lives and conditions of a number of people. It first changes their lives as such, and often requires further changes of life as a response to it. That is, the accelerated social change triggered by a disaster is drastic and essential (cf. Kreps 1985). Third is rituality: disasters not only challenge life conditions, but also shared understandings and interpretations of existence. Through their radicality they provide a blow to the fundamental unquestioned assumptions of humanity, as did the 1755 earthquake of Lisbon in its effects on European Enlightenment philosophy, politics, and religion (cf. Hamacher 1999). Thus, disasters are often responded to by demonization, emphasizing their unpredictable and malicious qualities. These three properties of disaster and catastrophe are also present in the etymologies of both terms: *catastrophe* (Greek): a sudden overturning; *desastro* (Latin): evil star.

The three "r" features entail consequences for the rhetorical and generally communicative practices that accompany a disaster. However, the temporal dimension (rapidity) might vary according to the type of disaster dealt with. There are sudden disasters, such as tsunamis, flash floods, earthquakes, airplane or train crashes, or nuclear accidents that happen suddenly and in a completely unannounced manner. When emergency units arrive, the cause of disaster per se is already over. Other types announce themselves over a long period of time or are creeping, such as pollution or global warming. The growing radicality of the disaster is cotemporaneous with the fight against it. A third type includes disasters that emerge, last for some time, and are over when they are successfully fought or have ended naturally. Examples are forest fires, droughts, volcanic eruptions, or slow river floods. Finally, since concepts such as disaster and catastrophe are meaningful and impressive, they are also popular. We might therefore possibly speak of metaphoric disasters, as when financial crises are termed disasters even though they are directly related to human action and do not necessarily deeply affect large groups of people.

The different temporal dynamics of disasters have implications for their course. In the case of sudden disasters, emergency crews fight the consequences triggered such as fires and hurt, homeless, and helpless people, while in the case of episodic disasters of the third type, they must also fight the disaster itself. Creeping disasters are still in the making, so what we fight, in fact, is their very beginning. Furthermore, disasters might also produce further disasters, as when a forest fire encroaches upon a chemical industrial plant and toxic fumes are set free. Disastrous consequences might equally be triggered by the media that report about them, as when people threatened by a tsunami begin to panic and produce traffic jams that culminate in crashes and people dying.

The communicative processes that accompany, or even constitute, disasters can be distinguished in five phases. First is an alarming, which is the first communicative process after the impression that "something big" is going on. The alarming might consist of a vocal or phone call for help identifying and socially determining a disaster. Examples that are well studied include emergency calls as well as black box recordings prior to airplane crashes (cf. Zimmerman 1992). Second, if an emergency unit is alerted, communicative processes that trigger the internal mobilization of the institution are launched. These processes further define the disaster in its degree. This kind of communication still awaits further study.[2] Third, when emergency units have arrived at the site of the disaster, communicative processes that coordinate the fight against it, and coping with it, are set into operation. In this phase, further assessments of the degree and consequences of the disaster are made. This type of disaster communication equally still awaits further study. Most of the studies on disaster communication conducted so far have focused on the fourth phase, the social and cultural effects that disasters have engendered, as, for example, in relation to the theodicy question, or in philosophy, politics, and literature (cf. Steinberg 2000). Evaluative discourses have mostly been centered on the individual and social-moral implications of a disaster that has struck: How do we have to change our lives? What does this disaster tell us? A fifth phase of disaster communication is concerned with learning from past experiences and making preparations and risk assessments for potential future events. Much of the disaster communication in books and professional institutions of disaster management is concerned precisely with the problem of enhancing the resilience of people and structures to resist possible disasters (cf. Heath and O'Hair 2009). Risk communication is concerned with the feasibility of the future and the solvability of problems. It is the area in which the narrative of modernity is most present—it is a discourse that does not content itself with licking one's wounds that are due to past disasters, but that instead upholds the grand narrative of the ascent of humanity.

## The Global Discourse on the 2004 West African Locust Disaster

The topic of the subsequent analysis is an event that occurred shortly before other critical global events such as the big tsunami in the Indian Ocean four months later and Hurricane Katrina one year later. In August 2004, the global media began to report about huge locust swarms that were destroying crops in West Africa.

This event was represented in the global media as a typical sudden natural disaster not incomparable to the hurricane and the tsunami. On 9 July 2004, the French newspaper *Le Monde* published an article titled "Locusts Launch Attack on Sahel." The English-speaking world reacted later: on 2 September 2004, the British *Telegraph* headlined "West Africa in Terror of Locust Plague." The event was characterized as an incident that struck unprepared and helpless people and that was completely unexpected. It was not long until words like "disaster" and "catastrophe" came up ("Catastrophe," *Libération*, 26 July 2004; "The Locust Disaster," *Le Monde*, 1 September 2004). Because of its force, references to biblical property and apocalyptic magnitude were soon made. "Plague" and "A Deluge of Locusts Lunges Out at Africa" were headlines of the French *Libération* (26 July 2004), the *New York Times* titled "Plague of Locusts Threatens West African Crops" (5 September 2004), and the British *Independent* headlined "Plague of Locusts Casts Shadow Over Africa" (20 August 2004). Later, IRIN, the publication service of the United Nations (UN) Office for the Coordination of Humanitarian Affairs, wrote "The Eighth Plague: West Africa's Locust Invasion" (1 December 2004), while the World Food Programme composed "Mali and Niger: Enough Locusts 'to Bring Job to His Knees'" (22 March 2005). As the plague extended via North Africa to countries in southern Europe as well as to the Near and Middle East, the global dimension of the crisis was emphasized. Media in China and India also began to report about it.

Massive emergency programs were finally established, and the "battle" (*Daily Mail*, 2 September 2004) and "war on locusts" (Abdoulaye Wade, Senegalese president at that time, 31 August 2004) was declared an international task, led by countries such as Algeria, Libya, Morocco, and France. The measures finally had success, and against all premonitions, the locust plague did not extend into 2005. At the end of 2004, a kind of aestheticization of the disaster in the global media ensued, when a picture of children running after locusts and playing with them in Dakar taken by Reuters photographer Pierre Holtz was awarded the second prize of the World Press Photo contest in the category "Nature."

Soon, however, this image of the disaster as an unforeseeable and natural disaster was criticized.[3] In fact, the Food and Agriculture Organization of the UN (FAO)—whose president, Jacques Diouf, is a Senegalese himself—had published locust warnings as early as September 2003 and asked for US$9 million to begin an early preventive fight. Senegalese president Abdoulaye Wade had launched another call for help in March 2004 in the French newspapers *Le Figaro* and *Le Monde*. None of these calls were responded to, and at the end the crisis cost international donors more than US$300 million, not only to fight the adult locust swarms, but also to combat the famine triggered by the plague.

In addition, critics emphasized that the crisis was anthropogenic rather than merely natural. First, obviously, the warning systems had failed, since there was no institutional response to the discovery that locusts were about to develop into a plague. Since the early 1960s the warning systems had functioned so well that only one plague had occurred, in 1988 to 1989, while between 1940 and 1963 there had been swarms every single year. Thus, the disaster of 2004 had not been a problem of risk recognition, but a problem of inadequate reaction. The second reason for the claim that the disaster was man-made rather that naturally created was the fact that measures of structural adjustment required by the International Monetary Fund (IMF) exacerbated the disaster. Experts of international institutions thought that only a free corn market would be able to balance out losses from drought and therefore forbade governments in the area to stabilize corn prices. Therefore, in 2005, when the first famines broke out, the rich southern neighbors of the infested countries—like Nigeria and Cote d'Ivoire—were able to buy up the scarce harvests in the region. Even in regions that had not been hit by locusts, corn became scarce, and the people had to be supported by nongovernmental organizations (NGOs). A third anthropogenic factor that supported the development of the plague was, finally, that locusts appear to be particularly eager to form swarms when their food is scarce, so that overgrazing and soil exhaustion in general contribute to the probability of locust development. When the ground is treated with fertilizers, for example, locusts encounter less advantageous breeding conditions. This connection might gain more importance in the future in the course of global warming.

A final critique uttered, but this is only a marginal point, was made by conspiracy theories that aligned the locust swarm, along with other extreme weather events such as Hurricane Katrina, the Indonesian tsunami, or global warming, with practices of weather designing putatively adopted by the US military as warfare strategies (cf. Chossudovsky 2004).

## The 2004 Locust Disaster in Senegal

In the previous section, I presented the discourse of the locust disaster in the global media. Let me now give you a short account of how the disaster developed and what occurred in Senegal aside from these global discourses.

Exceptional rains during the summer of 2003 throughout the northern Sahelian belt led to an augmented breeding of locust larvae. Some areas in the western Sahara received more than one hundred millimeters of rain where they normally get about one millimeter of rain in a year. The desert locust is usually a rather solitary and phlegmatic maverick, unable to fly, hopping around and avoiding contact with other hoppers.[4] But when the population density exceeds fifty individuals per square meter, the locust completely changes its phenotype. It becomes black and yellow instead of green; it grows wings, becomes hyperactive and social, and begins to coordinate and to form swarms. This change is due to serotonin production in the body, which is stimulated when hoppers come into bodily contact with each other. These changed, so-called gregarious locusts, instead of avoiding it, now actively seek bodily contact with other hoppers, which stimulates the production of serotonin in them, turns them gregarious, and makes them look for other hoppers, and so on. In other words, they create a feedback loop that leads to ever growing numbers of swarming locusts. The locust plague is a typical disaster that, like a forest fire, is based on an emergence effect with a specific threshold value leading to the self-sustainment of the disaster and making the fight against it more difficult.

When the locusts of the Sahelian belt turned into the gregarious form and grew into adults in 2003, they migrated north, where they again encountered favorable conditions, as rain had fallen well in the Maghrebian states in early 2004 as well. This made the swarms literally explode in number and magnitude. One swarm in Morocco was 230 kilometers long and 200 meters wide and contained an estimated number of 70 billion individuals. Such a mass of insects consumes about 140,000 tons of greens per day. When the swarms migrated south again in the summer of 2004 looking for new greenery, they moved directly into the developing West African crops and destroyed them. When in the beginning of 2005 they moved north once again, the North African states were well prepared and extinguished them with airplanes spraying pesticides; the wind and the low temperatures were also unfavorable for the locusts at that time.

During their stay in Senegal, three month's growth of crops was destroyed in thirty minutes, and of course, the affected populations were unhappy about the late start of the battle against the locusts and the heavy consequences of the swarm. The "yellow pests," as the locusts were called, even began to munch their way through the straw huts of the local farmers. In addition, the adult locusts laid eggs in the ground, and once they hatch after ten days of incubation, the concentrations of hungry young hoppers can reach ten thousand per square meter. Before they are fully grown, the locusts slowly move forward, like a rippling carpet of three hundred square meters, destroying everything in its way. However, these hopper bands are much easier to kill than the swarms of fully fledged flying locusts, which can move over one hundred kilometers per day and can only be sprayed with pesticides in the early morning when they settle to the ground before flying off again.

In Senegal, the fight against the locusts only slowly began to pick up speed. In August, three hundred thousand hectares of farmland had been invaded by locusts, but only a third of that area had been treated with insecticides. At the end of the year, 1.3 million hectares were pre-emptively treated, and only seven hundred thousand invaded. The battle was fought mainly by hand at the beginning, through digging trenches to bury them, with hatches, hoes, and improvised brushes, or with sticks and tin cans to drive them away with noise. Motor-driven spraying of pesticides only effectively began in late September.

On the other hand, the consequences of the spraying of pesticides were severe. Thirteen million liters of pesticides were sprayed, and more than 6.3 million liters of pesticides were left over at the end of the campaign. While at first there was not enough pesticides at hand, later, when the crops and graze lands were already destroyed by the locusts, there was too much, and the villagers wondered whether all the insecticides thrown at the locusts would poison the pasture for their livestock and their drinking water.

With around a dozen swarms per day and locality, that is, two hundred swarms in total in August 2004, the locusts destroyed about 25 percent of the crops and 40 percent of the grazing greens in Senegal—a damage of US$500 million to agricultural production. This seriously threatened the food security situation in the country, also by producing strong price movements in the markets and by creating an insufficient availability of grazing areas. This in turn entailed the selling of animals at very low prices in order to meet the subsistence needs of households. It also motivated severe tensions between the pastoralists and local farmers over resources. In the long run, it triggered an extensive migration to urban areas as well as to Europe and the United States.

The locusts have thus made the long-term food security of the local populations even more uncertain, by aggravating the vulnerability of households already living under precarious conditions, in regions where food insecurity is structural. Only a UN appeal in early 2005, when the situation was presented as a severe natural disaster in the global media, was able to persuade donors and prevent the worst.

As we can see in this example, two current trends in disaster research are confirmed. First is the need to think about them not as a locally isolated phenomenon, but to treat them as phenomena that are embedded in global processes of risk production and management (cf. Alexander 2006; Dombrowsky 2007; Letukas and Barnshaw 2008). Second is the idea to think about disasters as socially constructed realities in at least two ways: as a consequence of the advancement of science and technology in reflexive modernity, where greater possibilities of interfering in the natural world also create greater risks; and as socially, culturally, and rhetorically created phenomena insofar as nowadays it is less knowledge about natural processes that lead to disasters than malfunctioning institutions, late decisions, or bad strategies, as well as a lack of funds.[5]

## LOCAL DISCOURSES IN NORTHWESTERN SENEGAL ON THE 2004 LOCUST DISASTER

I would now like to shift the perspective toward the local practices of sense making and of dealing with uncertainty and risk in the context of the Senegalese locust disaster. In other words, I now turn to the local textures of political action and repertoires of social practice. The data that I discuss were collected during fieldwork from 2004 to 2006. They mainly consist of audio recordings of debates on the village square that were subsequently transcribed. I have chosen two conversations from one year after the disaster (20 and 28 June

2005) when, shortly before the rainy season, the villagers were about to decide whether and when to sow again. A third conversation is from two years after the disaster around the same time (4 July 2006). The conversations were originally held in Wolof. For better readability I have left out the Wolof transcript of the debates and only present the English translation.

The Wolof inhabit the acacia savannah region of northwestern Senegal and live off the cultivation of millet, sorghum, and beans for subsistence, and of groundnuts as cash crops, along with the raising of small livestock, petty trade, and remittances from abroad.

A first observation in regard to the data is that the Wolof cope with the disaster in a very rational way: there are no myths involved, there are no witchcraft accusations as described by Evans-Pritchard about the Azande (Evans-Pritchard 1937: 63–83), and there are no accusations of taboo transgressions and purity pollution as described by Mary Douglas (1966: 95–114).

## *Rhetorical Domestication: Low-Caste Locusts*

What are the textures of evaluation and risk assessment that the Wolof employ when talking about the danger of locusts? A first rhetorical strategy of dealing with locusts consists of irony and indirection (cf. Kuipers 2002 for an account about the function of humor in the evaluation of disaster).

20 June 2005, Excerpt 1
001  Majaw  Yibba Jóob said that he nearly sowed today. But he said that then he tied his sack up again. He said: "Alas! With these guys sitting on the trees and beguilingly rolling their eyes will our plants grow or won't they?"
002  Laay   Well, what I know is that everybody has to sow when he still doesn't know what God will do.
005  Majaw  No field owner ever knows that. [Laughs]
006  Laay   But if you don't sow, because you know that they are roaming around.... If you won't sow today, you will never sow, because they stay here and keep roaming around.
007  Majaw  Yibba Jóob has said: "These guys sit on the trees and roll their eyes beguilingly while they are coupling."
008  Laay   If God would only dispel them from here and they would go away.

Majaw refers to a friend of his who stopped sowing when he saw hoppers (that is, the non-gregarious form of the locusts) again in 2005. He quotes Yibba Jóob's formulation of the "guys ... beguilingly rolling their eyes" (*gaa yi*

... *regeju*) two times with an ironic and funny attitude. The expression *regeju* refers to the beauty ideal of showing the white sclera, which is done by young women who intend to seduce. It, however, also alludes to the caste differentiation of Wolof society, in which the caste of the griots (bards), in contrast to the caste of the freemen (nobles), is allowed more freedom to show emotions and initiate social activity (cf. Irvine 1990). Rolling one's eyes beguilingly is a low-caste activity—locusts are classified as low caste by Majaw. Laay, in 006, supports this perspective with his expression "roaming around" (*wendéelu*), as this expression is often used for the (originally Fulani) caste of woodcutters (*lawbé*) (cf. Meyer 2008). At the same time, through his sexual allusion, Majaw, of course, refers to the enormous ability of reproduction of these beasts, which, in fact, is the biggest danger for the farmers.

Later in this same conversation, further rhetorical devices are used, namely, depreciation and cursing.

20 June 2005, Excerpt 2
039 Laay But when they are on wet ground they couple. When they are on wet ground they couple.
040 Majaw They couple even more quickly on tilled soil. Gosh, these machines like to couple on top of it. This is really a devil's breed.
041 Ngaan They prefer wet ground.
042 Njaga That's what they like.
043 Tapha On wet ground, when they have coupled and when it rains ... when it rains ...
044 Majaw Then the guys emerge.
045 Tapha They emerge.
046 Majaw You know, may God forgive us, but even the caterpillars, even the caterpillars do have limits. But these owners, these owners of wings ...
048 Jajji No, you know, even caterpillars are better than this here. Caterpillars are certainly better than that what flies.

Majaw, in 040, compares locusts with machines, which refers to the apparatus the Wolof use to sow. It contains a wheel with hollow spikes in its middle that place one seed after the other at a specific distance from a container on its top. The metaphor again emphasizes the reproductive capability, speed, and unstoppability of the locusts, which remorselessly continue to lay their eggs in the ground in masses. In the same line, he curses them in religious terms, calling them a "devil's breed" (*doomi raam*). In line 047, Majaw describes the locusts metonymically as "owners of wings" (*boroom naaw yii*), focusing on another quality: their ability to fly and to create swarms that cloud the sun and make a loud noise, as well as their ability to displace themselves fast so that they are difficult to fight. Jajji, in 048, takes up this metonymic image in his expression "that what flies" (*liy naaw*). The metonymic expressions as well as the metaphor "machines" along with derisive ironic expressions emphasize the physical and materially irresistible qualities of the locusts.

Later, in line 071, Majaw calls the insects by their literal denomination "locusts" (*soccet*) for the first time in this conversation.

20 June 2005, Excerpt 3
071 Majaw But these locusts, may God dispel them. These locusts—horrible! Every farmer, when he only sees them ...

Line 071 includes a further metonymic expression, when Majaw evokes the horror that the locusts will produce in a farmer, "when he only sees them ..." (*baykat bu ko gis rekk ...*). There are more of these extended metonyms in lines 012, 072, and 074.

20 June 2005, Excerpt 4
012 Jajji As long as they are here, the minds of the people won't be at rest.
072 Jajji Laay, they are the only thing that scares a farmer.
074 Jajji They are the only ones that withdraw our vitality. They are the only ones that create discord among us.

Jajji here expands upon the power that the locusts have over the psychic as well as social sanity of the famers: they are able to create uneasiness, fear, and despair in the individual as well as conflict and desolation in the social group.

## *Dialectics of Concern: Hope and Fear*

A second set of rhetorical strategies to deal with disaster consists of expressions of hope and prayers to God. In the transcript of 20 June 2005 discussed above, which was recorded before seeding the fields, Majaw, in line 071, said in regard to the locusts, "may God dispel them" (*yalna yalla yobbu yëp*). However, expressions of hope and confidence and prayers to God are even more present after seeding, as the transcript of 28 June 2005 shows.

28 June 2005, Excerpt 1
001 Majaw There is no place in Senegal where rain didn't fall.
002 Daur The places that are not wet aren't numerous. Indeed, the diviners scored well. It will largely rain all over Senegal. A rain that covers everywhere.

| | | |
|---|---|---|
| 003 | Serin | That's how they said it. |
| 004 | Daur | Yes. |
| 005 | Serin | The 27th. |
| 006 | Daur | And everything else what they said, may it happen as they said it. They said that everybody who cultivates will have plenty and even those who don't cultivate. They foresaw a successful tilling. |
| 007 | Serin | When it thunders, it will be prosperous if there are no caterpillars, and if there are no thingy ... locusts. |
| 008 | Daur | Yes, that's what they said. |
| 009 | Serin | That's what they said. But the locusts, I fear that they will come in masses, they won't fail to appear. They will come in masses, since I saw them at the place under the jojoba tree where father used to lie down. |

Here, the farmers refer to their confidence in what the diviners have announced for the year.[6] Soon after, however, they remember the year before, when the rain fell equally well, but the locusts destroyed the harvest. In 009, Serin expresses his fear—the counterpart of hope—that this might happen again. In the following excerpts, prayer, as an exteriorization of their will, is dialogically expressed (as it is mostly done among the Wolof).

28 June 2005, Excerpt 2

| | | |
|---|---|---|
| 014 | Serin | May God prevent them, may God prevent. |
| 017 | Daur | May God— |
| 018 | Serin | —prevent— |
| 019 | Daur | —protect us from it. |
| 020 | Serin | So that it won't occur. |

28 June 2005, Excerpt 3

| | | |
|---|---|---|
| 033 | Daur | Hmm, may God help us so that there will be no need to do anything about it. |
| 034 | Serin | Amen! |

The wickedness of the locusts is contrasted with the mercifulness of God.

28 June 2005, Excerpt 4

| | | |
|---|---|---|
| 030 | Daur | The big swarm is really wicked. |
| 031 | Serin | Yes, but God is merciful. |

After a third prayer, in 053 Majaw expresses his hope again and speaks of the beauty of sprouting green when rain comes.

28 June 2005, Excerpt 5
049  Daur   It looks like a cloud, only flapping, horrible. May God help us that they just don't fly.
050  Serin  Amen. [Sighs]
051  Daur   May God help us that they don't come here.
052  Serin  Amen, may God help us.
053  Majaw  Today the grass and everything was beautiful. When it only sprouts it will be beautiful.

## *Distributed Epistemic Practices and the Spreading of Risk*

A third rhetorical topic concerns the ways of dealing with uncertainty. How do the Wolof debate about risk? How do they qualify information, and how do they take epistemic stances?

There is, for example, an interesting debate about whether to sow or not, and about the risk connected to that, right at the beginning of the conversation of 20 June 2005 (see above, excerpt 1). As Laay says, too much fear of the locusts and indecision about what to do would only lead to the incapacity to act. We can also see that the opening of a debate is often made by reference to what others have said or done. But then, the farmers also directly assess the risk, as in the conversation of 28 June 2005, when they debate the real problem and the real danger.

28 June 2005, Excerpt 6
015  Daur   Do you know what the real problem is?
016  Serin  Huh?
021  Daur   Those who only fly in swarms, departing from the north and entering the country from the outside.
022  Majaw  Entering the country from the outside.
023  Serin  Those coming out of the mountains.
024  Daur   Yes, those, which look like a cloud.
025  Serin  That's the ones that have troubled the country.
026  Daur   That's the real danger, that is the danger, but . . .
027  Serin  That's what came here and besieged the country.
028  Daur   But that's not a common grasshopper, that's not a grasshopper.

Shortly after, they evaluate the probability of the locusts already being in their area.

28 June 2005, Excerpt 7
045  Daur   But they are already much farther than [Morocco].

046  Serin  Yes, they probably are.
047  Daur   If they just agreed to stop there. They gather from Thies to behind Linguere.
048  Serin  Yeah!

Another topic of risk assessment is the help of political institutions, initiatives, or the state, as discussed in the conversation of 28 June 2005.

28 June 2005, Excerpt 8
032  Majaw  The Algerian president has said that they will do something about it.
033  Daur   Hmm, may God help us so that there will be no need to do anything about it at all.
034  Serin  Amen!
035  Majaw  He has said that he will do something about it. I don't remember anymore with whom.
036  Daur   That's what I hope for, Maj—, Serin.
037  Majaw  The mountains where they hatch out.
038  Daur   He said that seven countries would unite to think out a joint strategy. To find them where they hatch. They will find a solution that will bring us peace.
039  Serin  You are right. Just these mountains. If they went there and blocked the entries or powdered them inside, sprayed them.
040  Daur   Yes.
041  Majaw  Bombed them.
042  Serin  Yes, inside, only this would make them disappear.
043  Majaw  They really can restore well over there.
044  Serin  Yeah.

Finally, they also consider and discuss the possibility and the promises of changing their subsistence strategies, that is, moving from cultivation to the raising of livestock, as in the conversation of 20 June 2005 (for another account on the flexibility of farmers in the Sahelian area in regard to their subsistence strategies, cf. McCabe 2002). Here we can see how the disaster of the past year has already induced social change.

20 June 2005, Excerpt 5
075  Majaw  Yibba also said it today. He said: "I wanted to sow but to be honest I had bad premonitions." And then that he will buy sheep and raise sheep, he spoke of sheep today. [Laughs] Who sells his peanut seeds and begins to raise sheep, I say?

| | | |
|---|---|---|
| 076 | Njaga | The wet ground is really good, though, this wet ground. |
| 077 | Tapha | Around the village it is easy and comfortable to herd. |
| 078 | Njaga | The wet ground is not good. |
| 079 | Daur | Oh? |
| 080 | Tapha | Around the village it is comfortable to herd. |
| 081 | Jajji | Right this year it is comfortable to herd. |
| 082 | Majaw | Pshaw! This year is made for the farmers. |
| 083 | Jajji | This year is comfortable. |

In the introduction, I distinguished between several phases of disaster communication, one of them being alarming. Alarming includes a definition of what is a disaster and what is not. This is where uncertainty comes in. The Wolof—in a kind of distributed cognition—constantly and accurately monitor their environment to seek information about risks in order to subsequently discuss it with the other villagers. The village square is the place where decisions are made about whether the current situation might be severe (so that possibly governmental agencies will have to be mobilized) or not. For example, in the following excerpt from the conversation on 20 June 2005, they talk about whether the locusts are indeed coupling and—as entailed—reproducing, or not.

20 June 2005, Excerpt 6

| | | |
|---|---|---|
| 010 | Jajji | Do you listen? They said that they haven't coupled yet. They haven't coupled yet and they haven't yet descended to the ground to couple. |
| 011 | Njaga | Once they descend it will be wicked. |
| 012 | Jajji | As long as they are here, the minds of the people won't be at rest. |
| 013 | Majaw | But two persons have said it. |
| 014 | Jajji | What? |
| 015 | Majaw | Two persons said it. |
| 016 | Jajji | No, there is no one who saw the coupling. There has been no coupling yet. |
| 017 | Yoro | Father Jajji, I myself saw two of them that were coupling. |
| 018 | Jajji | OK, then I was wrong. |

Subsequently, they talk about whether the locusts are laying eggs.

20 June 2005, Excerpt 7

| | | |
|---|---|---|
| 019 | Laay | I saw them on my field when they were descending to the ground. |

| | | |
|---|---|---|
| 020 | Jajji | OK, descending to the ground, all right. |
| 021 | Laay | I didn't see them coupling, but I saw them descending. |
| 022 | Yoro | This morning in my field I found them on the ground. |
| 023 | Njaga | If they descend it's worse. |
| 024 | Laay | I saw some of them on the ground. |
| 025 | Yoro | I chased them off and all of them but two made "wrrrrom." I caught the two and separated them. When I let them go they weren't able to fly any more. |
| 026 | Majaw | When they couple they die. |
| 027 | Modou | When it couples, it can't fly. |
| 028 | Majaw | But it dies when it delivers. |
| 029 | Tapha | Yes, when it delivers it dies. |
| 030 | Njaga | When it delivers, it dies, but it delivers a lot. |
| 031 | Tapha | That's for sure, if only it delivers it dies. |
| 032 | Laay | I really saw them sitting on the ground. |
| 033 | Majaw | Yibba Jóob also said that there are people who said that they saw it. |
| 034 | Modou | It is coupling. [Laughs incredulously] |
| 035 | Tapha | When it lays eggs it dies. |
| 036 | Majaw | He said he saw it coupling, but Yibba didn't see it himself. |
| 037 | Tapha | And the eggs, when it rains ... |
| 038 | Majaw | But he said that he didn't see it. |
| 039 | Laay | But when they are on wet ground they couple. When they are on wet ground they couple. |
| 040 | Majaw | They couple even more quickly on tilled soil. Gosh, these machines like to couple on top of it. This is really a devil's breed. |

Thus, the men constantly seek knowledge of their environment, and they permanently adjust this knowledge among themselves, so that it is easier for them to assess the risk connected to investing in seeds and sowing. When the risk of the loss of the seeds is too high, they have to think about and discuss alternative action, as in excerpt 5 from 20 June 2005 (see above).

## *Disaster Evaluation: The Power of Fate*

A fourth topic concerns the moral and religious but sometimes also very personal evaluation of the past disastrous experience. Thus, while risk communication concerns the assessment of future action, evaluative communication concerns the past. One example of ironic self-evaluation is in the conversation of 20 June 2005, when Majaw quotes a religious song.

20 June 2005, Excerpt 8
056 Majaw   It is like that singer sang, you know?
058 Majaw   As Serin Tuba sang …
060 Majaw   As Musa Ka sang to Serin Tuba: [Sings] "If you gave us what we had …"
062 Majaw   [Sings] "… then we would be like we are. Haven't you perceived that we were accomplished?"
063 Jajji   [Sings] "If we had had it we wouldn't have done what we did."
064 Majaw   Yes. [Laughs]
066 Majaw   [Sings] "Haven't you perceived that we were accomplished?"
068 Jajji   Right.
069 Ngaan   That, if we only had it, we would be grateful toward God.

Jajji dialogically comes in, since the song is known to all of them. The excerpt comes right after excerpt 2 from the same day, in which the farmers speak about caterpillars, which are the usual vermin they are confronted with. How much better would this pest have been in comparison to the locust swarms!

But most of all, the third conversation, from two years after the swarms (4 July 2006), is concerned with the evaluation of the horrible past. Here, Laay narrates his personal experience of the locusts arriving in the village.

4 July 2006, Excerpt 1
001 Majaw   The rainy season, he said, also is like that. It makes budum, bum-bum bum-bum-bum, so that you just say: "Go!" Nothing disturbs it and everything seems to grow fine. That's like the year of the locusts. Sëriñ Modu himself commented it so. He said, all of a sudden, all of a sudden you lose hope in anyone and in the rainy season.
002 Laay    Oh, in that year I was harvesting a lot of millet. Really in that year one donkey carriage full full full full full with millet that was opulent opulent opulent opulent opulent opulent opulent. [Laughs] At that time I came back from the pilgrimage to Daaru Musti. They said the east is like that, the east is like that.
003         [Laughing]
004 Laay    The east will be wet through. I said: "Oh, it is noon." I said, let's inspect the house field. There were only a few. At that time, it was that we planned to provisionally harvest the millet the next day. When we went at it we ran ran ran. Every millet cob that we touched, five minutes later it was zinc white.
005 Majaw   Right.
006 Laay    Zinc!

| | | |
|---|---|---|
| 007 | Majaw | They start at the bottom. |
| 008 | Laay | Good Lord! |
| 009 | Majaw | And then climb up to the top. |
| 010 | Laay | And my millet was perfectly perfectly perfectly perfectly perfectly perfectly perfectly ripe. Really. |
| 011 | Majaw | If you had known it earlier, you would just have it cut and laid on the ground. |
| 012 | Laay | Yes, at that time, but you can't enjoy what has not yet become your fortune. Nobody can enjoy it. Good Lord! I would have been able to make a harvest so well well well. I am sure that I would have had two hundredweights of ripe millet. Two hundredweights of millet! That's like my harvest in this year. It is one donkey carriage full full full full full full, but still it may stay as it is. If a field is to be productive, it shall be. |
| 013 | Njaga | Yeah. |
| 014 | Laay | And if it won't succeed you will be tired and you won't have anything. To be honest I have tilled it roundly. The year before last when I tilled it, as it had lied fallow before, I needed three plough blades. And then when rain came and I sowed! [Laughs] How good life can be, gosh. |
| 015 | Njaga | Yeah. |
| 016 | Laay | Man oh man. |

Majaw's statement and Laay's account, narrated from the distance of nearly two years, start with the problem of a striking disaster and the loss of hope. Adopting a self-ironic stance, Laay presents a personal story formulated in hyperboles and dramatic repetitions that subsequently, especially in lines 012 and 014, is evaluated in more general terms. Especially his "you can't enjoy what has not yet become your fortune" (*ludul wërsag mëneesu ko lekk*) in line 012 shows how much the farmers think in terms of temporal organization and how they include the contingencies and uncertainties (in other words, the risks) of life in their thinking in a very fundamental way. Line 014 emphasizes the working morale and, most of all, the satisfactions of successful work.

### *Options for Action: Conflict and Revolution*

A fifth and final observation that I would like to make is the following: from the end of excerpt 5 of 20 June 2005 on, the men begin discussing the damage that grazing livestock is doing to their crops. In a discussion that is far too long to be represented here, they, instead of further talking about the threat of a new locust plague, now begin talking about herding and the dangers that grazing animals present to their crops. Traditionally, the Wolof are farmers, and the herders are the neighboring Fulani. Therefore, interethnic relations with their neighbors became an issue after the locust swarms. However, as the men said, some of the villagers had equally begun to invest more money in livestock instead of putting it into seeds. They therefore spoke about the possibility of letting animals graze on their fallow land. Subsequently, thinking of fallow land, they moved on to an agreement that the villagers had made about a portion of their common land that they intended to sell to another village and that they agreed to let lie fallow until then. The agreement had been breached by the son of the village chief, who had begun to cultivate this area, and by others of the more wealthy villagers, who had let their livestock graze on it. Some animals had subsequently entered neighboring cultivated crop fields and damaged them.

20 June 2005, Excerpt 9
191 Majaw They said that whoever owns a lamb might unbind it.
192 Jajji Yes, but we ... but we haven't heard of it. They have colluded and done it, but they ... as soon as we will have a dispute, they will see, what ... they will see!
193 Daur Yes.
194 Jajji We haven't heard of it.
195 Laay As it appears now ...
196 Daur Jajji ...
197 Laay We should be careful. The quarrel hasn't started yet.
198 Jajji Yes. The quarrel hasn't started yet.
199 Laay Let's wait and see.
200 Jajji Because they have colluded ... they have colluded and they went so far as to breach our agreement.

This point led the discussants to the topic of social inequality between the clans in the village. The clan of the village chief and the other clans were blamed for colluding in order to gain personal benefits. The traditional way of parceling out the community fields, which is done by the village chief, was eventually questioned.

20 June 2005, Excerpt 10
236 Tapha But this isn't right!
237 Modou In the afternoon there was a horse sowing.
238 Tapha As to me tomorrow ... tomorrow early in the morning ...
239 Daur Huh?
240 Tapha I will cultivate my field!

The interclan relations were suddenly in danger. Thus, as it appears, the locust disaster motivated the people of the village to complain about the current relations of existence (i.e., to criticize the most powerful and wealthy of the village) and created a will for social change, even if this implies social conflict.

20 June 2005, Excerpt 11

| | | |
|---|---|---|
| 289 | Yoro | As long as the fields won't be released … |
| 290 | Jajji | Pshaw! |
| 291 | Njaga | Yes. |
| 292 | Ngañ | This is how they do it. |
| 293 | Majaw | Even if they were released … |
| 294 | Ngañ | We have to go via the village chief. |
| 295 | Majaw | You see! You see! |
| 296 | Majaw | You see! Even if they were released! |
| | | [Section omitted] |
| 309 | Jajji | The fallow land, they have colluded in order to execute their plan. |
| 310 | Ngañ | Oh. |
| 311 | Jajji | Wait … just listen, man! |
| 312 | Daur | This is your clan! |
| 313 | Jajji | Yes, your clan only! |
| 314 | Daur | Ngañ! |
| 315 | Jajji | This is your clan only! |
| 316 | Daur | Ngañ, Ngañ, Ngañ. I am in front of this mosque! |
| 317 | Ngañ | Look, we talk of what we all had agreed upon here. Here we had agreed upon it! |
| 318 | Jajji | Oh, but this was only your clan! |
| 319 | Daur | In the name of Sëriñ Tuba, only those of this part of the village have negotiated the survey. |
| | | [Section omitted] |
| 342 | Jajji | Even if everybody cultivates, I, I don't need a field anymore. |
| 343 | Jajji | I don't need any. But what we say, they have colluded here. |
| 344 | Jajji | I will only till where I want to. |
| 345 | Daur | They have colluded, they have colluded. |
| 346 | Ngañ | What you say, we all spoke about it here, I say. |
| 347 | Jajji | You will have big problems in the future! |
| 348 | Ngañ | In this village, as to what we have agreed upon … |
| 349 | Jajji | Big problems! |
| 350 | Ngañ | Everything in this village has been openly discussed here. |
| 351 | Jajji | You will have big problems in the future! |
| 352 | Ngañ | You blame your relatives of collusion only now! |
| 353 | Daur | No, we don't blame your relatives of collusion. |

| | | |
|---|---|---|
| 354 | Ngañ | Oh, all of them, all of them. |
| 355 | Daur | They have fabricated the survey. |
| 356 | Ngañ | Everybody agreed to it! |
| 357 | Daur | They have fabricated the survey. |
| | | [Section omitted] |
| 388 | Jajji | They have colluded! |
| 389 | Jajji | First they talk loudly ... |
| 390 | Daur | They are double-tongued! |
| 391 | Jajji | First they talk loudly, they talk loudly, and then they do something else. |
| 392 | Jajji | May it hit their relatives. |
| 393 | Jajji | They talk about their things until ready. |
| 394 | Daur | Until they ... they ... |
| 395 | Jajji | They ... they ... they think the people were idiots! |
| 396 | Daur | And he says, they had openly talked about it here. |
| 397 | Daur | He doesn't tell the truth himself! |

Note that in line 352 Ngañ speaks of an inclusive "your relatives," which emphasizes the joint kinship of all the clans (Ngañ's kin are Daur's kin as well, according to Ngañ), while Daur in 353 accentuates their division by stressing that he blames only Ngañ's relatives (which are not Daur's, in his view). Thus, the crisis has the power to create mischief in the village.

Therefore, an important strategy in dealing with risk appears to be that fields of action that are open for intervention become relevant, while other realms—in our case, the fight against the locusts themselves—might not be considered in depth. Instead, the—from the perspective of the farmers—unalterable situation of disaster is used to raise topics such as social inequalities, problems, and conflicts that are open for change. Thus, risks that are generated by external factors appear to be domesticated by dealing with connected or loosely associated variables that are possible to manipulate, and that are culturally available for modification (cf. Paine 2002).

In contrast to the global discourses mentioned above that mainly dealt with either the scientific and technological aspects or the moral implications and meanings of the disaster from the perspective of a modernist narrative of human ascent, the Wolof farmers tried to find paths that are susceptible to their manipulation and influence. In putting social inequalities into the center of their action, they appear no less modernist than the Western global discourses. This affirms that the world risk society is a society of not only one kind of risk, but of plural risks and risk ideologies. We therefore should not only speak of "multiple modernities" (Eisenstadt 2000), but equally of a multiple world risk society that offers plural pathways toward the completion of the (apparently still unfinished) project of modernity.

## Conclusion

This chapter was a first exploration of how the people in Senegal in their everyday life deal with extreme events such as the locust plague in 2004 and how they cope with their uncertainty about whether and when this event will repeat. As we can see, people in Senegal do not just patiently wait for disasters to come, but actively assess their situation and its risks as well as their possibilities for action. Due to high potential follow-up costs, they are under constant pressure to act and therefore also to make joint decisions, or at least to come to joint epistemic stances, through rhetorical deliberation.

In their debates, communications about alarming, mobilization, disaster management, evaluation, and risk calculation constantly alternate. These debates serve to produce sensibilities for indicators of disaster, and keep individual as well as organized forms of reaction available.

As we can also see, disasters question existing forms of interpretation; they are shocking (cf. Clausen's radicality) and thereby produce a consciousness about the contingency of human existence. From the perspective of rhetoric, we can assume that rhetoric flourishes under these circumstances, as rhetoric is fundamentally concerned with uncertainty and contingency. On the other hand, disasters are precisely the kind of events that at first create speechlessness, since there is no foil for adequate rhetorical response, and where, consequently, new forms of rhetorics have still to be invented. Let me emphasize here that the Wolof farmers did not speak about "disaster" or the like. The Wolof word closest to it (*musiba*, "harm") was not used in the discussions. The global discourse that celebrated the disaster in a hysterical way appears to not have been the discourse of those who were affected by it, even though they were well-informed about it.

New rhetorics in turn activate social energies and processes of aestheticization that follow up any deep social shock. In our example, irony and metonym were among these forms. However, this is only a helpless way of coping with external forces that are beyond control. The realms where people have the possibility of "creative destruction" (from Marx through Schumpeter) are restricted. Among the Wolof, they mainly consist of either changing the subsistence strategy to herding or of emigration, and only a slight possibility of "revolution." There is thus not so much destruction—rather, the old ways of living continue to coexist with newly created and adapted forms. Vulnerability, to mention a much-discussed category in disaster anthropology (cf. Oliver-Smith and Hoffman 1999), is absorbed by flexibility in livelihood.

**Christian Meyer** is a professor of communication studies at the University of Duisburg-Essen (Germany). Recent publications include *The Rhetorical Emergence of Culture*, edited with Felix Girke (Berghahn Books, 2011); *Communication Wolof et Société Sénégalaise: Héritage et Création*, edited with with Anna M. Diagne and Sascha Kesseler (L'Harmattan 2011); "New Alterities and Emerging Cultures of Social Interaction," *Global Cooperation Research Papers* 3 (Käte Hamburger Kolleg Centre for Global Cooperation Research, 2013; http://www.die-gdi.de/uploads/media/Global-Cooperation-Research-Papers-3.pdf); and "Ethnography: Body, Communication and Cultural Practices," in *Body—Language—Communication*, volume 1, edited by Cornelia Müller, Alan Cienki, Ellen Fricke, Silva H. Ladewig, David McNeill, and Sedinha Teßendorf (Mouton de Gruyter, 2013).

## Notes

The transcripts on which the analysis is based were made with the help of Malick Faye. I am also grateful to the research group on "Communicating Disaster" (2010–11; Center for Interdisciplinary Studies, Bielefeld University) with whom, as a resident fellow, I had the opportunity to discuss the data. Special thanks go to Dieter Neubert (University of Bayreuth), who was member of the group and generously funded part of the transcription.

1. As Latour (1993: 6–7) says, "The ozone hole is too social and too narrated to be truly natural."
2. However, there are some studies on the functioning of "centers of coordination," as, for example, in the London Underground in the (nondisastrous) everyday (cf. Heath and Luff 1992).
3. In the subsequent paragraphs I refer mainly to the analyses of Enserink (2004), IRIN (2004), Lecoq (2005), and Thiam and Kuiseu (2005).
4. In the subsequent section I refer mainly to Despland, Rosenberg, and Simpson (2004), Enserink (2004), IRIN (2004), Lecoq (2005), Thiam and Kuiseu (2005), Ceccato and colleagues (2006, 2007), Sánchez-Zapata and colleagues (2007), Anstey and colleagues (2009), Bazazi and colleagues (2011), and Ma and colleagues (2011).
5. This, at least, is the sociological point of view that is increasingly adopted by aid institutions (who formerly viewed disasters mostly as natural incidents to be solved technically). In recent years, however, there are some voices that argue against a pure social constructionism and insist upon the natural, cultural, and social interwovenness present in disasters (Wilford 2008; Williams 2008; Law and Singleton 2009).
6. In Senegal, every year at the beginning of the rainy season, diviners (who stem from the ethnic group Sereer) foretell the future rainfall and other events in the country in a ritual called *xóoy* (invocation). The ritual is performed in different parts of the country. The most important one (which is the one referred to in this example) is held in Fatick.

# Bibliography

Alexander, David. 2006. "Globalization of Disaster: Trends, Problems and Dilemmas." *Journal of International Affairs* 59, no. 2: 1–22.
Anstey, Michael L., Stephen M. Rogers, Swidbert R. Ott, Malcolm Burrows, and Stephen J. Simpson. 2009. "Serotonin Mediates Behavioral Gregarization Underlying Swarm Formation in Desert Locusts." *Science* 323, no. 5914: 627–30.
Bazazi, Sepideh, Pawel Romanczuk, Sian Thomas, Lutz Schimansky-Geier, Joseph J. Hale, Gabriel A. Miller, Gregory A. Sword, Stephen J. Simpson, and Iain D. Couzin. 2011. "Nutritional State and Collective Motion: From Individuals to Mass Migration." *Proceedings of the Royal Society B: Biological Sciences* 278, no. 1704: 356–63.
Ceccato, Pietro, Michael A. Bell, M. Benno Blumenthal, Stephen J. Connor, Tufa Dinku, Emily K. Grover-Kopec, Chester F. Ropelewski, and Madeleine C. Thomson. 2006. "Use of Remote Sensing for Monitoring Climate Variability for Integrated Early Warning Systems: Applications for Human Diseases and Desert Locust Management." In *Proceedings of the International Geoscience & Remote Sensing Symposium, July 31–August 4, 2006, Denver, Colorado,* 270–74.
Ceccato, Pietro, Keith Cressman, Alessandra Giannini, and Sylwia Trzaska. 2007. "The Desert Locust Upsurge in West Africa (2003–2005)." *International Journal on Pest Management* 53, no. 1: 7–13.
Chossudovsky, Michel. 2004. "The Ultimate Weapon of Mass Destruction: 'Owning the Weather' for Military Use." Global Research, 27 September. http://globalresearch.ca/articles/CHO409F.html (accessed 30 June 2012).
Clausen, Lars. 1992. "Social Differentiation and the Long-Term Origin of Disasters." *Natural Hazards* 6: 181–90.
Danisch, Robert. 2010. "Political Rhetoric in a World Risk Society." *Rhetoric Society Quarterly* 40, no. 2: 172–92.
Despland, Emma, Jane Rosenberg, and Stephen J. Simpson. 2004. "Landscape Structure and Locust Swarming: A Satellite's Eye View." *Ecography* 27: 381–91.
Dombrowsky, Wolf R. 2007. "Lessons Learned? Disasters, Rapid Change and Globalization." *International Review of the Red Cross* 89, no. 866: 271–77.
Douglas, Mary. 1966. *Purity and Danger. An Analysis of the Concepts of Pollution and Taboo.* London: Routledge and Keegan.
Eisenstadt, Shmuel. 2000. "Multiple Modernities." *Daedalus* 129, no. 1: 1–29.
Enserink, Martin. 2004. "Can the War on Locusts Be Won?" *Science* 306: 1880–82.
Evans-Pritchard, Edward E. 1937. *Witchcraft, Oracles and Magic Among the Azande.* Oxford: Oxford University Press.
Hamacher, Werner. 1999. "The Quaking of Presentation." In *Premises: Essays on Philosophy and Literature from Kant to Celan,* ed. Werner Hamacher, 261–93. Stanford, CA: Stanford University Press.
Heath, Christian C., and Paul Luff. 1992. "Collaboration and Control: Crisis Management and Multimedia Technology in London Underground Line Control Rooms." *Journal of Computer-Supported Cooperative Work* 1: 69–94.
Heath, Robert L., and H. Dan O'Hair. 2009. *Handbook of Risk and Crisis Communication.* New York: Routledge.
IRIN. 2004. "The Eighth Plague: West Africa's Locust Invasion." Web Special of the publication service of the UN Office for the Coordination of Humanitarian Affairs.

December. http://www.irinnews.org.administrator.irinnews.org/pdf/in-depth/eighth-plague-irin-in-depth.pdf (accessed 3 June 2015).
Irvine, Judith T. 1990. "Registering Affect: Heteroglossia in the Linguistic Expression of Emotion." In *Language and the Politics of Emotion*, ed. Catherine A. Lutz and Lila Abu-Lughod, 126–61. Cambridge: Cambridge University Press.
Kreps, Gary A. 1985. "Disaster and the Social Order." *Sociological Theory* 3, no. 1: 49–64.
Kuipers, Giselinde. 2002. "Media Culture and Internet Disaster Jokes: Bin Laden and the Attack on the World Trade Center." *European Journal of Cultural Studies* 5, no. 4: 450–70.
Latour, Bruno. 1993. *We Have Never Been Modern*. Cambridge, MA: Harvard University Press.
Law, John, and Vicky Singleton. 2009. "Disaster: A Further Species of Trouble? Disaster and Narrative." In *The Social and Cultural Impact of Foot and Mouth Disease in the UK in 2001: Experiences and Analyses*, ed. Martin Döring and Brigitte Nerlich, 229–42. Manchester: Manchester University Press.
Lecoq, Michel. 2005. "Desert Locust Management: From Ecology to Anthropology." *Journal of Orthoptera Research* 14, no. 2: 179–86.
Letukas, Lynn, and John Barnshaw. 2008. "World-System Approach to Post-Catastrophe International Relief." *Social Forces* 87, no. 2: 1063–87.
Ma, Zongyuan, Wei Guo, Xiaojiao Guo, Xianhui Wang, and Le Kang. 2011. "Modulation of Behavioral Phase Changes of the Migratory Locust by the Catecholamine Metabolic Pathway." *Proceedings of the National Academy of Science* 108, no. 10: 3882–87.
McCabe, J. Terrence. 2002. "Impact of and Response to Drought among Turkana Pastoralists: Implications for Anthropological Theory and Hazard Research." In *Catastrophe and Culture: The Anthropology of Disaster*, ed. Susanna M. Hoffman and Anthony Oliver-Smith, 213–36. Oxford: James Currey.
Meyer, Christian. 2008. "Persuasive Interaktion und soziale Beeinflussung: Zur Mikrophysik der Macht in einem Wolof-Dorf Nordwest-Senegals." *Paideuma* 54: 151–72.
Oliver-Smith, Anthony, and Susanna M. Hoffman. 1999. *The Angry Earth: Disaster in Anthropological Perspective*. New York: Routledge.
Paine, Robert. 2002. "Danger and the Non-Risk Thesis." In *Catastrophe and Culture: The Anthropology of Disaster*, ed. Susanna M. Hoffman and Anthony Oliver-Smith, 67–89. Oxford: James Currey.
Perry, Ronald W., and Enrico L. Quarantelli. 2005. *What Is a Disaster? New Answers to Old Questions*. Philadelphia: Xlibris.
Quarantelli, Enrico L. 1988. *What Is A Disaster? Perspectives on the Question*. London: Routledge.
Sánchez-Zapata, José A., José A. Donázar, Antonio Delgado, Manuela G. Forero, Olga Ceballos, and Fernando Hiraldo. 2007. "Desert Locust Outbreaks in the Sahel: Resource Competition, Predation and Ecological Effects of Pest Control." *Journal of Applied Ecology* 44: 323–29.
Sauer, Beverly J. 2003. *The Rhetoric of Risk: Technical Documentation in Hazardous Environments*. Mahwah, NJ: Erlbaum.
Steinberg, Theodore. 2000. *Acts of God: The Unnatural History of Natural Disaster in America*. Oxford: Oxford University Press.
Thiam, Abou, and Julienne Kuiseu. 2005. "Heuschreckenplage im Sahel: Warten hat fatale Folgen." *Entwicklung und ländlicher Raum* 3: 27–29.

Wilford, Justin. 2008. "Out of Rubble: Natural Disaster and the Materiality of the House." *Environment and Planning: International Journal of Urban and Regional Research* 26, no. 4: 647–62.

Williams, Stewart. 2008. "Rethinking the Nature of Disaster: From Failed Instruments of Learning to a Post-Social Understanding." *Social Forces* 87, no. 2: 1115–38.

Zimmerman, Don H. 1992. "Achieving Context: Openings in Emergency Calls." In *Text in Context: Contributions to ethnomethodology*, ed. Graham Watson and Robert M. Seiler, 35–51. London: Sage.

CHAPTER 10

## *Too Too Much Much*
### Presence and Catastrophe in Contemporary Art

Monica Westin

■ ■ ■ ■ ■ ■ ■

In the Belgian countryside outside the city of Gent stands a small private museum devoted to contemporary art, with large glass double doors and oversized windows juxtaposed against a lush, green rural landscape. Inside, track lighting creates subtle spotlights on immaculate white gallery walls. But in 2010 the Museum Dhondt-Dhaenens, instead of displaying an orderly collection of paintings or sculptures, literally overflows with trash, specifically aluminum beverage cans. Crushed cans fill the entire space of the museum past the depth of a person's height, so that if you stood on the floor of the museum you would be completely covered; instead, you have to scramble over dunes of garbage as you move from room to room. The trash spills out in a sort of delta from the museum's front doors. Inside, the landfill is punctuated by objects like fossils in sediment: uncanny mannequins, partially buried or standing at attention; couches, chairs, and electronic appliances rising out of the heaps like mushrooms from a sodden forest floor; giant sculptures of soda cans confounding the scale of the human figure in the space (figure 10.1). The overall aesthetic experience is one of being swamped or engulfed by systems of consumption and reification. The museum setting both allows the drowning-by-landfill to feel meaningful and also implicitly questions the relationships between art institutions and the global systems that support art's superstructure.

Figure 10.1. Thomas Hirschhorn, *Too Too Much Much*, Museum Dhondt-Dhaenens, 2010. "Thomas Hirschhorn @ Museum Dhondt Dhaenens" by Lux & Jourik (happyfamousartists), licensed under a Creative Commons Attribution-NonCommercial-NoDerivs License 2.0. Original photo at https://www.flickr.com/photos/happyfamousartists/5231338479/in/photostream/.

## Material, Energy, and Excess

Thomas Hirschhorn's 2010 installation *Too Too Much Much* is the result of an attempt, in the words of the artist, "to give form to a kind of universal and conflictual hyperconsumption ... which goes beyond the usual facts and criticism of consumption" (Cruzvillegas 2010). Echoing Hirschhorn's own statement, art historian Pamela Lee describes his body of work as consistently putting forth "an argument about mediation, materialism, overproduction, and consumption: a primer on how to work *with* and *under* such conditions as our worldly horizon," where "we are implicated in the mess" of that world (Lee 2012: 109). Lee finds that this effect is largely based on the material Hirschhorn uses: "He works with a ... profligate range of materials ... whose representational force is held in check by the sheer excess of the matter itself" (Lee 2012: 110).

If Hirschhorn's argument in *Too Too Much Much* is about coming to terms with our never-ending crisis of consumption, and if his intention is for the force of the issue to act directly on the viewer, then the scale and materials of *Too Too Much Much* embody the problem of consumer behavior and the systems into which the consumer finds herself woven. *Too Too Much Much* thus addresses a cultural problem—catastrophic, excessive consumption—that is also a political problem and, in Hirschhorn's treatment, an aesthetic problem that the artist articulates through both the materials and the form of his installation.

Hirschhorn regularly uses cheap, mass-produced materials—cardboard, plastic, pages torn from magazines—for his sprawling installations, and much of his work's power and energy seems to be a result of his choice to abandon traditional artistic mediums of representation in favor of "everyday" tangible detritus, which seem to be able to turn an otherwise abstract issue (here the excessive consumption and production of material waste) into something like an embodied revelation for audiences. Hirschhorn has repeatedly described his use of these materials, in opposition to archival materials that would make his work more collectible and fluid within art markets, as a political decision.[1] In an interview with art historian Benjamin Buchloh, Hirschhorn describes the materials he chooses in terms of "energy" rather than aesthetics:

> I want to work on this notion of an exalted high art … I question that, and I criticize that. And that is why I create my work with my own materials … you could even say miserable [materials]—not only discouraging but miserable—and truly modest results. I try to give form to my ideas. And if I am to give them the kind of form I want, I have to work with materials that everybody knows. It's not a matter of antiaesthetics … it is a matter of a different purpose. If a woman puts tape around her suitcase because she fears that it might burst open, she doesn't think about whether it looks nice. She simply wants to fix something that presents a problem for her. And she thereby creates a form, or uses the materials that interest me for what is actually needed: energy … energy in the sense of something that connects people, that can connect you with others. That is why I also have to say programmatically, "Quality *no*, energy *yes!*" (Buchloh 2005: 89–92)

Hirschhorn's explanation of his materials as a means to harness and deploy social energy suggests that he understands his work to be engaged in "fixing things" through materials that offer direct encounters with the problems that interest him. In addition to the force of the literal materials, the scale in which these materials are presented produces the energy in *Too Too Much Much*: not just a few cans, but a hurricane of cans that burst from the seams of the museum, an institution that cannot contain them. The excess is manifold: wading through trash so deep the floor cannot be touched, the literal excess in audience experience "gives form," to use the artist's words, to the thematic excess underlying the catastrophe that Hirschhorn tries to presence through the artwork's energy.

## Art, Catastrophe, and Sublimity

Beyond the literal materials of the pieces, at least part of the installation's energy can be located in the tension between the modern art institution of the "white cube" gallery space of the museum and the veritable garbage dump (or recycling plant) Hirschhorn creates in it and overflowing from it. Hirschhorn seems aware of the ironies of using art as a platform for representing catastrophe, as well as the contrast created by the debased, "miserable" material against the pristine white nonspace of the gallery.[2]

As an institution, what we now think of as contemporary art—in particular the high-end art exhibited at biennales and museums and purchased at blue-chip galleries and auctions—has by definition not been part of the everyday. Its semiautonomous nature sets it apart from functional, daily life, and it is self-consciously framed as such.[3] Along the same lines, art generally gains its rhetorical power when it dehabituates from daily life; art's operations might be seen as fundamentally a radical decontextualizing. Art is thus art uniquely poised to try to represent catastrophe, which would seem to be definitionally that which fractures daily life—so when an artist takes catastrophe as the subject matter of his art, his job might seem to be halfway done: emergencies are, by definition, never habitual. But jot-for-jot representation of catastrophe is mere reportage, and art (again definitionally) does more; among many other things, art helps humans navigate social life by crystallizing complexity into an image or an icon—a persuasive emblem of ideology. When an artist attempts to do this with disaster or catastrophe, there is nothing to amplify and no element to exaggerate—the subject is already exaggerated. So what tactics might an artist employ in his effort to crystallize the complexity of catastrophe?

The tropes we often associate most directly with art made in and about the aftermath of disaster often include healing, memorial, testimony, and advocacy. One perennial theme in the art of catastrophe is the question of whether it can even be represented at all, resulting in art that seeks to create absences rather than presences and suggest the limits of our memories and imaginations. There is a long genealogy of art that self-consciously considers its own limitations in articulating and responding to different kinds of disasters. (Consider, for example, the conversations around representations of the Holocaust.)

But in the case of Hirschhorn's installation, art attempts to take on a phenomenon that is everyday and largely unseeable; the scale of production and consumption remaining only partially visible is crucial to both socioeconomic processes and the ideologies surrounding them. Hirschhorn attempts to convince us to see catastrophe in this at a time when we are experiencing the historical emergence of vocabularies invented to distinguish between hierarchies of catastrophes: the new "superstorms" that suggest we need to reimagine the scale of weather, for example, or the poet Jalal Toufiq's 2009 book about "surpassing disasters" (Hiroshima/Nagasaki is one of his cases). Against this backdrop, Hirschhorn's project is to embody and turn into a visible, experiential presence the largely unseen, unsettlingly *latent* nature of overconsumption.

The mundane nature of the catastrophe Hirschhorn presents is a deep irony that the artist references through his placement of human figures; the mannequins in the installation, which offer a dark commentary on human agency, provide direct allusions to the images of catastrophes that we thought *would* happen but did not. They immediately recall the crash test dummies that regularly provide our models for the emergencies to the human body we are prepared for. The most immediate historical context for the mannequins (and one that would be salient to Hirschhorn, given his birth in 1956) is the use of mannequins during midcentury atomic bomb tests to try to plan for a nuclear holocaust that failed to occur. Hirschhorn's Cold War mannequin imagery reminds us that the large-scale, fast apocalypses we expected in the twentieth century have more often turned out to be incremental, everyday cumulative effects that are more difficult to conceptualize as disasters.

Invisible, everyday catastrophes are paradoxical to us. We might, after Ariella Azoulay, call these kinds of insidious phenomena "near emergencies" on the "verge of catastrophe" that remain invisible except when they threaten to erupt into the kinds of catastrophes that stop our daily life and demand recognition, the kind that we make plans for and consider our reactions to (for example, the "global weirding" behind the "superstorms").

> The verge of catastrophe does not emerge, is not exactly an event, and has no power to create a difference. It exists on the surface, completely open to the gaze and yet evading it, because there is nothing to distinguish it from the surroundings in which it exists. Its contours are indistinct; one could easily fail to notice it … it meets all the conditions necessary to escape most existing systems of representation. (Azoulay 2012: 291)

In this light, Hirschhorn's project seems to be directing energy toward a looming, ever present force that needs to have emergency claims made for it, brought into presence.

The sublime is often overtheorized as an ahistorical experience, but in this case it seems unavoidable as a trope: the overcoming of some kind of perceptual limit to create an experience of simultaneous fear and (aesthetic) appreciation. Here the fear is that of the implacable—the unyielding, relentless desire of consumers and the machines that fuel those desires. The aesthetic appreciation in this sublime experience comes from the framing of the material as an art experience that asks to be read as exceptional: the unconventional use of the museum space as a site for massive containment of material, the encouragement of the audience to interact physically with the art, the actual spatiotemporal experience of the cans themselves.

The sublime also requires some kind of human figure to understand the scale of its force, which here takes the form of the uncanny figures of the mannequins. Art critics and theorists usually invoke the term "sublime" in modern and contemporary art to describe almost any kind of encounter with the infinite or ungraspable in the spectator:art:world relation—the visual representation/suggestion of the unrepresentable, in which the human figure, when it appears, does so on a dramatically small scale that is drastically overshadowed by the environment around it.

Notably, the sublime in modern and contemporary art almost always includes a self-conscious consideration of kinds of artificiality in regard to the human figure. The reemergence of the human figure writ large—but now increasingly in the form of mannequins and other unnatural human figures in contemporary art, as in Hirschhorn's piece—was the subject of a symposium titled "Art and Subjecthood: The Return of the Human Figure in Semiocapitalism" at the Institut fur Kunstkirtik during the summer of 2010, when Hirschhorn's piece was being exhibited. More recently, this issue of the human figure in contemporary art as a kind of uncanny relational sublime has been written about at length by Isabelle Graw, who co-organized the symposium. Graw considers the renewed attention to the idea of the subject, but what she calls a "distorted subject" in the form of mannequins, which she argues is a result of the changing role of the subject under capitalism: a "commodified quasi person ... mannequins are symptomatic of the unstable border between product and person" (Graw 2011: 245).

For better or worse, the current understanding of subjectivity as "produced" rather than "natural" has deeply affected the reintroduction of the figure into contemporary art, particularly in work that takes up a rhetoric of the sublime. The forces of the unmediated global market, which are, of course, part of Hirschhorn's critique, can produce the feelings of awe, terror, and overwhelmingness of the sublime. By reintroducing scale and questioning the ontology of the human figure, art can actually take up a project of critiquing this phenomenon.

## Metaphor, Abstraction, and Representation

All of my observations to this point have attempted to lay out the particular texture of Hirschhorn's articulation about catastrophic consumption. I want to turn next to a set of more specific vocabulary for describing the visual rhetoric of the artwork: the difference between metaphor, abstraction, and representation. Hirschhorn seems to be attempting to make a piece that can avoid being read as merely an *allegory* of excess, the way a work of "high art" (to use his words) might be interpreted. *Too Too Much Much* is insistent on being understood experientially and quite literally by the viewer.

I want to make a distinction between metaphor or allegory, which are firmly in the realm of symbolic representation, and an understanding of abstraction as distillation: that which lives in the uncanny space between the real and the representational. While *Too Too Much Much* can potentially be read as a symbol of superabundance and detritus—albeit a vivid metaphor—the way that it is experienced by the viewer and the intentions of the artist are more of a condensing of the real than its representation. To call the piece an allegory or a metaphor would be to ignore its purpose of re-creating an experience of excess consumption using the actual objects of that consumption—objects the audience themselves consume in "real life."

*Too Too Much Much* takes our knowledge of our role in unsustainable production and tries to make it present, "really real," for the viewers of the piece. In Hirschhorn's words, "I want my art to appropriate the world" (cited in Lee 2012, p. 106). Rather than creating a metaphor, Hirschhorn has created something more like a distillation of the real, an abstraction that is similar in form and material to the real thing. The concept of iconicity from semiotics is helpful; like the smoke from a fire, the cans are a symbol that nonetheless has a direct material relationship (one of *evidence*) to the real event.

This distilled quality of *Too Too Much Much* raises the question of what might be called the metaphoric and unravels some of the inherited binary between the real and the representational. I want to call this third space an effect of "presencing," a concept with a long history in rhetorical theory. The purpose or intention of this conception of presence is to create conviction through appeals to authenticity, framelessness, and reality effects, with its foundation in evidence. Hirschhorn's work is neither merely representational nor does it escape representation as a mode, though its primary motive is not to represent.

## Presence as Aesthetic Persuasion

Conceptualizing aesthetic presence first requires unthinking representation as the primary motive for art making, which can be difficult to do. Until now, I have used the words "represent," "representative," and "representational" in an art historical sense, where they are shorthand for pictorial representation, an inherently mimetic project. For most of art history, we have understood images and objects made by artists to be either direct or indirect acts of mimesis of nature or, since modernism, self-aware explorations of and arguments about specific media requiring interpretation on the part of the viewer. But entwined with this dominant narrative, there are numerous other genealogies of the arts that are created for different ends and effects. If Hirschhorn's art does attempt to create a "real" presence (here, that of consumption, otherwise latent or invisible in our daily lives), then it is part of a genealogy of art that also might include early Christian icons, understood to hold and invoke the real presence of saints lying dormant in the image until contemplated by the viewer; perhaps, even, the cave paintings of early humans (if we understand the images of animals as attempts to bring forth successful future hunts of real animals); and certainly the avant-garde turn to minimalist and conceptual art of the early 1960s, which had a direct influence on Hirschhorn's work. This strand of art history appears to stand in sharp contrast to the heritage of historically representative art, working instead to create an experience that is not sequestered or quarantined within art's semiautonomous framed zone, but rather part of and in interaction with the outside, everyday world. If art is usually understood to work via representation, then aesthetic presence seeks to work in more direct ways.

What Hirschhorn cannot do, what he can only gesture at in the sense of engulfment that *Too Too Much Much* creates, is take all the cans consumed—or even all the cans in Belgium used in a single day—and deposit them in one place. Consumption itself remains invisible to us in its true form and scale. We cannot access or even visualize the full extent of our personal consumption, let alone that of our apartment building or globalized city, and any attempt to show consumption will necessarily be a reduction of the real thing. Hirschhorn's cans are a representation of the sheer volume of the problem of consumption—they are a representation of scale. The world's production by nature covers up its own actions and remains largely invisible, despite our efforts to visualize it, and despite Hirschhorn's attempts at shock and power.

Whether or not *Too Too Much Much* is successful in convincing its viewers that it succeeds as a real-world intervention (conviction in the "realness" of what is being presenced is ultimately a matter of something like the viewer's faith, whether for Hirschhorn or religious icons), it does seem to carry a certain kind of rhetorical power that I have previously described in terms of iconicity. Considering this kind of art as exemplary of a particular rhetorical approach, we might imagine "presence" as a central tool that might occasionally have the ability to move rhetoric out of the realm of representation (though not entirely).

Presence has long been understood to be a species of rhetorical action, and the key definition for modern rhetoric of presence comes from Perelman and

Olbrechts-Tyteca's 1958 *The New Rhetoric*, in which they observe how choosing particular elements—data—to select and present to an audience "endows these elements with a *presence*, which is an essential factor in argumentation" (Perelman and Olbrechts-Tyteca 1958: 116). The rhetorician in this model works either to "make present, by verbal magic alone, that which is actually absent but what he considers important to his argument," or to make elements that are present enhanced (Perelman and Olbrechts-Tyteca 1958: 117). The point is obvious but deep; Perelman and Olbrechts-Tyteca give an example of a Chinese emperor who, when he saw an ox being taken to be sacrificed, insisted that a sheep be killed instead—merely because he could not see the sheep, while the ox was present for him. And while the concept of presence is technical in *The New Rhetoric*, it is not only literal; presence can extend from real objects to "a judgment or an entire argumentative development" (Perelman and Olbrechts-Tyteca 1958: 118), again relying on the logic that all argumentation involves selection and that presence is a means of selection.

While Perelman and Olbrechts-Tyteca focus on presence as a tool for focusing audience attention, I want to expand presence into the realm of evidence. Considering art that aspires to realization rather than representation reveals a rhetorical desire to overcome representation as well, through the "really real" objects of proof. The ultimate case of rhetorical presence would be rhetoric that overcomes its own context and breaks from its own frame: self-evidence. We might begin to ask whether perhaps a great many rhetorical strategies are in whole or in part avenues to achieving this kind of presence. Perfect rhetoric, of course, seems not to be rhetoric at all, but rather simply a presentation of the obvious thing that is already right before us. Presence helps to remind us that the line between real and representation is deceptively clearcut—and that what appears to be obvious through presence (proof, evidence) requires different faiths in order to be understood as real.

*Too Too Much Much* takes our knowledge of our role in unsustainable production and attempts to make it present, "really real," for the viewers of the piece who experience it. The viewer enters the rooms, wades through the trash, confronts the mannequins, and literally enters into a particular version of political texture through trash and production. This kind of texturing of the conceptual (here the concept involves the figure of the human and the scale of our consumption) with the material is necessarily nondiscursive in Hirschhorn's piece: simultaneous, not successive, taken in at once as a gestalt rather than "read" as a text, symbolizing the affective, ineffable, perhaps unsayable. It is inherently nonmetaphorical, involving a distillation of real things into a realm of abstraction that still feels unmediated to audiences, if it is successful. And if Hirschhorn is persuasive, it is because for particular viewers he collapses the distance between the concept and the experience of political interpellation:

being hailed as an always-already subject in a world that, in Lee's words, implicates us in its mess.

Ultimately, meditations on art like Hirschhorn's reveal the breadth and depth of our ongoing preoccupation with and reliance on this kind of presencing in a much larger realm of rhetorical action—and aesthetic projects—than might first appear, especially in instances in which we may not even be aware that our rhetorical proofs are resting on invocations of rhetorical presence. There are relatively low stakes involved in whether we are persuaded by the presence of Hirschhorn's cans that the artist is overcoming metaphor and representation itself in his installation—that is a matter for today's art critics and tomorrow's art historians. But much higher stakes are involved in arguments that create a sense that the "real" has been distilled and displayed for judgment: as when statistics, for example, are used to convince us of the reality of a social problem. Both the creation of conviction and the need for presence to always be a reduction work the same way in art and in everyday persuasion. The motive is the same: to collapse the distance between us and the thing itself—an impossible feat because the real simply does not have a presence for us (ironically, consumption as such is hard to find). So we reduce the invisible macroworld into a microworld that we can visualize, and in this sense reduction is always a kind of artifice. This attempt at collapsing distance is also an attempt to escape context; ultimate persuasion would free itself from all situational contexts in its creation of conviction.

A recuperated vision of presence also helps to derail the deceptive obviousness of presence as proof being used as a misleading short-circuit that moves contingent conditions in the realm of probability to apparent certainties that may not exist. On the other hand, just because presence is not as "real" as it purports to be does not mean it is not a powerful force; it is very possible for there to be a self-conscious knowledge that something is merely a distillation, or fundamentally rhetorical, but that does not diminish our ability to find power in it. Like a cave painting of a bear drawn to gather the power of the bear, or like a pile of cans created to gather and direct some of the power of our imagination about consumption, presence can gather its force indirectly, giving us the illusion of comprehension and order and creating an effect of abundant substantiation.

**Monica Westin** is a PhD candidate and university fellow at the University of Illinois at Chicago and a recent visiting student researcher in the Department of Rhetoric at the University of California, Berkeley. Her dissertation addresses the function of imaginary images in rhetorical theory and practice from Aristotle through the Second Sophistic. She writes regularly about visual art for *Artforum* and *BOMB,* among other places.

## Notes

1. Video interview for the Museum Dhondt-Dhaenens, http://www.museumdd.be/en/verleden/t4 (accessed 16 June 2015).
2. Hirschhorn regularly makes installations in nonartistic institutions, most famously his "monument" series to philosophers. His most recent monument, the *Gramsci Monument* from the summer of 2013, was constructed at the Forest Houses (part of the New York City Housing Authority's projects) in the South Bronx, where the artist remained present daily for months. The pavilion-like space received a mixed response from critics. Given Hirschhorn's movements in and out of art's institutions, it seems useful to consider what *Too Too Much Much* may have looked like had it been constructed in a nonart site: what is powerful and even fun in a museum setting is a depressing, cheap eyesore elsewhere.
3. Even in art that seeks to take on the everyday as its subject, this work is still predicated upon the radical way that institutionalized art has the power to draw attention and focus to a subject more than another platform could. A recent Whitechapel anthology on the everyday in contemporary art argues its rise "is usually understood in terms of a desire to bring ... overlooked aspects of lived experience into visibility" (Johnstone 2008: 12).

## Bibliography

Azoulay, Ariella. 2012. *The Civil Contract of Photography*. New York: Zone Books.
Buchloh, Benjamin. 2005. *An Interview with Thomas Hirschhorn*. October 113 (Summer 2005), 77–100.
Cruzvilllegas, Abraham. 2010. "Art:Interview, Thomas Hirschhorn by Abraham Cruzvillegas." *BOMB* 113 (Fall). http://bombmagazine.org/article/3621/thomas-hirschhorn. (accessed 16 June 2015).
Graw, Isabelle. "Ecce Homo," *Artforum* 2011, 241–247.
Johnstone, Stephen, ed. 2008. *The Everyday: Whitechapel Documents of Contemporary Art*. Cambridge, MA: MIT Press.
Lee, Pamela. 2012. *Forgetting the Art World*. Cambridge, MA: MIT Press.
Perelman, Chaïm, and Lucie. Olbrechts-Tyteca. 1958. *The New Rhetoric: A Treatise on Argumentation*. Notre Dame, IN: University of Notre Dame Press.
Toufiq, Jalal. 2009. *The Withdrawal of Tradition Past a Surpassing Disaster*. Forthcoming Books. http://www.jalaltoufic.com/downloads/Jalal_Toufic,_The_Withdrawal_of_Tradition_Past_a_Surpassing_Disaster.pdf (accessed 16 June 2015).

CONCLUSION

# WHAT NEXT?
## MODERNITY, REVOLUTION, AND THE "TURN" TO CATASTROPHE

*Ralph Cintron*

■ ■ ■ ■ ■ ■

In this concluding chapter I want to take up notions that my coeditor, Robert Hariman, and I have been discussing since we began to conceive of this project. All the contributors, some more than others, address in this volume the idea of texture/texturing and the idea of catastrophe. The latter idea in particular holds unusual theoretical potential. Although the authors of the volume may never quite say this, Hariman and I believe that collectively the chapters test the notion that the trope of revolution has been superseded by the trope of catastrophe as a primary means for imagining social change. This conclusion fleshes out that claim in a way that differs a bit from Hariman's introduction.

I want to begin with an anecdote that Naser Miftari and I developed one afternoon over the telephone as we were discussing his chapter for this volume. Miftari, a native of Kosovo, had taught me a lot about the Balkans when I spent a year there as a Fulbright Scholar. Something that I had noticed in those days was the regular use of the word *katastrofë*. It functioned as a popular go-to term, ubiquitously labeling everything that had gone wrong, or could go wrong, personally, socially, politically, economically. Years later, over the telephone, Miftari reminded me of this and pulled together in a single instant several decades of Balkan tragedy: "You know, Ralph, *katastrofë* (Albanian, singular; *katastropha*, Serbian, singular) was spoken across all the languages of Yugoslavia. Today it is still a popular word. Yugoslavia may have fallen apart, but that word still unifies us." So, a word that transcended geographies and languages is now the last unifier after the collapse of its sociopolitical order. I wonder as I start this conclusion if *katastrofë* unifies the planet.

If we think of the entire planet as more or less textured by disastrous political and economic actions, we begin to get a sense of the sheer precarity of the times. Texture, as suggested in the introduction, contains two possibilities. First, "texturing" captures a sense of "braiding" by which contrary elements are tentatively held together, as when both Left and Right use lobbying power to maintain elite interests. In this sense, the Left and Right are textured or braided together, meaning that political parties in democracies function like a loosely bundled oligarchy hidden behind a veil of democratic voting.[1] Second, texture and texturing also point to the importance of surfaces. "Just as material surfaces are rough or smooth, so are social surfaces rich or poor, relaxed or tense, bureaucratic or sentimental, and so forth, and each of these textures carries a history of how it got that way" (Hariman, this volume). Combining the two understandings of texture, we conclude that political actions are not the results of coherent theories or ideologies manifesting themselves, but rather the results of numerous oppositions, compromises, multiple motives, and temporal changes (micropolitics as opposed to theoretical politics) braided together so as to constitute a moment of political decision and action; and further, that these elements are legible on the surfaces of political actions. So, the meanings of the actions may be visible as part of the "style" of an event. Consider how the character of participatory democracy and the character of managerial, representative democracy become visible on the surfaces of their actions. For instance, Occupy's public deliberations were highly textured and socially engaged as seen in speaking order, the use of hand signals, and so on, but a more abstract, solipsistic style is visible on C-SPAN when representatives and senators address empty chambers of the United States House of Representatives and Senate.[2] These two ways of conducting deliberation represent different constraints, needs, intentions, and spatial characteristics. The first is marked by engagement and immediacy but gets little accomplished, while the second is marked by sterility but does the work of the country. Perhaps these paradoxes are paradigmatic of the sorts of social divides that are consequences of a democracy that has become by turns both increasingly managerial and populist.

However, more provocative than claims about texture is the notion that the trope of catastrophe has superseded the trope of revolution as the central dynamic for social change. As argued in the introduction, both terms have in their etymological roots a sense of overturning. "Catastrophe"—from the Greek *katastrephein*—is related through the verb to the rhetorical term *trope*, a "turning or transformation" as well as a "twisting." *Kata* is a preposition in Greek meaning "down" or "downward" or "against," as in "contrary to." Catastrophe, then, twists what is before us and points us downward. Like a trope, it changes how we understand. "Revolution" as a "rolling" is clearly both a turning and an overturning. Perhaps what disassociates these terms in popular thinking is the downward movement of catastrophe (in the sense of things becoming worse) and the upward movement of revolution (in the sense of things becoming better). That is, revolution, unlike catastrophe, has blown the sails of modernity ever forward insofar as it "overturns" tyranny. Virtue, then, buttresses revolution, even bloody ones, but catastrophe is either a slow, well-hidden violence (global warming) or a destruction that appears out of nowhere—and unlike biblical times, catastrophe is not on the side of justice. A goal of this conclusion, then, is to understand these terms as they relate to each other by suggesting that the trope of catastrophe has superseded that of revolution.

I start with some broad observations regarding the term "catastrophe." The term might be parsed three ways: (1) the catastrophic event itself; (2) the conditions leading to the event that are often revealed only because of the event; and (3) the discursive labeling of the event and its causal conditions, a labeling that, among other things, tries to provide an overview regarding our contemporary moment. With the latter, catastrophe "turns" into discourse, becomes a "turn of phrase," a trope that now becomes a supplement to reality and may, indeed, make it virtually impossible to talk of any other reality. As readers might guess, this is a major concern of this conclusion. For instance, 9/11 may have been, realistically speaking, a minor event, but its symbolic, discursive weight—including the subsequent memorial site—utterly refuses to be called minor. In contrast, Greenland's melting ice sheets and subsequent rising sea levels are different in terms of event and causal conditions, but it can be argued that the most significant difference occurs at the level of the symbolic/discursive. If 9/11 jelled almost instantaneously a centuries-old ideological position based on nation-states and war, melting ice sheets do not yet have a mature ideological/discursive interpretation, particularly for those living in the United States. That is, 9/11 had immediate rhetorical presence (meaning that the event itself and the conditions leading to the event became visible or interpretable because the discursive labeling of the event was already well in place), while melting ice sheets remain in a kind of rhetorical limbo (meaning that, again, particularly in the United States, the labeling of the event is still an unsettled matter and unable to provide a definitive interpretation to the event itself and its causes).[3]

Another related observation is that the labeling of catastrophe is seemingly far more pervasive than actual catastrophic events. In this sense, "catastrophe" and a host of related terms—such as "disaster" or some variant of "brokenness," as in the currently popular "X system is broken"—keep "turning" up. If the work of a turn of phrase is to "turn" our understanding, then many of the referents are at the mercy of the terms themselves. That is, all sorts of events, some significantly less catastrophic than others, get lumped together in a single discursive/symbolic field. We lose our sense of discrimination, most particularly because catastrophe, as a term, incites anxiety.[4] Further, such a pervasive condition also becomes rather quickly a money-making enterprise.

Consider some of the language used by the Global Conference on Disaster Management. This mini-industry of service providers must claim that disasters and catastrophes are in some sense technologically preventable, or if they should occur, that they are manageable. Hence, they must rely on earnest and realist arguments, but ultimately their logic, in order to sell, must be rooted in dark panic.

> Shockingly, less than 25% of Americans have a disaster plan in place for their family, home, and business. And it's only a matter of time until another major disaster will affect you and your loved ones. How it will affect you depends on one vital difference—PREPAREDNESS. As the number of declared emergencies have more than doubled in the past few years, being prepared is more important than ever.[5]

As we will see, "preparedness" contains many of the values of managerial modernity: control, orderliness, and so on. As long as these commonplaces are pervasive, catastrophe/disaster—as managerial modernity's necessary negatives—are also always available for deployment. That is, we do not need many actual catastrophes for catastrophe itself to become a pervasive, discursive condition—and a highly marketable one at that. Catastrophes structure news events because the animal in us seems to be deeply attuned to danger. Insofar as they structure our news media, they have become part of the pulse of our lifeworld. Indeed, we experience globality not with deep knowledge but mostly as an electronic body of information flows. We desire the exquisite detail of the latest measurement of danger from the "unfolding story": "the likelihood of the worst case scenario, the experts say, stands right now at 35 percent." As one catastrophe completes itself, we anticipate the next. The news frames a world in which order and disorder are deeply textured together, and this seems to satisfy a rather primal intuition that life is precarious. And rather thrilling because of it.

So how do we make sense of this repeating and commercialized story of catastrophe, this probably permanent condition of catastrophe, in the contemporary world? I suspect that catastrophe has something to do with the fraught term "modernity." Now, it would be a mistake in this short space to pursue ontologically the whole problem of modernity, postmodernity, and so on. Theorists know well that there were conflicting modernist strands, that modernity's origins do not have a clear date or geographic location, and that its all-encompassing nature makes modernity a poor conception for explaining anything specific. Nevertheless, what is useful about the term is how it functions heuristically as a way of talking about and imagining a significant chunk of world history as well as the here and now. "Modernity," whatever it might be ontologically, is today primarily an institutional form, a way of managing all dimensions of contemporary life. In this sense modernity is more like the acceptable and expected template for the management of populations and economies. Managerial modernity, then, for the most part advocates advancement, and advancement typically presumes some sort of accumulation of capital. It is thus possible to think of modernity as a kind of shorthand for signaling the work accomplished by capital accumulation. Should we, therefore, dispense with the term "modernity" altogether and simply refer to capital accumulation and its power to design and redesign our technological and physical landscapes? No. Simply making modernity another name for accumulated capital runs the risk of not seeing how historically modernity has also aspired to become a universal, planetary project. That is, it has aspired to occupy all geographies and to become a universal culture and ethics. Of course, today it is a vastly uneven project, split by wealth, technological access, and an assortment of other social divides including formal law versus customary practices. As a result we now live on islands of differences.

Nevertheless, we have also achieved significant connectivity. Connectivity, another word, perhaps, for globalization, is nothing less than modernity continuing to unfold across the planet, sometimes as an imposition that local populations do not want but more often as the imaginative horizon through which most peoples think of the real and the good. Through such thinking, "uneven modernity" begins to even itself out because so many aspire to it. It becomes, in effect, a kind of global common sense. So, modernity as a system of rational, moral management proves itself, according to many, when it delivers measurable, material improvement. This *mentalité* justifies such things as large-scale development projects; wage labor as opposed to subsistence economies; humanitarian interventions in the name of democracy and universal human rights; global wars on terror; the nation-state as the proper form for dividing the peoples of the earth; and so on. These, then, are discrete projections of today's institutionalized modernity. Through such schemas the whole planet is to be captured in order to create the greater prosperity for all—on this the Left and Right mostly agree. Their disagreements do not run deeper than arguing for different mechanisms to get there.[6] As Foucault says in *The Birth of Biopolitics*, "Dialectical logic puts to work contradictory terms within the homogenous" (2008: 42). Only the apocalyptic Left or Right might be willing to abandon modernity as such, but even then their theories are themselves projections of modernity. That is, to hate the whole of modernity is not possible, but one can hate those singular aspects produced by modernity that have injured one. The upshot here is that as people begin to invent and structure solutions to all their macro- and microinjuries, they can only invent from within the imagined horizons of the modernity that already constitutes us, for it is hard, even impossible, to invent outside the orbit of our encompassing present.

So, within this understanding of a hegemonic, managerial modernity, where does catastrophe sit? It would seem to hit viciously the very confidence that we maintain in our institutions; hence, the suppositions regarding our way of life. If modernity is a kind of enclosure inside of which we invent our realities and, hence, our lives, catastrophe has the potential to expose the operating system(s) as well as our dependency. In this sense catastrophe reveals. It reveals what revolution, as I will argue in more detail later in the paper, is no longer capable of revealing. And the more hyperbolic the catastrophe, the more truth is revealed—or so it seems. So, every catastrophe seems to have some sort of revelatory capacity that may reveal at several levels. At the most rudimentary level, the conditions themselves that were slowly building toward the event are revealed. Consider the crippling of the Fukushima Daiichi nuclear plant in 2011 and Hurricane Katrina in 2005. Quite a bit was known about both sites before the events hit. The dangerous geology underneath Fukushima Daiichi was well-known, and the dangers of nuclear power are so well-known that the heyday of its construction has long passed. As for New Orleans, the city had been in perpetual crisis waiting for the "big one" to expose existing weaknesses in the city's dike system and its social infrastructure. So in both cases the knowns were considerable, even if all the details of what might ensue were unknowable.

But at a still deeper level, what is revealed is the deep bind that characterizes technocratic knowledge and managerial modernity. Our modernist technologies are adaptations to the vast risks that they address. For instance, technology cannot overcome the riskiness of New Orleans, for it cannot achieve perfectibility over time. It cannot overcome the city's precarious geographic position or the government's unwillingness or inability to raise sufficient funds to repair the weaknesses of its infrastructure. Hence, our technical solutions are always adaptations to, and not a transcendence of, local constraints. Risk, then, is always encamped inside our technical solutions. Indeed, risk constitutes the solution itself insofar as any specific solution is built to address a specific sort of catastrophe, but then has difficulty accommodating the unpredictable, cascading catastrophes that can follow a single event. What catastrophe reveals at the deepest level, then, is that managerial modernity's promise to protect has already been compromised by its adaptation to and incorporation of vast stratums of risk inherent in all of modernity's operations. Modernity cannot create ideal protections, even though that is part of its ethos and authority. (The extent to which investigative committees looking into "what went wrong" miss this fundamental point is the extent to which managerial modernity furthers its delirious promise.⁷)

But there is more to say about the significance(s) of catastrophes within the modernist imaginary. What is quite clear in the Fukushima and Katrina disasters is that there is no clear distinction between natural and human-made catastrophes. Nature and the human are fully braided together—or to use one of the key terms of this volume, they are "textured" together. There is no distinction, because modernity has aimed its instruments of measure at all domains—the living and the nonliving, that which precedes the human and that which is human-made—and thus constructed an intricate network of relations. We might call this a vast commons through which a single event ripples to shape a variety of other events throughout the system. Hence, any "natural" catastrophe is simultaneously catastrophic for the invented world that today we call modernity. That is, if one of the foundational aspirations of modernity has been to order the world—or better put, to reveal the ordering of "nature" so as to bring it into line with human social ordering—then catastrophes smash any distinction between the two, revealing the deep symmetry that links them.⁸ Catastrophes, no matter their origins, signal a kind of across-the-board breakdown of the aspiration to order, control, and unify. Catastrophe as condition, then, marks the shortcomings of modernity's intuitions regarding truth, as well as its methods for doing so, or marks some glitch in its predictive power or its measuring instruments. In this sense, catastrophe summarizes the unevenness, the disenchantment, the incompleteness of modernity.

Modernity in its representation as ceaseless advancement toward an optimistic future is of particular interest for understanding the role of catastrophe. Sometimes this advancement looks to an invented past in order to keep moving forward, but the essential idea is a progression toward an ever better, transformed world. It is not as if modernity "knows" where it is going. In this sense it rests on a vast assumption: any increase in knowledge (in our ordering of the world, as mentioned earlier) serves the innate trajectory of modernity. In this sense modernity as progress accomplishes a kind of telos function. It ascends the past with the accomplishments of the present, and then ascends the present with projected accomplishments existing somewhere in the future. The future, because it is open-ended, can be the utter embodiment of hope, for we can stuff it with our imaginings of a better place that can redeem all the shortcomings that constitute the present. Sweatshop economies in emerging states (South Korea in the 1950s, for example) become redeemable if they can be understood as initiating the capital accumulation that in time can be poured into economies of innovation, in somewhat the same way that migrant parents can redeem their sacrifices if they see themselves as increasing the opportunities of their children. The future as the perennial site for social and personal advancement is the sine qua non of the modern ethos.

But, as we will see, the future is always a mixed bag. Sometimes it redeems, sometimes it does not. We build knowledge systems in the hope that they will guarantee a positive future. These knowledge systems are, in effect, technocratic ways of knowing that embody the telos function. What this means is that the past and present—if not exactly knowable—can be surveyed for "best practices" that can then be implemented in new contexts for a better future. That is the heart of technocratic knowing, and these technocracies are invested in the marketing of human care: increased longevity, higher standards of living, better-educated populations, and so on.

These reflections on technocratic knowing had their beginnings in my own fieldwork. I observed international technocrats engineering best practices into "emerging" democracies/economies so that they might become, someday, "mature" democracies/economies. The site was the former Yugoslavia after its breakup. What haunted the international effort and continues to do so in Kosovo is the idea of a "failed state" close to Europe marked by ethnic war, Islamic jihadists,[9] and high rates of joblessness (40 percent), meaning, in effect, a remittance-dependent economy (World Bank 2014).[10] But what are failed states? They are less ontologically real and more like existential self-doubts within modernity's Westphalian model of state sovereignty. Under the model, each state has sovereign control over territory, politics, and economy, and each state as rational entity functions in relation to other sovereign states via agreements and competitive self-interest that raises each state's standard of living and gross domestic product (GDP). Technically, failed states should not happen, particularly when they are constitutional, democratic states. As long as failed states can be thought of as consequences of the economic and political corruptions of authoritarianism, the telos function of "emerging" democracies/economies becoming "mature" ones remains safe. Hence, the international order is deeply invested in "stabilizing" Eastern Europe by eliminating from public life corruption and criminal networks and transforming political leaders from thugs into democrats. So the stakes are high, for the contemporary version of the Westphalian system represents how modernity organizes peoples on a global scale, and losing that foundation would be, indeed, catastrophic. International technocrats, then, tutor local technocrats in ways of knowing and best practices, and necessarily bury self-doubt behind earnest, determined faces.[11] (See Miftari, this volume, for his analysis of similar scenes.)

So, I have described modernity broadly as a system for the management of peoples and economies in order to make the following point: something, seemingly out of the blue, performs some sort of wreckage so that catastrophe becomes a setback in the tale of ascension. That is, a catastrophic event cannot exist outside some sort of built-up world, which includes, of course, some remarkable expectations regarding security, order, and a certain confidence about the future. Hence, there is no catastrophe *as such* without a certain set of socioeconomic infrastructures that are vulnerable to destruction, and without a set of ideologies and expectations about security, order, the future, and modernity as a capable, moral force. An observation to draw from this claim is that catastrophe indeed functions as a globalized trope enabling even further globalization, for even the least developed parts of the world are said to suffer from one catastrophe or another: a famine, locusts, an AIDS or Ebola epidemic. In these places it is thought that the infrastructures of the developed world are lacking—hence the catastrophe—because such people live closer to the bone with less security and more uncertain futures. In sum, in these places the possibility of large-scale loss has not been eradicated but is an expectation. Indeed, the Third World through its very label tells us that they are at the edges of the modernist project. Their suffering waits to be colonized. So, their catastrophes are reminders of the work to be done—or if the catastrophe in question is the result of the modernist project having gone wrong, then it becomes necessary to redouble the effort and make things right. Of course, the deep irony in any distinction between Third and First (and whatever else) Worlds is that catastrophe itself reveals a singular world in which the most severe breakdowns (financial catastrophes, for instance) start from within the most sophisticated and advanced systems that today govern the world's networks. From here the catastrophe ripples out and spreads. So, in all of these scenarios catastrophe reminds us of modernity's shortcomings even as it instigates more modernist ascension. Catastrophe tells us that the prowess of our knowledge and the capabilities of our institutions have not transcended human vulnerability, even though transcendence has always been modernity's goal.

When we examine catastrophe and its relation to economics, we seem to reveal even more precisely and profoundly the nature of our current modernity. Catastrophe today more often than not is framed through economic tropes. For instance, how do we determine the size and impact of a catastrophe? It typically includes an economic calculation, and it makes no difference, as I have been arguing throughout, whether the catastrophe began as "natural" or not, for both, despite their origins, can only exist today as a singular relation. The size and impact of a catastrophe, then, are calculated in highly conventional ways: by counting or estimating dead bodies, transforming the destruction and/or rebuilding into an economic sum, or both. Consider the Fukushima nuclear catastrophe, which started, of course, as an earthquake that led to a tsunami that then smashed into the nuclear reactor. The British newspaper the *Independent* captured the conventional framing while comparing the Fukushima and Chernobyl disasters: "Japan has estimated it will cost as much as £188bn to rebuild"; "there are a number of estimates of the economic impact [of Chernobyl], but the total cost is thought to be about £144bn." "Fukushima: two workers died inside the plant. Some scientists predict that one million lives will be lost to cancer; Chernobyl: It is difficult to say how many people died on the day of the disaster because of state security, but Greenpeace estimates that 200,000 have died from radiation-linked cancers in the 25 years since the accident" (McNeill 2011).

What is the significance behind these calculations and phrases like "economic impact"? They speak, I think, to a variety of things. First, econometrics is an ordering discourse by which we regain control over the sheer size of a disorder. In this sense managerial modernity reasserts itself even in the face of disorder and catastrophe. Second, at a deeper level we signal a very special relationship between nature and society, for it is the size of the destruction—and more broadly, the size of the economy—that tells us of the distance that separates the structure of our social system from the grip of nature. Let me explain: when we measure the size of an economy through such calculations as GDP and we then encounter a partial destruction of that economy—in other words, a catastrophe—what we seem to be measuring is the cushion between us and the violence of nature. That is, the size of the catastrophe measured economically shows us the size of that cushion, the size of all those protections by which we avoid our innate vulnerability to nature itself and to the inevitable vicissitudes that it represents. There is no surprise here, for economic growth is justifiable to the extent that nature can be represented as a set of vicissitudes that can do us in. With such a premise in place, "society," then, can be represented as a set of infrastructures constantly responding to and protecting us from as many vicissitudes as possible. The invention of such infrastructures as agriculture, industrialization, modern medicine, and so on depends on the conviction that each increases life chances that can be measured as reductions in child mortality, increased longevity, and increases in basic necessities and luxury items. At least, this is how Adam Smith in *The Wealth of Nations* declared it at a critical historical juncture that was witnessing a new leap in civilizational prowess:

> [Savage] nations ... are so miserably poor, that from mere want, they are frequently reduced, or, at least, think themselves reduced, to the necessity sometimes of directly destroying, and sometimes of abandoning their infants, their old people, and those afflicted with lingering diseases, to perish with hunger, or to be devoured by wild beasts. Among civilized and thriving nations, on the contrary, though a great number of people do not labour at all, many of whom consume the produce of ten times, frequently of a hundred times

> more labour than the greater part of those who work; yet the produce of the whole labour of the society is so great, that all are often abundantly supplied, and a workman, even of the lowest and poorest order, if he is frugal and industrious, may enjoy a greater share of the necessaries and conveniences of life than it is possible for any savage to acquire. (Smith 2003: 2)[12]

Nature and the savage seem to function as tropes of an original vulnerability, whereas wealth increase, as the premise and promise of modernity, seems to signal an essential distance from all that threatens to do us in. Smith's account of the savage in nature functioned as the invented common sense of his time. Our own era, due to the inroads of modernist anthropology, has mostly dropped the savage parts, but what persists into our own day are the nature parts, and this is why an encounter with catastrophe seems to contain the imprint of that long-standing relation between modernity and nature. Hence, when we measure catastrophe according to wealth destruction, we are in effect measuring the amount of infrastructure, social and material, that modernity has produced in order to protect ourselves from vicissitude. What these calculations represent, then, is the size of our dependency on modernity's ongoing production of wealth as the buffer against nature's potential power to reduce us to destitution.

If modernity is so deeply wedded to systems of mastery and if catastrophe, momentarily at least, reveals the sheer precariousness of all those systems, it should not be a surprise that we live in the midst of a kind of rhetorical overproduction of catastrophe. In this sense, catastrophe as a pervasive discursive condition speaks to an increasing nervousness about our material and existential well-being. It hyperbolizes our precariousness in order to mobilize action—but what actions are to be taken? As we have been saying throughout, the only answer can be more and more modernity in a face-off against vicissitude. If we want to find the generative, rhetorical force for the production of ongoing material ascension—which is nothing less than the production of our "civilization"—we might want to consider the hyperbolic function of catastrophe as global trope.

## Revolution and the Topos of the Future

Having sketched some preliminary notions about catastrophe and modernity, let us turn to the possibility that revolution as master trope signaling a primary means for social change has been superseded by another master trope, catastrophe. The gist of the argument can be grasped by returning to our earlier analysis of the future. That is, modernity's notion of ascension—the idea that the management of peoples and economies can be made ever better—requires a future to be ever present. Such a future motivates. It gives purpose and meaning to the present insofar as the present is the only site where the rhetorical and material production of the future can occur. New worlds are imagined and built in the name of the future. As stated earlier, even when modernity divides itself into a political Left and Right, it largely agrees—but for different reasons that we will soon touch upon—that the trope of the future is a guiding beacon. To be sure, however, the clearest mobilizations of the future as trope belong to the revolutionary Left. The Left narrative often constructs particular historical junctures where the future suddenly appears in the present. Narratives such as these seem to be somewhat teleological insofar as society at these moments witnesses the freedom and equality that is steadily becoming. Here is the melodrama, then, in which the future ruptures into the present. At its most extreme, as in the case of the French historian of the Revolution, Jules Michelet, the rupture is a kind of rapture.[13] In 1845 Engels expresses much the same in his own heated way, very much in the spirit of the French Revolution:

> The war of the poor against the rich now carried on in detail and indirectly will become direct and universal. It is too late for a peaceful solution. The classes are divided more and more sharply, the spirit of resistance penetrates the workers, the bitterness intensifies, the guerilla skirmishes become concentrated in more important battles, and soon a slight impulse will suffice to set the avalanche in motion. Then, indeed, will the war-cry resound through the land: "War to the palaces, peace to the cottages!"—but then it will be too late for the rich to beware. (1993: 302)[14]

This Left narrative of the future erupting into the present is always due to the force of the proletariat as a revolutionary class. Of course, if the writer is more of a populist, the proletariat becomes the "people," or, as with Hardt and Negri (2004), it becomes the "multitude." But the point is that the radical Left narrative evokes rather often a future suddenly entering the present. The masses at this moment realize a fullness of being, a complete change socially and subjectively, that otherwise cannot be expressed under hierarchical concentrations of power. So, if living under the present is marked by oppression, its displacement by the future is the experience of liberation itself, a liberation that is seemingly guaranteed at some point in the future if one believes that society is indeed moving along an evolutionary path. Cornelius Castoriadis calls these moments when the future realizes itself in the present "the switch plates in modern history" (1993: 149). And Jean-Luc Nancy suggests that these alterations of the present by the future are a kind of "going beyond in principle: to that which no prediction or foresight [*prévision*] is able to exhaust insofar as it engages an infinity in actuality" ([2008] 2010: 11). Both authors mark these melodramatic "switch plates" with specific dates. For Castoriadis, who was writing in 1968 and reflecting on prior moments, these dates are 1848 and 1871 (Paris); 1905 and 1917 (Russia); 1919 (Germany and Hungary); 1925 and 1927 (China); 1936 and 1937 (Spain); and 1956 (Poland and Hungary). For Nancy, the dates are "1789, the beginning of the French Revolution; 1848, the revolution that established the Second Republic in France; 1917, the Russian Revolution"; and 1968 ([2008] 2010: 4, 54). The future "descends" into the present at such moments, meaning that political life can no longer be connected to any state form but is, in effect, the realization of human potentiality. The fact that many of these dates overlap suggests that the radical Left narrative is quite coherent about the nature of the future and the forcefulness of its periodic descents. Indeed, within this narrative the past, present, and future seem to be teleologically cemented.

However, the Left narrative, as articulated by Castoriadis and Nancy, is already in deep trouble. Writing in May 1968, Castoriadis is well aware that the Left narrative has been undone by the privatization of capital.[15] And writing in 2008, Nancy makes it clear that political action today is in paralysis because it no longer has a "prime mover," except possibly "the growth of capital."[16] We can summarize this existential collapse by returning, again, to the trope of the future in the hands of the Left. The following contains the best articulation that I know of:

> What happens to political thought, practice, and imagination, when it loses hold on "the future"? It goes into crisis. The analytic, psychological, and libidinal structures of twentieth-century revolutionary politics were beholden to the temporal form of the future—it even gave the first movement of the avant-garde its name: Futurism. The future was on the side of the revolution. It was a great and empowering myth, but few believe it any longer: the future is over. Its last vestiges were squandered in the schemes of a heavily futurized financial capitalism. (Genosko and Thoburn 2011: 3)

In sum, the radical Left future has been undermined by an economic Right future. If the radical Left narrative announced a historical world process, the economic Right rushed in and over time reengineered it—or at least, that seems to be what Berardi (2011) fears has come true. There are a variety of dimensions to this takeover by the Right, and we will explore a few of these, but a critical point to make at the outset is that if the radical Left has exhausted itself as a motor of social change, we are mostly today left, as we will see, with capitalism as motor but, more seriously, catastrophic collapses, particularly the catastrophic collapses of capital.

There are several processes at work that undermine the heroic narrative of revolution. Let us consider democracy first before turning to capitalism.

(Ultimately the two must be considered together, because the first provides the legal expressions for the second, and each shapes the other. Of course, capitalism has and does graft itself onto other political forms—as in China, for example.) When democracy confronts tyranny, it does so as revolution. As Nancy describes it, "Democracy comes right out and demands a *revolution*: a shift in the very basis of politics, frank acceptance of the absence of foundation" ([2009] 2011: 63). Interestingly, democracy seems incapable of instituting a revolution against itself—or rather, it absorbs revolutionary churning by transforming it into more diluted forms. Elections and term limits for the executive are a type of churning, though severely diluted. In this sense, the revolution becomes suspended; violence against the democratic state becomes delegitimized insofar as both the state and citizenry agree that the legitimate expression of dissent is the vote. At a very deep level, elections become limited to second-order principles (voting the managing party in or out) as opposed to first-order principles (voting which ideas ought to rule over us). If all these are valid points, we can understand how the radical Left narrative of revolutionary change becomes attenuated over time not only because of the failure of its different sociopolitical experiments, but because democracy itself absorbs and dissipates the very idea of radical change—that is, revolution. Still, there are times when first-order principles and concerns suddenly erupt across our second-order lives. It is then that we seem to inhabit, for the moment, the sort of sociopolitical transcendence that Nancy seems to admire.

But such transcendence is not long-lasting, for it inhibits the emergence of a stabilizing order that enables things to get done. So order gets reintroduced; investments in such an order reemerge and grow; as these investments grow, resistance to disorder becomes more entrenched. That is, the transcendence of revolution, ultimately, is not everyone's cup of tea. Second-order principles return under the rubric of sanity, as well as public order and the rule of law, in order to sublimate first-order concerns. We saw some of this during the recent fiasco of Egypt's Arab Spring. On the surface it may have resembled a kind of democratic revolution opposing Mubarak's oppressive regime. But very quickly it became evident that a variety of forces were undercutting the emergence of revolution. If the revolution began in January 2011, a few close observers had already spotted that the Egyptian military, which is Egypt's oligarchic class, would not allow themselves to be outmaneuvered. Prescient commentaries written as early as June 2012 seemed to already know the future (Stacher 2012).[17]

A politics that rests on a horizontal distribution of power achieves the transcendence that Nancy admires. This transcendence is nothing less than a politics of enthusiasm rupturing across the social scene, for in the collapse of hierarchical relations there is the release of all manner of subjectivities. That which could not live is now seen as possible. The various Arab Springs seem to have felt something of this, and thus the revolution as topos or energy field will continue to work some sort of magic, but behind the enthusiasms lie the practical necessities of managing that hugely complex organ known as the state. The state as an organized system requiring management brings into being vertical accumulations of power, as Michels (2004) noted a century ago. That is, new oligarchies appear or merge with the old ones that remain. This passage is not just the fate of violent revolutions, but also all the forms of nonviolent change due to elections (Obama, Tea Party victories), reforms, and so on. Original enthusiasms give up the ghost and slide toward the ins and outs of management, which include compromises with deeply conflicting but equally vested interests, and though this inevitable disappointment is not necessarily a bad thing, it is the reason why many revolutionaries have theorized the possibility of continual revolution. Thomas Jefferson's notion that the Constitution should be written every twenty years is among the earliest examples.[18]

But here is the deepest and most ironic of twists: it is in capitalism itself, with such concepts as "creative destruction," that the vitality of revolution persists. And here we need to inquire into a certain relationship between Marx and Engels's brilliant phrase "all that is solid melts into air" and the economist Joseph Schumpeter's less arresting "creative destruction." "The bourgeoisie cannot exist without constantly revolutionizing the instruments of production, and thereby the relations of production, and with them the whole relations of society.... All fixed, fast-frozen relations, with their train of ancient and venerable prejudices and opinions, are swept away.... All that is solid melts into air" (Marx and Engels 1978: 476). For Marx and Engels, the constant churning of capitalist enterprise threatened both the laborer and the employer. The laborer's wages could be driven ever lower as the employer sought profit, but the employer also was in the gun sights of competitors seeking any possible advantage. The revolution of the proletariat would not only return the ownership of production to the laborer, and thus end the exploitation and vulnerability, but just as importantly, it would continue the expansion of human potential that capitalism itself had begun but could not finish.

This capitalist world of ceaseless churning was picked up whole by Schumpeter (1987), a free market economist who read Marx closely. His articulation of business cycles as embedded in creative destruction functions now as a classic understanding of capitalism. For Schumpeter, unimpeded churning was the only route for expanding human potential. The expansion of the "laborer's budget ... from 1760 to 1940" was due to a "history of revolutions" that "incessantly revolutionizes the economic structure *from within*, incessantly destroying the old one, incessantly creating a new one. This process of Creative Destruction is the essential fact about capitalism. It is what capitalism consists in and what every capitalist concern has got to live in" (1987: 83; emphasis in original). For Schumpeter it is the rawness of capitalist civilization—"the civilization of inequality" (425) rooted in a defense of property rights (142) and capital accumulation, another term for monopoly (106)—that must be preserved against forces such as the state that want to soften and regulate raw capitalism (424). For Schumpeter the collateral damage of creative destruction is eventually redeemed through the release of human potential via an ever broadening economic advancement; however, for Marx and Engels only the revolution of the proletariat can topple the current forms of oppression and thus release human potential materially and transcendentally, in Nancy's sense, as the release of new subjectivities.

How do we make sense of this? The trope of revolution would seem to have two axes. One is wedded to the political domain, while the other is wedded to technological innovation and its appropriation by capitalism. If modernity is compelled to stretch toward a horizon, it does so today through the marketplace, and it tells politics to follow. Capital destroys itself through a succession of innovations, for it is through this constant churning that we gain increases in efficiency, which lead to overall increases in material well-being. The authority of modernity rests on these basic premises and promises, and if they should falter, then modernity as ideology would give way, perhaps, to some sort of nonexpansionary ideology and economy. Modernity may have no final definition, but a nonexpansionary modernity seems almost like an oxymoron. At any rate, today political churning plays more the role of handmaiden, because politics *by itself* does not increase material well-being, though it certainly enables and consolidates it via property laws and so on. If at one point the trope of political revolution meant the shattering of the status quo in the name of some horizontal distribution of power, its reality has become increasingly conservative, constrained, as it were, by the imperative to increase material well-being. How do we solve poverty? The standard answer in a democracy is not revolution but, at most, some sort of protest that will become a lobby. But more often it is job creation, the expansion of the economy. So, when we talk of job creation increasing everyone's standard of living (human potential), we are admitting that politics should not sweep away the living order—or even, in an Aristotelian sense, define the life of the citizen. The proper role of politics, rather, is to technocratically adjust the mechanisms of the economy so that either more people get their "rightful" piece of the pie or the wealthy be allowed to concentrate capital because they are the "rightful" "job creators." Both the Left and Right here are under the imperatives of capitalist economics. That is, in democracies both the Left and Right are committed to second-order principles, not first-order principles. The upshot is that revolutionary churning, particularly in democracies, is useful to the extent that it overthrows the entrenched forces that restrict the cycles of innovation at the heart of capitalism. In this sense the trope of revolution has moved steadily out of the political domain into the economic. Furthermore, nationalist preoccupations with standards of living, as well as job seeking and job making, point to a kind of soft tyranny that is firewalled from political revolt. This soft, insidious tyranny occurs because employment has become the only route to survival, and because it monopolizes and defines our subjectivities, our notions of a meaningful life. We can revolt against tyrannical political systems and/or ideologies, but it is a different matter to revolt against a mechanism that provides both our survival and our meaningfulness. Now, this takeover of what it means to be human cannot bear high rates of unemployment that also spill over into high rates of criminality, for these begin to empty out the very promise and authority of managerial modernity. They represent the darkness that modernity must keep at bay and, in some ways, the "failed state" described earlier that worries the international order.

## Conclusion

The melodramas of revolution are, seemingly, no longer the major drivers of social change. Perhaps such a claim seems absurd given the recent Arab Spring upheavals, the uprisings in Venezuela, and what appeared to be, for a while at least, a liberatory revolution in the Ukraine aimed against patronage politics and economics. But underneath these events something else is at work, something even more fundamental. Schumpeter's creative destruction is one name for it. It too calls itself revolutionary. Ardent free marketers, for instance, praise the rough-and-tumble of businesses in competition and of entire economic sectors becoming new growth areas replacing older sectors (innovation!). In this sense capitalism churns social life, and the revolutionaries of the economic Right—like their counterparts on the Left—aspire to a future bounty that transcends the present. This is what the two camps share: the melodramas of revolution, the utopianism of the future. If what they share constitutes the two of them, then it is not surprising that they participate together in altering social relations. That is, capitalism's churning can alter social relations so dramatically that different political forms become necessary, such as democratic revolutions against despots (sometimes in the name of the "people," sometimes in the name of the bourgeoisie). Or capitalism's churning can also bring to the fore socialist revolutions of the proletariat, and more recently Islamist revolutions (insofar as these seem to be responses to the colonizing forces of secularist capitalism). In sum, revolution today can go in almost any direction: Left, Right, liberal, theocratic. When it occurs, it changes only the second-order principles of a world system whose first-order principles are determined by capital. The point here is worth repeating: revolution was once imagined as liberatory, as having the power to inaugurate a social order genuinely grounded on first-order principles. But today both revolution and reform have nothing to do with establishing first-order principles. Political change rearranges the chairs, the seating order of those already at the table. The table itself is littered with insurmountable worries regarding economic advancement, job opportunities, and a better life for both the population and the nation. Preserving capitalism's revolutionary potential is the first-order principle, the reigning monarch, who must be protected from political revolt.

Social change, then, under the guidance of creative destruction amounts to a series of improvisations off a central theme, modernity—that is, modernity as managerial system. Modernity in this sense is, for all practical purposes, synonymous with capitalism, and as it produces its efficiencies and technologies, it accelerates social changes. Many of these social changes are themselves resisted by capitalists, for each social change represents the potential destruction of someone's capital. Nimbleness, collusion, creative accounting, offshore banking, and lobbying are some of the weapons and defenses available to any accumulation of capital that is under threat. The larger point, however, is that social change due to creative destruction seems to consist of unending improvisation without ever abandoning the central theme, managerial modernity, which must constantly, in the eyes of the general public, enable the advancement of capital. In this sense it may very well be that modernity, as discussed earlier, is somehow firewalled against revolt because of its role in the provisioning of daily life. Framing it a little differently, modernity and its consort, creative destruction, are not bodies sitting in a palace and fearing dethronement. Rather, they represent an insidious tyranny that also invents and furthers our daily life.

What, then, of the relationship between catastrophe and this notion of social change that ultimately changes little? A catastrophe reveals some breakdown in the current political-economic regime. Repairing the breakdown can only occur within the logics of modernity and capitalism. As we have argued, a catastrophe wreaks damage that is measured in economic terms, and this metric tells us what is at stake. The economy is always at stake, and the economy fully incorporates catastrophe as part of the engine that drives it. In this sense social change, which cannot proceed without having at least one leg inside economic structures, is driven not only by routine creative destruction but also by catastrophes, which by definition are not routine. Indeed, in strong economies catastrophes can function as economic stimulus programs. In weak economies, such as Haiti, nothing ever quite recovers. The larger point is the revelatory capacity of catastrophe: not only does it reveal the inadequacies underlying the current order, but it also reveals the amount of infrastructure, measured monetarily, that cushions us from destitution. The power to repair is nothing less than the size of accumulated capital that can be brought to bear. There is nothing else separating managerial modernity from its collapse. This is why catastrophe holds the trump card between one state of being and the other. Its ultimate revelation, then, returns us to its etymological roots—if managerial modernity is an ascent, catastrophe reveals a "turn" pointing downward. Hence, every time catastrophe plays its trump card, it holds our attention.

So, what next? To offer something programmatic may indeed be practical, but it falls into the canonical history of modernist solutions. This is why Berardi's answer is stubborn, interesting, certainly anarchistic, and probably nihilistic:

> Only withdrawal, passivity, abandonment of the labor market, of the illusions of full employment and a fair relation between labor and capital, can open a new way. Only self-reliant communities leaving the field of social competition can open a new way to a new hope. This is why I prefer to say "autonomy" rather than "communism." Autonomy does not refer to creating a new totality, nor to a general subversion of the present, but to the possibility of escape, of self-reliance.... Passivity does not mean ethical resignation, but refusal of participation.... Activism is fake.... I don't see any conservatism or moralism in this, just the acknowledgement of the dead end we are facing. (Berardi 2011: 176–77)

We might follow Berardi, or we might argue instead for one of the themes that organizes this volume: texture. (Incidentally, despite the compelling nature of his writing, Berardi offers little proof for his claims, whereas the collective chapters of this volume are the beginnings of a kind of qualitative proof.) First, I agree with one of Berardi's central points, namely, that a politics of exhaustion is coupled to an explosion of the general intellect ("the info-overflow ... the intricacies of the ever-changing network, the virtual infrastructure of the swarm, the soul of the swarm" [2011: 175–76]). Second, I agree that it has become difficult to reduce the "info-swarm" to a specific solution that is somehow not already interconnected to all other catastrophes. Berardi lays before us the difficulty of knowing which action does no harm. Third, this state of not knowing, however, also implies an open-endedness that relates to my earlier claim, namely, that contemporary political actions are not the results of coherent theories or ideologies manifesting themselves, but rather the results of numerous oppositions, compromises, multiple motives, and temporal changes (micropolitics as opposed to theoretical politics) braided together. It is this braiding, this texturing of unpredictable elements incompletely understood, that makes the exhausted future of managerial modernity strangely productive. We do not know what local, small-scale, ad-hoc maneuvers can be braided to or already are braided within capitalism and managerial modernity. This is what a theory of texture points to. Unfortunately, the key here may be, indeed, that the small scale will never add up to any large scale. Again, we do not know. Hence, we cannot put a definitive period at the end of it all, for that would be saying too much …

**Ralph Cintron** teaches rhetorical theory and its intersections with political economy and urban theory in the Department of English at the University of Illinois at Chicago. In his secondary appointment in Latin American and Latino Studies at UIC, he teaches ethnographic methods and immigration studies. He has been a Rockefeller Foundation Fellow at SUNY Buffalo, a Fulbright Scholar (political science) at the University of Prishtina, Kosovo, and received honorable mention for the Victor Turner Prize for Ethnographic Writing (American Anthropological Association). He has been a Great Cities Institute Scholar and a Humanities Institute Fellow while at UIC, and is currently finishing a manuscript titled *Democracy as Fetish: Rhetoric, Ethnography, and the Oligarchic Condition*.

## Notes

1. The confluence of oligarchy and democracy is increasingly being demonstrated in political theory and economics (see Winters 2011; Piketty 2014).
2. Interestingly, this very question is posed on the website of the Dirkson Congressional Center: "Why is the Senate Chamber so empty when I watch C-SPAN?" Answer: "Perhaps one of the reasons the Golden Era of the Senate was so 'golden' was that the Senate had nowhere else to work at the time. On any given day, you'd find most of the senators at their desks in the chamber … writing, listening, debating, laughing, sleeping, franking [*sic*] mail. They were all present. No doubt, this was conducive to debate and resulted in some great discussions and arguments. The crowded chamber also provided a great show for the visitors in the gallery. Today, we have the Capitol, three Senate office buildings, and the Capitol Visitors Center. Senators are dispersed among committee rooms, hearings facilities, press briefings, and various offices. They come to the chamber to vote, to propose a bill, and to make a speech. The heart of the action today takes place on the periphery of the Senate Chamber rather than in the Senate Chamber—usually out of view of the C-SPAN cameras." See http://www.congresslink.org/print_expert_tenthingssenate.htm (accessed 2 July 2014).
3. This state of rhetorical limbo will not last long. It is becoming clearer that we are starting to see "climate migrants," poor, displaced coastal residents who have lost their fields to either salt or sea. Bangladesh is becoming a major flash point where one can start to see rising sea levels spawning new debates caused by global warming. Should wealthy polluting countries compensate poorer countries as they encounter this emerging catastrophe? Should the same wealthy countries accept populations who may become

stateless? How will the urban centers of these developing countries absorb even larger migrations of poor people? One estimate claims that "50 million Bangladeshis would flee the country by 2050 if sea levels rose as expected" (Harris 2014: 1).
4. The rhetorical mechanics by which some "catastrophes" become salient and others disappear from view are interesting. For instance, what makes 9/11 a pivotal American catastrophe but the 5,600 deaths of border-crossing migrants between 1998 and 2012 a near nonevent (Planas 2013)? Is it the sudden spectacle of the first versus the long duration of the second? Is it the toppling of the symbolic center of global finance versus marginalized, nondescript migrant labor? Surely, something about the futurism of virtual capital perceived as enormously productive versus unauthorized migrants perceived as illegal and even parasitic has much to do with noticing the former and not the latter. "Catastrophes" are not innately catastrophic but become catastrophes due to meanings already in place in social contexts.
5. Advertisement for Global Conference on Disaster Management, 26 September 2013, Chicago, Illinois.
6. This line of thinking runs contrary to theories of resistant multitudes as argued by Hardt and Negri (2004) and others. In my account, resistance is not "resistance as such" but another way to appropriate the modernist paradigm—that is, by placing the basic paradigm under more local control.
7. There is probably no finer document to understand this inability to reflect on the very premises of a "managerial modernity" than *The 9/11 Commission Report*. The refrain that the "nation was unprepared" is an implicit disavowal that risk constitutes the existence of managerial modernity. "Preparedness" presumes a kind of rational perfectibility that can understand the ways of precarity and uproot them. But if complete planning is not possible, then risk cannot be eliminated. At a still deeper level, every solution misapprehends, even though its public rhetoric is the exact opposite. In this sense, the constitutive nature of risk is revealed in the moment of catastrophe. Consider the promises and idealisms underwriting the following passage: "We learned that the institutions charged with protecting our borders, civil aviation, and national security did not understand how grave this threat could be, and did not adjust their policies, plans, and practices to deter or defeat it. We learned of fault lines within our government—between foreign and domestic intelligence, and between and within agencies. We learned of the pervasive problems of managing and sharing information across a large and unwieldly government that had been built in a different era to confront dangers" (p. xvi).
8. Claims in this paragraph stating that nature and the human are "fully braided" or "textured" together, and the development of "texturing" in Hariman's thinking in particular, echo current strands in political and rhetorical theory. I am thinking most particularly about the work that goes by the name of object-oriented ontology, network theory, ecological rhetorics, and material rhetorics generally. I do not have the space here to develop the connections, but I am sympathetic to theorists such as Thomas Rickert (2013), Diane Davis (2010), Jane Bennett (2010), and others. Rickert's exposition of "ambient rhetoric" is one of the clearest articulations. Here we see traditional divides between nature, technology, and the human—indeed, the entire surround—collapsing toward an interactive "pattern of life" (2013: 23). All interactants appear to be porous to each other or mutually inhabiting each other, as if we existed in a kind of general sensorium whose nerve endings are both human and nonhuman. In contrast to their work, this conclusion's articulation of catastrophe as an unraveling of

life and thing, of the human and nonhuman, picks up a long-enduring fear in human consciousness. I do not think that Rickert, Davis, or Bennett are especially attuned to that, but any deep networking of the human/nonhuman would, presumably, speed up and increase the wreckage of any major catastrophe. Increased enmeshment is, in effect, increased fragility. In sum, any supportive network for sustaining daily life would appear to be a house of cards.

9. In mid-August 2014 a number of international news outlets reported the arrest of forty Albanian Kosovars for involvement in the jihadist activities in Syria and Iraq as well as the death of sixteen Kosovars in those uprisings. See *Aljazeera* (2014) and a more detailed article published a few months later (Hopkins 2014).

10. "Kosovo remains one of the poorest countries in Europe, with a per-capita gross domestic product (GDP) of about €2,700 and about one-third of the population living below the poverty line—and roughly one-eighth in extreme poverty"—and this despite being "one of only four countries in Europe that recorded positive growth rates in every year during the crisis period 2008–12, averaging 4.5 percent" (World Bank 2014).

11. The interviews that I conducted in Kosovo between 2007 and 2008 among internationals tended to infantilize the locals as simply too invested in their old ways (communism being only one of those ways), while among the locals it was the incompetence of the internationals. One of the more interesting indictments came from a radical group, Vetëvendosje (Self-Determination), some of whose members were temporarily imprisoned by the international police. Paraphrasing from field notes, the essential point concerned the meaning of the vote. The members drew a distinction between first-order principles and second-order principles. First-order principles dealt with the fundamental organization of the society. Second-order principles dealt with the rotation of legislators whose wealth and power already depended on a set of first-order principles remaining in place. If the people could genuinely vote on first-order principles, their lives might change.

12. It is important to note that anthropology in the last half of the twentieth century attempted to reverse these long-standing notions of human precarity in the face of nature. The gist of the argument for Sahlins (1972), Woodburn (1988), and Gudeman (2001) has been that hunter-gatherers (Smith's savage) were historically far more productive, nutritionally healthier, more confident about their environment's ability to provide for their needs, and blessed with more leisure time than "modernity" has ever imagined.

13. Jules Michelet, more of a populist than a radical, captures in his writings of the 1850s this sense of the future. In the following passage he is reflecting on the Festival of Federation on 14 July 1790, which for him was the high point of the French Revolution: "We, worshippers of the future, who put our faith in hope, and look towards the east; we, whom the disfigured and perverted past, daily becoming more impossible, has banished from every temple; we who, by its monopoly, are deprived of temple and altar, and often feel sad in the isolated communion of our thoughts; we had a temple on that day" (1967: 450–51).

14. Here are the same tropes and narratives expressed in 2007 during and after the fires and riots of the *banlieues* of Paris: "Power is no longer concentrated in one point in the world; it is the world itself, its flows and its avenues, its people and its norms, its codes and its technologies. Power is the organization of the metropolis itself. It is the impeccable totality of the world of the commodity at each of its points ... Paris now

stands out only as a target for raids, as a pure terrain to be plundered and ravaged. Brief and brutal incursions from the outside strike at the metropolitan flows at their point of maximum density.... A day will come when this capital and its horrible concretion of power will lie in majestic ruins, but it will be at the end of a process that will be far more advanced everywhere else" (Invisible Committee [2007] 2009: 132).

15. "We have to understand what lies at the bottom of the proletariat's attitude: an adherence to modern capitalist society, privatization, the refusal to envisage taking charge of collective matters, and the race toward ever-higher levels of consumption are the key factors. Acceptance of the hierarchy—be it work or in the union and in politics—passivity and inertia, and the limitation of demands to economic issues correspond to these factors as the negative to the positive. To understand this we must understand what modern capitalism is, and go beyond a moribund traditional Marxism, which continues to dominate the minds of many living beings" (Castoriades 1993: 141).

16. "The reason why political action is paralyzed today is that it can no longer be mobilized on the basis of some 'prime mover' endowed with causal energy: there is no longer anything of the sort in political terms and politics as a whole must be remobilized from elsewhere. Nor does there exist any other economic prime mover apart from capital and the growth of capital, so long, at least, as economy itself continues to be thought as what moves politics and everything else by means of the choice that values equivalence, along with an idea of 'progress' that is supposed to give moral value to the indifference of this equivalence" (Nancy [2008] 2010: 29–30).

17. "Egyptians have gone to the polls five times since March 2011. Rather than elections' producing real choices, though, the military has used them to create an environment in which it can negotiate a pact with the winners. And the Muslim Brotherhood, which is trying to gain a lasting foothold in the system, has willingly participated. Yet it remains a comparatively weak actor, forced to compete on the military's uneven playing field.... Egypt's leading generals had a long-game strategy to capture control and they have emerged as the election's actual victors because they are poised to remain in charge of the country for the foreseeable future" (Stacher 2012).

18. In *Michael Hardt Presents Thomas Jefferson,* Hardt (2007) locates his brand of radical politics in one of the founding fathers of American democracy. What links Hardt to Jefferson is a shared faith that the masses have in them a kind of ineluctable perfectibility that will enable them to achieve the sort of deliberative powers demanded by self-rule and that will allow them to escape the tyrannies of elite rule. Again, these are the same notes that Nancy plays when he talks of transcendence and that I feature when criticizing the idea of political enthusiasm.

## Bibliography

*Aljazeera.* 2014. "Kosovo Arrests 40 over Iraq and Syria Combat." 11 August. http://www.aljazeera.com/news/europe/2014/08/kosovo-arrests-40-over-iraq-syria-combat-201481193132475992.html (accessed 20 August 2014).

Bennett, Jane. 2010. *Vibrant Matter: A Political Ecology of Things.* London: Duke University Press.

Berardi, Franco (Bifo). 2011. *After the Future.* Ed. Gary Genosko and Nicholas Thoburn. Trans. Arianna Bove, Melinda Cooper, Erik Empson, Enrico, Giuseppina Mecchia, and Tiziana Terranova. Edinburgh: AK Press.

Castoriadis, Cornelius. 1993. *Political and Social Writings.* Vol. 3, *1961–1979: Recommencing the Revolution: From Socialism to the Autonomous Society.* Trans. David Ames Curtis. Minneapolis: University of Minnesota Press.

Davis, Diane. 2010. *Inessential Solidarity: Rhetoric and Foreigner Relations.* Pittsburgh, PA: University of Pittsburgh Press.

Engels, Friedrich. 1993. *The Condition of the Working Class in England.* Ed. David McLellan. Oxford: Oxford University Press.

Foucault, Michel. 2008. *The Birth of Biopolitics: Lectures at the College de France.* Ed. Michael Senellart. Trans. Graham Burchell. New York: Palgrave.

Genosko, Gary, and Nicholas Thoburn. 2011. "Preface: The Transversal Communism of Franco Berardi." In *After the Future,* by Franco Berardi, pp. 3–7. Edinburgh: AK Press.

Gudeman, Stephen. 2001. *The Anthropology of Economy: Community, Market, and Culture.* Oxford: Blackwell.

Hardt, Michael. 2007. *Michael Hardt Presents Thomas Jefferson, The Declaration of Independence.* London: Verso.

Hardt, Michael, and Antonio Negri. 2004. *Multitude: War and Democracy in the Age of Empire.* New York: Penguin Press.

Harris, Gardiner. 2014. "As Seas Rise, Millions Cling to Borrowed Time and Dying Land." *New York Times,* 29 March, 1.

Hopkins, Valerie. 2014. "The One Muslim Country that Loves America Is Developing an Extremist Problem." *Foreign Policy,* 16 October. http://www.foreignpolicy.com/articles/2014/10/16/kosovo_balkans_iraq_syria_isis (accessed 6 February 2014).

Invisible Committee. (2007) 2009. *The Coming Insurrection.* Los Angeles: Semiotext(e).

Marx, Karl, and Friedrich Engels. 1978. "Manifesto of the Communist Party." In *The Marx-Engels Reader,* 2nd ed., ed. Robert C. Tucker, pp. 469–500. New York: W. W. Norton.

McNeill, David. 2011. "Why the Fukushima Disaster Is Worse Than Chernobyl." *Independent,* 29 August. http://www.independent.co.uk/news/world/asia/why-the-fukushima-disaster-is-worse-than-chernobyl-2345542.html (accessed 10 January 2014).

Michelet, Jules. 1967. *History of the French Revolution.* Trans. Charles Cocks. Chicago: University of Chicago Press.

Michels, Robert. (1962) 2004. *Political Parties: A Sociological Study of the Oligarchical Tendencies of Modern Democracy.* Trans. Eden and Cedar Paul. New Brunswick, NJ: Transaction Publishers.

Nancy, Jean-Luc. (2008) 2010. *The Truth of Democracy.* Trans. Pascale-Anne Brault and Michael Naas. New York: Fordham Press.

———. (2009) 2011. "Finite and Infinite Democracy." In *Democracy in What State?,* trans. William McCuaig. New York: Columbia University Press.

Piketty, Thomas. 2014. *Capital in the Twenty-First Century.* Trans. Arthur Goldhammer. Cambridge, MA: Belknap Press.

Planas, Roque. 2013. "Border Deaths Spike 27 Percent, Even as Immigration from Mexico Drops, Report Says." Latino Voices, *Huffington Post,* 20 March. http://www.huffingtonpost.com/2013/03/20/border-deaths-spike-27-percent-immigration-mexico_n_2915605.html (accessed 3 March 2014).

Rickert, Thomas. 2013. *Ambient Rhetoric: The Attunements of Rhetorical Being.* Pittsburgh, PA: University of Pittsburgh Press.

Sahlins, Marshall. 1972. *Stone Age Economics.* New York: Aldine.

Schumpeter, Joseph A. (1942) 1987. *Capitalism, Socialism, and Democracy*. London: Unwin Paperbacks.
Smith, Adam. (1776) 2003. *The Wealth of Nations*. New York: Bantam Dell.
Stacher, Joshua. 2012. "How Egypt's Army Won." *New York Times*, 29 June.
*The 9/11 Commission Report*. http://www.9-11commission.gov/report/911Report.pdf (accessed 8 March 2014).
Winters, Jeffrey A. 2011. *Oligarchy*. Cambridge: Cambridge University Press.
Woodburn, James. 1988. "'Sharing Is Not a Form of Exchange': An Analysis of Property-Sharing in Immediate-Return Hunter-Gatherer Societies." In *Property Relations: Renewing the Anthropological Tradition*, ed. Chris M. Hann. pp. 48–63. Cambridge: Cambridge University Press.
World Bank. 2014. "Kosovo Overview." http://www.worldbank.org/en/country/kosovo/overview#3 (accessed 8 August 2014).

# Index

■ ■ ■ ■ ■ ■

**A**
absolutism, 178
Active Distribution Network (ADN), 153, 161
activism, fair trade, 152, 154, 156. *See also* fair trade
Addams, Jane, 94, 102, 103
agency, concept of, 2, 3, 56–58
Agha, Asif, 50, 57, 58
agricultural standards, European Union (EU), 55
Ahearn, Laura, 56
AIDs epidemics, 239
American movies, influence of, 51, 52
Amharic language, 172
Amharization, 172
Andonovski, Zoran, 59, 60
Arab Spring, 106, 244
Arihood, Bob, 87
Aristotle, 194
art (contemporary), 220–30
   excess, 221–22
   presence as aesthetic persuasion, 226–29
   representation, 225–26
   sublimity, 223–25
"Art and Subjecthood: The Return of the Human Figure in Semiocapitalism," 225
*Art as Experience*, 98
assemblies, 174
atomic bombs, 224

**B**
Bakhtin, Mikhail, 14, 48, 49, 52
Balkans, 15, 71

Bárándy, Péter, 30, 33, 34, 42
Beck, Ulrich, 194
behavior, political, 4
Benjamin, Walter, 11
Big Lottery Fund of the National Lottery (BIG), 154
*The Birth of Biopolitics*, 235
Black Panther Party, 113
Boromisza-Habashi, David, 14
Bosnia, 50
bread riots, 106
brokenness, 233
Buchloh, Benjamin, 222
Bud Billiken Day parade, 122

**C**
Café Estima, 161
campaign coffee, 162. *See also* fair trade
capitalism, 9, 14, 245, 246
   neoliberal, ascendance of, 106, 108
   social movements, 118
   transitions, 107
case studies, overview of, 13–19
Castoriadis, Cornelius, 242, 243
catastrophe
   communications in, 82
   definition of, 10–13, 195, 232, 233
   discourse, 233
   Kosovo, 68–86. *See also* Kosovo
   social, 42
   turn to, 231–55
celebration of struggle, 114–16
Central Elections Commission (Kosovo), 80

centralization (Ethiopia), 171
Charities Aid Foundation, 155
Chernobyl (Russia) disaster, 240
Chicago Housing Authority (CHA), 122, 123. *See also* project heat
Chicago public housing, 122–148
    ethnographic context of project heat, 131–41
    historical context of project heat, 126–31
    overview of, 123–24
    project heat research methods, 124–25
Christianization, stimulation of, 172
chronotope, 47–67
    Bakhtin's concept of, 48, 49
    concept of agency, 56–58
    and everyday life, 48–52
    media, 52–56
    Say Macedonia! news scandal, 58–64
Cicero, 5
Cintron, Ralph, 19, 194
citizenship (rhetorical)
    Occupy Wall Street (OWS), 87–105
    within public culture, 100–04
civic art, rhetoric as, 5
clans, politics of, 77
classical rhetoric, 9. *See also* rhetoric
clientelism, 78
cofacilitators, 92
coffee, 149, 157
    campaign, 162
    Ethiopia, 183
    Mexico, 153
Cold War, 110
    Imagery (Hirschhorn), 224
collective association, 4
colonialism, 168
Comic Relief, 155
commodities, coffee, 149
Commonwealth Edison (Com-Ed), 122, 123
communal dilemmas (Hungarian), 25–46, 41
    cultural meaning of dilemma, 39–41
    language use as context, 29–39
communication, 6, 7, 27
    in catastrophes, 82
    disaster, 195–97
    new technologies, 113

communicative action, 41–43
conflicts, Balkans, 71
connectivity, 235
consumerism, ethics of, 163
consumption
    consumers (digital) and fair trade, 152–60
    contemporary art, 227
    ethics, 149–168
    market-driven social change, 157–60
    overconsumption, 224
    patterns, 108
    politics of fair trade, 163–64
corruption in Kosovo, 74
Council of Europe (COE), 59–64
Crapanzano, Vincent, 57
creative destruction, 245
Crimea, Russian conquest of, 3
crisis, life philosophy of, 21
critiques, 50
C-SPAN, 232
cultural hybridization, 2
culture
    and chronotopes, 65
    and mediation, 150
    concept of, 1, 6–8
    of Ethiopia, 170–73
    rhetorical citizenship within public, 100–04

**D**

Danisch, Robert, 15
Darwin, Charles, 12
decentralization, 107
Declaration of Independence (United States), 89
Declaration of the Occupation of New York City, 92, 97
Declaration of the Occupation of Wall Street, 90
Deleuze, Gilles, 110, 117, 118
democracy, 244
    election outcome stories as narratives, 79–80
    grassroots democratic structures, 116–17
    horizontal, 101
    identifying liberal democracies, 70–73

Kosovo, 68–86
Occupy Wall Street (OWS), 87–105
  phases of, 94–95
  politics in Kosovo, 76–79
*Democracy and Education,* 98
Department for International Development (DFID), 154, 155
Derg government (Ethiopia), 179
development strain (of fair trade), 152
Dewey, John, 94, 96, 97, 98, 100
digital consumers and fair trade, 152–160
digital rhetoric of fair trade, 149–68. *See also* fair trade
dilemmas (Hungarian)
  cultural meaning of, 39–41
  invocations, 41
  language use as context, 29–39
dilemmas, historical, 73
Diouf, Jacques, 198
disasters, 236. *See also* catastrophes
  definition of, 195–197
  regime-made, 11
  responses to, 18
discourse
  chronotopes of, 47–67
  ethnorhetorical approach, 26
  local discourses in Senegal, 201–15
  of catastrophe, 233
discrimination, 28
  loss of sense of, 234
disengaged electorates, Kosovo, 75–76
distribution patterns, 108
*Dnevnik* newspaper, 54, 60

E
Eastern Europe, stabilization of, 238
Ebola epidemics, 239
Ecocoff (EC), 154
economic determinism, 73
elections, 244
  in Kosovo, 78–80
elite, emergence of political, 69, 72, 73
Emerson, Caryl, 49
encounter, textures of, 174–77
engaged electorates, Kosovo, 75
enlightenment, 12
Enlightenment political philosophy, 100
ethics
  of coffee, 149
  consumerism, 163
  consumption, 149–68
  peasant, 172
Ethiopia, 17, 18, 183. *See also* Kara (Ethiopia)
ethnographic context of project heat, 131–41
ethnorhetorical approach, 26
European Commission, 155
European Enlightenment philosophies, 195
European Fair Trade Association (EFTA), 154, 156
European Union (EU)
  agricultural standards, 55
  presence in Kosovo, 70, 74
European Union Rule of Law Mission in Kosovo (EULEX), 68, 70, 73
events, narratives, 49, 52
Evolution, Theory of, 12
*Experience and Nature,* 98
Extension residents (Horner), 132, 135

F
face dilemmas, 34
fair trade, 17, 149, 150. *See also* consumption
  digital consumers and, 152–60
  historical framing of rhetoric of, 161–62
  market-driven social change, 157–60
  politics of, 163–164
  sugar, 158
Fairtrade Fairground, 58
Fairtrade Foundation (FTF), 154, 157
Fairtrade Mark, 161, 162
familism, 78
favoritism, 78
Federal Police (Ethiopia), 182
Fennell, Catherine, 16, 17
Fernandez, James, 178
flexibility, 107
Food and Agriculture Organization of the UN (FAO), 198
Fordist system, 108, 109, 141
former Yugoslav Republic of Macedonia (FYROM), 59. *See also* Macedonia
Foucault, Michel, 235
fragmentation, 107

frames
  political, 35
  theory of, 27
freedom of expressing opinions (Hungarian Constitution), 40
free trade, 151. *See also* fair trade
Frèkovski, Ljubomir, 60
French ideals (of democracy), 95, 96
French Revolution, 242, 243
Fukushima Daiichi nuclear plant (2011), 236, 237, 240
Fulbright Scholars, 231
Funke, Peter N., 16
futurism, 241–47

**G**
General Assembly of NYC, 87, 90, 96, 117
genres, 6
  public discourse, 48. *See also* discourse
geography, 4, 170–73
Giddens, Anthony, 109
Gilgel Gibe III Dam, construction of, 187–90
Girke, Felix, 17, 190
Global Conference on Disaster Management, 234
globalization, 9
  economics of, 150
  and fair trade, 149
global system integration, 2
governments
  Ethiopia, 179
  history of Ethiopia, 170–73
Graan, Andrew, 14
Graeber, David, 178
grassroots democratic structures, 116–17
grassroots rhetoric, 194–219
the great community, 96
Greece, 14
  failure to recognize Macedonia, 50
gross domestic product (GDP), 238, 240
Guattari, Félix, 110, 117, 118

**H**
Habermas, Jürgen, 21
Habesha, 173, 175
Hamar *woreda,* 179
Hariman, Robert, 175, 231

Harvey, David, 107
Hastrup, Kirsten, 186
hate law (Hungary), 29, 33
hate speech debate in Hungary, 28–29, 40, 41
Hegedûs, Lóránt, Jr., 37, 38, 39
hegemonies, 170, 189, 236
Henry Horner Homes housing complex (Horner), 123, 124–25
hidden transcripts, 7
Hirschhorn, Thomas, 19, 221
historical dilemmas, 73
historical struggles, megastructural solutions to, 186–90
history, Ethiopian, 170–73
Hobbes, Thomas, 100
Holocaust, 29, 30
Holtz, Pierre, 198
horizontal democracy, 101
horizontalism, 117
Horner, Henry, 123
Hull House, 96, 100
human dignity (Hungarian Constitution), 40
human rights, 40
Hungarian Constitution, 40
Hungarian Socialist Party, 33
Hungary
  cultural meaning of dilemma, 39–41
  hate speech debate in, 28–29, 40, 41
  language use as context, 29–39
  political expressions in, 25–46
Hurricane Katrina (2005), 197, 199, 236, 237
Hutcheon, Linda, 178, 181
hyperurbanization, 2

**I**
Ihaddik (Ethiopia), 179
imperialism, 177–186
Impetus Trust, 155
in-between states, 68–86
  identifying liberal democracies, 70–73
Independent Media Center (IMC), 114
individualization, 107
industrial vote theft, 79
Indymedia, 114, 117
infanticide, 177

inflation, 109
Institut fur Kunstkirtik, 225
Intercontinental Encuentro for Humanity and Against Neoliberalism (1996), 111
international community actors, Kosovo, 73–74
International Monetary Fund (IMF), 106, 198
irony, peripheral wisdom and, 177–86
irrigation (Ethiopia), 182

J
Jakimovski, Stevèe, 55
Jakuloski, Zvonimir, 59
Jameson, Frederic, 107

K
Kara (Ethiopia), 168–93
  culture of, 170–73
  map, 169
  megastructural solutions to historical struggles, 186–90
  people of, 17, 188
  peripheral wisdom and irony, 177–86
  textures of encounter, 174–77
*katastrofë,* 231, 232
Keynesian development, 141
Kosovo, 15, 68–86, 231, 238
  disengaged electorates, 75–76
  elections in, 78
  engaged electorates, 75
  identifying liberal democracies, 70–73
  international community actors, 73–74
  liberation of, 77
  outcome stories, 79–80
  political parties in, 74
  politics in, 76–79
  regions of, 77
Kovács, András, 35, 37

L
labor, 109
landscapes, 131
language use as context, 29–39
laws, hate (Hungary), 29, 33
leadership roles, Occupy Wall Street (OWS), 92
*Le Figaro,* 198

Left
  modernity, 235
  narrative of, 243, 244
  principles of, 246
Lekakis, Eleftheia J., 17
*Le Monde,* 197
Lenin, Vladimir, 113
liberalism, political, 43
liberalization, 3
*Libération,* 198
life philosophy of crisis, 21
lifestyle through development, 154. *See also* fair trade
literary composition, rhetoric as, 5
Local Advisory Council (LAC), 139
local discourses in Senegal, 201–15
locust plagues, 194–219, 199–201
  disasters, 195–97
  global discourse, locust disaster (2004), 197–199
  local discourses in Senegal, 201–15

M
Macedonia, 14, 15, 47–67
  chronotopes of everyday life, 48–52. *See also* chronotopes
  independence of, 50
  media chronotopes, 52–56
  Say Macedonia! news scandal, 58–64
  scandals, 53
*Magyar Hírlap* (daily newspaper), 38, 42
management, 238. *See also* modernity
market activities, 12
Marxism, 115
mass action, 47
mass injustice, 89
materials, art (contemporary), 221–22
Max Planck Institute for Social Anthropology, 190
media, 6
  chronotypes, 52–56
  Say Macedonia! scandal, 58–64
  scandals, 53
Menelik (Emperor), 168
metaphors, art (contemporary), 225–26
Mexico
  coffee (fair trade), 153
  Zapatista rebellion, 106, 111–13

Meyer, Christian, 18
Michelet, Jules, 242
MIÉP (Hungarian Justice and Life Party), 37
Miftari, Naser, 15, 231, 238
Millennium Development Goals of the United Nations, 173
Ministry of Foreign Affairs (MFA), 59, 61
mobilization practices, types of, 158
modern art, 225. *See also* art (contemporary)
modernity, 12, 82, 194, 231–55
   revolutions, topos of the future, 241–47
modernization, 3, 17
morality, 34
Morson, Gary, 49
movement politics, 106–21
   capitalism, 118
   celebration of struggle, 114–16
   grassroots democratic structures, 116–17
   nomadic movements, 110–11, 119
   organizational models, 113–14
   transitions from old left to new, 107–09
   Zapatista rebellion (Mexico), 111–13
movies, influence of, 51, 52
Mubarak, Hosni, 244
Museum Dhondt-Dhaenens, 220, 221

N
Nancy, Jean-Luc, 242, 243
*Nap-Kelte* (Sunrise) television program, 30–33
narratives, 48
   development of, 49
   election outcome stories as, 79–80
   events, 52
   fair trade, 151–152. *See also* fair trade
nation, concept of, 69
National Democratic Institute (NDI), 74
Negri, Antonio, 116
neoliberal capitalism, ascendance of, 106, 108
neoliberalism, 9
Netanyahu, Benjamin, 25
networks, 4
New Left, 108, 109, 112, 116

New Orleans, Louisiana, 236. *See also* Hurricane Katrina (2005)
*The New Rhetoric,* 228
news, 47, 52–56. *See also* media
   Say Macedonia! scandal, 58–64
   scandals, 53
the *New York Times,* 198
Nicaragua Solidarity Campaign (NSC), 152–53
Nietzsche, Friedrich, 110
nomadic movements, 106–21, 110–11, 119
   Zapatista rebellion (Mexico), 111–13
nongovernmental organizations (NGOs), 61, 162, 174, 176, 199
North Atlantic Treaty Organization (NATO), 77

O
Obama, Barack, 25, 245
Occupy Wall Street (OWS), 15, 16, 87–105, 110–11, 117, 232
   pragmatism and, 94–100
   processes, 89–93
   radical democracy, 89–93
   rhetorical citizenship, 100–04
   rights, 89–93
official transcripts, 7
oil shock (1973), 109
Old Left, 107–109, 112, 116
Omo Valley, 173
   Gilgel Gibe III Dam, construction of, 187–90
organizational models, movement politics, 113–14
overconsumption, 224
Oxfam, 155

P
parodies, 50
Partia e Fortë, 75
peasant ethics, 172
Pendarov, Todor, 55
peripheral wisdom and irony, 177–86
Petrov, Slavko, 55
phases of democracy, 94–95
police powers (Ethiopia), 177–86
political action, 6, 19–21. *See also* Occupy Wall Street (OWS)

consumption as, 149
political ambiguity, concept of, 69, 71, 72
political behavior, 4
political culture
  concept of, 1
  Kara, Ethiophia, 170
political elite, emergence of, 69, 72, 73
political experience, 9
political expressions
  in Hungary, 25–46
  language use as context, 29–39
political frames, 35
political interpellation, experience of, 228
political liberalism, 43
political parties
  Kosovo, 74
  Partia e Fortë, 75
political retexturing, 41
politicians, 3
politicization of risk, 139–41
politics
  concept of, 69
  of fair trade, 163–64
  in Kosovo, 76–79
  movement, 106–21
  of recognition scholarship, 143
  sensory, 122–48
  of trade justice, 150
population displacement, 2
populism, 9
power
  horizontal distribution of, 244
  peripheral wisdom and irony, 177–86
  relations, 4, 7
  textures of encounter, 174–77
pragmatism, relevance of, 87–105
preparedness, 234
presence as aesthetic persuasion (art), 226–29
processes, Occupy Wall Street (OWS), 89–93
production
  patterns, 108
  revolutions, 245
Professional Air Traffic Controllers Organization (PATCO), 109
project heat, 122–48. See also Henry Horner Homes housing complex (Horner)
protections, 236
Protestant revolution, 12
protests, World Trade Organization (WTO), 106, 110, 114
*The Public and Its Problems,* 98, 99
public deliberations, 232
public discourse, 47. See also discourse
public expression, 25. See also political expression
  outlaw of, 29
public housing, 16–17

**Q**
*The Quest for Certainty,* 96

**R**
radical democracy, Occupy Wall Street (OWS), 89–93
radicality, 195
Reading International Solidarity Centre (RISC), 153, 154, 155
Reagan, Ronald, 109
recognition scholarship, politics of, 143
regime-made disasters, 11
relativity, 178
religion, 4
representation, art (contemporary), 225–26
Republic of Macedonia. See Macedonia
resettlement schemes, 189
responses to disasters, 18
retexturing, political, 41
revolution, 10, 11, 12, 231–55
  topos of the future, 241–47
rhetoric
  consumers (digital) and fair trade, 152–60
  consumption, 149–68
  contemporary art, 220–30
  conventions, 6
  definition of, 3–10
  disasters, 195–97
  ethnorhetorical approach, 26
  grassroots, 194–219
  Habesha, 175
  historical framing of fair trade, 161–62

market-driven social change, 157–60
Occupy Wall Street (OWS), 87–105
of presence, 227
role of, 5
Rhetoric Culture project, 26
Right
   modernity, 235
   narrative of, 243
   principles of, 246
rights, Occupy Wall Street (OWS), 89–93
risk, social and sensory, 135–39
rituals, infanticide, 177
Rose, Nikolas, 135
Russia, 3, 12, 70
Russian Revolution, 12

**S**
Sarkozy, Nicolas, 25
scandals, 53
   Say Macedonia! news, 58–64
Schultz, Howard, 161
Schumpeter, Joseph, 245
Schwimmer, Walter, 59, 61
Scott, James C., 17, 181
sedentarization schemes, 189
Senegal, 18, 194–219
   disasters, 195–97
   global discourse, locust disaster (2004), 197–99
   local discourses in, 201–15
   locust plagues, 199–201
sensory politics, 122–48
   ethnographic context of project heat, 131–41
   historical context of project heat, 126–31
   project heat research methods, 124–25
   risk, 135–41
September 11, 2001, 233
Serbia, 70
   liberation of Kosovo, 77
Shankilla, 176
Shared Interest Foundation, 155
Simon, János, 35, 37
Skalnik, Peter, 170, 173
Sloterdijk, Peter, 12, 20
slow violence, 11
Smith, Adam, 240–41

social catastrophes, 42
   hate speech in Hungary, 28–29
social engineering, 69
social hierarchies, 4
socialism, 14
social justice, 152
social movements, 106–121
   capitalism, 118
   celebration of struggle, 114–16
   grassroots democratic structures, 116–17
   nomadic movements, 110–11, 119
   organizational models, 113–13
   transitions from old left to new, 107–09
   Zapatista rebellion (Mexico), 111–13
social risk, 135–39
social structures, 2, 3
solidarity
   Occupy Wall Street (OWS), 89
   strain (of fair trade), 152
South Omo region (Ethiopia), 170
sovereignty, concept of, 69
speech, freedom of, 29
stack takers, 92
Starbucks, 161
state
   concept of, 69
   Kara (Ethiophia), encounters, 181
   resistance of (Ethiophia), 173
Stewart, Kathleen, 9
stigmatization, 28
storytelling, 151
   strains of fair trade movement, 152
   trade injustice, 154
structural violence, 179
struggle, celebration of, 114–16
Students for a Democratic Society (SDS), 113
subjectivity, 178
sublimity, contemporary art, 223–25
sugar, fair trade, 158
superstorms, 223, 224
sweatshop economies, 237

**T**
Tea Party, 6, 245

*Telegraph*, 197
*terra nullius* arguments, 188
terrorist attacks (9/11/2001), 233
textures
  of civilizations, 11
  of encounter, 174–177
  of evaluation, 202
  of political practice, 2, 201
Thatcher, Margaret, 109
Theory of Evolution, 12
theory of frames, 27
Tompkins Square Park (New York City), 87
*Too Too Much Much*, 19, 221, 226. *See also* Hirschhorn, Thomas
Toufiq, Jalal, 224
town meetings (Kara), 174, 175. *See also* power
trade
  fair, 17, 149, 150. *See also* fair trade
  injustice, 154
Trade Justice Movement (TJM), 153, 154, 156
transcripts
  official and hidden, 7, 181
transition
  chronotope of, 50
  from old left to new social movements, 107–09
tribal zones, 168
tyranny, 233
  revolutions against, 247

**U**
Ukraine, 3
United Kingdom (UK)
  consumers (digital) and fair trade, 152–60. *See also* fair trade
United Nations (UN)
  Food and Agriculture Organization of the UN (FAO), 198
  Millennium Development Goals of the, 173
United Nations Interim Administration Mission in Kosovo (UNMIK), 70
United States (US)
  Declaration of Independence, 89
  recognition of Kosovo as state, 69, 74
  welfare, 124
*Utrinski Vesnik* report, 60

**V**
venture philanthropy, 155
violence, structural, 179
*Vreme*, 59, 60

**W**
Wade, Abdoulaye, 198
war crimes, Kosovo, 74
wealth, 4
*The Wealth of Nations*, 240–41
welfare (United States), 124
Wolfson, Todd, 16
Wolof farmers (Senegal), 195
World Bank, 238
World Social Forum, 110, 112, 115, 117
World Trade Organization (WTO) protests, 106, 110, 114
World War II, Hungary after, 29

**Y**
Yugoslavia, 71. *See also* Kosovo

**Z**
Zapatista Army of National Liberation (EZLN), 111, 118, 160
Zapatista rebellion (Mexico), 106, 111–13
Žižek, Slavoj, 111
Zuccotti Park (New York City), 87

www.ingramcontent.com/pod-product-compliance
Lightning Source LLC
Chambersburg PA
CBHW070915030426
42336CB00014BA/2419